Bytes, Bombs, and Spies

Bytes, Bombs, and Spies

The Strategic Dimensions of
Offensive Cyber Operations

Edited by
Herbert Lin and Amy Zegart

BROOKINGS INSTITUTION PRESS
Washington, D.C.

Library of Congress Cataloging-in-Publication data are available.
ISBN 978-0-8157-3547-2 (cloth. : alk. paper)
ISBN 978-0-8157-3548-9 (ebook)

9 8 7 6 5 4 3 2

Typeset in Adobe Caslon Pro

Composition by Westchester Publishing Services

To the men and women of U.S. Cyber Command

Contents

Figures and Tables

Acknowledgments

We are indebted to the authors of this volume for devoting their talents and time to offensive cyber operations—a topic that is cloaked in newness, uncertainty, and secrecy. The group first came together at a Hoover Institution workshop that we held in 2016. It was among the first unclassified, in-depth examinations of offensive cyber operations, and our colleagues were lured by an admittedly devious strategy that promised good food, better company, and little work. They now know that we lied. The food was good, the company better, but the workload was substantial. Each author has contributed chapters and in addition has reviewed the work of many others so that we could harness the group's collective wisdom throughout this volume. Two years, many revisions, and dozens of emails later, we are all still working, and learning, together. We could not ask for better collaborators.

Emily Goldman was a thought partner in this endeavor from its inception. Tom Berson, Joe Felter, Bill Perry, and Scott Sagan served as workshop discussants, offering generous feedback to many of the draft chapters. Sameer Bhalotra, Chris Painter, and Eli Sugarman offered incisive comments and questions throughout the workshop. Student rapporteurs Kim Chang, Sam Gussman, Wesley Tiu, and Aaron Zellinger ensured that we remembered all of the right things.

Taylor Johnson McLamb has provided pivotal research assistance from start to finish. Thanks also to the rest of the Hoover team: Caroline Beswick,

Taylor Grossman, Michelle Ritter, and Russell Wald. Without them, there would be no workshop or book.

Tyler Moore violated James Q. Wilson's admonition for all organizations: "Never do anything a first time." Thanks to his leadership, the *Journal of Cybersecurity* devoted its first special issue to offensive cyber operations and included earlier versions of several chapters appearing in this book. Bill Finan and his fine team at Brookings Institution Press did a masterful job of taking this book from idea to reality.

Our deepest thanks to the Lakeside Foundation, the Davies Family, Bob and Marion Oster, Hank J. Holland, and the Hoover Institution for supporting this project and so much more.

The leaders of three institutions have encouraged and enabled us to venture into cyberspace: Admiral Mike Rogers at U.S. Cyber Command, Tom Gilligan at the Hoover Institution, and Michael McFaul at Stanford University's Freeman Spogli Institute for International Studies.

We would each like to thank our families for supporting our long-running cyber partnership and all the Peking duck that comes with it, and our Stanford colleagues Rod Ewing, Andy Grotto, and Harold Trinkunas.

Finally, we thank the men and women of U. S. Cyber Command, cyberspace pioneers in every sense of the word. Their foundational work will last for generations to come, even as the technology changes daily. Our work to help them better understand and triumph in this evolving terrain is just beginning. We dedicate this book to them.

An earlier version of chapter 1 appeared in the *Journal of Cybersecurity* 3, no. 1 (March 2017), Special Issue on Strategic Dimensions of Offensive Cyber Operations, as "Introduction to the Special Issue on Strategic Dimensions of Offensive Cyber Operations."

An earlier version of chapter 3 appeared in the *Journal of Cybersecurity* 3, no. 1 (March 2017), Special Issue on Strategic Dimensions of Offensive Cyber Operations, as "The Role of Effects, Saliencies and Norms in U.S. Cyberwar Doctrine."

An earlier version of chapter 5 appeared in the *Journal of Cybersecurity* 3, no. 1 (March 2017), Special Issue on Strategic Dimensions of Offensive Cyber Operations, as "A Cyber SIOP? Operational Considerations for Strategic Offensive Cyber Planning."

An earlier version of chapter 6 appeared in the *Journal of Cybersecurity* 3, no. 1 (March 2017), Special Issue on Strategic Dimensions of Offensive Cyber Operations, as "Second Acts in Cyberspace."

An earlier version of chapter 9 appeared in the *Journal of Cybersecurity* 3, no. 1 (March 2017), Special Issue on Strategic Dimensions of Offensive Cyber Operations, as "Thermonuclear Cyberwar."

An earlier version of chapter 10 appeared in the *Journal of Cybersecurity* 3, no. 1 (March 2017), Special Issue on Strategic Dimensions of Offensive Cyber Operations, as "Cyberterrorism: Its Effects on Psychological Well-Being, Public Confidence and Political Attitudes."

An earlier version of chapter 11 appeared in the *Journal of Cybersecurity* 3, no. 1 (March 2017), Special Issue on Strategic Dimensions of Offensive Cyber Operations, as "Limiting the Undesired Impact of Cyber Weapons: Technical Requirements and Policy Implications."

An earlier version of chapter 12 appeared in the *Journal of Cybersecurity* 3, no. 1 (March 2017), Special Issue on Strategic Dimensions of Offensive Cyber Operations, as "Rules of Engagement for Cyberspace Operations: A View from the USA."

An earlier version of chapter 15 appeared in *The Virtual Weapon and International Order* (New Haven, Conn.: Yale University Press, 2017).

1

Introduction

HERBERT LIN *and* AMY ZEGART

In March 2016 we held a two-day research workshop on the strategic use of offensive cyber operations. The workshop brought together distinguished researchers from academia and think tanks as well as current and former policymakers in the Department of Defense (DoD) and the U.S. intelligence community. All discussions and papers were unclassified.

We organized the workshop for two reasons. First, it was already evident then—and is even more so now—that offensive cyber operations were becoming increasingly prominent in U.S. policy and international security more broadly. Second, despite the rising importance of offensive cyber operations, academics and analysts were paying much greater attention to cyber defense than to cyber offense. Consequently, key issues such as the conceptual underpinnings, doctrine, operational assumptions, intelligence requirements, organizational demands, and escalation dynamics of offensive cyber operations were understudied.

On the increasing prominence of offensive cyber operations for the United States, consider the following:

- The deployment and use of Stuxnet against Iranian centrifuges is widely credited with slowing Iran's progress toward acquiring a nuclear weapon before it was discovered in 2010.[1]

- Presidential Policy Directive 20 (PPD-20), which established U.S. policy for both offensive and defensive cyber operations, was leaked by Edward Snowden in 2013, and much of its content was described in news articles.[2] According to the *Guardian*'s reporting, offensive cyber capabilities can be used broadly to advance "U.S. national objectives around the world."[3]

- The Department of Defense Cyber Strategy, released in April 2015, focuses on "building capabilities for effective cybersecurity and cyber operations to defend DoD networks, systems, and information; defend the nation against cyberattacks of significant consequence; *and support operational and contingency plans*."[4]

- In a speech at Stanford University releasing the April 2015 cyber strategy, Secretary of Defense Ash Carter explicitly noted that one mission of the DoD is "to provide offensive cyber options that, if directed by the President, can augment our other military systems."[5]

- The DoD has publicly acknowledged using cyber weapons in its fight against the Islamic State of Iraq and Syria (ISIS). For example, in February 2016 Secretary of Defense Carter said that U.S. Cyber Command is conducting offensive cyber operations to cause ISIS to "lose confidence in their networks, to overload their networks so that they can't function, and do all of these things that will interrupt their ability to command and control forces."[6] He also noted that Cyber Command "was devised specifically to make the United States proficient and powerful in this tool of war." In April 2016, Deputy Secretary of Defense Robert Work said, regarding ISIS, "We are dropping cyber bombs. We have never done that before," and "Just like we have an air campaign, I want to have a cyber campaign."[7]

- During the 2016 presidential campaign, then-candidate Donald Trump promised to "make certain that our military is the best in the world in both cyber offense and defense."[8] Trump argued in the same speech that "As a deterrent against attacks on our critical resources, the United States must possess the unquestioned capacity to launch crippling cyber counterattacks. . . . America's dominance in this arena must be unquestioned."

On Inauguration Day the White House noted, "We will make it a priority to develop defensive and offensive cyber capabilities at our U.S. Cyber Command."[9]

- In March and April 2017 the *New York Times* published a number of articles describing U.S. efforts regarding certain "left-of-launch" ballistic missile defense methods targeting North Korea's program,[10] in particular cyber methods for compromising a missile before launch. On the basis of what *New York Times* reporters David Sanger and William Broad believed to be an unusually high failure rate of North Korean missile tests, they concluded that the United States had been conducting a cyber campaign against the North Korean missile development program.

- The Trump National Security Strategy of December 2017 states that "the United States will impose swift and costly consequences on foreign governments, criminals, and other actors who undertake significant malicious cyberactivities."[11]

More broadly, the attention paid to cybersecurity issues by policymakers has risen dramatically in the past few years. Cyber threats from China (for example, the 2015 theft of millions of records from the Office of Personnel Management), North Korea (the 2017 WannaCry ransomware attack that affected computers worldwide, including the United Kingdom's National Health Service), Russia (the 2017 NotPetya ransomware attack against Ukrainian institutions, including parts of its critical infrastructure), and Iran (the 2012 attack against Saudi Aramco that destroyed 30,000 computers) have provided strong signals to policymakers that offensive cyber operations are powerful instruments of statecraft for adversaries as well as for the United States. Cyber-enabled information operations, such as the Russian intervention in the U.S. presidential election of November 2016, have further raised the profile of the relationship between cyberspace and national security.

If recent history is any guide, the interest in using offensive cyber operations is likely to grow. Already, there is robust discussion about whether the current requirement articulated in PPD-20 for "specific presidential approval" of offensive cyber operations with significant consequences should be relaxed to allow greater delegation to theater combatant commanders. Strategically, greater receptivity to the use of offensive cyber operations may suggest that such operations could be the instrument of first military use if nonmilitary measures (diplomatic, economic, or legal measures) fail.

A logical consequence would also be continuing or expanded efforts to establish a ubiquitous presence on possible cyber targets, an outcome discussed at greater length by Chris Inglis (chapter 2 in this volume).

Other significant changes may also be in the offing. For example, greater receptivity to the use of offensive cyber operations may lead to a greater willingness to employ destructive or disruptive active defense measures, or to allow their use by the private sector in extremis. The U.S. government's Vulnerabilities Equities Process, which determines whether software vulnerabilities discovered by intelligence agencies should be disclosed to private sector vendors so that they can be patched, may also shift. Under the Obama administration, this process reportedly tilted toward disclosing vulnerabilities to companies. The rising use of offensive cyber operations may shift the calculus toward stockpiling vulnerabilities instead so that they can be used by the U.S. government in subsequent offensive operations. In addition, more open and vigorous support may be offered to efforts that promote exceptional access to encrypted files and communications for law enforcement and intelligence agencies.

Last, the elevation of U.S. Cyber Command from unified subcommand under U.S. Strategic Command to a full unified combatant command—mandated by Section 923 of the National Defense Authorization Act for FY 2017[12]—occurred on May 4, 2018.[13] The full operational implications of this organizational change will unfold over time, but it is possible that as a full unified combatant command, Cyber Command will have greater independent authority to conduct operations, both offensive and defensive, in cyberspace.

The increasing prominence of offensive cyber operations as instruments of national policy alone would warrant serious research conducted by independent scholars at universities and think tanks in the same way that a great deal of research has been conducted on defense-related topics such as missile defense, nuclear strategy, and naval operations. Because these topics are important to national defense and international security, they are appropriate for independent scholars to study, if only because independent perspectives contribute to the overall body of useful knowledge on which policymakers can draw.

To date, academics and analysts have paid much more attention to cyber defense than to cyber offense. One important reason underlying this imbalance is a high degree of classification about nearly every aspect of U.S. offensive cyber capabilities. Indeed, Michael Hayden, former director of both the National Security Agency and the Central Intelligence Agency, has noted that, as recently as the early 2000s, even the phrase "offensive cyber operations" was classified. Not what it might mean, or what the targets would be, or what technologies would be involved—merely the phrase itself.

High levels of classification and excessive secrecy are especially problematic when policymakers try to understand a new domain of conflict because secrecy inhibits learning across traditional boundaries, and new types of conflict necessarily require learning across traditional boundaries. Again, quoting Hayden:

> Developing policy for cyberops is hampered by excessive secrecy (even for an intelligence veteran). I can think of no other family of weapons so anchored in the espionage services for their development (except perhaps armed drones). And the habitual secrecy of the intelligence services bled over into cyberops in a way that has retarded the development—or at least the policy integration—of digital combat power. It is difficult to develop consensus views on things that are largely unknown or only rarely discussed by a select few.[14]

Thus we convened the 2016 workshop in large part to promote and demonstrate the realistic possibility of collaboration between government policymakers and independent nongovernment researchers working on strategic dimensions of offensive cyber operations on an unclassified basis. Although over the years a few scholars have ventured into the realm of strategy and doctrine around offensive cyber operations without access to classified materials, the vast majority have found it easier to stay away from the subject matter entirely. The result has been a deep loss for strategic thought and a stark contrast from the roles that key nongovernment researchers played in developing nuclear strategy during the Cold War.[15]

For example, Bernard Brodie developed the fundamentals of deterrence by threat of retaliation as an essential underpinning for nuclear strategy and also the importance of a secure second-strike capability (that is, deliverable nuclear weapons that could survive a first strike by an adversary) for strategic stability.[16] Herman Kahn introduced the key strategic notion of an escalation ladder as it might apply across the entire range of quite limited conventional conflict to all-out nuclear conflict.[17] Thomas Schelling and Morton Halperin developed influential theories for promoting arms control involving strategic nuclear weapons.[18]

The workshop focused on strategic dimensions of offensive cyber operations, which can be used across a wide range of scenarios and for a wide range of purposes. Tactical uses of a weapon (cyber or otherwise) focus on short-term, narrow goals—how to defeat the adversary in the next village tomorrow. Strategic uses of weapons, by contrast, focus on longer-term, more overarching goals and are designed to affect the broader dynamics between potential adversaries both on and off the hot battlefield.

Generally speaking, offensive cyber activities compromise the confidentiality, integrity, or availability of information. An activity that affects the confidentiality of information is considered a "cyber exploitation," while an activity that degrades the integrity or availability of information is considered a "cyberattack." In this volume we define offensive cyber operations more specifically as: the use of cyber capabilities for national security purposes intended to compromise the confidentiality, integrity, or availability of an adversary's information technology systems or networks; devices controlled by these systems or networks; or information resident in or passing through these systems or networks.

A good place to start thinking about offensive cyber operations in a strategic context is to consider some of the unique characteristics of cyber weapons and their operation in cyberspace.

- In cyberspace, instruments used to gather intelligence and inflict damage are difficult to distinguish. Because the same techniques are usually used to gain access to an adversary's systems and networks for intelligence gathering and for causing harm, an adversary that detects a penetration cannot be certain of the penetrator's intent and therefore may misperceive an attempted intelligence operation as an attack.

- Offensive cyber operations act most directly on intangibles—information, knowledge, and confidence. To be sure, cyber operations can cause tangible effects, as when the information in question is integral to the operation of devices or equipment that affect the physical world. But offensive cyber operations are fundamentally deceptive in nature—at a tactical level, no cyberattack tells the user of a computer "click on this link and your computer will be compromised by a malicious adversary." Human cognition is of course based on the availability of information—and if the humans involved doubt the provenance of the information available to them, their concerns may well prompt them to assume the worst.

- The effectiveness of a cyber weapon is a very strong function of the target's characteristics. In cyberspace, a small change in configuration of the target machine, system, or network can often negate the effectiveness of a cyber weapon against it. This is not true with weapons in other physical domains. Any ship hit by a torpedo with a sufficiently large warhead will be damaged, whether the ship is made of wood or steel. Anything within the crater of a nuclear weapon will be destroyed, regardless of how it was built. The nature of target-weapon interaction with kinetic weapons can usually be estimated on the basis of physics experimentation and calculation. Not so with cyber weapons. For offensive cyber operations, this extreme "target dependence" means that intelligence information on target characteristics must be precise, high-volume, high-quality, current, and available at the time of the weapon's use.

- Interaction with the target in advance of an actual cyberattack on it is often a prerequisite for an attack's success. That is, the attacker may have to prepare a cyber target well before the actual attack—for example, by surreptitiously installing a "back door" that will grant the attacker access at a later time for downloading a customized attack payload that takes into account new intelligence information that may then become available.

- Military planning often involves drawing up lists of targets that are well known and understood—military bases, headquarters buildings, ammunition and fuel storage facilities, telecommunications facilities, and so on. By contrast, many targets in cyberspace can appear and disappear from the internet with the flick of a switch.

These characteristics appear in the four interrelated themes explored by the chapters in this volume: (1) cyber strategy and doctrine for offensive use of cyber weapons, (2) operational considerations in using cyber weapons, (3) escalation dynamics and deterrence, and (4) the role and relationship of the private sector to offensive cyber operations. We selected these four themes because of their obvious importance to policymakers, because of their clear relevance to offensive operations in other domains, and because they will advance our understanding about what is and is not different when it comes to the strategic effects and impacts of offensive cyber operations, both now and in the future. In the chapters that follow, contributors go both deep and broad. Some offer specific expertise about individual country challenges (such as Adam Segal's examination of China in chapter 13). Others take a broader view of a conceptual challenge (such as Henry Farrell and Charles Glaser in chapter 3). Still other chapters focus on technical dimensions of cyber capabilities and how they might be utilized for precise targeting (Steven Bellovin, Susan Landau, and Herbert Lin in chapter 11) or sabotaging a missile development program (Lin in chapter 7). Together, the chapters offer what we hope is a compelling and comprehensive view of many of the key technical, political, historical, and legal dimensions of offensive cyber operations.

Cyber Strategy and Doctrine

Strategy and doctrine are foundational to achieving strategic effects of offensive cyber operations. In chapter 2, Chris Inglis sets the stage by examining the intelligence, surveillance, and reconnaissance (ISR) infrastructure needed to support an effective U.S. cyber strategy. He argues that ISR capabilities for cyberspace must be ubiquitous, real-time, and persistent. Capabilities must be ubiquitous because cyberspace is global, and the cyber targets that operational plans call for attacking are potentially located anywhere. They must be real-time because up-to-the-minute information on target characteristics is almost certainly necessary for an offensive cyber operation to be successful. And they must be persistent because operational preparation of the cyber battlefield is time-consuming and it is not known in advance when a given offensive cyber operation may need to be executed. The aspirational goal for ISR to support cyber operations is that it enables offensive cyber operations to sprint from a standing start at any given moment.

How should the United States choose between cyber and kinetic (or physical) responses to cyberattacks? Since the early 2000s, the United States has made a variety of statements addressing some aspects of this question. The 2004 National Military Strategy said explicitly that U.S. nuclear capabilities played an important role in deterring the use of weapons of mass destruction or effect, including "cyberattacks on U.S. commercial information systems or attacks against transportation networks"[19] that have a "greater economic or psychological effect than a relatively small release of a lethal agent."[20] The DoD's 2015 Cyber Strategy specifically states that the United States will respond to cyberattacks against its interests "at a time, in a manner, and in a place of our choosing, using appropriate instruments of U.S. power and in accordance with applicable law."[21] The 2018 Command

Vision for U.S. Cyber Command argues for a strategy of persistent engagement in cyberspace below the threshold of armed conflict.

In chapter 3, Henry Farrell and Charles Glaser take a step back from these pronouncements. Their starting premise is that decisions about deterrence and warfighting should be based on the effect a given U.S. attack will have, not the means by which that effect is produced. But, they note, perceptions matter as well: adversaries may perceive different forms of retaliation that do equal damage as differently punishing and differently escalatory. In particular, kinetic damage may be perceived as "more serious" than comparable damage caused by a cyberattack, thus reducing the likelihood and value of kinetic retaliation for deterring and responding to cyberattacks.

In chapter 4, Max Smeets and Herbert Lin review the March 2018 Command Vision for U.S. Cyber Command. Superseding the Command Vision released in June 2015, the new document demonstrates a marked change in Cyber Command's thinking and approach to engaging adversaries in cyberspace. Perhaps the most significant change is the acknowledgment that adversary cyber operations below the threshold of armed attack or the use of force (both terms recognized by the United Nations Charter) can still have strategic significance—small actions can create large consequences. In large part, the new Command Vision is the result of the observation that previous U.S. practices of restraint in cyberspace have not been sufficient to deter adversaries from below-threshold operations. The 2018 Command Vision articulates a new approach that is based on persistent engagement—that the United States must be willing to engage actively and affirmatively below the threshold if it is to compete successfully in cyberspace, and thus implicitly downplays the escalation risks inherent in a more active stance. Even the title of the 2018 Command Vision—"Achieve and Maintain Cyberspace Superiority"—sets up Cyber Command's aspirational vision in cyberspace.

Operational and Tactical Considerations

Operational considerations are implicated in the strategic use of weapons in that they speak directly to how military forces are employed to gain military advantages over an adversary and thereby attain strategic goals. Such considerations focus on the design, organization, and conduct of major operations and in-theater campaigns. Of course, the borderless nature of cyberspace makes the definition of "in-theater" problematic, a point suggesting that offensive cyber operations are themselves likely to be conducted without regard for national borders.

An operation plan is a complete and detailed plan for military operations that would be executed upon receipt of appropriate orders for particular military contingencies. In 2013 the *Guardian* reported that PPD-20 called for the identification of "potential targets of national importance" where offensive cyber capabilities "can offer a favorable balance of effectiveness and risk as compared with other instruments of national power."[22] Identification of such targets is analogous to the development of a target list for the Single Integrated Operating Plan for using strategic nuclear weapons, today known as OPLAN 8010, "Strategic Deterrence and Global Strike."

With the backdrop offered by PPD-20, Austin Long (chapter 5) uses the frame of nuclear planning processes to understand how strategic targeting using cyber weapons might occur, considering how the organizational processes used to plan for the use of nuclear weapons and to execute such plans could in fact be applied to cyber weapons as well. Long considers how and to what extent strategic influence emanating from an adversary complicates planning for strategic responses, in particular asking under what circumstances strategic influence could be regarded as a strategic cyberattack. He also discusses whether the oft-mentioned clandestine nature of offensive cyber operations has an impact on deterrence, drawing an analogy to Cold War strategic electronic warfare as precedents for that possibility.

In chapter 6, Martin Libicki considers the connection between tactics and the conduct of an extended cyber campaign that could have strategic impact. He notes that adversaries are likely to adapt as we conduct offensive cyber operations against them. Such adaptations could occur relatively quickly and may reduce the effectiveness of subsequent operations unless the initial operations are crafted carefully to minimize adversary opportunities to adapt.

In chapter 7, Herbert Lin looks at some of the technical issues that a program of cyber-enabled sabotage might entail if it were conducted against a nation's missile development program and considers its relevance to an operational ballistic missile defense. Although Lin's piece is not based on any specific knowledge regarding any particular nation's program, it is noteworthy that press reports in 2017 described a U.S. program using various cyber means to disrupt and delay the North Korean missile development program.

Escalation Dynamics

Escalation dynamics and deterrence refer to processes by which conflict can start, how smaller conflicts can grow into bigger ones, and how these processes can be interrupted to make the outbreak or escalation of conflict less likely.

As one important example, intelligence collection—one of the primary functions of certain types of offensive cyber operations—can easily lead to misperceptions with escalatory implications. Consider, for example, the sensitivity of nations to the security of their nuclear capabilities, which are regarded as the ultimate guarantor of their security against hostilities from other nations. Gathering intelligence that could shed light on an adversary's intentions is often regarded as enhancing stability, since it can provide reassurance about the putative intent of an adversary. But because it is often unclear in the initial stages of an offensive cyber operation whether such an operation is intended to gather intelligence or to prepare the cyber battlefield (and because offensive cyber operations are likely to be used early in a conflict),[23] cyber-enabled intelligence collection directed against nuclear command and control facilities—especially if noticed by an adversary during a crisis—may be misinterpreted as a sign that a preemptive attack on its nuclear capabilities is imminent, and thus undermine nuclear stability.

A second escalatory path may be the comingling of assets for command and control of nuclear and conventional forces. An adversary's command and control assets are explicitly called out as a target for U.S. offensive cyber operations in the DoD Cyber Strategy;[24] if the early phases of a conflict involve conventional forces (and hence the United States launches cyberattacks on the command and control assets for these forces), the adversary may well see such attacks as attempts to compromise the command and control of its nuclear forces—a perception that might lead to escalation of the conflict.

A third factor in unintended escalation is an inappropriate scope and nature of the rules of engagement for the use of cyber weapons. One basic rule of engagement for offensive cyber operations appears to be articulated in PPD-20. According to public news reports, PPD-20 directs that cyber operations "reasonably likely to result in significant consequences require *specific presidential approval*" (emphasis added) where "significant consequences" are known to include loss of life, serious levels of retaliation, damage to property, adverse foreign policy consequences, or economic impact on the country.[25]

A fourth factor that may drive escalation is public opinion and pressure on decision makers. Public opinion has certainly influenced decision makers to go to war—a fact known since the outbreak of the Spanish-American War in 1898.[26] Even if such pressures themselves are insufficient by themselves to cause war, they can create climates conducive to conflict escalation in which the perceived significance of small incidents grows out of all proportion to its actual significance—and there is no reason to suppose that conflict in cyberspace would be an exception.

Last, the use of a weapon that caused more damage than was intended by the attacker might cause unintended escalation of a conflict. Both PPD-20 and the DoD Cyber Strategy note that offensive cyber operations must be conducted in accordance with the laws of armed conflict (LOAC), just as all other U.S. military operations are conducted. To address issues of collateral damage, the DoD has established a "No-Strike and the Collateral Damage Estimation Methodology"[27] that requires commanders to compile a list of "no-strike entities" upon which kinetic or nonkinetic attacks would violate LOAC. Public reports also indicate that PPD-20 directs officials to weigh "the potential threat from adversary reactions" and "the risk of retaliation," both considerations in managing risks of escalation. Such considerations would help to shape the establishment of a restricted target list comprising valid military targets that for non-LOAC considerations, such as escalation, should not be attacked in certain specified ways. Mission-specific rules of engagement (also known as supplementary rules of engagement) account for no-strike entities and restricted targets.

These examples of possible escalatory pressures ground the discussion of the book's third theme—escalation dynamics in cyberspace—to which six chapters are devoted.

First, Jason Healey (chapter 8) examines historical case studies and finds that cyber conflict is more often escalatory than not. According to his analysis, U.S. cyber actions often lead to misinterpretations and overreactions by adversaries, resulting in those states increasing their own cyber capabilities as a result of fear in what might be called strategic escalation or the cyber manifestation of the security dilemma.[28] Thus, he argues, an open display of offensive cyber capabilities—advocated by many as a measure supporting deterrence—is likely to inflame relationships between states as a result of "worst-case" judgments on both sides.

Erik Gartzke and Jon Lindsay (chapter 9) raise another important question regarding escalation dynamics. Motivated by press reports regarding

U.S. attempts to compromise the North Korean missile development program and noting that cyber capabilities depend on concealing information about cyber vulnerabilities from the other side, they argue that if the latter has nuclear capabilities its confidence in its ability to use those capabilities may be excessively high, and that it will be less likely to back down in a crisis—thus increasing the likelihood that nuclear war will break out. They further distinguish between offensive cyber operations used for preventative counterproliferation and for preemptive counterforce, the former extending over a longer period of time than the latter. The persistence of such operations over longer times increases the likelihood that those operations will themselves be compromised, an outcome that would tend to undermine the further effectiveness of a preventive operation and increase the possibility that those operations could be used for preemption.

Michael Gross, Daphna Canetti, and Dana Vashdi (chapter 10) focus on the psychological harm and consequential impact of offensive cyber operations on public confidence in important national institutions, noting especially how the mystique and omniscience associated with cyber operations affect the risk perception of civilians and how access to the internet has become a prima facie requirement for realizing certain basic human rights, both of which open new avenues for cyber terrorism. They observe in experiments that in the face of hostile cyber activity, many citizens reevaluate their confidence in public institutions and increase their support for harsh military responses, tendencies that may well increase public pressures for cyber or even kinetic escalation.

Steven Bellovin, Susan Landau, and Herbert Lin (chapter 11) point out that with appropriate intelligence in hand, cyberattacks can be designed and conducted in a way that limits damage to the intended targets: discriminating cyber weapons are technically possible. The chapter also addresses technical means for limiting the proliferation of cyber weapons that could otherwise occur, a factor that can mitigate the security dilemma in cyberspace.

C. Robert Kehler, Herbert Lin, and Michael Sulmeyer (chapter 12) provide an overview of how the DoD normally conceptualizes such rules of engagement, but without reference to PPD-20. They note that the U.S. military seeks as much as possible to integrate cyber weapons into its operational toolkit within a common framework of principles that apply to all weapons, and that, from the DoD perspective, principles that inform rules of engagement for traditional kinetic weapons can and do inform rules of engagement that govern cyberspace operations as well. Nevertheless, several characteristics of operations in cyberspace and the use of cyber capabilities complicate the formulation of cyber-specific rules of engagement, including the borderless geography and range of effects possible on the internet, ambiguity of adversary intent arising from the difficulty of distinguishing between intelligence gathering for reconnaissance and preparation for attack, and difficulties of attribution in cyberspace. A paucity of historical experience with cyber operations in a military context will hamper the formulation of rules of engagement for cyber weapons; consequently, special efforts should be made to impart experience (such as might be developed through war gaming and tabletop exercises) to the appropriate leaders and commanders.

Finally, Adam Segal (chapter 13) offers a possible case study addressing the escalation potential of U.S. offensive cyber operations in a China-U.S. military confrontation. Segal notes that while China is increasingly a target-rich environment from both tactical and strategic perspectives, the use of offensive cyber operations against these targets is likely to be highly escalatory. Complications will arise from differing conceptions of deterrence and crisis management, a lack of transparency into the political control of cyber forces, and an expansive view of competition in cyberspace. Yet neither the United States nor China will eschew the use of offensive cyber operations, a point suggesting the importance of both sides considering measures that reduce the likelihood of escalation from tactical to strategic attacks undertaken through cyber means.

The Role of the Private Sector in Offensive Cyber Operations

The private sector is an important part of cyberspace. Unlike other physical domains, private actors in cyberspace can significantly influence the nature, execution, and prospects for success of offensive operations. It is uncontestable that cyber weapons are available to private actors, but the policy implications of such availability are controversial and widely debated. Each of the three chapters in this section tackles a different dimension of the private sector's role in cyberspace.

David Aucsmith (chapter 14) argues that because governments are incapable of defending cyberspace for all denizens, private parties must have the capability to defend themselves—a capability that necessarily includes the ability to inflict harm on attackers. However, the existing legal regime limits the actions private organizations can pursue in cyber defense. A variety of changes to the existing legal regime would allow private companies to take actions consistent with the self-defense constraints of necessity, proportionality, and immediacy, and improve an organization's ability to both defend itself and attribute actions to the aggressors. Lucas Kello (chapter 15) comes to the opposite conclusion in his chapter. Kello grants that the potential defensive and other benefits of cyber weapons in this role are significant, yet he finds that the risks to defenders, innocent third parties, and international conflict stability are greater.

Finally, in chapter 16, Irv Lachow and Taylor Grossman explore the critical roles that companies play in supporting offensive cyber operations, including intelligence/reconnaissance and planning and mission support for such operations. Cyber contractors provide U.S. and other militaries access to rapidly evolving technologies and necessary human talent. At the same time, the use of such contractors has international ramifications. For example, the availability of cyber contractors may affect the balance of power of states, as effective offensive cyber capabilities become available to nations willing to simply buy them. Cyber contractors involved in offensive cyber operations may face some uncertainties about their international legal status. And because their services are in principle available to any party willing to pay for them, a contracting company may find itself on both sides of a cyber operation.

Conclusion

It is only within the last few years that the Department of Defense has designated cyberspace a domain of conflict, and many policymakers are struggling with how best to integrate offensive cyber capabilities with other instruments of military and national power. Taken as a whole, the chapters in this volume suggest that thinking about offensive cyber operations as instruments of national policy need not require de novo construction. Indeed, many of the questions and issues that attend to the strategic dimensions of offensive cyber operations arise in other kinds of military operations. However, because the cyber domain is unlike other domains of conflict in important ways, it is not surprising that some of the answers and responses to these questions and issues in the cyber domain are different. More clearly delineating what's new and what isn't in offensive cyber operations is an important step forward.

Notes

1. See, for example, William J. Broad, John Markoff, and David E. Sanger, "Israeli Test on Worm Called Crucial in Iran Nuclear Delay," *New York Times*, January 15, 2011; and "Iran's Natanz Nuclear Facility Recovered Quickly from Stuxnet Cyber Attack," *Washington Post Foreign Service*, February 16, 2011. However, estimates vary about the extent of delay in the Iranian nuclear program that Stuxnet caused.

2. The leaked PPD-20 can be read in full at https://fas.org/irp/offdocs/ppd/ppd-20 .pdf. As noted in the main text of this chapter, PPD-20 has also been the subject of news articles and editorials, including Glenn Greenwald and Ewen McAskill, "Obama Orders U.S. to Draw Up Overseas Target List for Cyber-Attacks," *Guardian*, June 7, 2013; "Cyberwar: The White House Is Thinking Ahead," Editorial, *Washington Post*, June 16, 2013; Bill Gertz, "Cyber War Details Revealed," *Washington Free Beacon*, June 11, 2013 (http://freebeacon.com/national-security/cyber-war-details-revealed/); and Mark Clayton, "Presidential Cyberwar Directive Gives Pentagon Long-Awaited Marching Orders," *Christian Science Monitor*, June 10, 2013. Because those with clearances are allowed to read press stories reporting on leaked classified documents but not to read these documents themselves outside of cleared facilities, references to PPD-20 in this introduction should be understood as being derived from these articles and not from the original document. In addition, papers in this collection written by individuals who have had proper access to classified cyber-related documents have passed through DoD security review; these papers contain no references to PPD-20, and no individuals with security clearances had any input into this introduction.

3. In May 2018 it was reported that the Trump administration is considering rescinding PPD-20 to streamline decision making and facilitate the faster approval of offensive cyber actions. Chris Bing, "Trump Administration May Throw Out the Approval Process for Cyber Warfare," *Cyberscoop*, May 2, 2018 (www.cyberscoop.com/ppd-20-white-house -national-security-council-cyber-warfare-tactics/).

4. *Department of Defense Cyber Strategy* (April 2015) (www.defense.gov/Portals/1 /features/2015/0415_cyber-strategy/Final_2015_DOD_CYBER_STRATEGY_for _web.pdf); emphasis added.

5. Ash Carter, "Remarks by Secretary Carter" (Drell Lecture, Stanford Graduate School of Business, Stanford, California, April 23, 2015) (www.defense.gov/News/News -Transcripts/Transcript-View/Article/607043).

6. Sean Lyngaas, "The Business of Federal Technology," *FCW*, February 29, 2016 (https://fcw.com/articles/2016/02/29/carter-isis-networks.aspx).

7. Ryan Browne and Barbara Starr, "Top Pentagon Official: 'Right Now It Sucks' to Be ISIS," CNN, April 14, 2016 (www.cnn.com/2016/04/13/politics/robert-work-cyber -bombs-isis-sucks/).

8. Daniel White, "Read Donald Trump's Remarks to a Veterans Group," *Time*, October 2, 2016 (http://time.com/4517279/trump-veterans-ptsd-transcript/).

9. The White House, "Making Our Military Strong Again," January 20, 2017.

10. William J. Broad and David E. Sanger, "U.S. Strategy to Hobble North Korea Was Hidden in Plain Sight," *New York Times*, March 4, 2017; David E. Sanger and William J. Broad, "Trump Inherits a Secret Cyberwar against North Korean Missiles," *New York Times*, March 4, 2017; David E. Sanger and William J. Broad, "Hand of U.S. Leaves North Korea's Missile Program Shaken," *New York Times*, April 18, 2017.

11. White House, *National Security Strategy of the United States of America*, December 2017 (www.whitehouse.gov/wp-content/uploads/2017/12/NSS-Final-12-18-2017-0905.pdf).

12. U.S. Congress, *National Defense Authorization Act for Fiscal Year 2017*, January 4, 2016 (www.congress.gov/114/bills/s2943/BILLS-114s2943enr.pdf).

13. Katie Lange, "Cybercom Becomes DoD's 10th Unified Combatant Command," May 3, 2018 (www.dodlive.mil/2018/05/03/cybercom-to-become-dods-10th-unified-com batant-command/).

14. Michael V. Hayden, "The Making of America's Cyberweapons," *Christian Science Monitor*, February 24, 2016.

15. The points made in this paragraph and additional discussion of the deleterious effects of overclassification regarding offensive cyber operations can be found in Herbert Lin and Taylor Grossman, "The Practical Impact of Classification Regarding Offensive Cyber Operations," in *Cyber Insecurity: Navigating the Perils of the Next Information Age*, edited by Richard M. Harrison and Trey Herr (New York: Rowman & Littlefield, 2016), pp. 313–27.

16. Bernard Brodie, *The Absolute Weapon: Atomic Power and World Order* (New York: Harcourt, Brace, 1946); and Bernard Brodie, *Strategy in the Missile Age* (Princeton University Press, 1959) (www.rand.org/pubs/commercial_books/CB137-1.html).

17. Herman Kahn, *On Escalation: Metaphors and Scenarios* (New York: Praeger, 1965).

18. Thomas Schelling and Morton Halperin, *Strategy and Arms Control* (New York: Twentieth Century Fund, 1961).

19. Joint Chiefs of Staff, *The National Military Strategy*, 2004 (http://ssi.armywarcollege .edu/pdffiles/nms2004.pdf), p. 12.

20. Joint Chiefs of Staff, *The National Military Strategy of the United States of America*, 2004 (http://ssi.armywarcollege.edu/pdffiles/nms2004.pdf), p. 1.

21. *Department of Defense Cyber Strategy*, p. 11.

22. Greenwald and McAskill, "Obama Orders U.S. to Draw Up Overseas Target List."

23. Herbert Lin, "Reflections on the New DOD Cyber Strategy: What It Says, What It Doesn't Say," *Georgetown Journal of International Affairs* 17, no. 3 (2017), pp. 5–13.

24. *Department of Defense Cyber Strategy*, p. 14.

25. See, for example, "Cyberwar: The White House Is Thinking Ahead"; and Greenwald and McAskill, "Obama Orders U.S. to Draw Up Overseas Target List." All references to PPD-20 in this chapter are based on these public news reports and not on any classified document that may have been leaked into the public domain.

26. Office of the Historian, U.S. Department of State, "U.S. Diplomacy and Yellow Journalism, 1985–1898" (https://history.state.gov/milestones/1866-1898/yellow-journalism).

27. Chairman of the Joint Chiefs of Staff, Instruction, *No-Strike and the Collateral Damage Estimation Methodology*, October 12, 2012 (https://info.publicintelligence.net /CJCS-CollateralDamage.pdf).

28. See, for example, Ben Buchanan, *The Cybersecurity Dilemma: Hacking, Trust, and Fear between Nations* (Oxford University Press, 2017).

2

Illuminating a New Domain

The Role and Nature of Military Intelligence,
Surveillance, and Reconnaissance in Cyberspace

CHRIS INGLIS

Cyberspace—the word confounds and provokes in equal measure.

While many definitions of cyberspace argue the fine points of its composition, texture, and context, it is clear by any definition that the domain comprises far more than technology alone. In its simplest form, cyberspace can be considered a melding of technology that stores, processes, and presents information and people whose choices largely direct the execution of the many and varied functions that take place in and through it. Several consequences derive from this reality, foremost among them is that cyberspace constantly evolves, driven by the ebb, flow, and unceasing injection of new technologies, constantly evolving patterns of use, and the individual actions of hundreds of millions of users. And although this inherent complexity and

The opinions expressed in this chapter are those of the author and do not necessarily reflect the views of the United States Naval Academy, the Department of the Navy, or the National Security Agency.

dynamism of cyberspace is rightly perceived as a great good for the billions of people who have come to expect steady advances in the capabilities made available to them by the cyber domain, these same features offer a lucrative and high-leverage means for people and organizations to misappropriate, degrade, or destroy assets and critical functions located in or dependent upon this shared space.

The May 2017 WannaCry ransomware attack that affected hundreds of thousands of computers around the world is a case in point.[1] Designed and implemented by North Korean government hackers,[2] the virus exploited a vulnerability in some Microsoft operating systems that allowed the attacker to take control of a victim's computer, encrypt many of the victim's data files, and issue a demand for a ransom payment as a condition of removing the encryption and restoring the victim's files to usable condition. Two factors were required for a successful attack. First, the victim's operating system had to be susceptible to the software flaw that made the attack possible (specifically, one produced by Microsoft; operating systems produced by other computer software vendors, such as Apple, were not at risk from this particular attack). Second, the victim's operating system had to be one that had not been updated with a "patch" issued by Microsoft in April 2017 that closed the vulnerability exploited by WannaCry (victims who were running pirated versions of Microsoft software were therefore particularly at risk since they do not receive continuing support from Microsoft). Thus, while a technology flaw in the operating system made the attack possible, the actions of both the attacker and the victim were considerably more influential in determining the actual success or failure of the attack. The North Koreans targeted a vulnerability in human procedure as much as or more than one found in the underlying technology. Users who had ensured their software was up to date with the latest patches staved off the attack. Users who had not found themselves vulnerable to the malicious actions of an adversary who made critical files inaccessible and demanded ransom money to restore the system to good order. In the end, the melding of technology and people determined the outcome of an encounter that played out hundreds of thousands of times across the latter half of May 2017.

Cyberspace may then be seen as a system of systems whose properties are attributable to human behavior(s) as much as to technology, one that is largely devoid of physical boundaries or buffer zones that would afford some measure of time to detect and interdict oncoming threats to assets stored in or dependent on cyberspace. Lacking these margins, initiative and agility are often ceded to the adversary, who gets to pick the means, place, and time of an attack, which can then be effected with sufficient speed to cause a defense based principally on detection of ongoing attacks and a reactive response to fail. A state of perpetual preparedness and situational awareness on the part of the defender is the necessary foundation for success in anticipating, detecting, and defending against the actions of a cyber aggressor.

But the challenge of effecting speed, precision, and (desired) impact in cyberspace operations is not confined to defense alone. The dynamism of cyberspace cuts both ways, challenging the aggressor attempting to prosecute a sustained *campaign* (measured by success that is sustained beyond the initial opening tactic) in the face of a now alerted and often unpredictable defender. For these reasons, maintaining the precision and staying power of an attack beyond an opening phase, across the dynamic realms of cyberspace, is a daunting proposition that must also be addressed in the foundations of supporting intelligence, surveillance, and reconnaissance (ISR).

U.S. Cyber Command's Role and Its Implications Going Forward

Following on the heels of Secretary of Defense Robert Gates's June 2009 direction to create U.S. Cyber Command, the U.S. Department of Defense (DoD) brought the command into being in the spring of 2010 with the mission to organize and conduct cyber operations on its behalf. The practical origins of the command's creation go back well more than a decade before Gates's memo as the DoD experienced a number of cyber events, from data theft to system disruption, that steadily increased the department's perception of its own vulnerability to cyber threats.

The culmination of that experience was evidenced in both organization and doctrine that reflected the DoD's expectations that it would be called on to defend the private sector as much as or more than its own systems. In an essay published in *Foreign Affairs*, then–deputy secretary of defense William Lynn III described a foreign government's penetration of U.S. classified systems in October 2008 as an "important wake-up call" and described cyberspace as a "new domain of warfare," marking it as a "fifth domain" of prospective U.S. military operations alongside land, sea, air, and space.[3] As DoD strategy documents were modified to reflect the decision to treat cyberspace as a domain of operations,[4] the department made clear that it expected to be called on by its civilian masters to defend U.S. and allied interests increasingly dependent on, or resident in, cyberspace.[5]

While the DoD considered several models for assigning and organizing prospective cyber missions, the department ultimately concluded that cyber capabilities were sufficiently different from traditional military capabilities that they called for the creation of a physically distinct organization that could focus intellectual and material resources on defining, building, and employing cyber doctrine and capabilities. Reflecting the relative immaturity of U.S. military cyber doctrine and its nascent cyber capabilities, the command was established as a subunified combatant command, tethered to a full-fledged unified command, United States Strategic Command, whose public mission statement is "Deter strategic attack and employ forces as directed to guarantee the security of the U.S. and its allies."[6] The steady maturation of both cyber doctrine and capabilities was reflected in President Trump's August 2017 order that U.S. Cyber Command be "elevated" to the status of a "combatant command" in its own right, initiating its separation from U.S. Strategic Command and a transition to generating and delivering cyber capabilities for the U.S. Department of Defense. That official transition occurred on May 4, 2018.

The U.S. Strategic Command fact page for U.S. Cyber Command lists three main focus areas: "Defending the DoDIN [Department of Defense Information Network supporting the global operations of the DoD in peace and war], providing support to combatant commanders for execution of their missions around the world, and strengthening our nation's ability to withstand and respond to cyber attack."[7] A fourth responsibility of Cyber Command to support U.S. and allied deterrence efforts may be inferred and will also levy expectations on ISR support, reinforcing requirements derived from its primary missions.

The then-commander of U.S. Cyber Command, Admiral Mike Rogers, added greater fidelity to this characterization in his June 3, 2015, Commander's Vision and Guidance for U.S. Cyber Command:

> Our mission in cyberspace is to provide mission assurance for the operation and defense of the Department of Defense information environment, deter or defeat strategic threats to U.S. interests and infrastructure, and support the achievement of Joint Force Commander objectives. Our challenge is to protect the things we value—freedom, liberty, prosperity, intellectual property, and personal information—without hindering the free flow of information that fosters growth and intellectual dynamism.[8]

Three key aspects of the resulting Cyber Command mission warrant highlighting:

1. Cyber Command is responsible for developing and deploying defensive capabilities in direct support of the DoDIN, *and* for participating in the defense of the "nation" and allies against cyberattacks;

2. Cyber Command is responsible for developing and executing offensive capabilities in support of national objectives (sometimes through other combatant commanders);

3. Cyber Command is held to a high standard of precision in the application of its capabilities as reflected in Admiral Rogers's statement that its activities must not hinder "the free flow of information that fosters growth and intellectual dynamism."[9]

Cyber Command's challenge of operating within, through, and from its assigned domain—cyberspace—is by no means straightforward or fully resolved. The department's development of doctrine and capabilities for cyberspace operations has been challenged by several factors, not least of which are: the paucity of directly applicable analogs from other operational domains (sea, land, air, and space); the ambiguous jurisdiction of the cyber domain, one shared between civilian, and various public sector institutions, including the military; the challenge of distinguishing between defensive reconnaissance and its near-twin, reconnaissance supporting incipient attack; and the lack of clear-cut differences between DoD and private sector capabilities and, in a similar vein, clean margins between areas of responsibility as the DoD attempts to sustain, monitor, and, if needed, restore and defend *key terrain* in cyberspace.[10]

These expectations, combined with the realities of its operational domain, create a high bar for U.S. Cyber Command.

• Its participation in the defense of the nation in cyberspace mandates that it be in a position to provide responsive capabilities *when called upon* through the traditional tasking process of the U.S. government in support of the defense of infrastructure and systems that are largely sustained and operated by the private sector. This, in turn, requires Cyber Command to recognize threats in real time to networks that it does not control or have the authority to patrol (in order to enable responsive support).

- Its mandate to prepare and, on order, deliver offensive capability in support of national objectives also requires U.S. Cyber Command to be cognizant of campaign plans, relevant indications and warnings (especially in cyberspace), and the doctrine, routines, rules, and current topology of potential adversary systems and capabilities. Although some of the intelligence sought will reveal insights that remain valid for long periods of time (for example, adversary doctrine), other facets (such as adversary capabilities and tactics) will change more frequently, especially in the midst of an ongoing campaign. Equally important, the cyberspace environment, which comprises large swaths of private sector–provisioned commodity technology and systems, constantly changes in both its substance (technology) and patterns of use (human behavior). The sum of these change dynamics requires ISR that places a high premium on *currency*: real-time, comprehensive intelligence that keeps pace with domains, tactics, and actors whose salient characteristics constantly change.

- Its mandate to achieve precision in the application of its capabilities calls for an ability to see and discriminate between legitimate targets and protected persons, capabilities, and infrastructure at network speed (that is, in real time). Note that the execution of campaigns (as opposed to one-time strikes) will require that this comprehensive fidelity be sustained over time.

Taken in sum, the framing of Cyber Command's mission requires that it have real-time, fine-grained, and current knowledge about adversary forces, capabilities, routines, operating venues, and intentions. While ISR has always been an important *contributor* to mission success for Department of Defense missions, it is, without a doubt, an *essential predicate* and enduring companion to mission success in the cyber realm. Whether operating in time of peace, contingency, or conflict, the demands for ISR in support of cyber operations are much the same: requiring a high intelligence operations tempo that enables the command to go from a standing start to a precise and responsive engagement in the shortest possible time.[11] Equally important is ISR's role in detecting emergent conditions that inform decisions of policymakers and operational commanders in time to act and prevail, preserving the advantages of initiative and maneuver for the United States and its allies.

Two key differences between ISR that supports the DoD's traditional (noncyber) and cyber missions thus emerge. First, given the dynamic mix of technology, software processes, and human action that make up the undulating landscape of cyberspace, cyber ISR quite literally defines the landscape on which cyber operations will take place as much as or more than it describes current conditions in an otherwise stable environment. Second, the means and methods that constitute the ability to conduct cyber ISR are largely the same as the capabilities employed to deliver a discernible (to the adversary) cyber effect. A common view among U.S. Cyber Command's initial planning staff in 2009–10 was that the first 90 percent of cyber reconnaissance (i.e., ISR), cyber defense, and cyberattack consisted of the common work of finding and fixing a target of interest in cyberspace.[12] The remaining 10 percent of a given cyber action was deemed to be all that separated the three possible outcomes of reconnaissance, defense, and attack.

Before proceeding on to the topic of how best to shape cyber ISR, a brief treatment of tactics and strategy is in order.

Tactical and Strategic Foundations

Although cyberspace tactics can be defined as a fluid set of activities where the defense and offense of friendly force(s) (referred to as "blue" forces in DoD parlance) share resources, insights, and leverage, it is useful to consider the unique circumstances of each, which will, in turn, help them identify the ISR best suited to their work.

The Challenge of Defense: Deterring, Anticipating, Detecting, and Countering Adversary Action(s)

Tactical advantage in cyberspace has long been ceded to the aggressors who can choose the means, time, and place of their transgression, leveraging cyber deficiencies in technology and people in order to seize *and* retain the initiative in a domain where speed and agility matter.

Aggressors who achieve a degree of surprise greatly intensify the defender's challenge to characterize the event, precisely locate its constituent components, attribute actions as necessary, mitigate, and recover. The principal issue will be one of speed—wherein the party able to confidently maneuver at greater speed enjoys strategic advantage over the other.

An aggressor's ability to employ large numbers of devices, an inherent advantage derived from operating in and through cyberspace, yields even greater leverage that magnifies the agility and effects of an attack. When an aggressor uses the anonymity that comes from working among large populations along with the rich set of capabilities that serve to misattribute and cloak actions taken in and through cyberspace,[13] the aggressor enjoys a significant advantage against defenders who rely solely on their ability to detect and respond at the moment of attack.

In its most challenging manifestation, aggressor strategy in cyberspace thus leverages the following characteristics:

- Pre-attack systemwide probing and analysis across technology and people to find critical weak points and flaws that provide favorable opportunities for an attack.

- Diffusion of attack forces that are broadly distributed across physical and virtual geography, able to concentrate and converge their fire at a given point of application. This derives from the adversary's ability to coherently command and control numerous devices concentrating fire on a given target.

- Agility derived from choosing, without advance notice, the means, time, and place of exploitation to surprise, outmaneuver, and out-run victims.

- Jumbled, often incoherent, jurisdiction dividing the efforts of defenders, deriving from diverse ownership and management responsibilities inherent in the construction and operation of cyberspace.

- Anonymity, derived from hiding among large populations or active efforts to cover one's trail in order to diffuse or avoid attribution and attendant consequences.

Strategies to defend assets held in, or dependent upon, some aspect of cyberspace must deal with these inherent adversary advantages head-on. Failure to do so explains much about failures in strategies largely consisting of "detect and respond" tactics.

Leaving aside the essential foundations of resilience in hardware, software, and procedures (all elements of the practice of "information assurance" whose purpose it is to make systems more resilient to attack), traditional defense strategies have often centered on defending perimeters and choke points, locations where an adversary can presumably be identified, constrained, and defeated. Such a defensive strategy is usually based on the availability of discriminants such as reliable choke points and adversary use of a given and detectable piece of malware, tactic, or point of origination.

This, in turn, requires some foreknowledge of the adversary's "line of march" and the nature of the event that will trip the defensive action and a consequent focus on examining transactions to match against the tripwire at the chosen choke points.

To be successful in "detect and respond" scenarios, the defender needs to have near perfect knowledge about potential adversary tactics and signatures (for example, the ability to recognize a segment of code known to have malicious purpose and effects), and these need to be observable at the chosen point of examination. Moreover, the defender needs to be able to cover the spread of attacking forces that are likely to emanate from widely dispersed sources and provide important leverage to the attacker. Over time, adversaries have strived to counter such knowledge by adjusting their tactics in ways that are sufficient to bypass or overwhelm the defender's screen, or to subtly modify their malicious code to bypass a signature-based defense. The summary effect is that the defense is often focused on scanning for previously observed malicious behaviors and therefore points its defense at fixed positions, rather than predicting the adversary's broader intentions and behavior and tracking real-time anomalies and behavioral flows. This is not to say that blocking malicious activity at available choke points is not helpful. It is simply insufficient. In the ideal situation, the ability of defenders to *anticipate* will hang on the ability to determine the character, capabilities, and likely future actions of the aggressor, rather than on the ability to identify his tools and observable signatures alone. To be clear, each of these tactics—detection of anomalies, behavioral characterization, and anticipation—makes a valuable contribution to defense, but wresting initiative back from aggressors will require a significant move to anticipation, with increased use of big data analysis and predictive techniques to enable decisions inside, or ahead of, the decision cycle of the adversary or his tools.

The demands of each of these defensive tactics on intelligence are quite different.

- Transaction processing requires a steady feed of (transaction) discriminants, which may be received as a "push" of quantitative data harvested from sensors deployed across networks of interest as well as forensic analysis.

- Behavioral detection requires a real-time feed and synthesis of discriminants associated with entities operating in or on the margins of a given system. The data necessary to feed this approach are best when they are holistic, covering adversaries, behaviors, and the status of protected entities (for example, data, software, and at times the infrastructure that stores and processes them).

- Anticipation (prediction) requires the aggregation, synthesis, and analysis of all source intelligence (derived from network surveillance, human sources, publicly available data sources, and reporting from friendly intelligence organizations across the private sector and governments) covering adversary capabilities, intentions, goals, norms, and values (the latter three providing insight into expected behaviors in a given situation).

- Leveraging the available forces equally requires timely and accurate detection of adversary command and control elements and an ability to anticipate (predict), as well as the ability to track and react.

Autonomous collection, aggregation, and synthesis can be quite helpful across the spectrum of these ISR outcomes, especially in enabling humans with analytic capacity to spend more time on discerning and gaming adversary strategy. Indeed the ever more numerous and sophisticated body of sensors deployed across cyberspace infrastructure is generating an enormous amount of environmental data about real-time conditions in the domain, including the processes used by persons actively directing cyber action(s) and standing tasks. When combined with increasingly sophisticated analytics, getting ever closer to artificial intelligence, such data offer the opportunity to establish robust situational awareness of conditions that constitute both the trip wires and the grist of information needed for cyber ISR.

Such real-time cognizance requires constant ISR that is at once comprehensive and anticipatory.

- *Comprehensive* ISR must cover adversary aspirations, capabilities, modalities, and current disposition.

- *Anticipatory* ISR must be able to predict and discern aggressor actions with sufficient advance warning so that deterrence can be bolstered, defensive actions can be arrayed and adjusted over time, and counterforce application (offense) can be applied with the highest possible leverage and greatest effect. Failure to achieve this will cede initiative to the aggressor in an environment where speed and congestion favor the aggressor.

The challenge of attribution must also be addressed, both to ensure the legitimacy of any response and to assist in crafting tactics that are optimized to counter and defeat the actor in question. Despite its long-standing identification as a major strategic thrust of U.S. national security strategy,[14] attribution remains uneven and widely perceived as weak. As noted in the 2003 U.S. Strategy to Secure Cyberspace: "The speed and anonymity of cyber attacks makes distinguishing among the actions of terrorists, criminals, and nation states difficult, a task which often occurs only after the fact, if at all."[15] This challenge is made unnecessarily difficult by a propensity to view attribution as a post-event phenomenon, essentially condemning the defense to a foot race where the aggressor begins the race "at speed" and the defender from a "standing start." Again, this realization should drive defenders to a preference for real-time, or *ahead-of-time*, and comprehensive ISR.

This chapter does not cover deterrence in any great detail, beyond noting that deterring potential aggressors depends heavily on the perceived (that is, in the mind's eye of the aggressor) ability of a defender to survive and attribute attacks, and the defender's willingness and ability to respond to attacks.

The Challenge of Offense: Sustaining Offensive Campaigns in the Face of a Staunch Defense and Changing Conditions

While the ability to surprise and gain tactical advantage is inherently ceded to the first mover, the challenge of sustaining an offensive campaign in dynamic conditions is by no means trivial, especially in the face of a highly motivated, even if reactive, defender who can be expected to challenge the aggressor's initiative(s) and modify the environment in an attempt to frustrate or defeat him.

The key to sustaining tactics across offensive cyber campaigns is often described as one of sustaining the efficacy of tools under varying conditions caused by the defender's response and the natural variability and dynamism of cyberspace. This description inappropriately pins the burden on technology alone. A better strategy is to consider the "tools" in play as the sum of the technology, the intelligence needed to aim and deliver cyber effects (more broadly: ISR), and the skills, judgment, and tactics of people committed to the "fight." This approach properly emphasizes all of the circumstances in a campaign, giving equal importance to ISR, operator skills and judgment, and the technologies they employ.

The Requirements for ISR

Combining the requirements for defense and offense yields the broad out-lines of the ISR needed to support effective operational campaigns. As I de-scribe in greater detail later in this chapter, the key differences between ISR that supports DoD operations in the physical (noncyber) world and ISR in and through cyberspace can be found in the fact that the cyber landscape (1) is considerably more dynamic (hence the need to achieve and sustain real-time situational awareness); (2) interleaves friendly, hostile, and neutral ac-tors; and (3) is a domain where attribution is often derived from long-standing observation instead of easily and quickly made objective discriminants.

Cyber ISR should therefore meet the following substantive, temporal, and contextual requirements. Hypothetical examples illustrate the intended meaning of each requirement (using the imagined adversary state of Zendia that puts the United States, its private sector, and its allies at risk through its conduct of continuous cyber espionage and episodic cyber disruption and destruction).

Substantive Requirements

Provide details on tactics, capabilities, and preferred behaviors (doctrine) goals and intentions of prospective adversaries, reflecting the commander's need to understand adversary doctrine, behaviors, and modalities as much as or more than adversary order-of-battle, tools, and foundational tactics. *Hypothetical example: The Commander of U.S. Cyber Command needs regular updates on the assigned roles, plans, capabilities, and current actions of the cyber forces of Zendia.*

Given that some of this information may well be visible only when friendly networks are targeted by an adversary, this requirement immediately calls into question the authority, or even the propriety, of the operational forces seeking to obtain, analyze, and hold such information from networks they might be expected to protect or through which they will operate. They may have no jurisdiction in those networks, and those networks are likely to be governed by laws and policies designed to protect the privacy of their own actors. This issue is covered in a following section.

Temporal Requirements (Timeliness)

- Understand a prospective adversary's intentions and actions *before* under-taking cyber actions that require immediate, "at speed" responses. *Hypo-thetical example: Information on Zendian cyber forces, capabilities, and oper-*

ations is a standing requirement, in peacetime, regardless of contingency, and in conflict. It is far more efficient to anticipate and thwart an adversary's action before it occurs, using instruments of power that minimize the possibility of escalation. Effective ISR must understand the adversary's posture, actions, and behaviors in real time. The goal is to move from ISR that *responds* well to ISR that predicts well and sustains that insight over time.

- General characterizations that extrapolate insights from past episodes will not suffice. Operational forces with missions that require real-time response must understand the *actual* conditions in which they will be expected to operate as well as the actual disposition and activities of prospective adversaries. Given the agility required by the environment, this cannot be based solely an ability to "react well" from a cold start.

Contextual Requirements (Agility)

The agility required for operational forces—in both defensive and offensive roles—requires an intimate interplay between ISR and cyber operations, both to enable operational forces to stay abreast of adversary actions and to effect synergy between the find, fix, and act components of the cyberspace operation. *Hypothetical example: U.S. cyber ISR must find and stay in continuous ISR contact with Zendian cyber forces to ensure it has current working knowledge of Zendian intentions, capabilities, strengths, and weaknesses.* ISR assets and personnel must be organic (integrated with both defensive and offensive U.S. cyber operators and fully knowledgeable about friendly force intentions, strategies, and disposition) to keep pace with changing conditions and needs.

In summary, the requirements for ISR require a high level of effort before an event, essentially a "move to contact before contingency and conflict" strategy that develops and sustains near real-time cognizance of environments, actors, routines, and actions in conditions that range from peace to crisis to conflict.

The Challenge of Ambiguity and Shared Spaces

The challenges of effecting reliable and capable ISR support to defensive and offensive operations are exacerbated by two limitations on the freedom of action of ISR forces.

Ambiguity of Intentions

One challenge concerns the ambiguity of an action attendant to its context. The context of a given action in cyberspace determines its outcome. Procedures of monitoring, defense, and attack that are virtually identical in one context can produce vastly different outcomes at the last moment in another context. The actor's intent is often unknown until very late in a sequence of actions.

For the defender, the challenge is to predict an aggressor's downstream moves—that is, to correctly interpret which of several possible "next moves" an aggressor intends to make.

For the attacker, the challenge is to get the defender to misinterpret his actions. This may be desirable (if surprise is the goal), but undesirable if the defender misreads a limited action as an existential threat, thus escalating a situation in a manner unintended by the attacker. One exceptional challenge here is the possibility that an effort to conduct surveillance in support of establishing defensive indications and warning (I&W) is interpreted as probing in preparation for an offensive action.

Shared Spaces

The second factor derives from the large intersection between operating environments and the "global commons" in which the preponderance of infrastructure is privately owned and innocent parties with no role in the campaign, even as they live alongside aggressors and defenders. Legal restraints deriving from U.S. and international law and international frameworks constrain the introduction of military operations into the realm of cyberspace without necessary and proportionate cause.[16] This restraint is particularly acute in peacetime, when the requirements for indication and warnings create an expectation that ISR will detect and thwart cyber aggression at the earliest possible moment, when perceived "necessity" is wanting.

The following challenges therefore arise and must be addressed:

- ISR outside of exigent conditions is generally constrained by law, treaty, and convention to respect the sovereignty of nations, the property of private parties, and the privacy of protected persons.

- Leaving aside potential legal constraints, ISR outside of DoD "owned networks" needed to posture the defense can be mistaken for the leading edge of an offensive campaign.

- The context needed by U.S. decision makers regarding adversary intentions with respect to networks defended by the DoD will often be impossible to determine using data provided by DoD or government-controlled sources alone.

- U.S. (DoD) ISR of adversary systems that support both tactical (example: routine administrative and/or command and control of logistics) and strategic (example: nuclear command and control) capabilities run the risk of being perceived as "worst-case threats"—for example, ISR intended to understand and/or hold tactical capabilities at risk may be perceived as ISR intended to hold strategic capabilities at risk, in the worst case eliciting a strategic response to a perceived existential threat. Moreover, U.S. efforts to limit or de-escalate offensive actions may not be evident if tactical and strategic systems on either side of a given contingency are combined (for example, a limited attack on a system supporting critical or strategic capabilities may not be perceived as "limited" in the absence of clear unambiguous signaling that can only exist outside the channel(s) of the attack vector).

- Real-time cognizance of adversary intentions, means, and attribution is extremely difficult if attempts to understand adversary behavior are initiated only in reaction to a specific event. In such circumstances, initiative, speed, and cover are ceded to the adversary. The ability to anticipate and "respond well" will require pre-event ISR that discerns the character of the environment, notable actors, and incipient actions.

Mitigating the Concerns: Foundations of a Viable ISR Strategy

Given the challenges cited in the previous section, the following recommendations are designed to address the need for comprehensive and anticipatory ISR. The recommendations are presented in three groups: those that deal with changing the character of ISR to match the unique character of cyberspace; those that focus on establishing international understanding, consensus, and norms for cyber ISR; and those that leverage non-DoD resources to complement, augment, and extend DoD capabilities.

The preponderance of these recommendations should be read as improving ISR to support a robust defense of cyberspace or assets that depend on it. Indeed, only one of the recommendations specifically refers to cyber offense, for several reasons: First, the preponderance of DoD's cyber mission is necessarily to effect a robust defense, applying offensive power as a tool of last resort if, as, or when directed by the civilian authority. Second, the situational awareness needed by DoD's offensive cyber missions is largely similar in character, if not in specifics, to that required for the DoD's defense of non-DoD systems, both of which can be expected to take place on or through the shared infrastructure of cyberspace. And finally, the large multi-use, multi-stakeholder shared infrastructure results in a significant, though not complete, overlap in ISR requirements supporting cyber defense and offense. To that end, extensions from the ISR support required to support DoD's defensive cyber mission(s) to enable its offensive mission(s) are noted in the recommendation bearing on cyber offense.

Recommendations to Improve Speed, Fidelity, and Coherence of ISR as a Full Partner to Cyber Operations

Embrace real-time, pre-event ISR as the necessary foundation for agility, precision, and timeliness for all U.S. cyber operations and mitigate challenges of jurisdiction and restricted U.S. ability to develop intelligence in and from systems that it is expected to help defend but does not control.

- Real-time and comprehensive cognizance can be achieved through the integration of three sources:

    (i) *DoD organic resources.* These resources collect, synthesize, and analyze data from sensors deployed on:

    - DoD-owned or -controlled networks that can identify anomalies and flows used to complement and/or initiate additional collection from sources collecting data outside of DoD-controlled infrastructure. Emphasis should be given to correlating events in the broadest possible context to discern the actions of malicious parties operating across DoD, partner, and adjacent networks over time, rather than a garrison-only focus that attempts to discern the context of an aggressor's actions using DoD data alone. These data are principally useful in preparing the defense of DoD-owned/controlled networks, but they can also make a valuable contribution to the situational awareness of partners engaged in defending their adjacent systems, and will inform the tactics and strategies of DoD offensive forces that need to characterize the capabilities and modalities of presumed or prospective adversaries.

- Adversary networks that are surveilled under (1) standing intelligence authority(ies) that permit government surveillance of legitimate foreign intelligence targets pursuant to the production of intelligence that supports all instruments of government power (principally conducted by the U.S. intelligence community) and (2) emerging rules governing U.S. Cyber Command's focused surveillance of prospective adversaries, in advance of a decision to conduct cyber operations outside of DoD-owned or -controlled networks.

(ii) *Partner information* shared under various bilateral, multilateral, or statutorily permitted frameworks (for example, under authorities permitted by the U.S. Cyber Information Sharing Act of 2015). Privacy protections and concerns over legal liability occasioned by exposing adversary successes on networks owned by potential contributors of such data may limit the quantity and fidelity of the data provided to consortiums engaged in sharing. This fact underpins a later research and development recommendation to yield needed context and character for otherwise incomplete data sets. Those concerns aside, and given the natural limits of DoD organic capability to collect information, these sources are an essential component of the "big picture" needed by U.S. Cyber Command to achieve comprehensive real-time cognizance of the actions and intentions of prospective adversaries. The alliances at issue here vary in the ease with which they may be constructed and sustained. As a consequence, efforts to build coalitions in the past have been uneven in their value. The key will be to view them as essential, more than simply valuable, components of the DoD's situational awareness and to build partnerships that are of sufficient mutual benefit that will be sustained over time.

(iii) *Commercially available threat information* that can be harvested and analyzed more economically in the private sector (note that the classic definition of threat is intended here—focused on the actions, capabilities, and intentions of actors in cyberspace, rather than on the flaws of software or hardware they might theoretically hold at risk). This rich source of data can yield a comprehensive picture within the necessary constraints of law and jurisdiction while building trust and confidence that can be leveraged across the full range of peacetime and contingency operations.

Given legal and technical limitations in the DoD's ability to aggregate comprehensive and pristine characterizations of network activity across the span of networks on which they might be expected to conduct cyber operations, research and development must give a high priority to data analytics that can collect, synthesize, and analyze diverse, imperfect (incomplete), and limited-content data sets (likely to comprise more metadata than content) to produce a characterization of present behaviors, future trends, and probable actions by relevant actors. Absent this capability, DoD and U.S. intelligence community (IC) ISR efforts will be constrained to a reactive intelligence strategy owing to the restrictions on their ability to collect, manipulate, and report rich information outside of their jurisdiction. There is a considerable body of this work under way within the private sector, the DoD and the IC.[17]

Fully employ peacetime authorities to monitor and characterize potential adversary aims, capabilities, and actions as a basis for responsive cyber offense if and when directed by the appropriate authority.

This recommendation draws on traditional military theory that intelligence preparation of the environment is fundamental to success in complex operations where timeliness, precision, and attention to proportionality in the application of military force are required.

These requirements are particularly important in cyberspace where protected persons, allies, and foes share a common infrastructure and must deal with moment-to-moment changes in the state of technology and systems, as well as adversary agility, which significantly increase the challenge of applying rational and effective offensive cyber power.

Aggressively pursue threats across jurisdictional boundaries through collaboration and the enhancement of "hot pursuit" authority.

Collaboration that connects the threads of aggressor activity across the jurisdictional boundaries of network owners should be the governing principle here. DoD organizations should aggressively patrol owned networks and pursue threats under still maturing rules of hot pursuit and through collaborative relationships with adjacent network owners.

- Rules for hot pursuit in cyberspace are not yet well defined or widely embraced as a consensus goal. The concept of hot pursuit is also distinct, as in other jurisdictions, from the right of self-defense: hot pursuit refers to crossing into the territorial jurisdiction of a third party to engage a clear and present threat. While this activity might be conflated with pre-emptive engagement of potential adversaries, the burden of responsibility under proposed hot pursuit rules for cyberspace will require that the defender have and demonstrate high confidence that their actions are taken in response to, and only to counter, adversary initiative. Territorial jurisdiction concerns aside, proscribing a hot-pursuit option cedes advantage to adversaries who can exploit the dissonance between physical jurisdictions and a cyber action. Near-term progress in advancing this goal requires legal work to define appropriate implementations of hot pursuit in cyberspace. The precedent needed is likely to be found in laws governing counterterrorism, where a growing body of legal scholarship and international law lays out the case for states to use force against nonstate actors and to breach the territorial sovereignty of foreign states in response to terrorist attacks.[18]

- Collaborative relationships with adjacent network owners are a more straightforward but nonetheless still immature practice. Although sharing of vulnerability information (such as information on security weaknesses in hardware and software) is relatively mature, sharing of threat information (regarding malicious actors who are actively engaged in cyber aggression) lags considerably, making robust collaboration in cyber defense even more challenging. Much of this immaturity can be laid at the feet of concerns over legal liability, but the 2015 U.S. Cyber Information Sharing Act provides broad relief from liability and leaves experience as the principal limiting factor. The DoD, acting through U.S. Cyber Command, should establish physical venues and collaborative arrangements for the real-time sharing of threat data on actors and capabilities. The recent creation in the United Kingdom of the National Cyber Security Centre (NCSC) provides an exemplar of collaboration between the private and public sector.[19]

Sustain a high level of operations tempo in both peace and contingency.

Proactive, anticipatory cyber cognizance across all of the activities recommended here should be perceived as the standard posture, with a bias toward enabling collective defense rather than preparing for offensive action.

The benefit of a faster operations tempo will have two advantages. The first is to improve the fidelity and currency of DoD situational awareness of the status of networks it is called on to defend or hold at risk, with attendant improvements in the probability of success. The second is to signal potential adversaries the resolve of the United States to defend its interests, thereby deterring those adversaries through the increased risk of detection, raising costs borne by adversaries for the construction of tactics and strategies they would bring to bear in any action they might undertake, and the resulting deterrence effects yielded by both. Given the possibility that a faster operations tempo might be read by potential adversaries as an escalation above an otherwise stable baseline, these operational adjustments must be accompanied by careful messaging and an enduring commitment to sustain the new steady state of greater vigilance and vigorous defense. Rapid, unwarned changes in operational tempo will almost certainly alarm a potential adversary as much as they might deter.

Use all components of the cyber ISR toolkit (people, technology, and doctrine that codifies the required and expected practices), with a special focus on people and doctrine.

Significant attention should be focused on the doctrine and training governing the values, behaviors, and accountability of U.S. cyber personnel. They are the critical core of the cyber operations weapons system. Their agility, initiative, and probity will fuel U.S. and allied capabilities while building confidence in the precision and control of U.S. cyber capabilities.

Recommendations to Establish, Communicate and Implement Norms for ISR That Ensure Freedom of Action in U.S. Cyber ISR and Supported Operations

Increase transparency in the conduct of military operations.

- Take confidence-building measures: building and sustaining alliances, publicly declaring priorities, and sharing periodic threat and trend reports with the public sector and allies. DoD cyber actions, and those of U.S. Cyber Command in particular, must be continuous rather than episodic in substance and perception. This is best accomplished by increasing the visibility and perceived value of its work.

- Conduct exercises in plain view to establish understanding of DoD capabilities and rhythms, and to set expectations across supported populations, allies, and potential adversaries.

Embrace, publicly support, and visibly share operational norms beyond the United States.

- Establish broad understanding of U.S. norms and the department's commitment to support them across supported populations, allies, and adversaries. The declaration and practice of these norms will set expectations among the public, allies, and potential adversaries and will establish a foundation for deterrence.

- Publicly embrace norms advanced by U.S. diplomatic efforts and the U.S. International Strategy for Cyberspace.[20] Consistent with public testimony of the State Department before the Senate Foreign Relations Committee on May 14, 2015, these may include:

  - Proscribing intentional damages to critical infrastructure or efforts that otherwise impair the use of that infrastructure to provide services to the public.

  - Proscribing activity intended to prevent national computer security incident response teams from responding to cyber incidents (outside of conditions of war).

  - Cooperating in a manner consistent with domestic law and international obligations with requests for assistance from other states in investigating cyber crimes, collecting electronic evidence, and mitigating malicious activity emanating from its territory.

  - Proscribing cyber-enabled theft of intellectual property by nations, including trade secrets or other confidential information, with the intent of providing competitive advantages to their companies or commercial sectors.

The DoD's embrace of these norms is in keeping with their articulation as a U.S. government policy. They do not constrain DoD activities under the law of armed conflict or in legitimate, necessary, and proportional, self-defense actions. Together with DoD's cyber doctrine and publicly visible actions as recommended in the preceding sections, they support public understanding of the roles, lines of operation, and the limits of both to the private sector, and to state and nonstate actors whose misperceptions about all three constitute a potential source of surprise and instability for any level of DoD activity.

*Lead by example to reduce the propensity for miscalculation, modifying archi-
tecture and doctrine to reduce ambiguity in interpreting the actions of cyberspace actors.*

Tactical systems should be disentangled from strategic and critical systems. Systems that support routine administrative and logistical operations
and routine command and control should be separate from those systems that
support strategic capabilities such as nuclear command control, for two reasons. Separate operations will allow for a greater concentration of effort and
return on investment in the defense of systems that support strategic capability. And as an underpinning to declared U.S. policy, separate operations
will make it clear to adversaries that any cyber activity targeted at strategic
systems is unacceptable.

There may still be ambiguity in the minds of potential cyber adversaries
regarding distinctions, and signaling, between U.S. surveillance that supports defensive operations (traditional I&W) and surveillance related to
preparation-of-battlefield ISR.[21] A policy that declares the U.S. intention
to achieve a high level of cognizance and greater collaboration with the private sector and allies, as well as the signaling conveyed by reasonable transparency and stability in the level of cyber operations, will serve to mitigate, though
not wholly remove, these concerns.

Wherever possible, the United States should employ offensive cyber power
(or actions that may be interpreted as the leading edge of offensive cyber
operations) in conjunction with other instruments of power to reduce the
possibility of adversary misinterpretation of U.S. intentions. Given the
ambiguity of signaling in cyber actions across the spectrum of vigorous
defense, proactive intelligence gathering, and imminent offensive cyber operations, signaling outside of cyberspace should complement signals observed in and through cyberspace.

Recommendations to Identify and Leverage Non-DoD Partners, Data Sets, and Capabilities

*Enrich the collection of information on threat actors through the robust use of
cyber honeypots,[22] the fullest possible sharing of data between public and private sector organizations, and greater use of network hunting and redteaming.*

- The key here is to combine information collected under standing authorities (typically apportioned on the basis of network ownership or

control and/or user consent agreements) to yield a picture of adversary behavior that transcends the traditional jurisdictions of networks based on ownership.

- The DoD must lead by example by vigorously patrolling DoD-owned networks (especially through hunting and penetration testing), collaborating proactively and visibly with partners, and declaring a policy to fully use its peacetime intelligence authorities to understand and track the actions of presumed or prospective aggressors.

- Privacy concerns may require anonymization of collected data shared across jurisdictions, but even metadata will contribute to the collective understanding of the scope, scale, and nature of cyber threats.

Build and sustain collaborative partnerships that reduce the possibility of surprise and increase the probability of mutual support.

- Foster close working relationships with organizations in the private sector, combat support agencies, and the larger IC that foster the timely (ideally real-time) exchange of threat indicators characterizing behaviors and capabilities. (These will include the organic Cyber Command assets, the U.S. intelligence community, private sector threat information providers, private sector network owners and managers, and allies.) Privacy concerns will necessarily constrain these efforts but can only be understood and reconciled through an aggressive effort to partner within the rule of law, treaties, and international convention.

- Create interdependence between the U.S. private and public sectors, and between U.S. and appropriate foreign military partners. Again the United Kingdom's National Cyber Security Centre can serve as an example of real collaboration between government and the private sector. This interdependence will facilitate the ability of these systems to deliver under all conditions and establish shared norms for thresholds for warning and action.

- The use of organizational embeds (e.g., exchange officers and liaisons) and cross-organizational exercises will build confidence and needed muscle memory for crisis and contingency situations.

Conclusion

The agility, diversity, and strategic capabilities of potential adversaries in and through cyberspace can only be understood, mitigated, and addressed through an identical and, when needed, overmatching U.S. ability to anticipate, outmaneuver, and defeat threats in their incipient phase. The need for persistent surveillance as an enabler of mission success is both operationally justified and legally and practically constrained by factors related to overlapping jurisdictions, shared infrastructure, and the inherent ambiguity of cyberspace actions.

The U.S. Department of Defense, working in concert with other U.S. government, private sector, and allied partners must establish the ISR feeds and collaborative partnerships needed to support responsive, precise, and proportionate cyber actions that contribute to the achievement of U.S. and allied ends while not unnecessarily (unintentionally) raising concerns or precipitating escalations by other actors in the space.

The key to reconciling these multiple aims—responsive ISR, unambiguous signaling, and effective cyber operations—is to establish new norms of U.S. ISR in its operational signatures, operations tempo, transparency, collaboration, integration of ISR and operational activities, and professional training standards. These will form a mutually supportive framework of capabilities and messaging that improves the intrinsic power and ultimate effect of ISR and the operations they are intended to enable.

Notes

1. See "WannaCry: Understanding and Preventing the Global Ransomware Attack," Aldridge Company, May 24, 2017 (http://aldridge.com/wannacry-understanding-preventing-global-ransomware-attack) for further details on the nature and impact of this virus.

2. In a White House press briefing on December 19, 2017, the president's Homeland Security and Counterterrorism adviser, Thomas Bossert, announced his agency's conclusion that North Korea executed the WannaCry attacks of May 2017.

3. Quoted in William J. Lynn III, "Defending a New Domain: The Pentagon's Cyberstrategy," *Foreign Affairs* 89, no. 5 (September/October 2010), pp. 97–108.

4. Strategic Initiative 1 of the July 2011 *Department of Defense Strategy for Operating in Cyberspace* states that the DoD will "treat cyberspace as an operational domain to organize, train, and equip so that DoD can take full advantage of cyberspace's potential" (https://csrc.nist.gov/CSRC/media/Projects/ISPAB/documents/DOD-Strategy-for-Operating-in-Cyberspace.pdf).

5. The *Department of Defense Cyber Strategy*, published in April 2015, laid out five strategic goals, the third of which is "Be prepared to defend the U.S. homeland and U.S. vital

interests from disruptive or destructive cyber-attacks of significant consequence" (www .defense.gov/Portals/1/features/2015/0415_cyber-strategy/Final_2015_DoD _CYBER_STRATEGY_for_web.pdf).

6. U.S. Strategic Command internet home page (www.stratcom.mil). The Strategic Command's priorities are further cited as "strategic deterrence, decisive response when deterrence fails, and sustainment of a resilient, equipped and trained combat ready force."

7. U.S. Strategic Command Fact Page for U.S. Cyber Command, as of January 10, 2016 (www.stratcom.mil/factsheets/2/Cyber_Command/).

8. Admiral Michael Rogers, Commander U.S. Cyber Command, "Beyond the Build: Delivering Outcomes in Cyberspace," June 3, 2015 (www.defense.gov/Portals/1/features /2015/0415_cyber-strategy/docs/US-Cyber-Command-Commanders-Vision.pdf).

9. This constraint is equivalent to a determination of acceptable collateral damage allowed in traditional military operations.

10. There is, in addition, the attendant difficulty of basing a relationship between military and civil sector responsibilities on "by degree" considerations as an alternative to physical distinctions in jurisdiction (such as transferring responsibility along the continuum from peace to war).

11. The DoD's tactical airlift community refers to this phenomenon as "idling at 100 percent," a term denoting the fact that C-130 engines run at 100 percent of their rated speed at all times, creating an ability for immediate power generation by simply changing the pitch of the propeller to take larger or smaller bites of the air.

12. The military term of art "find and fix" means to locate an activity of interest and then focus military capabilities on it with sufficient precision that the target will be at the nominal center of any military action.

13. An example is the so-called Onion Router (Tor), available as a commodity service on the internet to anyone who wants to obscure their true identity or location.

14. "Improve capabilities for attack attribution and response" was cited as one of "six major actions and initiatives to strengthen U.S. national security and international cooperation." The White House, *National Strategy to Secure Cyberspace*, February 2003, p. xiii (www.us-cert.gov/sites/default/files/publications/cyberspace_strategy.pdf).

15. Ibid., p. viii.

16. The U.S. Constitution's Third Amendment provision on "anti-quartering" has been interpreted by some to imply a requirement for a zone of privacy separating military operations from private domestic systems. More consequential are the provisions of the Fourth Amendment, which constrains the government's ability to "search and seize" information owned by or pertaining to U.S. persons while allowing, under case law, an exemption to the warrant requirement for exigent circumstances where either evidence or a suspect might disappear before a warrant could be obtained. A leading U.S. case on this is *United States* v. *Santana*, 427 U.S. 38 (1976) (www.loc.gov/item/usrep427038/).

17. Both the Intelligence Advanced Research Projects Activity (IARPA) and the Defense Advanced Research Projects Agency (DARPA) sponsor significant research along these lines.

18. Christian J. Tams, "The Use of Force against Terrorists," *European Journal of International Law* 20, no. 2 (2009), pp. 359–97.

19. Established in early 2017, the United Kingdom's NCSC is a physical center that supports a collaborative endeavor between the U.K. government and the private sector designed to "help protect our critical services from cyber attacks, manage major incidents and improve the underlying security of the U.K. Internet." See website of the NCSC at www.ncsc.gov.uk/.

20. The White House, *International Strategy for Cyberspace, Prosperity, Security and Openness in a Networked World,* May 2011 (https://obamawhitehouse.archives.gov/sites /default/files/rss_viewer/international_strategy_for_cyberspace.pdf).

21. Again, this author sees no distinction between the terms "computer network exploitation" (CNE), "preparation of the battlefield," and "operational preparation of the environment" (OPE). These are sometimes used to distinguish between Title 50 intelligence and Title 10 operational authorities. In practice, they are the same activity.

22. Cyber honeypots are decoy servers or systems set up to attract the attention of malicious actors and gather information regarding their attempts to take unauthorized actions within or against a system.

3

How Effects, Saliencies, and Norms Should Influence U.S. Cyberwar Doctrine

HENRY FARRELL *and* CHARLES L. GLASER

How should the United States respond if an adversary employs cyberattacks to damage the U.S. homeland or weaken its military capabilities? Closely related, what threats should the United States issue to deter these attacks? The most obvious answer may be that cyberattacks should be met with cyber retaliation. Careful examination of these questions shows, however, that under a variety of conditions the United States should retaliate with conventional military attacks—that is, kinetic attacks. On the flipside, are there situations in which the United States should employ cyberattacks to improve its prospects for success in a conventional war?

To analyze these questions, we draw upon and combine three logics: effects, saliencies, and norms. We begin with a basic effects-based logic—that is, decisions about deterrence and warfighting should be based on the effect a U.S. attack will have, not on the means by which that effect is produced; if kinetic retaliation and cyber retaliation would inflict comparable costs, then there is no obvious reason to favor one over the other. We then draw upon the concepts of focal points and saliencies to add useful distinctions. This is necessary because the pure effects-based logic is likely too sparse—states may perceive different forms of retaliation that do equal damage (that is, are equally costly) as differently punishing and differently escalatory. Finally, we consider the possibility that norms against certain types of cyberattacks should impose limits on U.S. cyber doctrine. Although such norms have not yet been established, beyond those that apply generally to the laws of war, we discuss a couple of possibilities, as well as the barriers to their achievement.

Current U.S. cyber doctrine is consistent with an effects-based approach, making clear that the United States envisions the possibility of kinetic attacks in response to cyberattacks: "The United States will continue to respond to cyberattacks against U.S. interests at a time, in a manner, and in a place of our choosing, using appropriate instruments of U.S. power." On the flipside, the strategy also suggests that the United States might rely on cyberattacks to contribute to U.S. efforts that have not yet involved cyberattacks: "The United States military might use cyber operations to terminate an ongoing conflict on U.S. terms, or to disrupt an adversary's military systems to prevent the use of force against U.S. interests." The strategy emphasizes that cyber capabilities will be integrated with the full range of other U.S. fighting capabilities: "DoD should be able to use cyber operations to disrupt an adversary's command and control networks, military-related critical infrastructure, and weapons capabilities. . . . To ensure unity of effort, DoD will enable combatant commands to plan and synchronize cyber operations with kinetic operations across all domains of military operations."[1] Less clear is whether U.S. doctrine narrows this effects-based approach by taking into account saliencies and norms (except for the laws of armed conflict).[2]

Influential analyses of cyber strategy question a purely effects-based approach, pointing out that a kinetic response to a cyberattack could constitute a dangerous escalation. This alternative perspective argues that other considerations—beyond the amount of damage that an attack would inflict—may influence an adversary's understanding of and reaction to an attack. For example, Herbert Lin cautions that "nations involved in a cyber-only conflict may have an interest in refraining from a kinetic response—for example, they may believe kinetic operations would be too provocative and might result in an undesired escalation of the conflict."[3] Martin Libicki offers a similarly cautious perspective; while not ruling out kinetic responses, he argues that a kinetic response "would trade the limited risks of cyberescalation with [sic] the nearly unlimited risk of violent escalation."[4]

The first section of this chapter develops the effects-based logic for cyberwar. Although U.S. doctrine incorporates this approach, application of basic deterrence theory enables us to develop a more nuanced effects-based doctrine. We distinguish between counterforce and countervalue cyberattacks and explore their implications for retaliation. Further, we argue that a potentially important difference between kinetic and cyberattacks should be included in a sophisticated analysis: even if cyber and kinetic attacks are expected to inflict the same damage, the effects of the cyberattack will be less certain. This difference in uncertainty and predictability has a variety of implications for cyber doctrine.

The second section addresses the possibility that saliencies exist, or could be established, in the cyber environment that would require the United States to modify the effects-based approach. For example, a retaliatory attack that *econ* inflicts extensive economic damage but no physical damage is likely to be *US.* understood differently from an equally costly attack that does inflict physical *lives* damage; there is likely a salient difference between economic and physical damage. Consequently, the United States should not envision these attacks simply as equally damaging. We believe that a cyber doctrine that fails to incorporate saliencies risks overlooking the escalatory potential of certain types of retaliatory attacks. More specifically, there are likely to be situations in which kinetic retaliation will be more escalatory than a comparably costly cyber response. This has specific implications for the argument that the United States should retaliate against cyberattacks on democratic institutions and practices. Without a salient understanding of what such attacks involve, and which ones merit which kind of response, *such retaliation may be more escalatory* than anticipated. The third section explores possible norms that could constrain U.S. doctrine. We believe that a norm prohibiting cyberattacks against critical infrastructure, including even limited cyberattacks, is likely worth pursuing. We then discuss the possibility of an arms control arrangement in which major nuclear powers agree not to plan or launch cyberattacks against each other's nuclear command and control.

Logic and Implications of the Effects-Based Approach

Adversaries may use cyberattacks to weaken U.S. military capabilities and to inflict damage on U.S. society, such as crippling its electric grid, disrupting its financial systems, and undermining other components of key infrastructure.

Defense alone ineffective

The United States can try to defeat these attacks by reducing software vulnerabilities, diversifying key cyber systems, and increasing awareness of attacks. However, for a variety of reasons, the United States will be unable to make its cyber systems completely invulnerable to attack. Consequently, the United States will need to rely also on deterrence of cyberattacks.[5]

Deterrence Basics

The cost-benefit logic of deterrence should apply, at least in principle, to cyberspace (although as many have argued, questions of attribution will complicate many deterrence-based arguments). The key questions for U.S. policy concern which deterrent threats or actions will prevent other states from behaving contrary to U.S. interests without leading to retaliation that makes U.S. deterrent policies self-defeating. Exploring this set of issues requires understanding what other states care about, and which threats are hence most likely to deter them without leading to unwanted escalation.

An effects-based approach starts from the claim that states care primarily about the *extent* of the damage that is inflicted, not about the *means* used to inflict it. For example, if an adversary undermines the functioning of a dam and causes severe flooding, it matters little whether the adversary employed a cyber weapon or a kinetic weapon—the state suffers the same damage and the same costs.[6] If this perspective is correct, the state should envision its adversary in the same way. Deterrence then depends upon the state's ability to inflict damage on the adversary or to deny the success of the adversary's attack. The adversary should therefore care little whether these effects are achieved by cyber or kinetic means. Thus, at least as a first-order approximation, whether the adversary is deterred should depend on its anticipation of effects and damage, not on the means by which the state promises to achieve them.[7]

The preceding points have direct implications for both deterrence by punishment (threatened costs) and deterrence by denial (threatened defeat of the adversary's attack).[8] *Deterrence by punishment* relies on "countervalue" attacks—that is, attacks on targets of inherent value, as opposed to military targets, which are valued because of their ability to perform military missions. Valuable targets include a state's people, possibly its leadership, and its economy, as well as the infrastructure that supports the state's people and its economy. Deterrence by punishment will succeed if the adversary believes the threatened costs are sufficiently large and sufficiently likely to be inflicted. In the nuclear realm, holding the adversary's cities hostage—that is, vulnerable to retaliation—is considered the basic requirement for deterring the adversary's nuclear attacks on one's own cities. The strict parallel in the cyber realm would be to threaten cyber retaliation that would inflict comparable damage to the same type of targets that the adversary had attacked with cyber weapons.

The effects-based logic suggests, however, that we need to scrutinize this parallel much more carefully. From this perspective, there is no obvious reason that the United States *needs* to deter countervalue cyberattacks with the threat of cyber retaliation. Because deterrence works by threatening costs with sufficient credibility, not by threatening specific types of attacks, this type of retaliation-in-kind is not necessary for deterrence to be effective.

There are many examples from the Cold War that are consistent with this basic point. For example, the United States relied on tactical nuclear weapons to bolster its ability to deter Soviet conventional land attack. These weapons would have inflicted more damage than conventional weapons, but the point here is that the United States did not rely solely on retaliation-in-kind. The United States has retained the option of employing nuclear weapons to deter biological weapons attacks, among other reasons because it does not possess biological weapons. Studies of other U.S. options for deterring biological weapons attacks have identified a range of conventional options, including invading the attacker's country.[9] All of these arguments are grounded in an effects-based logic. There does not appear to be a first-order reason that the United States should not rely on the same logic in planning to deter countervalue cyberattacks.[10]

If the United States wanted to make clearer that it was threatening or attempting to inflict comparable damage (for example, to avoid further escalation) through kinetic retaliation, it could attack targets that were similar to those its adversary had destroyed with cyberattacks. For example, if the adversary's cyberattack had destroyed part of the U.S. electric grid, oil refineries, or pipelines, the United States could retaliate against these infrastructure targets in the attacker's homeland. Alternatively, the United States could threaten to cause damage that was quite different from that inflicted by the cyberattack. For example, except when facing a major power, the United States could threaten to invade the attacker's country or impose a new regime, if the country launched an extremely destructive countervalue cyberattack against the United States. These costs would be very different from those imposed by the adversary's cyberattack, but the costs do not have to be of a similar type for an adversary to be deterred. In the effects-based approach, the key consideration for the United States should not be whether to respond in kind—using the same means or aiming for a similar target—but rather which threatened response is likely to be most effective.[11] The decision should take a variety of factors into account, including credibility, expected effects, predictability of effects, and the availability and vulnerability of targets.

For all except possibly the most devastating cyberattacks, the United States would be able to inflict comparable damage with kinetic attacks against critical targets in the adversary's homeland.[12] Depending on the nature of the adversary's economy and the extent to which it depends on vulnerable information networks, the United States might also have the ability to inflict comparable damage with a cyberattack.[13]

A key potential shortcoming of kinetic retaliation must therefore lie in the adversary's assessment of U.S. credibility—that is, the adversary's assessment of the United States' ability and willingness to inflict retaliatory damage by kinetic attack.[14] These shortcomings need to be compared with the credibility challenges inherent in cyber retaliation, which are likely substantial.

To lay the groundwork for this comparison, we first consider the barriers to making cyber retaliatory threats credible. Generally speaking, the threat of cyber retaliation is less credible than the threat of kinetic retaliation because a state will have greater difficulty demonstrating its cyberattack capabilities before a conflict begins. States can reveal their conventional and nuclear capabilities by developing, testing, and deploying forces, demonstrating their effectiveness against relevant types of targets, and engaging in training and exercises, all of which are observable (to varying degrees) by their adversaries. In contrast, an adversary will have far less evidence of the extent and effectiveness of U.S. offensive cyber capabilities. Not only are they entirely invisible, but they may be untested against adversary systems, leaving the adversary with some doubt about their effectiveness, and in turn about the credibility of U.S. threats.[15] Testing cyber weapons against the adversary's systems, especially ones that it views as especially valuable and important, would be risky because, if detected, the adversary would likely view the test as highly provocative. In addition, testing a cyber weapon could reduce its future effectiveness by alerting the adversary to the vulnerability that the attacker plans to exploit. Doubts about the attacker's offensive cyber capabilities could be further increased by the limitations of relying on one-shot or target-customized weapons, which could well be useless after the first attack.[16] Thus conventional responses will often be easier for an adversary to assess.

cyber credibility

How does the credibility of kinetic retaliation compare? First, the adversary might doubt the appropriateness of a conventional response, believing that retaliation-in-kind is the most obvious response. Although this is a reasonable consideration, an effects-based perspective suggests that it should be largely discounted: why should the means that the United States employed to inflict damage influence the adversary's assessment of the United States' ability to inflict a given level of damage? If anything, the analysis so far suggests that conventional retaliation has important advantages. For the already noted reasons, the adversary will have less doubt about the U.S. ability to launch an effective conventional attack than an effective cyberattack. Second, uncertainty about the scope of the effects that a cyberattack would inflict—especially the possibility that it would do far more damage than intended—could make U.S. leaders reluctant to order such an attack. Recognition of this complexity-induced reluctance could, in turn, reduce the credibility of U.S. countervalue cyber retaliation.

Third, the relative vulnerability of the United States to cyberattacks could favor conventional retaliation. The United States is a densely networked society, with a rich variety of targets for countervalue cyberattacks. Some potential adversaries may not be so rich in cyber vulnerabilities. In this case, if the adversary believed that the United States expected retaliation-in-kind (which we have argued is not a clearly logical position), then the adversary would find U.S. conventional threats more credible, because the United States is less vulnerable to conventional retaliation than to cyber retaliation.

Fourth, the adversary might question whether the United States would be willing to escalate to conventional retaliation if it thought that the United States believed that conventional retaliation would escalate the conflict and lead to still more damaging attacks. Once again, from an effects-based perspective there is not an obvious reason for this belief. It is possible, however, that more subtle understandings of escalation thresholds or steps in an escalation ladder could support this concern. They might explain, for example, why the Obama administration reportedly "authorized planting cyberweapons in Russia's infrastructure . . . that could be detonated if the United States found itself in an escalating exchange with Moscow" in the wake of Russian election hacking.[17] In the following section on saliencies we explore whether this type of distinction might exist between the specific effects of cyber and kinetic attacks, and whether the United States has the ability to influence these understandings.

Similar considerations apply to the most extreme form of kinetic retaliation—nuclear retaliation. The possibility of a nuclear attack in retaliation for a cyberattack was raised in the 2018 Nuclear Posture Review (NPR). The report states:

> The United States would only consider the employment of nuclear weapons in extreme circumstances to defend the vital interests of the United States, its allies, and partners. Extreme circumstances could include significant non-strategic attacks. Significant non-strategic attacks include, but are not limited to, attacks on the U.S., allied, or partner civilian population or infrastructure, and attacks on U.S. or allied nuclear forces, their command and control, or warning and attack assessment capabilities.[18]

Nonstrategic attacks could include cyber, space, chemical, and biological weapons capabilities, as well as large-scale conventional attacks. Although there has been some disagreement over whether the NPR is referring to cyberattacks in this passage about non-nuclear strategic attacks,[19] cyber is likely the only non-nuclear capability that could inflict massive population damage or severely undermine U.S. command and control (C2).

The statement applies to two quite different types of cyberattacks—countervalue attacks against the U.S. population and infrastructure, and counterforce attacks against nuclear C2. The discussion here applies to both types of attacks, although in different ways. One of the doubts raised about nuclear retaliation against a countervalue cyberattack is that it would be disproportionate; some experts believe that a cyberattack against U.S. infra-structure would kill far fewer people than a nuclear attack. If, however, these experts were wrong and the damage involved truly massive loss of life, then, according to an effects-based approach, nuclear retaliation—possible with a small nuclear weapon—should be viewed as an option. Moreover, a nuclear retaliatory threat might not need to be highly credible because the United States would clearly be threatening to inflict enormous costs. Still open, though, is the question of whether the nuclear retaliatory threat would be sufficiently credible. The point raised earlier, that the United States could be deterred from escalating to a conventional attack, applies in spades to a nuclear attack: if a cyberattack were launched by a nuclear power, the United States might be deterred from escalating to a nuclear attack by the adversary's ability to match or exceed its nuclear response. Recognizing this possibility, the adversary might doubt the credibility of even an explicit threat to escalate to a nuclear attack. And here again, the question of saliencies—specifically crossing the nuclear threshold—could play a significant role in U.S. decisions about this type of escalation.

Cyber counter-C2 attacks pose a different type of danger. Instead of trying to coerce the United States by inflicting costs, with the threat of more to come, a counter-C2 attack makes sense only as part of an effort to significantly reduce or entirely disable the U.S. nuclear retaliatory capability. The fear is that disrupting nuclear C2 might either prevent the United States from being able to launch its weapons or delay its ability to retaliate for long enough that the attacker could employ other weapons to destroy the U.S. nuclear forces. In most scenarios an attack against nuclear C2 would be a component of a war plan designed to start an all-out war. Nuclear retaliation will be feasible for the United States only if it is able to avoid being completely crippled by the cyberattack. If it is, or if the adversary believes it is, then the threat of U.S. nuclear retaliation against the adversary's population and infrastructure should be a highly effective deterrent. In this case, the United States would necessarily be relying on a combination of *deterrence by punishment* and *deterrence by denial*. If the United States could not defend its nuclear C2 sufficiently to convince its adversary that a cyberattack would not be completely successful, then its threat of deterrence by punishment would lack credibility. Whether nuclear retaliation would cross a saliency and therefore reduce its credibility is a trickier issue: although the adversary would not have used nuclear weapons, its cyberattack would have damaged U.S. nuclear capabilities, thereby at least blurring the distinction.

To sum up, the effectiveness of the U.S. deterrent will be enhanced by leveraging both its (known) kinetic prowess and its (partly unobservable) cyber prowess to make deterrent threats. Precisely how to use both sets of assets requires addressing trade-offs: not specifying in advance which it might use increases the range of retaliatory options the adversary must take fully into consideration; on the other hand, making specific threats if specific types or levels of fighting occur puts the United States' reputation on the line, which can contribute to the credibility of specific threats. One thing that is likely, though, is that the United States should rely, at least partly, on its kinetic options, as it already does. Whether nuclear responses should be included is a much more complex question.

Deterrence by denial works by an entirely different logic: in this approach, the United States deploys capabilities to convince its adversary that the probability that its attack will succeed is low; this reduces the adversary's expected benefits from the attack and can therefore result in successful deterrence. Even more than deterrence by punishment, the type of scenario plays a critical role in evaluating the choice between cyber and conventional denial.

If the United States is preparing for a cyberattack that does not inflict physical damage, then the denial capability will typically be cyber; that is, because the attack is against cyber systems, the way to defeat it will ordinarily be some type of cyber capability, whether defense, redundancy, or an offensive cyberattack that disrupts the adversary's attack (although some forms of physical protection, such as disconnecting systems from the internet and other networks may also be efficacious).

If, however, the United States is preparing for a cyberattack against U.S. military capabilities, its options are quite different. Deterring cyberattacks in isolation is probably not the key to deterring this type of attack. Both the United States and its adversary are likely to envision countermilitary cyberattacks as an integral part of their conventional fighting capability. Within types of weaponry and warfare, the United States has traditionally distinguished between conventional and nuclear warfare, and also made distinctions between chemical and biological weapons. In contrast, in the context of countermilitary attacks, cyberattacks should not be considered a different type of warfare. Instead, countermilitary cyberattacks should be viewed as a component of conventional warfare.

This thinking would be in line with current categorizations, which include, for example, electronic warfare assets as an element of conventional capabilities. Similarly, imagine a cyberattack that damaged U.S. conventional command and control capabilities. Why should the United States' response to this attack, or its deterrent threat that is designed to prevent the attack, be different if the damage is done by a kinetic attack than by a cyberattack?

If the preceding line of argument is correct, then the challenge the United States faces in deterring countermilitary cyberattacks is to deter the adversary's overall conventional attack, including the offensive cyber capabilities that would be a component of this attack. This overall deterrent will depend on relative U.S. cyber capabilities, including both its ability to defend against the adversary's cyberattacks and its ability to use offensive cyberattacks to weaken its adversary's overall conventional capability. But deterrence will depend still more broadly on how the United States' conventional capabilities compare with its adversary's. The adversary could be deterred from launching a conventional attack, including its countermilitary cyber component, if the United States has the ability to win a conventional conflict, even if its adversary enjoys a cyber advantage. And, more in line with standard worries, an adversary that enjoys a net advantage in countermilitary cyber capabilities might not be deterred, even if U.S. conventional forces are otherwise clearly superior, because it believes cyberattacks will enable victory in the conventional war. In any event, the point here is that the impact of cyber capabilities on deterrence should be understood in terms of their net impact on overall U.S. conventional capabilities.

Given that expectations about the combined impact of conventional and cyber capabilities should determine the effectiveness of the U.S. ability to deter by denial a conventional war, including cyberattacks, the United States should choose the mix of conventional and cyber capabilities that will have the best prospect for defeating the adversary's attack and, closely related, for deterring that attack in the first place. The proper mix of U.S. conventional and cyber assets is likely to vary across specific conventional war scenarios.

Once again, relying heavily on conventional capabilities has one clear advantage: the United States is likely to have greater confidence in these capabilities. As a result, its adversary may view conventional forces as a more convincing deterrent.

Implications for Deterrence of Uncertainty about the Effects of Cyber Retaliation

One important difference between conventional attacks and cyberattacks is that the effects of cyberattacks are uncertain.[20] Their unpredictability reflects the nature of cyberattacks, which typically target complex software architectures that are connected to other computers through the internet. There are three aspects of cyberattacks, and of cyberspace more broadly, that make them so unpredictable.

First, the complexity of the targeted software itself could render an attack unpredictable simply by obscuring what would happen when the software system is interfered with or disrupted. Second, because most computer systems are connected to other computer systems through the internet, some kinds of attack can spread across these computers. The complexity and interconnectedness of the systems make it hard to predict the extent and speed of an attack's spread or the impact on each computer. Third, corruption of computers could generate physical effects that cascade well beyond cyberspace and are themselves difficult to predict. For example, a cyberattack against computers that control a limited portion of the electric grid could lead to much more far-reaching damage if local outages create other outages across the grid in a cascading process.

A well-known example of unpredicted spread of a cyber virus is Stuxnet: the attack ended up infecting many "innocent" computer systems in Iran and elsewhere, although it did not inflict physical damage beyond the Iranian nuclear complex.[21] Unconfirmed reports suggest that other cyberattacks have had unexpectedly extreme consequences (such as briefly taking out an entire country's internet access, more or less by accident).[22] Reports suggest that the unpredictable collateral damage of a large-scale U.S. cyberattack on Iran played an important role in war-planning discussions.[23] It is also plausible that attacks that were intended to have large-scale consequences have fizzled or failed because the targeted system did not respond in the predicted ways. Such failed attacks will often be invisible to everyone except the attackers.

Reflecting this uncertainty, the variance in the damage inflicted by a cyberattack is likely to be greater than by a kinetic attack.[24] In other words, the distribution of damage that would be inflicted by many types of cyberattacks is likely less tightly clustered around the hoped-for or planned damage than the damage from many types of kinetic attacks.

Uncertainty about the damage a cyberattack would inflict could make kinetic threats more effective deterrents than cyber threats. The effectiveness of deterrent threats depends on a state's ability to carry out the threat: deterrence by denial is less likely to succeed if one's adversary believes a threatened response will not achieve its military objective; and deterrence by punishment is likely to fail if the adversary doubts the state's attack will inflict the promised damage.

Moreover, except in an all-out war, a state will want to be confident that its attack will not inflict more damage than intended, because doing so could raise the probability that the adversary would escalate still further. For both of these reasons—credibility and escalation control—cyberattacks appear to be less effective than kinetic attacks as a deterrent.

However, in some circumstances the unpredictability of a cyberattack could make it *more* attractive than a kinetic attack. Building on Thomas Schelling's discussion of "the threat that leaves something to chance," we might imagine that an "attack that leaves something to chance" could be an effective deterrent under some circumstances.[25] The threat that leaves something to chance promises some probability of a very costly outcome when the decision to carry out the action is not under the control of the threatener. In situations in which the threatener would also be hurt by the action that inflicts great damage, or by the adversary's likely response, the threat that leaves something to chance can be more credible because the threatener may be willing to run some probability of suffering the damage, but not unwilling to suffer it with certainty. The threat would also be more credible if the threatener were unable to turn off the threat; otherwise the target of the threat might wonder whether the threatener might pull back its threat.

The "attack that leaves something to chance" would work by a related but somewhat different logic. An attacker that launched a cyberattack that might impose extremely high costs would demonstrate its resolve (that is, the extent of its interest) in prevailing in the conflict and thereby gain a bargaining advantage in a limited war. Although the attacker would be unwilling to inflict the costs with certainty, owing to the high probability of costly escalation, it is willing to take a chance or run the risk of inflicting these costs. And, by the nature of the effects of the cyberattack, once the attack is launched, the attacker cannot prevent the worst outcome from occurring, which should reinforce the target's judgment about the attacker's resolve. As a result, in certain situations, a cyberattack that is, on average, expected to inflict the same amount of damage as a kinetic attack could be the more effective tool for compelling intrawar deterrence and bargaining.[26]

Finally, it is possible that the ambiguities and uncertainties associated with cyberattacks will sometimes have another advantage. Policymakers and analysts have devoted enormous attention to the "attribution problem"—the difficulty of attributing cyberattacks to their attackers. This could be a major problem for deterrence, but could in some circumstances be a blessing. Difficulty identifying one's attacker provides states with greater freedom of action in choosing how or whether to respond to an attack. Consider the difference between a physical attack and a cyberattack that destroys or degrades an important asset belonging to an adversary. An adversary that ignores a physical attack will appear feckless or weak. If it is capable of responding, it will likely do so both to demonstrate resolve to possible attackers and to avoid criticism from domestic audiences. In contrast, a state that is attacked will have more leeway in deciding how to respond to certain cyberattacks. Even if the state knows who the attacker is, the attacker does not necessarily know that it knows, nor do other states necessarily know that it knows. Thus the lack of common knowledge and difficulty of attribution reduces the state's ability to deter cyberattacks, but for closely related reasons could allow the state to avoid a potentially costly response. The state can act as though it does not know who the attacker was and decline to retaliate without doing great damage to its reputation for resolve.

Thisiswhat I was looking for

Salience and Focal Points

The effects-based approach provides a relatively simple framework for thinking carefully about offensive capacities and deterrence in cyberspace. The approach, however, does not provide a sufficiently rich description of how states are likely to actually understand cyberattacks, especially in comparison with other types of attacks. It could be that states do not view all equally damaging attacks as equal. To understand this possibility, we turn to the concepts of focal points and saliencies, which capture the implications of states' shared understandings of actions, and in turn their reactions to others' actions and their expectations about how other states will react to them.

Imagine a scenario in which the New York Stock Exchange suffers a cyberattack that prevents stock trading for a period of weeks, thereby inflicting significant damage on the U.S. economy. Imagine further that the United States responds with a kinetic attack aimed at the central business district of the adversary's capital, which inflicts damage to property equivalent in value to the economic damage of the cyberattack, without any people being wounded or killed. Under this scenario, would others (adversary and other states) consider the U.S. retaliation to be commensurate, or would it be seen as escalatory?

An effects-based account would consider this response to be commensurate. Our intuition, however, is that this conclusion is wrong. Other states, including the adversary, would likely consider the retaliation to be a substantial escalation.

Yet there are other circumstances in which our intuition suggests that responding with a kinetic attack would not be viewed as escalatory. Imagine for example, that the initial attack was on military rather than civilian assets—say, for example, an adversary attacked and disabled an important military system using cyber means (as Israeli forces reportedly did in an air raid on Syria, in which they fooled the Syrian air defense system).[27] Here we suspect that a kinetic response aimed at a military system of similar importance would not be regarded as escalatory, or at the least would be seen as ambiguous.

The analytic challenge posed by intuitions like these is knowing whether they are widely shared. Intuitions may differ importantly from person to person and from state to state, which increases the probability of misunderstanding and hence of unintended escalation. Thomas Schelling's arguments about salience and focal points are valuable intellectual tools for exploring and possibly clarifying these intuitions. These can help both to sharpen analysis among observers and increase predictability in interstate relations. During the Cold War, analysts believed that developing a common vocabulary and understanding of how actions might be interpreted could contribute to stability during crises and limited wars.

Salience results from focal points, which serve as an implicit solution to coordination games. In the context of a specific situation, focal points possess a kind of "prominence, uniqueness, simplicity, precedent, or some rationale that makes them qualitatively differentiable from the continuum of possible alternatives."[28] If one imagines a coordination problem in which actors need to converge upon one of many possible solutions in order to coordinate properly, then actors will plausibly turn to shared focal points in order to predict how other actors might behave in order to reach an equilibrium. In Schelling's famous example, students who had to decide where to meet in New York at a given time, without any information as to which of the many thousands of possible locations in New York would be appropriate, are likely to converge on Grand Central Station as the meeting point. Here they draw on forms of information that are external to the intrinsic strategic situation in order to successfully resolve it. An actor is drawn to the focal point solution because of her belief that (1) other actors are likely to view the feature as a focal point and (2) other actors are likely to expect that the given actor also sees the features as a focal point, and so on, which creates common knowledge and hence generates converging expectations.

Such information might come from prominent features of the landscape such as rivers; the political status quo; differences between types of weapons—for example, conventional versus chemical versus nuclear;[29] labels associated with specific strategies, culture, and institutions;[30] or other distinguishing aspects of the situation that actors face which are not givens of the strategic structure of the situation itself.[31] These are the various factors that make focal points *salient*, enabling actors to converge on common understandings in ambiguous situations.

Notably, salience and focal points can play an especially important role in deterrence, compellence, escalation control, and limited war. Saliencies provide distinctions between specific categories of action, some of which are viewed as escalatory while others are viewed as restrained, some of which are viewed as requiring a harsh response while others are viewed as tolerable, some of which are expected while others are surprising. Possibly the clearest saliency in current weaponry and war is between conventional weapons and so-called weapons of mass destruction, with the conventional-nuclear divide being the sharpest. As both rationalists and constructivists have observed, states draw a sharp distinction between conventional and nuclear weapons. The distinction is not based entirely on the damage that a nuclear weapon would inflict. The United States can build nuclear weapons that would do less damage than the largest conventional explosives and far less damage than the overall damage inflicted by large-scale conventional bombing.

Instead, as Schelling described it, the understanding that nuclear weapons are "simply different and generically different" is based on an argument that "emphasized bright lines, slippery slopes, well defined boundaries, and the stuff of which traditions and implicit conventions are made."[32] Crossing the nuclear saliency by using even a single small nuclear weapon is believed to greatly increase the probability of further nuclear use and possibly of massive nuclear war. Among other reasons, this is because once nuclear weapons are used there may not be any "natural" place for the warring parties to stop.

If settled and relevant cyber focal points exist, then states will look to these saliencies to predict how other states will interpret a cyberattack. This may render some cyberattacks more escalatory or threatening than comparably damaging kinetic attacks, and vice versa. Hence, if saliencies exist in cybersecurity, then an effects-based approach to deterrence is incomplete: actors may respond to an attack in ways that the simple effects-based account would not predict because the attack crosses a salient dividing line. This, for example, could explain why actors might converge on agreement that a kinetic response to a cyberattack on civilian infrastructure, even if no one were killed, would be escalatory. It might also explain why actors could agree that a kinetic response to an attack on military infrastructure would not be escalatory. Clearly, working out the contours of the perceived landscape of possibilities that make one distinction focal and the other not is essential in designing U.S. cyber strategy.

Recent research finds that the American public does, in fact, view damage inflicted by cyberattacks differently from comparable damage inflicted by conventional and nuclear weapons. In an experiment that described an event in which the two types of attacks did similar damage, participants were less willing to escalate to a kinetic attack in response to a cyberattack than they were to match a kinetic attack.[33] If this response turns out to be accurate, widespread, and deeply entrenched, a potential cyber attacker might question the credibility of U.S. threats to escalate to a conventional or a nuclear attack.

Consider a few possible reasons why a kinetic response to a cyberattack might be considered escalatory. First, it could result from the belief that cyberattacks and kinetic attacks are fundamentally different in *kind*, such that one is considered fundamentally acceptable and the other is considered unacceptable. If this idea were generally accepted, then the effects-based doctrine that we outlined initially would be largely useless, since it would be undermined by an understanding that there is a crucial qualitative difference between all cyber and kinetic attacks. However, if we are not alone in our intuition that a kinetic response to a cyberattack on military infrastructure is nonescalatory, it would seem unlikely that such a sweeping and general distinction applies.

Second, it could be that the focal point turns on a perceived difference between physical and nonphysical *damage*. This would imply that forms of cyberattack might be considered equivalent to kinetic attacks when they do direct physical damage. For example, an attack on a dam's control system that created major flooding might be seen as equivalent to a direct kinetic attack that produces the same flooding. If this were the key distinction, then we might expect differentiation between different kinds of cyberattacks, depending on the type of damage they inflict. For example, attacks that damage information systems or electronic commerce would be viewed as noncomparable to kinetic attacks, while cyberattacks that do direct physical damage would be viewed as comparable.

Third, the distinction could turn on whether the cyberattack inflicts easily observable damage. The losses from a crippled stock exchange are plausibly less visible than the losses from a kinetic attack that does immediately observable damage to buildings and infrastructure. Here, cyber weapons that do observable damage (which might be physical, but might also involve purely virtual effects with easily observable consequences) might be viewed as equivalent to kinetic attacks that are equally visible.

Fourth, we expect there to be a relevant distinction between a cyberattack that inflicts physical damage on military assets and one that inflicts physical damage on civilian assets. As we have noted, we suspect that kinetic countermilitary responses to substantial cyberattacks on military targets are less likely to be viewed as escalatory.

Fifth, states are likely to distinguish between cyberattacks that kill people and those that do not. A cyberattack would not kill people directly, but could

result in physical damage that would cause people to die. Even visible physical damage that is very costly might be considered less escalatory than an
attack that kills people but is otherwise not very costly. It is less clear whether
a cyberattack that imposes material costs on people—for example, by depriving them of electricity—but does not kill anyone would be viewed as more
escalatory than an attack that inflicts great financial harm but does not have
immediate material consequences for people's lives. This set of distinctions
applies just as directly to the differential effects of kinetic attacks; that is,
the distinction is not special to cyber.

Still other potential saliencies may exist. It is possible to distinguish between attacks that occur during wartime and during peacetime. Kinetic attacks on civilian infrastructure may be less likely to be viewed as escalatory
if states are already involved in armed hostilities. There is also the possibility that states will view cyberattacks that temporarily interrupt the operation of systems—for example, an attack that takes down the electric grid
but does not permanently damage it—as less escalatory that a kinetic attack
that does permanent damage, even if the two attacks inflict equal economic
costs.

Given that states' understandings of cyberwarfare are at an early stage,
the United States should consider whether there are possibly feasible focal
points that it would like to help establish. Because we believe that agreed
upon saliencies have the potential to reduce undesired escalation in wars that
involve cyberattacks, establishing shared understandings could be in all states'
interests. The United States should also consider whether other actors—
adversaries, allies, or nonstate actors—may also be seeking to establish focal
points, and what those focal points might be. Not all focal points will be
desirable. Some may limit U.S. freedom of action by making certain types
of attacks more escalatory than they would be if the focal point did not exist
or, closely related, if the United States was known to have rejected the contested focal point.

This discussion raises the question of how, if at all, the United States can
contribute to the establishment of focal points in cyberwar. One approach
may be negotiations or possibly official dialogues in which states share which
saliencies, if any, they believe operate or can operate in cyberwar. But active
efforts to build focal points need not be limited to negotiations and discussions of the issue. In fact, it may well be that threatened actions, actual actions (and nonactions), and the interpretations of actions will contribute more
to the establishment of saliencies.

One potential source of influence on focal points is U.S. cyber doctrine. Current U.S. doctrine makes clear that the United States retains the option to employ a kinetic response to a cyberattack. In effect, the doctrine denies that, at least in broad terms, there is a salient difference between cyber and kinetic attacks. This preservation of flexibility over responses to cyberattacks has not received harsh criticism from other states, or even any sustained opposition from civil society. It is likely too early in the cyber age to know whether this reflects acceptance and recognition of the lack of a broad salient distinction between cyber and kinetic attacks. A broader evaluation and discussion of salience in cyberwar—within the U.S. government, with experts outside the government, and between governments—might help establish greater clarity before the test of war brings its own form of clarity to these issues.

In evaluating its possible interest in the creation of saliencies, the United States should consider the disadvantages of its current cyber doctrine. By reserving for itself the right to retaliate against cyberattacks using noncyber means, the doctrine provides other states with some justification for behaving in the same way. For example, if Iran had been capable of launching a kinetic attack against the U.S. homeland in retaliation for the physical damage that the Stuxnet virus inflicted on its nuclear complex, would the United States be willing to accept that this was a reasonable form of retaliation, or would it have viewed it as highly escalatory?[34] At the least, it is more difficult for the United States to complain about other states responding to cyberattacks with kinetic force if it reserves the same option for itself. Similarly, the NPR's position that the United States might turn to nuclear retaliation in response to cyberattacks could have the same unintended consequence. Of course, these would only be a problem if the United States plans to launch cyberattacks against an adversary's society; we do not know whether this is an option the United States possesses or is considering.[35]

A second potential source of influence on the understanding of focal points will likely be U.S. (and other states') actions in response to large-scale cyberattacks that variously inflict economic, physical, or military damage. To the best of our knowledge, there has not been a kinetic response by a state to a cyberattack. This fact, however, provides relatively little information about existing saliencies because the United States has not suffered a cyberattack that was sufficiently large and costly to initiate what would traditionally be considered an interstate war, in which kinetic retaliation might appear to be the "natural" response. The United States has suffered cyberattacks below this level and employed nonkinetic forms of retaliation. For example, it has indicted Chinese "military hackers" for hacking, espionage, and other offenses.[36] It also imposed sanctions against North Korea after Sony's servers were hacked, and, according to one prominent member of Congress, cut off North Korean access to the internet for a period of time.[37] Drawing insights from these cases about the existence of saliencies is further complicated by the possibility that a saliency was crossed, but the United States was deterred from inflicting the more costly or escalatory retaliation that might then have been appropriate.[38] Whether a saliency is crossed is only one factor in a state's decision to escalate. Escalation might not be the state's best option if the risks are too high. Thus a state's reactions may not align neatly with its saliencies.

Another set of problems reflects the extent to which saliencies are relatively clear, and recognizable to all states. When saliencies are murky, they are more likely to lead to misunderstanding, failed efforts to coordinate, and unanticipated escalation. Again, the United States could think more systematically about how to communicate the differences between different kinds of attacks, and how seriously it is likely to respond to them. One way in which the United States does this is by designating specific assets as part of "critical infrastructure," meaning that it views them as crucial and will respond harshly to attacks on them. However, critical infrastructure is defined increasingly broadly in U.S. official documents; for example, it includes movie studios. Given that the United States does not in fact depend on movie studios in the ways that it depends on the power grid, such a broad definition of critical infrastructure is likely to weaken its deterrent value.

The United States faces similar problems in deterring attacks on noncritical infrastructure as it does in deterring attacks against assets or allies that are of only modest strategic value. It encourages adversaries (if they would benefit from a potential attack) to call the United States' bluff. Doing so obliges the United States either to expend resources on a retaliatory attack that is not justified by the stakes, or alternatively, not to respond and risk having adversaries conclude that its commitments to defend more assets are similarly weak. There is little upside in defending marginal parts of an infrastructure, and considerable downside.

The recent suggestion by the Department of Defense's Task Force on Cyber Deterrence that the United States should seek to deter "sustained campaigns to undermine U.S. . . . political institutions (e.g., elections), and social cohesion"[39] notably extends the notion of cyber deterrence to cover activities that have not traditionally been considered military or even covert attacks (we discuss these at length later in the chapter, but introduce them here because they map onto other arguments about saliency). This means that the argument runs up against somewhat similar objections that it stretches the notion of military deterrence to protect targets that may or may not be of vital strategic importance. Indeed, it may be difficult to pin down what potential targets would undermine "social cohesion," let alone categorize unacceptable attacks against them.

It will thus likely be very difficult in the short term to develop a typology that generates salient understandings of which actions are likely to lead to U.S. retaliation and which actions are not. Although some actions (such as hacking the servers of U.S. political parties or penetrating U.S. voter registries) are relatively straightforward to categorize, others, including so-called Russian influence operations on social media are not. These latter actions could be categorized as cyberattacks, or as "information warfare," resembling the propaganda of previous eras rather than aggressive attacks,[40] or as "common knowledge attacks."[41] Without a clear scheme of categories (which could rest on one of these arguments, or on a different argument entirely), it is difficult to decide how, or even whether, the U.S. government should retaliate against such actions. Generating global acceptance for any saliencies or norms that could justify retaliation and deterrence will be extremely difficult.

The preceding discussion leads us to the following conclusion: U.S. cyber doctrine should strive to take saliencies and focal points into account. The effects-based argument implicitly assumes that all effects can be aggregated into a single value. Essentially, each type of damage, including human lives, can be given a dollar value, and all of the costs can be added together to determine an attack's total cost and effect. Appreciating the potential impact of saliencies requires us to reject this approach. Instead of aggregating across types of damage, we believe it is necessary to identify the different dimensions along which states and individuals distinguish types of damage and then cautiously rank the severity and information content of an attack. Different types of damage may simply be different—physical or not, human lives lost or not, easily observable or not, military or not, temporary or permanent. All of these may influence how an adversary understands an attack. An attacker will need to incorporate these dimensions into its decisions about what type of threat to make and how to retaliate if deterrence fails. As a result, in some but not all situations kinetic responses to costly countersociety cyberattacks will be inappropriate, or at least more escalatory than the effects-based approach would indicate. Nuclear responses are likely to generate even larger retaliation.

Norms

Another potential limit to the effects-based doctrine involves norms. Norms are internalized, and at least to some degree do not involve a means-end distinction, which makes it nearly impossible to incorporate them into an effects-based argument. Focal points and salience operate through a strategic logic that can be carried through by rational ends-focused actors. In contrast, internalized norms are *non-consequentialist*; that is to say, they involve judgments as to whether actions are innately appropriate or inappropriate, regardless of their consequences.[42]

For example, the previously discussed distinction between nuclear and conventional weapons is plausibly not only a focal point, but also a partly internalized norm. The first use of nuclear weapons is regarded as a taboo that can be violated only under extreme circumstances. The developing norm was recognized early in the nuclear age and has become more deeply established over time.[43] The animus against nuclear weapons stems not only from logic but also from "moral discourse about nuclear weapons" that was often viscerally hostile to the effects-based logic of deterrence.[44] Nuclear weapons came to be seen as profoundly different from ordinary weapons, and their first use came to be viewed as unacceptable.

An important question is whether there are norms of cyberwar that could or should place limits on U.S. cyber doctrine. Put another way, are there offensive cyberattacks that the effects-based approach supplemented by saliencies would prescribe, or at least not proscribe, that the United States would be unwilling to launch because they are normatively inappropriate? The answer—at least for the moment—appears to be no. As discussed earlier, there may be cyber saliencies that the United States should not cross because doing so would unduly increase the probability of escalation. In contrast, there do not appear to be offensive cyberattacks that the United States believes it would simply be *wrong* to launch, except for those that violate standard laws of war.

The United States has engaged in some informal norm-building efforts in cybersecurity. In part this is because one of the key alternatives for limiting an adversary's capabilities—formal cyber treaties—would usually be exceedingly difficult, and likely impossible, to verify. Compared to nuclear and conventional weapons, cyber capabilities are much more difficult for an outside observer to monitor. In addition, many of the capabilities an adversary could use to launch an offensive cyberattack could also be used to defend against one. Once an attack is launched, the state might not be able to identify the perpetrator with a high confidence, and even if it could, might not be capable of proving it to other states. Finally, even if all of these barriers could be overcome, it is far from clear that the United States would be willing to trade away its offensive cyber capabilities in return for its adversaries forgoing theirs. For all of these reasons the United States has not focused much energy on achieving formal treaties (which could have normative consequences as well as legal consequences and associated sanctions). Instead, the United States has looked to informal and quasi-formal understandings that rely on the identification of appropriate standards and the shaming of those who do not live up to those standards.

The most visible exercise in attempted norm building is not in cyber-offensive operations as such, but in cyber exploitation—cyber operations that are aimed at extracting information rather than paralyzing, degrading, or damaging assets.[45] The United States holds that there is a basic distinction between purely commercial cyber exploitation (securing commercial secrets that are then shared with favored domestic businesses—which it considers illegitimate) and regular cyber exploitation (gathering information relevant to national security—which the United States considers legitimate). Other countries, including prominently China, have disagreed. This disagreement may partly reflect different relationships between the state and the private sector: the United States does not have a history of strong direct state involvement in directing commercial activity; in contrast, many other countries do not have such an arm's-length relationship between the state and the private sector, which helps explain why their perspectives differ.[46]

Serious disagreements between the United States and China have resulted. As already noted, the United States, lacking the multilateral international instruments to express its displeasure, turned to domestic law enforcement—for example, to seek indictments against Chinese nationals that it claims have conducted commercial spying, and threatening sanctions. Although these indictments are highly unlikely ever to result in successful prosecutions, they carry some weight in signaling U.S. normative priorities and in shaming China.

Such pressures have led the United States and China to reach an understanding under which China has agreed "[not to] conduct or knowingly support cyber-enabled theft of intellectual property, including trade secrets or other confidential business information, with the intent of providing competitive advantages to companies or commercial sectors."[47] Although the informal agreement lacks explicit enforcement mechanisms, it has apparently led to some reduction in cyber exploitation of U.S. companies.[48]

This reduction may be the result of norms in action. According to this explanation, U.S. legal action shamed China and led to a shift in China's public position on commercial cyber exploitation.[49] There is, however, an alternative explanation, which holds that China is employing external pressures created by the United States to gain domestic control of actors who are pursuing their own economic interests with inadequate regard for China's overall strategy.[50] The available evidence is ambiguous and could be interpreted as supporting either of these explanations (or perhaps some combination).

There is even less normative agreement regarding cyberattacks. UN reports have agreed that international law applies to cyberspace but have provided little guidance on their implementation. The reports do not address the application of international humanitarian law to cyberspace.[51]

To end our discussion of norms, we identify a norm that the United States should consider promoting and a norm that would be difficult for the United States to promote. Although we believe the first norm, a prohibition on attacking critical infrastructure, would be potentially valuable, we do not advocate it; instead we encourage further exploration. The second norm, a prohibition against interference in democratic politics, might have some advantages for the United States, but is likely infeasible; consequently, the United States will likely have to depend on defense instead of norms.

A Norm That Would Ban Attacks on Critical Infrastructure

The rationale for a norm that bans attacks on critical infrastructure is that such attacks might inflict crippling economic damage that far exceeds that of a feasible conventional attack.[52] The publicly available scholarship disagrees on whether large-scale counterinfrastructure cyberattacks could have such severe and even crippling consequences for civilian infrastructure.[53] Without taking a position on the destructive potential of such attacks, we can make a qualified argument. If such attacks are a plausible danger, then the United States should consider supporting development of a norm against cyberattacks that target infrastructure that is critical to the operation of states, including electric grids, oil refining facilities, and backbone financial networks. The United States and other countries appear to be moving in this direction. The United Nations Group of Governmental Experts included among its "recommendations for consideration by States for voluntary, non-binding norms, rules or principles of responsible behaviour" that "a State should not conduct or knowingly support ICT activity contrary to its obligations under international law that intentionally damages critical infrastructure or otherwise impairs the use and operation of critical infrastructure to provide services to the public."[54]

A possible criticism is that a limited counterinfrastructure attack—for example, one that targeted only facilities in a geographically limited region—would not do catastrophic massive damage and therefore should not be subjected to this normative prohibition. However, a few rejoinders carry weight. To start, this type of limited attack could reduce the barriers to additional similar attacks, possibly leading to unlimited cyberwar. As with limited nuclear use, once the saliency is crossed there may not be a "natural" place to reestablish tacit limits on countervalue cyberattacks. In practice, an unavoidable complication that is not present in the nuclear case is that the line between counterinfrastructure attacks and other cyberattacks may be less clear than the nuclear-conventional divide. Efforts to establish this norm would have to engage this complexity, among others. Another counterpoint is that a limited counterinfrastructure attack could result in more far-reaching damage than the attacker intended: an attack against a specific region could cause cascading damage that flows from the interconnectedness of critical systems or through the unintended spread of the cyber weapon itself. Thus states should recognize that limited attacks against critical infrastructure are too risky and should stigmatize them. In the terminology of our earlier discussion, "attacks that leave something to chance" should be rejected as an unacceptable tactic in intrawar bargaining.

Another criticism is that states often violate norms, specifically those against harming noncombatants. Hence one might argue that norms are effectively worthless. However, in wars of attrition, states have often not violated the norm against targeting civilians until late in the war, when their qualms are overwhelmed by their determination or even desperation to win.[55] If the same logic applied to cyberwar, then a norm against counterinfrastructure attacks could contribute to delaying these attacks and possibly thereby avoiding them.

A norm against attacking critical infrastructure would augment the effects-based approach and would be grounded in the potential effects of such an attack. At least until recently, major powers were incapable of inflicting crippling damage against an adversary's critical infrastructure, and thereby its society, with conventional weapons before gaining control in a total war. At a minimum, this level of damage could not be inflicted quickly. By making this option available, attacks on critical infrastructure would appear to create a new danger that is large enough for states to judge it unacceptable.

The prospects for developing this norm are improved by the typical interest of norm entrepreneurs in threats to people's lives, especially large threats. The United States is hampered in many of its efforts at norm building by distrust and strong disagreement from the technology community and other states.[56] However, there is scope for agreement over norms against cyberattacks that would result in significant loss of civilian life, as reflected by the agreement of states that the ordinary laws of war ought apply to cybersecurity. This could potentially be expanded into a set of norms against the use of cyber weapons against critical infrastructure, even though many of the deaths might result from indirect effects of such an attack. Over time, if states observed this norm, it could become internalized, resulting in the delegitimization of cyberattacks against civilian infrastructure.

A Norm That Would Prohibit Interference in Democratic Politics

The United States could, as a response to recent efforts by Russia to influence its politics through "bots" and other measures, try to persuade other states to agree to a norm against political interference. However, this second norm would be difficult to implement in an international system where there are deep disagreements about the appropriate sources of domestic order.

The best outcome for the United States would be a norm that specifically precludes the use of online communication and social media to interfere in democratic politics. It is more or less unthinkable, though, that major U.S. adversaries such as China and Russia would agree to such a norm: it would both constrain them and implicitly disparage their systems of rule, without providing them any significant protections. China is an authoritarian state, and Russia's "managed democracy" is notably illiberal. In a brief era after the end of the Cold War it was possible to craft norms at the regional level in Europe that invoked democracy to justify significant forms of monitoring and moderate intervention.[57] Unfortunately, this temporary consensus on the benefits of democracy has not lasted.

It would likely be easier for the United States to get Russia, China, and other states to agree to norms that militated against foreign online intervention in domestic politics more generally, without specifying whether those politics were democratic or nondemocratic. Indeed, Russia and China have repeatedly pressed in international forums to define "information security" so as to preclude such interference.[58] However, this would also require the United States to refrain from supporting activities and technologies that were intended to spread democracy to nondemocratic countries, working against long-held principles of U.S. foreign policy, which arguably reflect deeply held values in American society. This about-turn in U.S. policy would likely be enormously controversial among the public, influential members of the U.S. foreign policy elite, U.S. technology companies, and allies.

The difficulty of either building saliencies or creating norms to ameliorate these attacks suggests that the United States ought to turn to different policy options—in particular, defense. Successful deterrence does not require common priorities, but it does require common understanding of each other's priorities and a clear set of shared concepts to avoid ambiguity and mistakes. Defense may be possible even without these shared understandings and even when it is difficult to create a shared intellectual vocabulary with other powers (although it does require clarity about what one is defending and how best to do so). Some defensive options are straightforward in principle: for example, more secure voting systems and mandates for basic security practices such as two-factor authentication for politically sensitive databases and servers could greatly alleviate the risk of attacks. In practice, however, even simple measures are more complicated than they first appear.

For example, experts agree in general how to defend against direct cyberattacks on voting; use ballot machines that keep unalterable written records and later do random sampling to ensure that the electronic results match the paper records. However, it has proven difficult to create commonly applied standards that reflect this expert consensus. Responsibility for maintaining voting systems is split among the federal, state, and local levels; but while state-level officials strongly resist federal mandates, state governments are often unwilling to pay. This decentralized system reflects the need for local knowledge in other aspects of the voting process, but makes it hard to apply a uniform approach, especially given other funding priorities.

Furthermore, some aspects of democratic processes are more difficult to defend. Some attacks on voting systems or voter registration records are intended less to change the result than to undermine confidence in the fairness of the vote. In the words of one group of experts, "Simply put, the attacker might not care who wins; the losing side's belief that the election was stolen from them may be equally, if not more, valuable."[59] Defense against such attacks is complex since, if they become publicly known, they may destabilize confidence even if they do not penetrate the system and change records.

It is more difficult again to defend against attacks that use social media or other online means to spread dissent and confusion and hence damage democratic decision making. Such attacks turn some of the strengths of democratic systems against themselves, weaponizing open communications in order to increase disagreement and weaken civil society. Crafting even semi-viable defenses will require consideration of the complex trade-offs between commercial freedom to set rules for social media sites, the role of government in shaping communications policy, and the legal principle of lack of "intermediary liability," which immunizes e-commerce firms from many legal risks and gives them little incentive to police the behavior of their users.

Even scholars have only the murkiest sense of how information and democracy go together, so making better policy will not be possible without a great deal of intellectual spade work. And this lack of intellectual clarity means that other approaches such as deterrence are even less likely to work.

Arms Control

A rather different type of restriction on U.S. cyber doctrine could result from an arms control agreement to forgo certain types of cyberattacks. As recommended by Richard Danzig, we believe that the United States should seriously explore the possibility of an agreement that would prohibit cyber intrusions into the command and control systems of the major powers' nuclear forces.[60] The effectiveness of a state's nuclear deterrent depends critically on its ability to credibly threaten retaliation, which requires not only that its force survive an attack, but also that its ability to launch those forces survives. Vulnerable C2 can undermine a state's nuclear deterrent and create dangerous dynamics during a crisis.[61] A state, however, could believe that holding its adversary's C2 vulnerable would provide strategic advantages, especially if it were also able to target much or all of the adversary's nuclear force. Given the potential advantages of being able to attack the adversary's nuclear C2, but also the risks, a state might be willing to forgo the ability to launch this type of a cyberattack if and only if its adversary were willing to do so as well. Because intelligence-gathering efforts would likely be indistinguishable from preparation for a cyberattack against nuclear C2, mutual restraint would almost certainly need to include both.

A state would likely only engage in this mutual restraint if it believed it had a high probability of verifying the adversary's restraint—that is, of detecting cyber intrusions into its nuclear C2 system and identifying the intruder. While the feasibility of detection and attribution is primarily a technical issue, one factor that would favor feasibility is timing: various types of preparation for a counter-C2 attack would almost certainly be required during peacetime; consequently, a country would likely have a substantial amount of time to inspect for intrusions. Finding a single serious intrusion would probably be sufficient to bring its own restraint to an end. The adversary's recognition of this likelihood could deter it from violating the mutual restraint on preparing cyberattacks against nuclear C2.[62]

An alternative to an arms control agreement would be a norm against nuclear C2 attacks. However, whether a norm against counter-C2 cyber would be valuable and can be developed is less clear. Regarding its value, one could argue that if verification is possible, then a norm is unnecessary; this has been the model for past arms control agreements. Regarding its feasibility, counter-C2 cyber capabilities would have to achieve a special status, one that makes them clearly more dangerous than other types of counternuclear and counter-C2 weapons. The United States has built these capabilities into its war plans. Some features of cyber might distinguish it from these other weapons—most obviously, the greater uncertainty that cyber counter-C2 weapons might create about the vulnerability of an adversary's nuclear retaliatory capability. However, at most this is likely to be a difference in degree, not in kind, which suggests the prospects for developing this norm are poor.

Conclusion

This exploration of an effects-based approach strongly suggests that a U.S. doctrine for cyberwar needs to understand and incorporate the focal points, and the related saliencies, that will influence adversaries' interpretation of a U.S. attack. The effects-based approach provides a useful starting point. It makes clear why we should not assume that cyberattacks must be deterred by and responded to with cyber means. And some of its more specific findings remain unchanged by the introduction of focal points and saliencies. However, for a variety of situations and types of attacks, U.S. appreciation of saliencies will support a cyberwar doctrine that differs from a doctrine based on a purely effects-based approach. In broad terms, the impact of including saliencies in our analysis is to reduce the role of kinetic retaliation in U.S. cyberwar doctrine. A next step in advancing this analysis is to ask whether we have identified the key possible saliencies in cyberwar, and to explore how widely and deeply they are held by individuals and states' decision makers. Because we are so early in the era of cyberwar, states' beliefs and understandings are weakly formed and will evolve with experience. Relatedly, because we are in a formative stage, U.S. policies have the potential to influence the development of certain saliencies; others are likely to stand quite separate from U.S. policy.

Whether norms have the potential to significantly shape U.S. cyberwar doctrine is less clear. Nevertheless, a norm against cyberattacks on critical infrastructure deserves attention because they have the potential to cause catastrophic damage. In contrast, a norm against cyberattacks on nuclear C2 appears both infeasible and, even if achieved, too likely to be ineffective to place any hope in. An arms control agreement designed to prevent intrusion into nuclear command and control systems appears more promising. Clearly, the United States will need to employ a diverse range of policy tools in response to the spectrum of cyber threats it faces.

Notes

1. *Department of Defense Cyber Strategy*, April 2015, pp. 11, 5, 14 (www.defense.gov /Portals/1/features/2015/0415_cyber-strategy/Final_2015_DoD_CYBER _STRATEGY_for_web.pdf).

2. Ibid., pp. 11, 5, 14, 6.

3. Herbert Lin, "Escalation Dynamics and Conflict Termination in Cyberspace," *Strategic Studies Quarterly* (Fall 2012), p. 65.

4. Martin C. Libicki, *Crisis and Escalation in Cyberspace* (Santa Monica, Calif.: RAND, 2012), p. 78.

5. This section draws on Charles L. Glaser, *Deterrence of Cyber Attacks and U.S. National Security*, Report CW-CSPRI-2011-5, July 1, 2011.

6. Our discussion here assumes that the state can determine who launched the attack; that is, we are putting aside the standard attribution problem. Given that our focus is on what type of retaliation the state should threaten or launch (or both), little is lost by assuming that the state knows the identity of the attacker. In contrast, whether the attacker would be able to determine that the state, not some other actor, retaliated could be an important factor influencing the state's choice between cyber and kinetic retaliation. Although we touch on this issue at the end of the section, it deserves more attention.

7. This deterrence logic has a direct parallel in the applicability of international law to cyberattacks; see Harold Koh, "International Law in Cyberspace" (remarks at Fort Meade, Maryland, September 18, 2012) (www.harvardilj.org/2012/12/online_54_koh/).

8. Glenn H. Snyder, *Deterrence and Defense* (Princeton University Press, 1961).

9. Victor A. Utgoff, "Nuclear Weapons and the Deterrence of Biological and Chemical Warfare," Occasional Paper 36 (Washington: Henry L. Stimson Center, October 1997).

10. However, as we explore in the following section, some considerations are consistent with an effects-based approach that should constrain U.S. retaliatory options to certain types of cyberattacks.

11. Whether the U.S. retaliation should be proportional is an important question in deterrence theory, but not a central issue for the choice between kinetic and cyber retaliation. Threatening to inflict much greater damage than one's state suffered can be an effective deterrent if the threat is highly credible. However, in some situations threats that are "too" large will lack credibility; threats to inflict a smaller amount of damage could therefore be the more effective deterrent. From the effects-based perspective, whatever amount of damage is best for deterrence could be threatened by either cyber or kinetic means.

12. There is substantial disagreement about the damage that a sophisticated adversary could inflict with a cyberattack against the U.S. homeland. Some experts argue that extremely high levels of damage are possible; see William A. Owens, Kenneth W. Dam, and Herbert S. Lin, eds., *Technology, Policy, Law, and Ethics Regarding U.S. Acquisition and Use of Cyberattack Capabilities* (Washington: National Academies Press, 2009): "While the immediate effects of cyberattack are unlikely to be comparable to the effects of weapons of mass destruction (for example, nuclear, chemical, or biological weapons), a large-scale cyberattack could massively affect the functioning of a society and lead to many indirect casualties. Conversely, it is possible to imagine that certain cyberattacks might be executed on a smaller scale and with a lower degree of lethality than might be expected if kinetic weapons were used for equivalent military purposes. Thus the policy implications of cyberattack have certain commonalities across the range from non-lethal engagements to wars involving the use of weapons of mass destruction" (p. 26). Others argue that the threat of wide-scale cyberattack has been overrated; see, for example, Jerry Brito and Tate Watkins, "Loving the Cyber Bomb: The Dangers of Threat Inflation in Cyber Security Policy," *Harvard Law School National Security Journal* (2011), pp. 40–84. The authors find that "Cybersecurity is an important policy issue, but the alarmist rhetoric coming out of Washington that focuses on worst-case scenarios is unhelpful and dangerous. Aspects of current cyber policy discourse parallel the run-up to the Iraq War and pose the same dangers. Pre-war threat inflation and conflation of threats led us into war on shaky evidence. By focusing on doomsday scenarios and conflating cyber threats, government officials threaten to legislate, regulate, or spend in the name of cybersecurity based largely on fear, misplaced rhetoric, conflated threats, and credulous reporting" (pp. 83–84). See also Eric Gartzke, "The Myth of Cyberwar: Bringing War in Cyberspace Back Down to Earth," *International Security* 38, no. 2 (2013), pp. 57–60. We do not seek to adjudicate this argument in this chapter. In the absence of any evidence of a wide-scale cyberattack or attempted cyberattack having occurred, it is hard to be sure how severe the consequences would be, since large-scale damage would likely result from cascading effects, unknown interdependencies, and other phenomena that are complex in the technical sense of that term. However, for the sake of analysis, we look at the *possibility* that such an attack could occur.

13. An important issue that we turn to later is the relatively uncertainty of the damage that would be generated by the two different types of attacks.

14. A second potential shortcoming, which is the focus of the following section, is that kinetic retaliation might cross an important saliency and therefore result in larger escalation.

15. Under one interpretation such problems mean that the revelations by Edward Snowden about U.S. cyber capabilities may actually have increased the credibility of U.S. cyber threats; see Adam Segal, *The Hacked World Order: How Nations Fight, Trade, Maneuver, and Manipulate in the Digital Age* (New York: PublicAffairs, 2016).

16. Martin C. Libicki, *Cyberdeterrence and Cyberwar* (Santa Monica, Calif.: RAND, 2009), pp. 57–59. It is true, however, that the United States' reputation for being highly capable in information technology, and in cyber more specifically, could mitigate or reduce this potential credibility problem.

17. Greg Miller, Ellen Nakashima, and Adam Entous, "Obama's Secret Struggle to Punish Russia for Putin's Election Assault," *Washington Post*, June 23, 2017.

18. U.S. Department of Defense, *Nuclear Posture Review*, February 2018, p. 21.

19. See Patrick Tucker, "No, the U.S. Won't Respond to a Cyber Attack with Nukes," *Defense One*, February 2, 2018 (www.defenseone.com/technology/2018/02/no-us-wont -respond-cyber-attack-nukes/145700/.WqVq-Ey2GpY.email).

20. There is a wide belief in the literature that cyberattacks have more unpredictable consequences than conventional attacks. See, for example, Owens, Dam, and Lin, *Technology, Policy, Law, and Ethics*; and Libicki, *Cyberdeterrence and Cyberwar*.

21. David Kushner, "The Real Story of Stuxnet," *IEEE Spectrum*, February 26, 2013 (https://spectrum.ieee.org/telecom/security/the-real-story-of-stuxnet).

22. Spencer Ackerman, "Snowden: NSA Accidentally Caused Syria's Internet Blackout in 2012," *Guardian*, August 13, 2014.

23. David E. Sanger and Mark Mazzetti, "U.S. Had Cyberattack Plan if Iran Nuclear Dispute Led to Conflict," *New York Times*, February 16, 2016.

24. This will, however, vary somewhat with the type of kinetic attack. For example, a precise kinetic attack against a portion of a state's electric grid could generate a cascade of blackouts comparable to a cyberattack that damaged the same portion of the grid.

25. Thomas C. Schelling, *The Strategy of Conflict* (Harvard University Press, 1960), chap. 8; and Thomas C. Schelling, *Arms and Influence* (Yale University Press, 1966), pp. 121–22. We are grateful to Scott Sagan for noting the difference between the attack and the threat that leave something to chance.

26. Interestingly, the deterrent value of threatening an attack that leaves something to chance (to be distinguished from actually launching such an attack) is not clearly greater than the comparable kinetic threat: although the target would recognize the possibility of suffering greater than the average damage, it would also be aware that the cyberattack might inflict less than the average damage. Risk-averse states would see the cyber threat as more costly, while risk-acceptant states would see it as less threatening than the comparable, more certain, kinetic threat.

27. Richard A. Clarke and Robert K. Knake, *Cyber War: The Next Threat to National Security and What to Do about It* (New York: HarperCollins, 2010), pp. 1–9.

28. Schelling, *The Strategy of Conflict*, p. 70.

29. Ibid., pp. 67–76.

30. David M. Kreps, "Corporate Culture and Economic Theory," in *Perspectives on Positive Political Economy*, edited by James E. Alt and Kenneth A. Shepsle (Cambridge University Press, 1990), pp. 90–143; Judith Goldstein and Robert O. Keohane, "Ideas and Foreign Policy: An Analytical Framework," in *Ideas and Foreign Policy: Beliefs, Institutions, and Political Change*, edited by Judith Goldstein and Robert O. Keohane (Cornell University Press, 1993), pp. 3–30.

31. Another type—skewed distributions in which some solutions are mentioned far more often than others—is explored in Robert Sugden, "A Theory of Focal Points," *Economic Journal* (February 1995), pp. 533–50.

32. Thomas C. Schelling, "An Astonishing Sixty Years: The Legacy of Hiroshima" (Nobel Prize Lecture, Oslo, December 8, 2005).

33. Sarah E Kreps and Jacquelyn Schneider, "Escalation Firebreaks in the Cyber, Conventional and Nuclear Domains: Moving beyond Effects-Based Logics," January 17, 2018 (htpp://dx.doi.org/10.2139/ssrn.3104014).

34. We do not mean to suggest by using this example that Iran did not employ kinetic retaliation against the United States or its allies because of this distinction. Among other possibilities, Iran might have been deterred by the possibility of U.S. escalation.

35. Cyberattacks against nuclear C2 are the other key possibility; because these are attacks against nuclear capabilities, the threat of nuclear retaliation may play a smaller role in influencing an adversary's expectations.

36. Department of Justice, "U.S. Charges Five Chinese Military Hackers with Espionage for Cyber Attacks against U.S. Corporations and a Labor Organization for Commercial Advantage" (press release, May 19, 2014) (www.justice.gov/opa/pr/us-charges-five-chinese-military-hackers-cyber-espionage-against-us-corporations-and-labor).

37. Chris Strohm, "North Korea Web Outage Response to Sony Attack, Lawmaker Says," Bloomberg, March 17, 2015 (www.bloomberg.com/politics/articles/2015-03-17/north-korea-web-outage-was-response-to-sony-hack-lawmaker-says).

38. On the United States being deterred, and also for criticism of its mild responses, see Jack Goldsmith, "The DNC Hack and (the Lack of) Deterrence," *Lawfare*, October 9, 2016 (www.lawfareblog.com/dnc-hack-and-lack-deterrence).

39. Defense Science Board, *Final Report of the Defense Science Board (DSB) Task Force on Cyber Deterrence* (Department of Defense, Task Force for Cyber Deterrence, 2017), p. 9.

40. Herbert Lin and Paul Rosenzweig, "Information Warfare and Cybersecurity Are Different, Related and Important," *Lawfare*, January 17, 2018 (www.lawfareblog.com/information-warfare-and-cybersecurity-are-different-related-and-important).

41. Henry Farrell, "Common Knowledge Attacks upon Democracy" (unpublished paper, 2018).

42. Jon Elster, *The Cement of Society: A Survey of Social Order* (Cambridge University Press, 1989).

43. Nina Tannenwald, *The Nuclear Taboo: The United States and the Non-Use of Nuclear Weapons since 1945* (Cambridge University Press, 2007).

44. Ibid., p. 372.

45. Owens, Dam, and Lin, *Technology, Policy, Law, and Ethics*, pp. 1–12.

46. China is not the only important example. France, too, has acquired a reputation for flexibility in the sharing of commercially valuable information with businesses, some of which were formerly state owned and still retain strong state connections.

47. Jack Goldsmith, "What Explains the U.S.-China Cyber 'Agreement'?," *Lawfare*, September 26, 2015 (https://www.lawfareblog.com/what-explains-us-china-cyber-agreement).

48. The ability to reach an informal agreement likely resulted partly from the process it put in place: repeated discussions between the United States and China (and perhaps other actors) about what the norm entails. The informal agreement requires both countries to consult with each other regularly about enforcement activities, creating a "high level

joint dialogue mechanism." See White House, "Fact Sheet: President Xi Jinping's State Visit to the United States," September 25, 2015. On the importance of this type of process, see Martha Finnemore and Duncan B. Hollis, "Constructing Norms of Global Cybersecurity," *American Journal of International Law* 110, no. 3 (2016), pp. 425–79.

49. Assistant Attorney General for National Security John P. Carlin, "Remarks on the National Security Cyber Threat" (lecture, Harvard Law School, December 3, 2015) (www.justice.gov/opa/speech/assistant-attorney-general-national-security-john-p -carlin-delivers-remarks-national); Baker S. Steptoe Cyberlaw Podcast, Episode 82: An Interview with Jim Lewis (www.lawfareblog.com/steptoe-cyberlaw-podcast-episode-82 -interview-jim-lewis).

50. Jack Goldsmith, "U.S. Attribution of China's Cyber-Theft Aids Xi's Centralization and Anti-Corruption Efforts," *Lawfare*, June 21, 2016 (www.lawfareblog.com/us -attribution-chinas-cyber-theft-aids-xis-centralization-and-anti-corruption-efforts); David Sanger, "Chinese Curb Cyberattacks on U.S. Interests, Report Finds," *New York Times*, June 20, 2016.

51. Elaine Korzak, "International Law and the UN GGE Report on Information Security," *Just Security* (New York University Law School), December 2, 2015.

52. For a similar and more developed recommendation, see Richard J. Danzig, "Surviving on a Diet of Poisoned Fruit: Reducing the National Security Risks of America's Cyber Dependencies" (Washington: Center for a New American Security, July 2014), pp. 24–26 (www.cnas.org/publications/reports/surviving-on-a-diet-of-poisoned-fruit-reducing-the -national-security-risks-of-americas-cyber-dependencies); see also Herbert Lin, "A Virtual Necessity: Some Modest Steps toward Greater Cybersecurity," *Bulletin of the Atomic Scientists* 68, no. 5 (2012), pp. 81–86, which focuses on the possibility of an arms control agreement, not a norm.

53. Owens, Dam, and Lin, *Technology, Policy, Law, and Ethics*; Brito and Watkins, "Loving the Cyber Bomb"; and Gartzke, "The Myth of Cyberwar."

54. United Nations Group of Governmental Experts, "Report of the Group of Governmental Experts on Developments in the Field of Information and Telecommunication in the Context of International Security," A/70/172 (New York, June 2015), pp. 17, 18.

55. Alexander B. Downes, *Targeting Civilians in War* (Cornell University Press, 2008).

56. Henry Farrell, "Promoting Norms in Cyberspace," Council on Foreign Relations Cyber-Brief (Washington, 2015).

57. Gregory Flynn and Henry Farrell, "Piecing Together the Democratic Peace: The CSCE, Norms and the 'Construction' of Security in Post-Cold War Europe," *International Organization* 53, no. 3 (1999), pp. 505–35.

58. Jack Goldsmith, "Cybersecurity Treaties: A Skeptical View," *Taskforce on National Security and Law* (Stanford, CA: Hoover Institution, 2011) (http://media.hoover.org /sites/default/files/documents/FutureChallenges_Goldsmith.pdf).

59. Scott Shackelford and others, "Making Democracy Harder to Hack: Should Elections Be Classified as 'Critical Infrastructure?," *University of Michigan Journal of Law Reform* 50, no. 3 (2016), pp. 16–75.

60. Danzig, "Surviving on a Diet of Poisoned Fruit," pp. 26–27.

61. On the vulnerability of nuclear command and control, and the dangers it can create, see Ashton B. Carter, John D. Steinbruner, and Charles A. Zraket, eds., *Managing Nuclear Operations* (Brookings Institution Press, 1987); for a recent analysis of these dangers in U.S. nuclear strategy toward China, see Charles L. Glaser and Steve Fetter,

"Should the United States Reject MAD? Damage Limitation and U.S. Nuclear Strategy toward China," *International Security* 41, no. 1 (2016), pp. 49–98.

62. For an argument that even passive intrusion into command and control systems could be regarded as a grossly provocative action, see Robert D. Williams, "(Spy) Game Change: Cyber Networks, Intelligence Collection, and Covert Action," *George Washington Law Review* 79, no. 4 (2011), pp. 1162–1200.

4

A Strategic Assessment of the U.S. Cyber Command Vision

MAX W. E. SMEETS *and* HERBERT LIN

On April 15, 2010, Lieutenant General Keith Alexander appeared before the Committee on Armed Services in the United States Senate to review his nomination to become the first commander of the U.S. Cyber Command and also lead the National Security Agency (NSA).[1] During the hearing, General Alexander noted that serious challenges await: "While cyberspace is a dynamic, rapidly evolving environment, what will never change will be an unwavering dedication by both Cyber Command and the National Security Agency to the protection of civil liberties and the privacy of American citizens."[2] He told the committee that there is "much uncharted territory in the world of cyber-policy, law and doctrine."[3]

Four years later, on March 11, 2014, the Senate Armed Services Committee held a nomination hearing for Vice Admiral Michael S. Rogers to succeed Keith Alexander as head of the NSA and U.S. Cyber Command. In advance of the hearing he was asked about the major challenges that would confront the commander of U.S. Cyber Command. "I believe the major challenge that will confront the next Commander, U.S. Cyber Command will be dealing with the changing threat in cyberspace. Adversaries today seek persistent presences on military, government, and private networks for purposes such as exploitation and potentially disruption. We as a military and a nation are not well positioned to deal with such threats," Rogers stated.[4]

On March 1, 2018, Lieutenant General Paul Nakasone appeared before the same committee to become the third commander of U.S. Cyber Command (and director of the NSA).[5] Most of the questions the committee asked Nakasone were on the Cyber Command's readiness and response to the Russian interference in the U.S. election.[6] In line with this trend, Senator Ben Sasse asked: "In the cyber space, are our problems primarily technical, or are they primarily strategic and will?" "Senator," General Nakasone responded, "I would offer that we have a number of different capabilities, and I don't think that our problems are either of those. I think that what we have to do is continue to determine what is the best way forward here, what fits within our national strategy, and then act on that, Senator."[7]

The purpose of this chapter is to assess to what degree U.S. Cyber Command now has a clear vision of the best way forward. Is cyberspace closer to being "well-charted territory" for the U.S. government? And has the United States found a (potential) way to deal with the variety of cyber threat actors that are said to (co)exist in this space?[8] Our assessment focuses primarily on the 2018 U.S. Cyber Command vision entitled "Achieve and Maintain Cyberspace Superiority," which lays out the potential benefits and risks of following this strategy.

Our main finding is that, with the publication of the most recent vision, U.S. Cyber Command has for the first time articulated a comprehensive strategy that is well adapted to the unique "symptoms" of cyberspace. Yet we also argue that the "medicine" the Cyber Command prescribes to effectively deal with the symptoms needs to be further scrutinized; indeed, the "side-effects" of the strategy are still ill-understood. We described multiple possible scenarios and provide several recommendations.

The remainder of this chapter proceeds as follows. We briefly discuss the history and mission of U.S. Cyber Command. Next we introduce the 2018 vision and compare it with the 2015 vision. The following sections review how the new vision will likely be implemented within a changing institutional landscape, assess the strategy and provide a scenario-based analysis of the possible short-term and long-term strategic effects of the vision's implementation, and list several important factors—not discussed in the scenarios—that may influence the potential course of action. The final section provides several recommendations.

History and Mission of U.S. Cyber Command

In mid-2009, Secretary of Defense Robert Gates directed the commander of U.S. Strategic Command (USSTRATCOM) to establish a subunified command, Cyber Command.[9] According to Michael Warner, the U.S. Cyber Command historian, "the creation of USCYBERCOM marked the culmination of more than a decade's worth of institutional change. DoD defensive and offensive capabilities were now firmly linked, and, moreover, tied closely, with the nation's cryptologic system and premier information assurance entity, the NSA."[10] With the establishment of the new command came a new seal, which has the following code written in its inner gold ring: 9ec4c12949a4f31474f299058ce2b22a.[11] The odd string is the MD5 cryptographic hash of the unit's mission statement:[12] U.S. Cyber Command "plans, coordinates, integrates, synchronizes and conducts activities to: direct the operations and defense of specified Department of Defense information networks and; prepare to, and when directed, conduct full spectrum military cyberspace operations in order to enable actions in all domains, ensure U.S./Allied freedom of action in cyberspace and deny the same to our adversaries."[13]

Since 2009, U.S. Cyber Command has grown significantly to execute this mission. Table 4-1 provides a brief overview of the U.S. Cyber Command's budget, workforce, and development.

A New Vision: Persistence through Superiority

U.S. Cyber Command published its first "vision" in 2015, which recognizes that, when it comes to cyber operations, "We as Department are still in the early stages of this journey."[14] It has a strong focus on specifying U.S. Cyber Command's role within the Department of Defense and stresses the role of partnerships and the development of capability and force.[15] The document can better be described as an elaborate mission statement, rather than a strategy. Its most explicit discussion of what that entails is found at the start of the document: "Our mission in cyberspace is to provide mission assurance for the operation and defense of the Department of Defense information environment, deter or defeat strategic threats to U.S. interests and infrastructure, and support achievement of Joint Force Commander objectives." And the ultimate goal of the Cyber Command is to protect "freedom, liberty, prosperity, intellectual property, and personal information."[16] The document does not say how it aims to "deter" or "defeat" actors in cyberspace. Similarly,

TABLE 4-1 U.S. Cyber Command in Numbers

		Description
Time line	**2009**	In October, initial operational capability was achieved.[a]
	2017	On August 18, announcement that U.S. Cyber Command will be elevated to the status of a full and independent Unified Combatant Command.[b]
	2018	On May 4, transition to Unified Combatant Command completed.[c] On May 17, full operational capability achieved for U.S. Cyber Command.[a]
Budget and workforce	**$600 million**	Spending on programs and projects for the fiscal year for 2018.[d] The budget was $120 million in 2010 and $509 million for 2015.[e]
	1,060	Full-time staff (military members and civilians, plus contractors).[d]
	5,070	Service members and civilians in the Cyber Mission Force (CMF).[d]
	133	CMF teams on May 2018 (from September 2018, full operational capability of 133).[f] In 2015 it was at half of its target.[e]

a. U.S. Department of Defense, "Cyber Mission Force Achieves Full Operational Capability," May 17, 2018 (www.defense.gov/News/Article/Article/1524747/cyber-mission-force-achieves -full-operational-capability/).

b. Jim Garamone and Lisa Ferdinando, "DoD Initiates Process to Elevate U.S. Cyber Command to Unified Combatant Command," August 18, 2017 (www.defense.gov/News/Article/Article /1283326/dod-initiates-process-to-elevate-us-cyber-command-to-unified-combatant -command/).

c. Katie Lange, "Cybercom Becomes DoD's 10th Unified Combatant Command," *DODLive*, May 3, 2018 (www.dodlive.mil/2018/05/03/cybercom-to-become-dods-10th-unified -combatant-command/).

d. Statement of Admiral Michael S. Rogers before the Senate Committee on Armed Services, February 27, 2018.

e. Joe Gould, "Constructing a Cyber Superpower," *Defense News*, June 27, 2015 (www .defensenews.com/2015/06/27/constructing-a-cyber-superpower/).

f. Max Smeets, "U.S. Cyber Command: An Assiduous Actor, Not a Warmongering Bully," *Cipher Brief*, March 4, 2108 (www.thecipherbrief.com/us-cyber-command-assiduous-actor-not -warmongering-bully).

it does not describe any mechanisms for protecting the essential values, or at what costs.[17]

The new 2018 vision, entitled "Achieve and Maintain Cyberspace Superiority," does provide a coherent plan for directing U.S. Cyber Command's activities in cyberspace. The document offers "a roadmap for USCYBERCOM to achieve and maintain superiority in cyberspace as we direct, synchronize, and coordinate cyberspace planning and operations to defend and advance national interests in collaboration with domestic and foreign partners."[18] Taken as a whole, the new command strategy emphasizes continual and persistent engagement against malicious cyberspace actors. One could summarize the vision using Muhammad Ali's famous phrase: "Float like a butterfly, sting like a bee." The U.S. Cyber Command aims to move swiftly to dodge blows of opponents, while simultaneously being attentive to and creating openings to strike.[19]

The emergence of this new vision recognizes that previous strategies for confronting adversaries in cyberspace have been less than successful. Table 4-2 provides a brief comparison of the main imperatives of the two visions. As the report notes:

> Adversaries direct continuous operations and activities against our allies and us in campaigns short of open warfare to achieve competitive advantage and impair U.S. interests. . . . Our adversaries have exploited the velocity and volume of data and events in cyberspace to make the domain more hostile. They have raised the stakes for our nation and allies. In order to improve security and stability, we need a new approach.[20]

The 2015 vision observes that cyberspace is an ever-changing space of constant contact and activity.[21] Yet, whereas in the 2015 vision it is a mere throwaway comment, this observation has become the foundation of the 2018 vision to seek superiority through persistent engagement.

Another key change in the vision is the acknowledgment that activities in cyberspace that do not rise to the level of armed conflict (as traditionally understood in international law) can nevertheless have strategically significant effects. The document notes:

> The spread of technology and communications has enabled new means of influence and coercion. Adversaries continuously operate against

TABLE 4-2   Comparison of Vision I and Vision II of
U.S. Cyber Command

	Vision I	Vision II
Title	Beyond the Build: Delivering Outcomes through Cyberspace	Achieve and Maintain Cyberspace Superiority
Publication year	2015	2018
Commander	Admiral Michael Rogers	Admiral Michael Rogers
Office	Obama administration II	Trump administration
Imperative I	Defend the nation's vital interests in cyberspace	Achieve and sustain overmatch of adversary capabilities
Imperative II	Operationalize the cyber mission set	Create cyberspace advantages to enhance operations in all domains
Imperative III	Integrate cyberspace operations in support of joint force objectives	Create information advantages to support operational outcomes and achieve strategic impact
Imperative IV	Accelerate full-spectrum capability and capability development	Operationalize the battle space for agile and responsive maneuver
Imperative V		Expand, deepen, and operationalize partnerships

us below the threshold of armed conflict. In this "new normal," our adversaries are extending their influence without resorting to physical aggression. They provoke and intimidate our citizens and enterprises without fear of legal or military consequences. They understand the constraints under which the United States chooses to operate in cyberspace, including our traditionally high threshold for response to adversary activity. They use this insight to exploit our dependencies and vulnerabilities in cyberspace and use our systems, processes, and values against us to weaken our democratic institutions and gain economic, diplomatic, and military advantages.[22]

Overall, it should be noted that, in theory, a strategy of persistence could be the most defensive one. Think about how Muhammed Ali famously dodged punches from his opponents: the other guy in the ring is desperately punching, but Ali persists, wearing him out and mentally dominating his opponent. A strategy of persistence could also be the most aggressive one. Think about Ali's practice of constantly punching his opponents, leaving them no opportunity to go on the offense—and sometimes he knocked them out.

A New Vision in a Changing Institutional Landscape

In addition to coinciding with a new administration, the new vision came into being in an evolving institutional landscape that will directly affect its implementation and further development.[23] This includes three (ongoing) institutional changes: (1) U.S. Cyber Command decoupling from Strategic Command, (2) a change of "cyber guards," and (3) a maturing U.S. Cyber Command.

First, in August 2017, the Department of Defense (DoD) initiated the process to elevate U.S. Cyber Command to a unified combatant command,[24] and the official elevation of the command took place on May 4, 2018.[25] Proponents argue that this elevation will speed up U.S. Cyber Command's operational approval and coordination.[26] The official DoD statement also said that it "will help reassure allies and partners and deter adversaries" as the elevation demonstrates increased U.S. resolve.[27] Alternatively, the decoupling of U.S. Cyber Command from USSTRATCOM might help to dispel the notion that adversaries should or can be deterred in cyberspace. After all, USSTRATCOM's official role is strategic deterrence, whereas the U.S. Cyber Command vision seeks to move away from the deterrence paradigm and focus on strategic persistence to achieve superiority.[28]

Second, U.S. Cyber Command's elevation coincided with the confirmation of General Nakasone. It remains unclear in which direction Nakasone will steer the agency. The prepared statement of his testimony before the committee closely matched the vision's "new thinking" on persistence, noting that "operating and aggressively defending our networks is a foundational mission . . . we need to impose costs on our adversaries to ensure mission success by persistent delivery of cyberspace effects in defense of our nation and in support of our combat forces."[29] Yet his answers in the Q&A mostly reflected "old thinking" within the cyber deterrence paradigm. For example, Nakasone talked about the need to build up a diverse set of capabilities to deter cyberattacks.[30]

Third, the vision will be implemented against the backdrop of an ever-expanding U.S. Cyber Command capacity. On May 17, 2018, the Cyber Mission Force (CMF) attained full operational capability of all 133 teams.[31] This means that in three years the organization doubled in capacity: in March 2015 it was about half of its target.[32] U.S. Cyber Command has also opened its new Cyber Center and Joint Operations Center (ICC/JOC) at Fort Meade.[33]

Finally, the possible splitting of NSA and U.S. Cyber Command remains an unresolved issue.[34] The NSA and U.S. Cyber Command have been "dual-hatted" since the inception of the latter in 2009.[35] The splitting of the dual-hat role has been considered for years.[36] Although there has been an expectation that the role would eventually be uncoupled, a logical recommendation following the vision would be to maintain the dual-hat arrangement. After all, "seizing the initiative" in cyberspace requires the need to constantly move between different types of computer network operations (CNO).[37]

A Scenario-Based Analysis of Cyber Persistence

U.S. Cyber Command's new vision, a high-level document, is far from comprehensive. It may serve as a starting point for the U.S. government to adjust its strategic behavior in cyberspace, but U.S. Cyber Command will have to do a lot more heavy intellectual lifting to identify and address critical stumbling blocks it is likely to encounter in its implementation. This section highlights some of those and further develops the U.S. Cyber Command research agenda through scenario-based analysis.

At the outset, it is important to describe what U.S. Cyber Command seeks to achieve. Its ultimate objective is to "gain strategic advantage," which according to Richard Harknett and Michael Fischerkeller can be interpreted to mean changing the distribution of power in favor of the United States.[38] This is in line with the observation made by Harknett that the cyber activity of adversaries that takes place below the threshold of war is slowly degrading U.S. power—both state and nonstate actors.[39] More generally, the premise underlying U.S. Cyber Command's vision is depicted in figure 4-1.

The notion is that the U.S. government's position has slipped over the years and that therefore international stability has increased. The series of cyberattacks that took place in the early 2000s with highly disruptive consequences—including the hacking of the Democratic National Committee (2016), WannaCry (2017), and NotPetya (2017)—underline this view. These attacks suggest that adversaries have grown bolder and potentially also more capable. This new status quo is deemed unacceptable by the United States, a situation also more broadly recognized in the 2017 National Security Strategy and the 2018 National Defense Strategy.[40]

FIGURE 4-1   Main Observation Underlying
U.S. Cyber Command's 2018 Vision

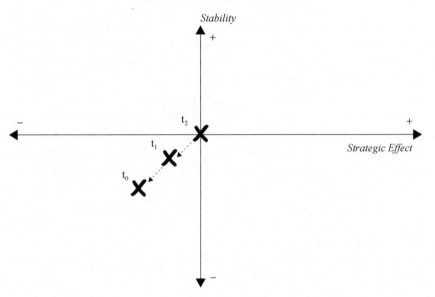

* t_0 refers to the current time period. t_1 and t_2 refer to two unspecified points in the past.

The best-case scenario following the command vision is therefore that the U.S. government achieves the end it desires and dramatically improves the ("general" or "cyber") distribution of power—that is, it achieves superiority through persistence.[41] More specifically, the way the U.S. Cyber Command aims to gain strategic effect is to seize the initiative, retain momentum, and disrupt adversaries' freedom of action.

Yet we need to be clear about the possible consequences of seeking this objective: a United States more powerful in cyberspace does not necessarily mean one that is more stable or secure. As used here, stability is a subset of the broad view of cyberspace that includes freedom, liberty, prosperity, intellectual property, and personal information.[42]

More formally, there are four possible scenarios, as shown in figure 4-2:

1. Win/Win: The strategy will lead to a more favorable distribution of power as well as a more stable and secure cyberspace and world.

2. Win/Lose: The strategy will lead to a more favorable distribution of power but also a growing degree of hostility in cyberspace and the world.

FIGURE 4-2   Potential Trade-Offs in Objectives for U.S. Cyber Command

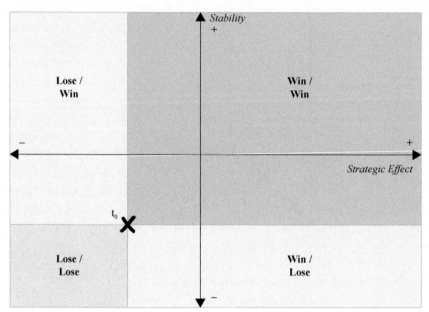

*t_0 refers to the current time period.

3. Lose/Win: The strategy will not lead to a more favorable distribution of power, but it does ensure a more stable and secure cyberspace and world.

4. Lose/Lose: The strategy will not lead to a more favorable distribution of power and will lead to a growing degree of hostility in cyberspace and the world.[43]

To gain a better understanding of which scenario is most likely, we address each in turn, providing an overview of the mechanisms that could cause the United States to end up in each situation.[44] For each scenario we take the following mechanisms into consideration: (1) threat perception of other (relevant) actors, (2) the ability of the United States to take away the initiative, and (3) the ability of the United States to seize the initiative. On the former, "Scholars in international relations have long given threat perception a central role in theories of war, deterrence, alliances, and conflict resolution," Janice Gross Stein notes.[45] Threat perceptions are subjective, but have "real" implications. Indeed, as Raymond Cohen writes: "Threat perception is the decisive intervening variable between action and reaction in international crisis."[46] How other actors, both adversaries and allies, will perceive U.S. (intended) actions in cyberspace will therefore have a decisive influence on how the strategy plays out in the future. In addition, the success of the U.S. Cyber Command strategy depends on its ability to dominate cyberspace and reduce the opportunity of adversaries to (re)act.

An important limitation of this scenario-based analysis is that we only project what could happen if the United States were to *change* its current approach.[47] In line with the above discussion of the U.S. government's perception of a degrading status quo, there are equally risks to *not* changing the course of action (which some would describe as "inaction"). Indeed, it is highly unlikely that, if the command scrapped its vision and proceeded on course, we would end up in a better situation in the (near) future.

First, there could be convergence of goals (win/win); superiority in cyberspace will in the long run also lead to a more stable environment, less conflict, norms of acceptable behavior, and so on. In fact, some argued at the first U.S. Cyber Command symposium that strategic persistence might first worsen the situation before making it better.[48] This notion is depicted as arrow A in figure 4-3. The figure also shows two other potential win/win scenarios.

The first scenario (arrow A) is possible when: (1) U.S. Cyber Command initially is unable to seize the initiative from a capacity perspective but becomes increasingly better at it in the future; and/or (2) other actors increase their hostility in the short term, but become less hostile in the long run. The first condition may well hold; as was noted, U.S. Cyber Command is still developing its cyber capacity. Even though the CMF has achieved full operational capability, it will take time for the new workforce to operate capably and for all units to coordinate effectively.[49] The second condition is much less likely to hold: other actors are likely to adapt to U.S. activities over time, and the number of actors in this space (with hostile intent) will increase. *FireEye* has reported on the "rise of the rest," stating: "While Russia and China remain atop the list of the most sophisticated cyber adversaries, *FireEye* has been observing an uptick in the number of state-sponsored cyber espionage campaigns from other countries."[50]

Another scenario, parsimoniously depicted as arrow C in figure 4-3, is interesting to consider as well. This situation could, perhaps paradoxically, be described as "deterrence through a strategy of persistence." The condition that would likely underlie this scenario is that the main threat actors are initially cautious to act following the release of a new U.S. vision. We

FIGURE 4-3   Win/Win Scenarios for U.S. Cyber Command

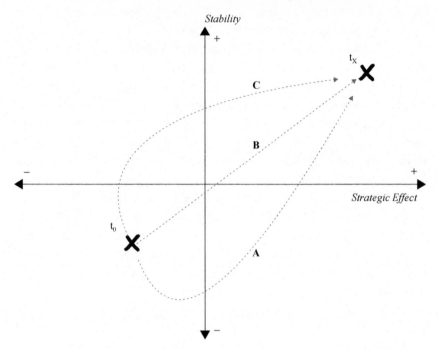

* t_0 refers to the current time period. t_x refers to an unspecified time in the future.

believe it to be unlikely that other actors will wait and see which way the wind blows. An excerpt from Nakasone's nomination hearing is telling:

> SENATOR SULLIVAN: They [our adversaries] don't fear us.
> GENERAL NAKASONE: They don't fear us.
> SENATOR SULLIVAN: So, is that good?
> GENERAL NAKASONE: It is not good, Senator.[51]

Following up on Senator Dan Sullivan's question, Senator Sasse asked: "And three years ago at the OPM hack we had Obama intelligence chiefs up here, primarily before the Homeland Security Committee, and we asked them the exact same questions: Is there any response from the United States Government that's sufficient to change the Chinese behavior? And they said absolutely not. Do you think there's any reason the Chinese should be worried about U.S. response at the present?" Nakasone responded: "Again, I think that our adversaries have not seen our response in sufficient detail to change their behavior."[52] In line with this comment, it is unlikely that the vision alone will be sufficient or threatening enough to have this type of response.

Second, it is worth considering several "escalation scenarios"—lose/lose and win/lose as shown in figure 4-2. One could equally argue that a strategy of superiority through persistence comes with a set of ill-understood escalation risks about which the vision is silent. It is noteworthy that neither "escalate" nor "escalation" appears in the new strategy document.[53] As Jason Healey has argued:

> The vision . . . ignores many of the risks and how to best address them. Most importantly, the vision does not even recognize the risk that more active defense—in systems and networks in other, potentially friendly nations—persistently, year after year, might not work and significantly increases the chances and consequences of miscalculations and mistakes. Even if they are stabilizing, such actions may be incompatible with the larger U.S. goals of an open and free Internet.[54]

To address these concerns in a more detail, figure 4-4 depicts five types of escalation scenarios: examining the arrows from right to left (A → E), they go from bad to worse. Arrows A and B both depict scenarios in which the United States achieves its ultimate objective, but has to pay a price for it. Arrows C–E depict a situation in which following the strategy does not make anything better.

In situations A and B the adversaries become more aggressive and conduct attacks that are highly disruptive to society.[55] These behaviors could be the result of either an increased *willingness* to do so or an increased *capacity*. With respect to the latter, the U.S. vision—and associated changed course of action—may encourage other actors to grow increase spending on offensive cyber operations. The conventional proliferation literature on weapons of mass destruction (WMD) includes extensive examination of the role of special interests in stimulating demand for weapons development.[56] The notion is that the new U.S. vision can be used by those groups within a country that favor a growing cyber command to justify or lobby for greater military spending.[57]

Situations A and B, as shown in figure 4-4, may also come about because of adversaries' growing incentive to conduct offensive cyber operations of a highly disruptive nature. In this case, the heightened hostility might be a

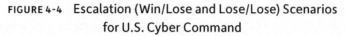

FIGURE 4-4 Escalation (Win/Lose and Lose/Lose) Scenarios for U.S. Cyber Command

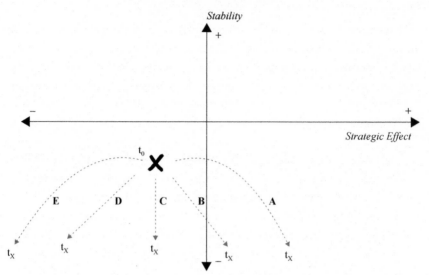

* t_0 refers to the current time period. t_x refers to an unspecified time in the future.

sign that the U.S. strategy is effective. Consider, for example, the current war against the Islamic State of Iraq and Syria (ISIS): losing territory and grip in the Middle East, the terrorist organization is said to be keen to recruit followers in Europe and other places in the world to conduct lethal attacks outside of Iraq and Syria. Attempts to perpetrate mass killings are a way to show they still need to be feared (and potentially to bolster recruitment), but they do not change the balance of power (BoP) in the region. Actors in cyberspace might become more noisy and aggressive purely to increase friction, gain attention, and so on—and perhaps also to influence public opinion in the hope the United States will change its strategy.

Arrows C–E paint a picture of the most grim possible scenarios, with the U.S. strategy failing on all accounts. These worst-case scenarios might partially result from the causal mechanisms on adversaries' capacity building described above for situations A and B. They also come about owing to U.S. failure to seize the initiative. This type of failure could stem from a multitude of sources.

First, a failure to seize the initiative may be due to a misunderstanding of the required means. The Cyber Command vision has remained silent on the available arsenal of capabilities. Scholars, however, have offered some examples of what this could entail. Michael Sulmeyer argues that the United States should "hack the hacker": "It is time to target capabilities, not calculations. . . . Such a campaign would aim to make every aspect of hacking much harder: because hackers often reuse computers, accounts, and infrastructure, targeting these would sabotage their capabilities or render them otherwise useless."[58] Such activities would indeed increase the friction that adversaries encounter in conducting hostile cyber activities against the United States.

It remains to be seen, however, whether that approach will result in persistent strategic advantage. The mixed results from the takedown of WebStresser, the largest service providing distributed denial of service (DDoS) available on the market, illustrate the issue. Europol shut down the website's infrastructure in late April 2018, at a time when the online service had more than 136,000 users.[59] According to Link11, a cybersecurity firm based in Germany, a week after the takedown of the portal the DDoS attacks fell 60 percent across Europe.[60] But a different firm, Corero Network Security, claimed that DDoS attack volumes actually increased the week after the shutdown.[61]

Second, the United States might overplay its hand. Muhammad Ali boxed sixty-one matches as a professional. He would not have won fifty-six of those fights if he had fought all of his opponents at the same time. U.S. Cyber Command is operating in a space in which it has to seize the initiative against a large and ever-growing number of actors. The dangers of fighting on multiple fronts, even for the most capable actors, are well known from conventional warfare. Because the number of (potential) cyber fronts is several orders of magnitude greater than the number of conventional warfare fronts, the risks of overextension have become exponentially higher too.

Superiority through Persistence: Against Whom, for Whom, and What Else?

The scenarios described in the previous section provide an overview of several causal mechanisms that could have implications for the new vision. Several other important factors may influence the potential course of action as well. This section discusses four additional considerations that are largely left undiscussed in the vision.

First, the scenario-based analysis did not distinguish between different types of adversaries. Yet even if the United States were able to seize the initiative against one actor, it might not be able to do so against *all* actors. It has been argued that the United States has historically focused on the large states in the international system. As Thomas Barnett writes in a well-known *Esquire* article:

> Ever since the end of World War II, this country has assumed that the real threats to its security resided in countries of roughly similar size, development, and wealth—in other words, other great powers like ourselves. During the Cold War, that other great power was the Soviet Union. When the big Red machine evaporated in the early 1990s, we flirted with concerns about a united Europe, a powerhouse Japan, and—most recently—a rising China. What was interesting about all those scenarios is the assumption that only an advanced state can truly threaten us. The rest of the world? Those less-developed parts of the world have long been referred to in military plans as the "Lesser Includeds," meaning that if we built a military capable of handling a great power's military threat, it would always be sufficient for any minor scenarios we might have to engage in the less-advanced world. That assumption was shattered by September 11.[62]

In the same vein, there is likely no one-size-fits-all way to implement strategic persistence in the cyber domain.[63] Note that several reports, including one from former secretary of defense Ash Carter, have argued that U.S. Cyber Command contributions in the campaign against ISIS have been minor.[64] It is unclear to what degree this alleged underperformance is the result of the United States preparing for the wrong threat. In any case, it does provide a valuable lesson about the difficulty of being effective in cyberspace against all types of threat actors.[65]

Second, much has been written on cyber deterrence in recent years. Given the low signal-to-noise ratio of policy discussions on this topic, the vision understandably and reasonably tries to shift the focus of cyber strategy toward an approach that is more closely matched to the realities of today. However, in being entirely silent about the topic of deterrence, it might go too far, and it implies that concepts of cyber deterrence have no relevance to U.S. cyber policy. It is likely that some form of deterrence is still needed to address low-probability cyber threats of high consequence.

Third, the U.S. Cyber Command vision acknowledges the importance of increasing the resilience of U.S. cyber assets as an important aspect of sustaining strategic advantage. But the only words in the document about doing so say that U.S. Cyber Command will share "intelligence and operational leads with partners in law enforcement, homeland security (at the federal and state levels), and the Intelligence Community."[66] Greater resilience of U.S. cyber assets will enhance our ability to bring the cyber fight to adversaries by reducing their ability to gain benefits by escalating in response, and yet the coupling between cyber defense and offense goes unmentioned.

Fourth, the vision correctly notes that "cyberspace threats . . . transcend geographic boundaries and are usually trans-regional in nature." It also notes "our scrupulous regard for civil liberties and privacy."[67] But U.S. guarantees of civil liberties and privacy are grounded in U.S. citizenship or presence on U.S. soil. If cyber adversaries transcend geographic boundaries, how will the command engage foreign adversaries who operate on U.S. soil? The vision document is silent on this point, even though it could have significant implications on its course of action.

Conclusion and Recommendations

The purpose of this chapter is to provide a brief overview of the U.S. Cyber Command strategy. In the constantly changing terrain of cyberspace in which "everyone is everyone's neighbor," the United States seeks (cyber) superiority through persistence, as stated in the 2018 vision. The ultimate goal is to maintain or favorably change the balance of power by seizing the initiative in cyberspace. We noted, however, that it remains unclear what will be sacrificed in pursuit of this optimal outcome.

From an operational perspective, we recommend that the U.S. Cyber Command give high priority to the following two aspects when implementing the strategy: prioritization and operational speed.

First, in seeking to engage on so many levels against so many actors, prioritization has to become a top issue in implementing the new vision. Priorities should not be decided on the basis of state actor versus nonstate actor, or nation-state versus criminal, hacktivist, or something else. Instead, in line with the vision's objective, prioritization decisions should be made on the basis of BoP-relevant actor versus BoP-irrelevant actor.[68] As said, this does however not mean that the United States should act in the same way against all BoP-relevant actors.

Second, operational speed and agility will manifest differently against different opponents; moreover, significant government reorganization will be required to increase operational speed and agility. What Muhammad Ali was most famous for—and what remained constant throughout all of his matches—was his amazing speed. The United States seems to be aware of the importance of threat actor prioritization and operational speed, as both are mentioned in the strategy.

The scenario-based analysis in this chapter aims to provide more insight into how the new strategy might play out. More research should be conducted on time frames for implementation, operational codes, and other external factors.

Notes

1. United States Senate Armed Services Committee, "Stenographic Transcript before the Committee on Armed Services United States Senate Nominations General Keith Alexander," U.S. Senate Committee on Armed Services, April 15, 2010 (www.armed -services.senate.gov).

2. Ibid. Also see Brian Prince, "Serious Challenges Await Head of Cyber Command," *eWeek*, May 12, 2010 (www.eweek.com/blogs/security-watch/serious-challenges-await -head-of-cyber-command).

3. Similar statements about the lack of strategic thinking have been made over the years. For example, former NSA and CIA director Michael Hayden noted: "From their inception, cyber weapons have been viewed as 'special weapons,' not unlike nuclear devices of an earlier time. But these weapons are not well understood by the kind of people who get to sit in on meetings in the West Wing, and as of yet there has not been a Herman Kahn [of *On Thermonuclear War* fame] to explain it to them." Michael V. Hayden, *Playing the Edge, American Intelligence in the Age of Terror* (New York: Penguin Press, 2016).

4. United States Senate Armed Services Committee, "Advance Questions for Vice Admiral Michael S. Rogers, USN Nominee for Commander, United States Cyber Command," March 11, 2014, pp. 7–8 (www.armed-services.senate.gov/imo/media/doc/Rogers_03-11 -14.pdf).

5. United States Senate Armed Services Committee, "Stenographic Transcript before the Committee on Armed Services United States Senate Nominations for Lieutenant General Paul Nakasone to be Commander of the U.S. Cyber Command and Director of the National Security Agency and Chief of the Central Security Service," March 1, 2018 (https://assets.documentcloud.org/documents/4407097/United-States-Senate-Armed -Services-Committee.pdf) (hereafter "Nakasone Hearings").

6. Ibid., See the opening statement of Senator Inhofe, and questions of Senators Hirono, Gillibrand, Graham, Blumenthal, Warren, and Donnelly. All asked about or commented on the Russian disinformation campaign during the 2016 presidential election.

7. Ibid.

8. The new U.S. strategy is important because it may directly enable or contain the actions of other actors, both adversaries and allies. It is also relevant for its indirect effects: given the position of the United States in the world, other governments will likely attempt to learn from any changes in U.S. thinking and adapt their policies as well.

9. For a pre-institutional history of the U.S. Cyber Command, see United States Strategic Command, "JFT-CND/JTC-CNO/JTF-GNO: A Legacy of Excellence," December 30,

1998/September 7, 2010 (https://nsarchive2.gwu.edu//dc.html?doc=2849764-Document -05). For a more general history of U.S. cyberwar, see Michael Warner, "Cybersecurity: A Pre-history," *Intelligence and National Security* 27, no. 5 (2012), pp. 781–99; and Fred Kaplan, *Dark Territory: The Secret History of Cyber War* (New York: Simon & Schuster, 2016).

10. Michael Warner, "U.S. Cyber Command's Road to Full Operational Capability," in *Stand Up and Fight: The Creation of U.S. Security Organizations, 1942–2005*, edited by Ty Seidule and Jacqueline E. Whitt (Carlisle, Pa.: Strategic Studies Institute and U.S. Army War College Press, 2015), chap. 7.

11. The official document of STRATCOM on the seal does not explain the code; it only states, "The eagle, our national symbol, is revered for the keen eyesight that allows it to pierce the darkness and remain vigilant. The two swords on the shield represent the dual nature of the command to defend the nation and, if necessary, engage our enemies in the cyber domain. The lightning bolt symbolizes the speed of operations in cyber, and the key illustrates the command's role to secure our nation's cyber domain." Strategic Command, "United States Cyber Command," March 2015 (www.stratcom.mil/Portals/8 /Documents/CYBERCOM_Fact_Sheet.pdf?ver=2018-04-18-172134-583).

12. An MD5 algorithm is a common hash function used in cryptography. Coincidentally and ironically, the U.S. intelligence community seems to have been interested in MD5 hashes at the time the U.S. Cyber Command was set up. In fact, one of the most complex espionage platforms ever developed, allegedly by the United States, Flame had as one of its most interesting features that it reengineered a certificate that could be used to sign Windows updates. As researchers from Kaspersky Lab note, "The certificate relied on an MD5 signature, which the attackers managed to fake, indicating they had the ability to break arbitrary MD5 hashes." In other words, Flame marked the death of MD5. See Mary-Beth Samekh, "Lessons learned from Flame, three years later," *Securelist*, May 29, 2015 (https://securelist.com/lessons-learned-from-flame-three-years-later/70149/); Alexander Gostev, "The Flame: Questions and Answers," *Securelist*, May 28, 2015 (https:// securelist.com/the-flame-questions-and-answers-51/34344/).

13. Noah Shachtman, "Crack the Code in Cyber Command's Logo (Updated)," *Wired,* July 7, 2018 (www.wired.com/2010/07/solve-the-mystery-code-in-cyber-commands -logo/); Noah Shachtman, "Code Cracked! Cyber Command Logo Mystery Solved," *Wired*, July 8, 2018 (www.wired.com/2010/07/code-cracked-cyber-command-logos-mystery -solved/). Even though the following operations order is heavily redacted, it provides the most detailed (publicly available) overview of the relevant tasks of U.S. Cyber Command: United States Cyber Command, "USCYBERCOM Operations Order (OPORD) 11-002, Operational Gladiator Shield (OGS)," May 19, 2011 (https://nsarchive2.gwu.edu//dc.html ?doc=2692120-Document-12).

14. United States Cyber Command, "Beyond the Build: Delivering Outcomes through Cyberspace," June 3, 2015 (www.defense.gov/Portals/1/features/2015/0415_cyber-strategy /docs/US-Cyber-Command-Commanders-Vision.pdf).

15. The focus on capability development (instead of strategy development) is in line with Rogers's nomination testimony in front of the Armed Services Committee: "If confirmed as the Commander, U.S. Cyber Command, my priority will be to generate the capabilities and capacities needed to operate in this dynamic environment and to provide senior decision makers and my fellow operational commanders with a full range of options within the cyber arena. I will partner aggressively with others in doing so, particularly with our allies and partners, those in the private and academic sectors, within the

Department of Defense, and agencies and organizations across the U.S. Government as well as the Congress." Michael S. Rogers, "Confirmation Hearing: Opening Statement to the U.S. Senate Armed Services Committee," March 11, 2014 (www.americanrhetoric .com/speeches/michaelrogersopstsarc.htm).

16. Ibid., p. 2.

17. Also, at a high-level event of the Aspen Institute, just after the vision was released, Admiral Rogers provided little strategic insight on these issues. In a conversation with David Sanger, he only expressed his concern about several cyber operations of adversaries and talked about the command's capability and force buildup (the "cyber mission force"). See Aspen Institute, "Beyond the Build: Leveraging the Cyber Mission Force," July 23, 2015 (http://aspensecurityforum.org/wp-content/uploads/2015/07/Beyond-the-Build-Lever aging-the-Cyber-Mission-Force.pdf).

18. United States Cyber Command, "Achieve and Maintain Cyberspace Superiority" (https://assets.documentcloud.org/documents/4419681/Command-Vision-for-USCYBER COM-23-Mar-18.pdf), p. 2.

19. For more details, see Richard J. Harknett, "United States Cyber Command's New Vision: What It Entails and Why It Matters," *Lawfare*, March 23, 2018 (www.lawfareblog .com/united-states-cyber-commands-new-vision-what-it-entails-and-why-it-matters).

20. United States Cyber Command, "Achieve and Maintain Cyberspace Superiority."

21. Also see U.S. Cyber Command Combined Action Group, "Beyond the Build: How the Component Commands Support the U.S. Cyber Command Vision" (Washing-ton: National Defense University Press, January 1, 2016) (http://ndupress.ndu.edu/Media /News/Article/643106/beyond-the-build-how-the-component-commands-support-the -us-cyber-command-vision/).

22. Although the document never says so explicitly, it clearly contemplates U.S. Cyber Command conducting many activities below the threshold of armed conflict as well. As Harknett notes, "This insight moves away from the conventional bifurcation of looking at cyber activity as 'hacking' and binning it as either nuisance (crime) or as a potential sur-prise attack against critical infrastructure. Instead, the strategy focuses on adversarial cyber operations for what they are—well thought out campaigns seeking to degrade U.S. power and advance their own relative capacities, while avoiding significant American re-action." Harknett, "United States Cyber Command's New Vision."

23. It is unlikely these institutional changes had an impact on the vision's content.

24. Jim Garamone and Lisa Ferdinando, "DoD Initiates Process to Elevate U.S. Cyber Command to Unified Combatant Command," *Department of Defense News*, August 18, 2017 (www.defense.gov/News/Article/Article/1283326/dod-initiates-process-to-elevate -us-cyber-command-to-unified-combatant-command/).

25. Katie Lange, "Cybercom Becomes DoD's 10th Unified Combatant Command," *DODLive*, May 3, 2018 (www.dodlive.mil/2018/05/03/cybercom-to-become-dods-10th -unified-combatant-command/).

26. Michael Sulmeyer notes that the elevation of U.S. Cyber Command might not ac-tually change much: "I am of the view that a stove-piped Joint Staff had more to do with delays and miscommunication than anything else; nor could I ever find a function Cyber Command might be asked to execute that could *only* be performed by a full, unified com-mand (like Strategic Command) but not by a sub-unified command (like Cyber Command). We looked at this several times during the last administration: If the secretary of defense wanted the sub-unified command to execute, they could and would. It wasn't a problem, so elevating the command wasn't necessary." Also, some have argued that the U.S. Cyber

Command indeed has been ineffective or overdue in its response to cyber threats. It is unclear, however, to what degree this was due to the organizational setup in the past—that is, that U.S. Cyber Command's commander has to go through STRATCOM's chain of command. See Michael Sulmeyer, "Much Ado about Nothing? Cyber Command and the NSA," *War on the Rocks*, July 19, 2017 (https://warontherocks.com/2017/07/much-ado -about-nothing-cyber-command-and-the-nsa/). On U.S. Cyber Command's "slow-start," see Ellen Nakashima and Missy Ryan, "U.S. Military Has Launched a New Digital War against the Islamic State," *Washington Post*, July 15, 2016.

27. Garamone and Ferdinando, "DoD Initiates Process to Elevate U.S. Cyber Command."

28. Also see Brad D. Williams, "Meet the Scholar Challenging the Cyber Deterrence Paradigm," *Fifth Domain*, July 19, 2017 (www.fifthdomain.com/home/2017/07/19/meet -the-scholar-challenging-the-cyber-deterrence-paradigm/).

29. In addition to these points, Nakasone said he was taught two other important lessons over the past decade: defending the nation requires a "whole-of-nation approach" and "while technology drives change in cyberspace, it's the people . . . who guarantee our success." See U.S. Senate Armed Services Committee, "Nakasone Hearings."

30. Also, in response to a question from Senator Harry Reed, Nakasone talked about the continuing need and challenges of attribution. Ibid.

31. U.S. Department of Defense, "Cyber Mission Force Achieves Full Operational Capability," May 17, 2018 (www.defense.gov/News/Article/Article/1524747/cyber-mission -force-achieves-full-operational-capability/).

32. Admiral Michael S. Rogers, USN, "Testimony on United States Cyber Command in Review of the Defense Authorization Request for Fiscal Year 2019 and the Future Years Defense Program," February 27, 2018 (www.armed-services.senate.gov/hearings /18-02-27-united-states-cyber-command); Joe Gould, "Constructing a Cyber Superpower," *Defense News,* June 27, 2015 (www.defensenews.com/2015/06/27/constructing-a-cyber -superpower/).

33. Rogers, "Testimony on United States Cyber Command," Statement before the Senate Committee on Armed Services, February 27, 2018 (www.armed-services.senate .gov/imo/media/doc/Rogers_02-27-18.pdf.

34. When the senators asked Nakasone about this at the nomination hearing, he avoided providing an answer: "I don't have a predisposed opinion on this. I think we begin with the question: What's best for the nation? And I think that's critical for us to consider. Is it best for the nation that the Nation Security Agency and U.S. Cyber Command stay together under one leader? Or is it time now that we think about a separate National Security Agency and a separate combatant command?" U.S. Senate Armed Services Committee, "Nakasone Hearings."

35. As Andy Greenberg notes, "For the first time since those two roles were combined in 2010, the man leading them may be more comfortable with the latter—leaving the NSA with the unfamiliar feeling of being the not-quite-favorite-sibling." Andy Greenberg, "The Next NSA Chief Is More Used to Cyberwar Than Spy Games," *Wired*, March 3, 2018 (www.wired.com/story/paul-nakasone-nsa-cyber-command/).

36. For recent discussions on the benefits, risks, and legal hurdles, see Sulmeyer, "Much Ado about Nothing?"; Robert Chesney, "Should NSA and CYBERCOM Split? The Legal and Policy Hurdles as They Developed over the Past Year," *Lawfare*, July 24, 2017 (www.lawfareblog.com/should-nsa-and-cybercom-split-legal-and-policy-hurdles-they -developed-over-past-year); Max Smeets, "Organisational Integration of Offensive Cyber

Capabilities: A Primer on the Benefits and Risks," 9th International Conference on Cyber Conflict, Tallinn, Estonia, 2017 (https://ieeexplore.ieee.org/document/8240326/).

37. This also leads to questions about the potential use of offensive cyber capabilities under title 10 and title 50. CNO consists of computer network defense (CND), computer network attack (CNA), and computer network exploitation (CNE). For a good discussion of how these activities overlap, see Matthew Monte, *Network Attacks and Exploitation: A Framework* (Hoboken, N.J.: Wiley, 2015); Hayden, *Playing the Edge.*

38. Richard J. Harknett and Michael P. Fischerkeller, "Deterrence Is Not a Credible Strategy for Cyberspace," *Orbis* 61, no. 3 (2017), pp. 381–93. See also Richard J. Harknett and Joseph S. Nye Jr., "Is Deterrence Possible in Cyberspace?," *International Security* 42, no. 2 (2017), pp. 196–99.

39. Harknett, "United States Cyber Command's New Vision."

40. Donald J. Trump, *National Security Strategy of the United States of America*, The White House, December 2017 (www.whitehouse.gov/wp-content/uploads/2017/12/NSS -Final-12-18-2017-0905.pdf); Department of Defense, *Summary of the 2018 National Defense Strategy of the United States of America: Sharpening American Military's Competitive Edge* (www.defense.gov/Portals/1/Documents/pubs/2018-National-Defense-Strategy -Summary.pdf).

41. The U.S. military makes an important distinction between superiority and supremacy. In the context of cyberspace, as the vision states, "superiority is the degree of dominance in cyberspace by one force that permits the secure, reliable conduct of operations by that force, and its related land, air, maritime, and space forces at a given time and place without prohibitive interference by an adversary." Cyberspace supremacy, following JP 1-02, would be the degree of cyberspace superiority wherein the opposing force is incapable of effective interference through cyberspace. Inherently, given the low barriers of entry for actors to conduct offensive cyber operations, supremacy would seem to be nearly impossible to achieve. See U.S. Cyber Command, "Achieve and Maintain Cyberspace Superiority"; Department of Defense Dictionary of Military and Associated Terms, Joint Publication 1-02, November 8, 2010/February 15, 2016 (https://fas.org/irp/doddir/dod/jp1_02.pdf).

42. This broad view is in line with the 2015 vision and President Obama's often-cited statement: "America's economic prosperity, national security and our individual liberties depend on our commitment to securing cyberspace and maintaining an open, interoperable, secure, and reliable Internet." The White House, Statement by the President on the Cybersecurity Framework, February 12, 2014 (https://obamawhitehouse.archives.gov/the-press -office/2014/02/12/statement-president-cybersecurity-framework).

43. Of course, it is possible to conceive of more complex scenarios. For example, persistence might have a strategic effect in the short term and the long term, but not in the medium term. We list only these four scenarios to avoid making the discussion unnecessarily complex.

44. We limited our discussion to scenarios 1, 2, and 4, and leave out 3 for reasons of space and word constraints.

45. Janice Gross Stein, "Threat Perceptions in International Relations," in *The Oxford Handbook of Political Psychology*, edited by Leonie Huddy, David O. Sears, and Jack S. Levy (Oxford University Press, 2013).

46. Raymond Cohen, "Threat Perception in International Crisis," *Political Science Quarterly* 1 (1978), p. 93; also see Robert Jervis, *Perception and Misperception in International Politics* (Princeton University Press, 1976); Robert Jervis, "War and Misperception," *Journal of Interdisciplinary History* 18 (1988), pp. 675–700; Joseph Nye Jr., "Transformational Leader-

ship and U.S. Grand Strategy," *Foreign Affairs* 85 (2006), p. 139; Barry Buzan, "Will the 'Global War on Terror' Be the New Cold War?," *International Affairs* 82 (2006), pp. 1102–18.

47. We thank Emily Goldman and Michael Warner for pointing out this limitation.

48. Max Smeets, "U.S. Cyber Command: An Assiduous Actor, Not a Warmongering Bully," March 4, 2018, *Cipher Brief* (www.thecipherbrief.com/us-cyber-command -assiduous-actor-not-warmongering-bully).

49. After all, offensive cyber operations are as much based on tacit knowledge, learned through practice, as they are on explicit knowledge.

50. Sarah Geary, "Rise of the Rest: APT Groups No Longer from Just China and Russia," *FireEye*, April 26, 2018 (www.fireeye.com/blog/executive-perspective/2018/04 /rise-of-the-rest-apt-groups-no-longer-from-just-china-and-russia.html).

51. U.S. Senate Armed Services Committee, "Nakasone Hearings."

52. Ibid.

53. Fears of escalation account for much of the lack of forceful response to malicious cyber activities in the past, and it can be argued that such fears have carried too much weight with policymakers; but ignoring escalation risks entirely does not seem sensible either.

54. Jason Healey, "Triggering the New Forever War, in Cyberspace," *Cipher Brief*, April 1, 2018 (www.thecipherbrief.com/triggering-new-forever-war-cyberspace); see also Jason Healey, "U.S. Cyber Command: 'When Faced with a Bully . . . Hit Him Harder,'" *Cipher Brief*, February 26, 2018 (www.thecipherbrief.com/column_article/us-cyber -command-faced-bully-hit-harder).

55. Healey also says that actors may gain more capabilities—for example, states like China might scale faster by relying on artificial intelligence. Yet, to understand the impact of the strategy, it is important to distinguish between those actions that are a (direct) response to the U.S. implementation of the new vision and those that occur whether or not the United States implements this strategy. See Healey, "Triggering the New Forever War, in Cyberspace."

56. Matthew Evangelista, *Innovation and the Arms Race: How the United States and Soviet Union Develop New Military Technologies* (Cornell University Press, 1988); Etel Solingen, "The Domestic Sources of Nuclear Postures," Policy Paper (San Diego: Institute of Global Conflict and Cooperation, October 1994); Scott Sagan, "Why Do States Build Nuclear Weapons: Three Models in Search of a Bomb," *International Security* 21, no. 3 (Winter 1996–97), pp. 54–86.

57. As Scott Sagan notes, the reverse argument has also been made for the Nuclear Proliferation Treaty (NPT): "The NPT regime is not just a device to increase states' confidence about the limits of their potential adversaries' nuclear programs; it is also a tool that can help to empower domestic actors who are opposed to nuclear weapons development." Sagan, "Why Do States Build Nuclear Weapons?," p. 72.

58. Michael Sulmeyer, "How the U.S. Can Play Cyber-Offense: Deterrence Isn't Enough," *Foreign Affairs*, March 22, 2018.

59. Catalin Cimpanu, "Europol Shuts Down World's Largest DDoS-for-Hire Service," *Bleeping Computer*, April 25, 2018 (www.bleepingcomputer.com/news/security/europol -shuts-down-worlds-largest-ddos-for-hire-service/). Note that this was a coordinated takedown led by Europol, but it was not the only organization involved in the operation.

60. Nicholas Fearn, "DDoS Attacks in Europe 'Down 60 Per Cent' following Web-Stresser Takedown," *Inquirer*, May 3, 2018 (www.theinquirer.net/inquirer/news/3031691 /ddos-attacks-in-europe-down-60-per-cent-following-webstresser-takedown).

61. Andrew Lloyd, "DDoS Attacks Rose in 2nd Half Of April 2018 after Webstresser Take-Down," *Information Security Buzz*, May 7, 2018 (www.informationsecuritybuzz .com/expert-comments/ddos-attacks-rose-in-2nd-half-of-april-2018-after-webstresser -take-down/).

62. Thomas P. M. Barnett, "Why the Pentagon Changes Its Maps," *Esquire*, September 10, 2016 (www.esquire.com/news-politics/a1546/thomas-barnett-iraq-war-primer/).

63. Indeed, Muhammad Ali also boxed differently against different opponents, especially taller ones.

64. Ash Carter, "A Lasting Defeat: The Campaign to Destroy ISIS," Belfer Center for Science and International Affairs, Harvard Kennedy School Report (October 2017) (www.belfercenter.org/LastingDefeat).

65. Of course, we may also debate to what degree the United States has been effective against nation-state actors such as Russia, China, North Korea, and Iran.

66. U.S. Cyber Command, "Achieve and Maintain Cyberspace Superiority."

67. Ibid.

68. It is best to consider these categories to be "ideal-types" on the far end of each spectrum, instead of conceiving them as binary categories. A potentially distinct category to include is BoP-enabling actors.

5

A Cyber SIOP?

Operational Considerations for Strategic Offensive Cyber Planning

AUSTIN LONG

For the first three decades of the nuclear age, discussion of nuclear strategy (particularly academic discussion) overwhelmingly focused on theoretical aspects of deterrence and certain stylized properties of weapons (such as yield and accuracy). Critical issues of command, control, communications, and intelligence (C3I), as well as targeting and planning operations, were frequently ignored or elided. This was in part due to the dearth of information available about these topics, sometimes even for those with security clearances.[1] Yet it also reflected a general view that nuclear weapons were radically different than conventional weapons.[2]

Beginning in the 1970s, scholars began to appreciate the importance of C3I, targeting, and operational issues for nuclear war.[3] This appreciation greatly improved the discourse on nuclear strategy as discussion became less abstract, even at the unclassified level. By the end of the Cold War, scholars were even able to attempt unclassified models of the Single Integrated Operational Plan (SIOP), the U.S. nuclear war plan.[4]

Discussion about cyberwar and offensive cyber operations (OCO) has thus far mirrored the early nuclear age, often neglecting C3I and operational issues in favor of more theoretical debates.[5] This chapter is an effort to move discussion of strategic cyberwarfare toward operational and tactical considerations. It takes the lexicon of nuclear operations as its starting point, while acknowledging the differences between nuclear and cyber operations. It does so from a U.S. perspective, as the author's experience is with the U.S. military and intelligence communities. Those communities are also not incidentally the world's most capable cyber actors.[6] However, much of the logic should apply to all forms of strategic OCO.

The chapter proceeds in six parts. First, it describes the main categories of targets for OCO and the nature of effects cyber operations could generate on those targets. Second, it discusses the intelligence requirements for OCO. Third, it argues that the relative ease of offense versus defense (the offense-defense balance) for OCO, an important component of strategic planning, varies depending on the target. Fourth, it describes the C3I requirements for OCO in the context of strategic warfare. Fifth, it discusses the distinction between theater and strategic cyber operations, which has C3I implications. It concludes with thoughts on the future of strategic OCO.

The primary focus of this chapter is on strategic OCO for military purposes. This distinguishes it from OCO for covert action or pure intelligence collection purposes. However, given the paucity of strategic OCO to date, some of the illustrative examples draw on historical cases of OCO for covert action (for example, Stuxnet).

Targeting OCO: Strategic Guidance for Planning

Borrowing from the nuclear lexicon, there are two broad categories of targets for OCO: countervalue and counterforce. Countervalue targets have no significant military utility but are of significant other value to the targeted state. Examples include general industrial targets and financial systems. Countervalue targeting is typically considered to be consonant with a strategy focusing on deterrence (or possibly compellence) by punishment—that is, making the cost of taking (or not taking) an action higher than the expected value of the alternative course of action.[7]

Counterforce targets are those with significant military utility. This covers a wide array of targets, from C3I systems to nuclear and conventional forces to some war-supporting industries (for example, a munitions plant).

Counterforce targeting has potential utility for deterrence by punishment but also deterrence by denial. Deterrence by denial seeks to deter a potential adversary from taking action by increasing the risk that action will simply fail to achieve an objective. Many states place some value on their military capabilities, so holding them at risk can impose costs while at the same time increasing the risk that the state will not achieve its military objectives.[8]

There are a variety of targets that straddle the divide between the two categories, at least in some contexts. For example, commercial electrical power production facilities and civilian communications infrastructure may have significant nonmilitary utility but also military utility in some contexts. Some states may rely heavily on both to support integrated air defense operations, for example. Conversely, targeting enemy leadership and internal security services may have military utility but potentially even greater value for deterrence or compellence. Most regimes place a premium on survival.

Strategic OCO planners will require guidance from senior leadership on the objectives and priorities of targeting. In the nuclear realm this is provided in a series of documents, beginning with the president's guidance through the National Security Council, which is then elaborated by the secretary of defense's guidance, which has historically been referred to as the Nuclear Weapons Employment Policy (NUWEP). These documents are then used by the chairman of the Joint Chiefs of Staff to develop the Nuclear Supplement to the Joint Strategic Capabilities (recently changed to Campaign) Plan (JSCP-N), which gives detailed instruction to U.S. Strategic Command (STRATCOM) on targeting and planning requirements.[9] This hierarchy of documents is evolving, but the basic concept will probably remain the same. Presidential guidance sets broad objectives and priorities, while the secretary of defense and the chairman of the Joint Chiefs of Staff refine this guidance for planners.

It is unclear at the unclassified level if a similar set of guidance documents exists to guide strategic OCO. News reports indicate that some presidential guidance on developing a target list for OCO was provided in 2012 by Presidential Policy Directive 20 (PPD-20).[10] However, it is not apparent whether cyber equivalents of the NUWEP and JSCP-N exist. Whether they do or not, it is worth considering what guidance such documents must provide to strategic OCO planners.

First, guidance documents should provide the objectives to be achieved through strategic targeting of OCO. In the nuclear case those objectives, in available declassified versions, have been threefold. The first is to deter attack or coercion based on the threat of attack on the United States and its allies. The second is to control escalation if deterrence fails. Escalation control is to be achieved by limiting the scope of response and selecting targets that leave some adversary targets hostage to the threat of future attack. The third, if escalation control fails, is to conduct general war to achieve maximum U.S. power relative to the adversary. This is to be achieved by destroying targets critical to the adversary's postwar status while limiting damage to the United States and its allies through counterforce operations and retaining a reserve force for use after the conclusion of hostilities.[11]

For a cyber equivalent to the SIOP (that is, a plan for strategic OCO), planners need similar objectives. Deterrence is an obvious parallel objective between nuclear and cyber, but deterrence of what? Are strategic OCO intended primarily to deter adversary OCO, or are such operations part of a broader set of deterrent capabilities, including nuclear forces? The latter seems more likely, but this is a policy choice different administrations may answer differently.

The 2016 Russian cyber efforts against the U.S. election complicates this policy choice. Although the effort did not inflict any physical damage, it nonetheless had potential strategic consequences. Should this be considered a strategic attack that strategic OCO planners should deter? Or is it a counterintelligence and law enforcement issue rather than a military planning issue? At present, policy appears to define it as the latter, but this may require further consideration.[12]

Likewise, the 2018 Nuclear Posture Review raises the possibility of nuclear response to strategic OCO by declaring:

> The United States would only consider the employment of nuclear weapons in extreme circumstances to defend the vital interests of the United States, its allies, and partners. Extreme circumstances could include significant non-nuclear strategic attacks. Significant non-nuclear strategic attacks include, but are not limited to, attacks on the U.S., allied, or partner civilian population or infrastructure, and attacks on U.S. or allied nuclear forces, their command and control, or warning and attack assessment capabilities.[13]

Although this statement does not specifically note attack by OCO, it seems likely that a non-nuclear strategic attack could include OCO. Certainly it seems likely that the drafters of the Nuclear Posture Review were aware of potential OCO threats to critical infrastructure. Only a few weeks after the release of the Nuclear Posture Review, the U.S. Department of Homeland Security released a report noting, "Since at least March 2016, Russian government cyber actors . . . [have] targeted government entities and multiple U.S. critical infrastructure sectors, including the energy, nuclear, commercial facilities, water, aviation, and critical manufacturing sectors."[14] The Nuclear Posture Review also highlights risks associated with targeting adversary command and control with OCO, which it seems the United States at least would view as non-nuclear strategic attack.

If deterrence fails, OCO planners need subsequent objectives. Here the parallel with nuclear operations, at least those from the Cold War context, may be less obvious. Is the next objective for strategic OCO the control of escalation? It could be, but this might vary by adversary and scenario. Failure of deterrence regarding a great power like Russia or China might lead to a subsequent objective of escalation control, but North Korea or Iran might be different, with the objective being the prompt neutralization of adversary strategic capabilities in order to limit (or eliminate) damage from enemy attack, particularly nuclear attack. This damage-limitation argument has been proposed by multiple defense analysts.[15]

Regardless, OCO could be a component of either objective but would be planned very differently. For escalation control, planners would need to define targets that punish the adversary and/or deny objectives in order to demonstrate U.S. resolve. Yet the targets would have to demonstrate resolve without giving the adversary an incentive to escalate. The need to strike this balance—producing effects sufficient to show resolve without risking escalation—will be challenging to policymakers and planners alike. Inadvertent escalation was a major worry in the late Cold War with conventional and nuclear forces, a concern that has returned in East Asia and potentially the eastern and southern flanks of the North Atlantic Treaty Organization (NATO).[16] The addition of OCO further compounds this problem by creating new pathways to inadvertent escalation. On the other hand, it may also present opportunities for escalation control that do not exist in nuclear strategy.

For example, countervalue targets are, in nuclear strategy, not often considered for escalation control. This is principally because they are associated with civilian populations, either directly or indirectly. For example, a major automotive factory or steel mill might be a lucrative countervalue target, but such targets are typically close to an urban work force. A nuclear strike that destroyed such a target would kill many civilians and give the adversary a strong incentive to escalate in retaliation.

In contrast, OCO can potentially be used against such targets with much lower collateral effect on the civilian population. Assembly lines could be disabled or even destroyed with few if any fatalities. Financial firms and telecommunications likewise could be targeted discriminately, at the firm level or even below firm level, where countervalue targeting could be used to harm particular assets valuable to a regime—bank accounts of leaders, for example.

If countervalue OCO offers new opportunities to control escalation, counterforce OCO may make such escalation more likely in some contexts. A historical parallel to counterforce OCO and inadvertent escalation was concern about the impact of electronic warfare in a conventional battle in Europe on Soviet early warning of a U.S. strategic nuclear attack, particularly one directed at the Soviet strategic nuclear arsenal.[17] Electronic warfare in this context was not intended to threaten Soviet strategic forces but could nonetheless generate pressure for nuclear use if the Soviet leaders became fearful that their forces were vulnerable.

Soviet exercises reflected this fear. In a 1984 Soviet strategic exercise, U.S. bombers exploited damage to the Soviet air defense as well as the massive volume of electronic warfare to strike key Soviet command centers. This initial attack was promptly followed by a devastating attack on Soviet strategic nuclear forces.[18] Thus conventional air operations, including electronic warfare, in an actual war may have made the Soviets extremely concerned about the survival of their nuclear forces and thus could have pressured them to use nuclear weapons first.

Strategic counterforce OCO could create similar fears, as attacks on even nonmilitarily critical systems (such as power supplies) could affect military capabilities or stoke fears that military networks had likewise been compromised. Indeed, OCO effects could be more escalatory than traditional electronic warfare, which even if it compromises air defense is nonetheless often observable—radar operators will often know they are being jammed even if they can do nothing about it. Counterforce OCO, if done well, could compromise systems without the target knowing. An adversary thus might not be able to distinguish between a system failure due to OCO and a natural system failure. In a crisis or conventional war, if some component of an adversary's command and control failed, it could easily be misinterpreted as successful OCO and create escalatory pressures. Targeting strategic counterforce

OCO for escalation control without risking inadvertent escalation may thus be a major planning challenge.

In contrast, strategic counterforce OCO may be very useful for achieving damage-limitation objectives, particularly against a regional power such as North Korea. Indeed, former deputy assistant secretary of defense John Harvey has called for a comprehensive effort to negate North Korea's nuclear arsenal, including:

> cyber capabilities to disrupt warhead arming and firing systems, or cause flaws to be introduced into warhead designs, so that any arriving warheads are duds. On this last point, foreign "assistance" to North Korea's nuclear program is a problem, but it is also an opportunity. Under such conditions, North Korea's leaders would no longer "own" their nuclear weapons—in a sense, we would. A bit fanciful? Not necessarily. The technologies, subsystems and capabilities exist today to address each one of these goals notwithstanding the need for a bit of luck here and there. It is well within the realm of technical possibility.[19]

Thus the target choice would be less restricted in planning for damage limitation than in escalation control. Essentially everything would be fair game. Yet establishing the accesses needed for OCO could be escalatory, as discussed in the next section.

A final objective might be the maintenance of a cyber "reserve" force. This may or may not be important to policymakers and planners, as the need to maintain a reserve would depend substantially on the uniqueness of accesses and exploits as well as the importance of the conflict. If the exploits and accesses were unique or highly specific to the target—for example, an indigenous Iranian air defense server system—then there might be little technical reason to reserve an attack capability for future conflict. On the other hand, a more widely applicable OCO capability in terms of exploits and accesses—for example, a widely used supervisory control and data acquisition (SCADA) system—might be best kept in reserve. Much would depend on the context of use, so planners would need to think through options as they related to both overall objectives and specific option planning.

In addition to overall objectives, guidance to strategic OCO planners should include direction on the desired attack structure and related operational priorities. In the nuclear context, attack structure in available declassified records had four elements: limited nuclear options (LNOs), selected attack options (SAOs), major attack options (MAOs), and regional nuclear options (RNOs).[20] This structure provides a useful starting point for thinking about the structure of strategic OCO plans.

LNOs were intended as the initial mechanism for nuclear response while controlling escalation. Although details about the nature of any preplanned LNOs are not available at the unclassified level, the guidance indicated they should signal U.S. commitment to a conflict and should focus on improving the military balance in a local conflict. A cyber equivalent, perhaps a limited cyber option (LCO), would target adversary systems of local military utility while attempting to limit the risk of escalation. The latter objective would require both a quantitative limit on the size of the attack and a qualitative limit on the military value of the target.

An example target of an LCO is a system that contributes to adversary offensive targeting capability. This could be an adversary's over-the-horizon targeting system, such as a satellite constellation or over-the-horizon radar. Such systems are a vital part of an adversary's ability to track and target U.S. forces at long range but could potentially be discretely targeted in a way that is unlikely to impair the adversary's strategic early warning or attack assessment.

In terms of scale, the Stuxnet attack on Iranian centrifuges would have been an exemplary LCO. It was confined to specific industrial control systems used by Iranian centrifuges in a limited number of facilities. Even then, the malware spread beyond the targeted facilities but did not cause widespread collateral effects.[21] To be clear, Stuxnet was not an LCO, having been intended to achieve its limited aims in a covert manner, while an LCO could be much more overt. However, Stuxnet demonstrates the ability to conduct OCO in a discrete and discriminate fashion.

In contrast to an LNO, a nuclear SAO would be a significantly larger target set, such as an adversary's long-range strike aircraft. This would require comprehensive targeting of all airbases, including dispersal bases. A cyber SAO intended to achieve the same effect would target both airbase air traffic control and logistics systems as well as the avionics of adversary strike aircraft (all to the extent possible). The risk of escalation from SAOs is higher than that associated with LNOs (indeed an SAO could be thought of as an aggregation of LNOs). Yet the military impact would be substantially higher, providing policymakers with stronger options.

Cyber SAOs also potentially provide unique opportunities for escalation that would be more difficult or even impossible for conventional or nuclear forces. One might be an SAO targeting adversary capabilities for information and population control (e.g., regime-controlled media outlets, internal security databases, and censorship/surveillance capabilities). A cyber SAO against this target set offers the ability to create effects without civilian loss of life and potentially the ability to introduce new information into the adversary state. This could be either false information (created, for example, by corrupting internal security databases with fictitious information) or true information (such as a more accurate representation of events in the regime's media).

A possible similar cyber SAO would target adversary OCO capabilities. This would include C3I for OCO, along with specific facilities known to generate OCO exploits or tools. Although OCO can be conducted in a distributed fashion, there are nonetheless likely to be a variety of critical nodes in C3I. For example, as of 2013, a large number of Chinese cyber operations originated from a single building.[22]

As noted, cyber SAOs also present the opportunity for countervalue attacks that inflict very limited civilian collateral damage (civilian deaths). One example could be an SAO on an adversary's financial system—banks and capital markets. Another could be an attack on the electrical power production system, though this would likely cause indirect civilian deaths from the loss of power to critical systems with limited backup (traffic control, for example).

MAOs represent the ultimate escalatory options for policymakers. If SAOs are analogous to aggregated limited options, then MAOs are aggregations of SAOs. An example is a comprehensive attack on all adversary military systems, including nuclear, conventional, space, and cyber. In addition, MAOs in the nuclear context can include attacks on countervalue targets, so presumably any countervalue cyber SAOs could be combined into an MAO.

Finally, RNOs are intended to respond to theater contingencies with theater forces. As we discuss later, theater cyber forces are growing, so the possibility of regional cyber options (RCOs) could be growing as well. Yet part of the desire for RNOs was the belief, correct or not, that responses from theater forces would be seen as less escalatory than responses with strategic forces. It is not clear that adversaries will even be able to distinguish OCO conducted by "theater" forces from those conducted by "strategic" forces, particularly given that cyber force assigned to a regional combatant commander may not be co-located with that commander.

Yet RCOs may be distinguishable by limiting geographic scope and effect rather than by geographic origin. It may therefore fill a gap between LCOs and cyber SAOs. For example, an RCO might be created as part of a regional combatant commander's war plan that attacks a broad target set, such as air defense systems, in a limited geographic area (such as the most likely point for conventional conflict with an adversary). Though not as distinct from strategic OCO as its nuclear equivalent, RCOs of this type would allow a commander to present leadership with an option that combines military utility with somewhat limited escalatory risk.

In addition to providing guidance on types of cyber options, policymakers must provide guidance on damage expectancy for cyber options. Is the goal of a given option to produce relatively transient and/or reversible effects? If so, within what parameters (for example, disrupt the functioning of a system for hours, days, or weeks)? If not, how much effort should OCO planners put into ensuring that effects are difficult to reverse, with the high end for such expectancy being physical destruction of critical system components?

This guidance will likely be affected by how policymakers envision cyber options interacting with other military options. One example would be options targeting adversary nuclear forces. It is unlikely, though not impossible, that policymakers would be willing to target adversary nuclear forces with cyber options alone. Cyber options targeting adversary nuclear forces (and attendant C3I) would therefore only be expected to achieve transient effects and, ideally, improve the ability of conventional or nuclear strikes to destroy those nuclear forces (for example, by revealing the location of mobile nuclear forces while disrupting their ability to move and launch). Even a transient effect of a few hours in this instance could vastly improve the efficacy of other military options. Such counter-C3I options against Soviet strategic targets using electronic warfare were apparently developed during the late Cold War.[23]

The countervalue equivalent of this damage expectancy is similar to a denial-of-service effect. Here the target system held at risk would be unavailable for some period of time but would eventually return to full operational status. The 2007 wave of distributed denial-of-service (DDoS) attacks on Estonian government and commercial websites is an example of this level of damage expectancy.[24]

At the other end of the spectrum, a cyber SAO targeting regime information and population control mechanisms might ideally produce permanent effects, at least for some systems. Permanent loss of servers used to maintain censorship and surveillance programs would impose very significant costs on any adversary that values such programs. The same would be true of servers associated with adversary OCO.

The countervalue equivalent of this damage expectancy is the physical destruction or permanent disabling of the target system. One reported example is the targeting of a German integrated steel mill reported in 2014. An operation targeting the mill's industrial control systems led to an inability to safely shut the mill down and "massive damage to the whole system."[25] The server and computer damage caused by the North Korean OCO against Sony is also at this end of the damage expectancy spectrum.[26]

Along with the spectrum of effects ranging from disruption and denial of service to physical destruction, OCO presents an additional category of potential "damage" expectancy distinct from any offered by nuclear or conventional weapons. This is the opportunity for deception by introducing false information into adversary networks.[27] Successful deception could be more militarily useful for some targets than disruption or destruction. For example, adversary systems that provide position, navigation, and timing (PNT) information will likely enable precision strike capabilities. The premier examples are satellite-based PNT systems like the U.S. Global Positioning System (GPS) and similar Russian GLONASS and Chinese Beidu systems.[28] Such systems rely on ground control stations to precisely monitor and control satellites, which in turn transmit signals to users.

Simply disrupting or destroying PNT systems would force adversaries to use alternative methods, such as shifting to nonprecision munitions, which would degrade performance. But subtly altering data in the monitoring and control system might degrade performance more as the adversary would be unaware of the problems in the PNT system and therefore continue to rely on it even as it provided inaccurate data. Thus rather than moving from accurate to less accurate weapons (if PNT were disrupted or destroyed) the adversary would have accurate weapons that consistently missed their aimpoint by small but militarily important distances (a dozen meters perhaps) without initially understanding why the weapons were not destroying their targets.

Before proceeding, it is worth noting that one of the difficulties of developing cyber options for deterrence is the difficulty of credibly communicating those options to adversaries. For example, imagine the United States had a very credible cyber option to permanently disable most or all of the servers supporting the so-called Great Firewall of China.[29] This option might have significant deterrent value if communicated, but as noted in the next section, such an option would entail developing very detailed intelligence about the targeted servers and exploiting vulnerabilities in the server system to obtain access. Credibly communicating the ability to attack this system would, in addition to provoking China, likely reveal aspects of the access method. At a minimum, it would increase Chinese efforts to detect vulnerabilities in the system. In other words, revealing the deterrent threat might fully or partially vitiate its efficacy, in contrast to most nuclear or even conventional deterrent threats.

Decision makers may be more likely to reveal or risk revealing some OCO capabilities than others. Some OCO capabilities may be more valuable than others, particularly if they are unique. Those that are not unique are therefore more readily put at risk for deterrence.[30] The context for putting the capability at risk may matter a great deal as well.

Electronic warfare provides an example of some of these tensions. In the 1960s the U.S. military and intelligence community developed a capability to trigger the identify-friend-or-foe transponder on export-model Soviet MiG fighters. This capability, code named COMBAT TREE, gave U.S. fighters equipped with the system a decisive advantage against these aircraft. As U.S. losses in the air war over North Vietnam mounted in 1967, there was a debate about using COMBAT TREE against North Vietnamese MiGs. Some officials were apparently reluctant to use the system in North Vietnam because it would risk revealing the capability, which could be vitally important in a war in Central Europe. Eventually the military decided to employ the system despite the risk, given that U.S. forces were at war. However, they would likely have been reluctant to risk revealing the system just for deterrence.[31]

Targeting OCO: Intelligence Requirements

The intelligence requirement for nuclear options is not trivial, but it is relatively straightforward. The central requirement for nuclear targets is a list of targets that meet the criteria required in the guidance. This has been known as the National Strategic Targets List, a database of thousands of relevant targets.[32]

Each target on the list has specific intelligence requirements. These include the nature of the target, the precise location of the target (for fixed targets anyway), the vulnerability of the target to nuclear effects, and depending on the target, the extent of active defenses that must be suppressed to reliably attack the target. During the Cold War, among the most difficult fixed targets were underground hardened command and control sites around Moscow, a city protected by extensive active defenses.[33] Yet the intelligence requirements once the sites were located were relatively modest.

In contrast, the intelligence requirements for cyber options are immense, as the delivery mechanism is entirely dependent on intelligence collection. First, the target and its vulnerabilities must be identified, then a malware payload exploiting those vulnerabilities developed, and access routes into the target established.[34] This can be extraordinarily difficult, even for advanced cyber actors, depending on the characteristics of the target.[35] Many targets may not be connected to any external networks or may function on dedicated land networks, which does not present an insurmountable barrier but does require very extensive intelligence development to cross.[36] Other targets may only be accessible through radio frequency operations. The U.S. Air Force has publicly acknowledged using its Compass Call jamming aircraft to target a variety of networks for exploitation.[37]

For example, cyber options targeting missile systems (for example, surface-to-air missiles or ballistic missiles) would require an understanding of both the C3I network supporting missile operations and ideally the missile system itself. The latter would require foreign military exploitation—the acquisition and experimentation with examples of the system itself. This is a capability the United States is investing heavily in, but does require examples of the foreign technology (or intelligence access to detailed technical specifications).[38]

For some systems this may be relatively easy for the United States. As an example, Greece, a NATO ally, has acquired the Russian S-300 surface-to-air missile (NATO designation SA-10 Grumble). Exploitation of the export variant of S-300 would be trivially easy. During the Cold War the United States also benefited from the exploitation of aircraft from defectors, such as the 1976 defection of Viktor Belenko in an advanced MiG-25 Foxbat interceptor.[39] In other cases, intelligence from sources provided similar insights, such as Adolf Tolkachev's detailed technical information on Soviet airborne radar.[40]

For many systems of interest, exploitation of a full system will be impossible. For example, no samples of adversary intercontinental ballistic missiles (ICBMs) are likely to be available to exploitation. Yet subsystems or analogous systems could be available. For example, the Soviet/Russian Topol and Topol-M (NATO designation SS-25 Sickle/SS-27 Sickle-B) mobile ICBMs use a transporter erector launcher (TEL) based on more widely distributed designs that originated from a firm based in what is now Belarus.[41] This commonality could potentially permit development of accesses and exploits of these systems.

The challenge of targeting intelligence and gaining access to some targets helps clarify one of the persistent questions about OCO: Is cyber an offense- or defense-dominant operating environment?[42] Many experts argue that the cyber environment is offense-dominant and therefore fraught with risks of escalation and security dilemmas. In this environment, efforts to improve one's own security through offensive cyber capabilities may imperil others and lead to arms races and instability.[43]

Yet others have observed that the conduct of OCO is often enormously challenging. Erik Gartzke and Jon Lindsay highlight the fact that deception, which is an effect of OCO, can be used by a clever defender to cripple offensive activity.[44] Some have also noted the enormous effort needed to establish the accesses and exploits required for OCO against hard targets such as the SCADA systems in Iran's Natanz uranium enrichment plant.[45] Even the use of airborne platforms like Compass Call to establish access creates a high barrier to entry for OCO; only a handful of nation-states operate such sophisticated electronic warfare assets.[46] For these observers, the cyber environment could very well be defense-dominant, with only very well resourced actors capable of any but the most rudimentary OCO.

How can these divergent perspectives be reconciled? First, one of the issues in assessing the offense-defense balance in the cyber operating environment is the different terminology used by technologists and hackers on one side and political scientists and defense analysts on the other.[47] Technologists often refer to offense as dominant if, given sufficient resources and time, an attacker can penetrate a system. This seems to be the meaning intended in a 2013 Defense Science Board Report that claimed, "With present capabilities and technology it is not possible to defend with confidence against the most sophisticated cyber attacks."[48] The report classifies such sophisticated attackers as those that "can invest large amounts of money (billions) and time (years) to actually create vulnerabilities in systems, including systems that are otherwise strongly protected . . . today limited to just a few countries such as the United States, China, and Russia."[49]

Yet when political scientists refer to offense as dominant, they mean the offense is, dollar for dollar, easier than defense.[50] If an attack requires years of work and billions of dollars to overcome a defense that cost (only) millions of dollars, political scientists would characterize the environment as highly defense-dominant. Defense dominance does not therefore mean offense is impossible; it just means attackers will have to spend disproportionately more than the defender to achieve success.

The Defense Science Board report notes a variety of defensive measures can, at manageable cost, thwart even "actors who are organized, highly technical, proficient, well-funded professionals working in teams to discover new vulnerabilities and develop exploits."[51] Moreover, even for the most sophisticated attackers (which the report terms Tier V–VI) these defenses, "when properly deployed, . . . make an attacker's task of moving data throughout the systems, while remaining undetected, much more difficult. Our goal is to raise the costs for the Tier V–VI attackers to succeed, limiting the number of operations they can afford to attempt."[52] This assessment seems in accord with a political scientist's definition of defense dominance. Thus the same report argues that high-confidence defense is impossible against sophisticated actors, but that relatively inexpensive efforts can thwart most attackers and limit attack options even for the most sophisticated. Clarity of terminology therefore matters a great deal. For purposes of this discussion, offense-dominant means it is cheaper on the margin to attack than defend, not just that an attacker with enough time and money will get through.

The offense-defense balance as it pertains to OCO should therefore not be taken as a given for the entire operating environment. Rather, borrowing from the work of Stephen Biddle, the offense-defense balance for OCO should be conceived at the *operational* rather than the *environmental* level.[53] The offense-defense balance is likely to be highly dependent on the target and objectives of OCO.

For example, imagine an air defense system connected by a combination of dedicated fiber-optic lines and encrypted microwave datalinks. OCO against such a system would be possible, but just establishing access might require some combination of physical operations to insert corrupted hardware into the fiber system or the actual radar or missile system, kinetic attack against fixed nodes, and advanced electronic attack against the datalinks (probably airborne). Developing the malware payload would likewise require obtaining some sample of the code used in the system.

These things are no doubt possible. A news report on one such program, the U.S. Air Force's Project Suter, describes "the magic":

After pinpointing the target antennas, Suter then performs its real magic—beaming electronic pulses into the antennas that effectively corrupt, if not hijack, the processing systems that present the enemy operators with their physical picture of the battlefield. Unlike classic jamming or EMP [Electromagnetic Pulse] attacks, these data streams do not flood enemy electronics with excess "noise" or power, but instead insert customised signals, including specialised algorithms and malware, into the vulnerable processing nodes.[54]

The introduction of malware from Suter sounds like OCO, and according to news reports the use of OCO for air defense suppression was considered in 2011 for both the raid into Pakistan that killed Osama bin Laden and the Libya air campaign. It is not clear if these options were Suter based or much more extensive. OCO options were apparently rejected for a variety of reasons, including the timeline to prepare options (a testimony to the need for extensive intelligence preparation) and the existence of other options for defense suppression.[55]

Yet if Suter and similar programs require hundreds of millions (or even billions) of dollars of investment and lengthy preparation to work against even relatively unsophisticated air defenses like Libya's and Pakistan's, one can hardly claim these OCO are offense-dominant. A similar argument can be made about the Stuxnet attack. Offense is possible against targets with limited or no connectivity to the outside world, but the defense will be dominant. Even modest efforts at defense make OCO against these targets impossible for all but the most capable (and patient) cyber attackers.

In contrast, commercially available systems with frequent or continuous connection to commercial communications (such as phone, fiber, or Bluetooth connections) are likely to be relatively easy targets for OCO. Here the offense may be dominant, particularly for reasonably sophisticated attackers capable of doing even modest reconnaissance (on social media for example). These would include a variety of important targets, including the SWIFT system of interbank transfers as demonstrated by the recent cyber heist from the central bank of Bangladesh.[56]

Several insights into the limits of OCO can be derived from a general understanding of intelligence requirements. First, the ability to develop new OCO options during a crisis in anything like real time—a process STRATCOM refers to as "adaptive planning"—will be circumscribed.[57] Accesses to systems will in many instances require precrisis exploitation. If this exploitation has not taken place, then OCO options will frequently just not be available. The only exception might be targets vulnerable to disruption by denial-of-service attacks.

However, vulnerability will likely vary by target. Targets where offense dominates—mostly countervalue targets like SWIFT—may be significantly easier for adaptive planning. Payloads focused on widely used commercial software could be stockpiled (and maintained as software is upgraded or patched) for use in adaptive planning. Access to systems frequently or continuously connected to commercial communications could potentially be established relatively quickly (days rather than months), making adaptive planning of countervalue OCO options possible. Where defense dominates—mostly against counterforce targets like air defense—adaptive planning may be an impossibility on anything like crisis or conflict timelines.

Second, given the requirements for access, the number of cyber options that can be developed will be more limited than nuclear or conventional options. As noted, for any specific target of nuclear or conventional attack, the intelligence requirements are limited, while attack systems are highly fungible: the same nuclear weapon can be used to attack a wide array of targets. In contrast, accesses and vectors for cyber OCO are not likely to be very fungible. An exploit attacking communications links for a surface-to-air missile system may provide little or no utility for attacking a ballistic missile (unless perhaps they use very similar transport systems).

The combined limits on adaptive planning and fungibility between accesses and exploits means policymakers must provide much more detailed guidance on priorities to OCO planners than they do for nuclear or conventional weapons. Thus if policymakers want to be able to hold electric power generation rather than banking at risk with OCO, this level of specificity must be provided in guidance to OCO planners. Planners can then prioritize target development for these systems over, for example, information about adversaries and population control. This may be less true for many countervalue targets, but will certainly be the case with many counterforce targets.

In addition to guidance, OCO planners must be given the authority to develop access to and exploitation of desired targets. Attempting to establish access, if discovered, can be provocative, so policymakers must measure the utility of any given OCO option against the escalation risk not just of executing the option but simply developing accesses for it. For example, an adversary could consider extremely provocative any effort to gain access to its national-level C2, including nuclear C2.

According to open-source reports, the United States could have the insight to attempt such an NC2 exploit against China. A Chinese defector may have provided the United States with extensive information on the security of Chinese leadership facilities and the Chinese nuclear C2.[58] Such information could allow the United States to develop cyber options against Chinese targets, yet the escalatory risk of doing so would be large given the possibility that its efforts to develop access and exploits could be discovered.

In contrast, many countervalue targets will likely be only modestly provocative, as penetrations are relatively common. Balancing the potential utility of OCO options against both the intelligence investment required to develop access and the risk of attempting to develop access presents a major challenge, particularly relative to development of nuclear and conventional options. This balancing merits a major interagency review, akin to similar efforts in the nuclear realm during the 1970s or more recent efforts conducted as part of Nuclear Posture Reviews.[59]

C3I for a Cyber SIOP

C3I requirements for strategic OCO mirror some, though not all, of the requirements for nuclear operations. For nuclear operations the main requirements are "that NC3 nuclear command, control, and communications must be reliable, assured, enduring, redundant, unambiguous, survivable, secure, timely, flexible, and accurate."[60] In addition to C3, nuclear forces require an intelligence component for early warning, to assess incoming attacks (at a minimum to distinguish very large from very small attacks), and to perform postattack evaluation of both incoming strikes from adversaries and outgoing strikes.[61]

The C3 requirements for OCO are the same as for NC3, but perhaps not as stringent. For example, the survivability requirement for NC3 is extreme—a minimum warning nuclear attack by a major power. Unless OCO is a major component of U.S. retaliatory capabilities for such an attack, OCO C3 need not be as survivable as NC3. Moreover, the forces that execute OCO may not be nearly as survivable as some elements of U.S. nuclear forces, making highly survivable C3 for OCO a poor investment.

As an example, the U.S. Air Force planned to contribute thirty-nine teams to the Cyber Mission Force as of May 2014, of which nineteen were teams that could have an OCO mission (the other twenty are cyber protection teams). Those teams were allocated to just five bases (two of which are in the greater San Antonio area).[62] A handful of nuclear strikes, and possibly even a robust conventional strike, could destroy or disable the entire Air Force contribution to OCO. In contrast, Air Force ICBMs, 450 of which are distributed in hardened silos, would require hundreds of nuclear weapons to destroy. In short, C3 need not be more survivable than the actual forces, whether nuclear or cyber. OCO forces may be significantly more vulnerable than nuclear forces, so C3 need not be highly survivable.

On the other hand, the C2 issues associated with OCO forces assigned to regional combatant commanders noted earlier create issues for the overall OCO C3 structure. If OCO forces assigned to a regional combatant commander are not co-located with the command headquarters, C3 must be sufficiently survivable to prevent the easy severing of combatant commanders from OCO forces. Only two of the Air Force teams potentially capable of OCO were planned to be located outside the continental United States (in this case in Hawaii, where the Pacific Command is headquartered). The other teams, in Texas and Georgia, could be assigned to support distant commands, such as the European Command (EUCOM), making them highly reliant on classified communications systems.

If C3 for OCO is based on the standard Department of Defense protocol for Top Secret/Sensitive Compartmented Information (TS/SCI) it may not meet this standard of survivability.[63] First, Department of Defense TS/SCI networks rely heavily on Defense Intelligence Agency (DIA) Regional Support Centers, of which there were only five in 2004, according to unclassified sources.[64] A relatively finite number of conventional strikes could therefore significantly damage not only U.S. OCO forces, but also the C3, allowing distant combatant commanders to effectively communicate with them.

Second, even short of conventional strikes on the United States, C3 may be vulnerable to adversary attack. Recent media reports have highlighted Russian efforts to map, and potentially target, undersea military communications cables in the Atlantic.[65] Severing these cables would greatly degrade but not eliminate C3 on networks linking EUCOM to U.S.-based cyber forces. Satellite communications can provide a substitute, albeit at a lower data rate, for the cables.

However, both Russia (and China) are reported to be developing a wide array of abilities to target U.S. space assets, including communications satellites. These include direct kinetic attacks (antisatellite missiles), electromagnetic attacks (jamming satellite links), and even OCO attacks of their own.[66] A combination of severing trans-Atlantic cables with even limited attacks on communications satellites could seriously impair OCO C3 from EUCOM without striking any ground targets.[67]

Vulnerability of C3 in the nuclear realm led to significant concerns about strategic stability, as it created incentives for preemptive attack. Preemption, by disrupting C3, could yield significant military benefits, which in turn would make crises less stable—the nuclear equivalent of the World War I mobilization mania.[68] Similar vulnerability of C3 for OCO, combined with the potential vulnerability of OCO forces themselves, may create crisis instability if one or both sides perceived utility in making a preemptive attack.

Yet the utility of preemption may be more limited, as cable-based communication within the United States may be less vulnerable than trans-Atlantic cables. OCO forces based in the United States could thus be directed by U.S. Cyber Command/STRATCOM rather than EUCOM, a less efficient C3 arrangement perhaps, but better than nothing. Yet the severing of links between Europe and the United States could degrade access to some targets for OCO even if C3 is maintained.

The intelligence requirements for OCO are difficult but better understood in some ways. Early warning of adversary OCO is well appreciated as a critical but difficult component of cyber defense. For example, the U.S. Intelligence Advanced Research Projects Agency (IARPA) is seeking to invest in novel ways to develop cyber early warning.[69]

Potentially more challenging is the ability to assess the effectiveness of OCO. Briefing a group of pilots about to conduct airstrikes that, despite imagery showing an intact air defense system, it is all right to proceed because OCO has disabled missiles and radars would be challenging, to say the least. What if the adversary has created a false image of effective OCO in order to lure aircraft into an ambush?

Given this potential for deception by adversary defense cyber operations, assessing the effectiveness of OCO probably requires a "dual phenomenology" approach.[70] This would mean that, after initial indications of successful OCO from OCO forces, another intelligence collection platform would confirm the result. In the case of the Suter program, the results of the introduction of malware are reported to be independently assessed by U.S. electronic warfare aircraft such as the RC-135 Rivet Joint.[71]

Similar intelligence collection may be required to verify the efficacy of other types of OCO. For example, OCO against targets with visual signatures (for example, an electric power grid) could be verified by overhead imagery. Much more difficult would be verifying OCO against a regime's internal security databases, though perhaps communications intelligence (COMINT) could detect an adversary's discussions of the attack. This too, however, could be part of a deception operation.

Theater and Strategic OCO: A Blurry Firebreak

One of the central distinctions in the nuclear era was between theater nuclear forces (and operations) and strategic nuclear forces. The SIOP was developed to govern strategic forces while theater forces were governed by the relevant theater commanders. The Supreme Allied Commander Europe (SACEUR), the American general commanding NATO forces, had a plan for the coordinated delivery of NATO theater nuclear forces. Below SACEUR's level, various tactical commanders could potentially be authorized to use nuclear weapons for relatively limited tactical effects.[72]

Over time, U.S. leaders became increasingly uncomfortable with tactical commanders having delegated authority to use nuclear weapons. The potential for escalation and other strategic effects from tactical nuclear use, combined with a general decision by the U.S. Army to refocus on conventional military operations after 1960, limited the development of very serious thinking about tactical nuclear use. Yet the boundary between theater and strategic was often opaque or arbitrary. For example, one of the long-standing distinctions in plans was geographic, with SACEUR's plans from the 1960s onward limited to NATO and Warsaw Pact territory outside the Soviet Union, while the SIOP would handle targets inside the Soviet Union. Yet this distinction began to blur as longer-range theater forces, such as the Pershing II intermediate range ballistic missile and Gryphon ground-launched cruise missile, were deployed in the early 1980s.[73]

OCO, in contrast to nuclear operations, has long been viewed as primarily (though not exclusively) strategic. While U.S. regional combatant commanders have long had an information operations capability that includes electronic warfare, military deception, and special technical operations and is thus capable of some OCO (or OCO-like) functions, the remit for such operations remains limited. Indeed relatively early in the development of OCO the joint task force charged with such operations was placed under U.S. Strategic Command. When that organization evolved into U.S. Cyber Command it remained a subunified command under STRATCOM.

At present the authorization for OCO, like nuclear operations, remains with the U.S. National Command Authority (NCA—that is, the president and the secretary of defense).[74]

Yet the trajectories of the two types of operations may be radically different. While nuclear operations became increasingly centralized in the early decades of the nuclear age, OCO is beginning to be decentralized. The current plan for a Cyber Mission Force (CMF) envisions a number of Combat Mission Forces that "will support combatant commands by generating integrated cyberspace effects in support of operational plans and contingency operations." These presumably could include OCO for theater purposes. U.S. Cyber Command will retain a National Mission Force, which will likewise presumably conduct strategic OCO.[75]

As a series of wargames and reports have noted, the existence of theater cyber forces will require a change in C2 and potentially a willingness to delegate authority to conduct OCO to commanders below the NCA level.[76] In terms of C2, many analysts agree that theater cyber forces should fall under a cyber (or information) component commander. This C2 architecture would parallel the special operations model, where each regional commander has a theater special operations command (TSOC), which is organized by the U.S. Special Operations Command but operationally controlled by the regional commander.

Yet C2 organization without authorities to both prepare for and execute theater-level OCO will not produce a meaningful capability. As described, there are real limits on the ability to effectively plan and target OCO absent extensive intelligence collection and target development. However, the risks of inadvertent escalation that leaders worried about with theater nuclear operations are at least as prominent with theater OCO. Leaders may be unwilling to delegate the authority necessary for theater OCO, limiting the utility of theater cyber forces, regardless of C2 architecture.

At the same time, some capabilities that strongly resemble OCO may be included as a subset of more traditional elements of theater forces. For example, electronic warfare, the use of the electromagnetic spectrum for offensive or defensive purposes, is a standard element of a regional combatant commander's forces. Yet sophisticated electronic warfare programs use the generation of false signals and in some cases employ malware.

The boundary between electronic warfare and OCO may be clearer at the classified level, but it merits significant consideration. If programs like Suter are considered OCO, then they will likely require authorization by the

NCA, which may in turn reduce the effort regional combatant commanders expend on incorporating them fully into their operational plans. Why rely on a capability requiring authorization that may not be forthcoming in a conflict? Alternately, if Suter and similar systems are simply a form of electronic warfare, policymakers may be unpleasantly surprised to discover their use in a conflict without NCA-level authorization.

This question is becoming increasingly important as the U.S. military articulates doctrines that call for greater reliance on OCO. The U.S. Air Force and Army are cooperating to produce a "multidomain" doctrine, which will almost certainly have an OCO element.[77] The operational boundaries within OCO should be carefully delineated as part of the development of regional cyber C2.

The Future of Strategic Offensive Cyber Operations

The U.S. government will have to grapple with all of the foregoing operational considerations for OCO. It should therefore pursue a cyber posture review in parallel to other strategic reviews, such as the Nuclear Posture Review and the Missile Defense Review. This review would provide the critical guidance for developing OCO and C31 targeting.

For an administration seeking to capitalize on U.S. strengths in OCO, this review might generate guidance that assumes escalation risk by seeking to develop options against critical adversary assets such as national and nuclear C2. In contrast, an administration concerned about the potential for inadvertent escalation caused by seeking to develop access to critical C2 might impose strict targeting limits on OCO, such as greatly confined regional scope for such operations.

Similarly, an administration may embrace an OCO posture focusing on deterrence by punishment through countervalue retaliation. It might also impose damage expectancy focusing on destruction rather than disruption. Alternatively, it may eschew countervalue OCO in favor of counterforce targeting, emphasizing the disruption of adversary OCO C3 and force structure in order to prevail in a short but sharp conventional conflict.

Central to any future for strategic OCO is a vision of the role of OCO in the broader U.S. defense strategy. At the time the nuclear SIOP was developed, U.S. strategic nuclear forces were the force of last resort and the lynchpin of U.S. extended deterrence.[78] After the end of the Cold War, nuclear weapons became less central to U.S. military posture and the SIOP was officially retired in 2003, replaced by other operational plans.[79] In contrast, the role of a cyber SIOP in U.S. military posture is just beginning.

Notes

1. On the limitations even analysts with security clearances faced, see Austin Long, *Deterrence from Cold War to Long War: Lessons from Six Decades of RAND Research* (Santa Monica, Calif.: RAND, 2008), pp. 28–31; Janne Nolan, *Guardians of the Arsenal: The Politics of Nuclear Strategy* (New York: Basic Books, 1989); Franklin C. Miller, "Masters of the Nuclear Weapons Enterprise," in George Butler, *Uncommon Cause: A Life at Odds with Convention*, vol. 2 (Denver: Outskirts Press, 2016), pp. 1–21.

2. Marc Trachtenberg, "Strategic Thought in America, 1952–1966," *Political Science Quarterly* 104, no. 2 (1989), pp. 301–34.

3. John D. Steinbruner, "National Security and the Concept of Strategic Stability," *Journal of Conflict Resolution* 22 (1978), pp. 411–28; Ashton B. Carter, John D. Steinbruner, and Charles A. Zraket, eds., *Managing Nuclear Operations* (Brookings Institution Press, 1987).

4. Lynn Eden and Steven E. Miller, eds., *Nuclear Arguments: The Major Debates on Strategic Nuclear Weapons and Arms Control* (Cornell University Press, 1989).

5. Richard A. Clarke and Robert K. Knake, *Cyber War: The Next Threat to National Security and What to Do about It* (New York: Ecco, 2010); Joel Brenner, *America the Vulnerable: Inside the New Threat Matrix of Digital Espionage, Crime, and Warfare* (New York: Penguin, 2011); Lucas Kello, "The Meaning of the Cyber Revolution: Perils to Theory and Statecraft," *International Security* 38 (2013), pp. 7–40.

6. See Kaspersky Lab, "Equation Group: Questions and Answers," February 2015 (https://media.kasperskycontenthub.com/wp-content/uploads/sites/43/2018/03/08064459/Equation_group_questions_and_answers.pdf). Many observers have concluded that the Equation Group is affiliated with, or a component of, the U.S. National Security Agency.

7. Glenn Snyder, *Deterrence and Defense: Toward a Theory of National Security* (Princeton University Press, 1961). For a short primer on deterrence theory generally, see Long, *Deterrence from Cold War to Long War*.

8. Ibid.; also see Desmond Ball and Jeffrey Richelson, eds. *Strategic Nuclear Targeting* (Cornell University Press, 1986).

9. Hans M. Kristensen, "The U.S. Nuclear Posture after the 2010 Nuclear Posture Review and 2013 Nuclear Employment Strategy," Federation of American Scientists, 2013 (https://fas.org/programs/ssp/nukes/publications1/Brief2013_Georgetown.pdf).

10. Glenn Greenwald and Ewen MacAskill, "Obama Orders U.S. to Draw Up Overseas Target List for Cyber-attacks," *Guardian*, June 7, 2013 (www.theguardian.com/world/2013/jun/07/obama-china-targets-cyber-overseas).

11. National Security Agency (NSA), "Policy Guidance for the Employment of Nuclear Weapons," April 3, 1974 (http://nsarchive.gwu.edu/NSAEBB/NSAEBB173/SIOP-25.pdf).

12. Greg Miller and others, "Obama's Secret Struggle to Punish Russia for Putin's Election Assault," *Washington Post*, June 23, 2017.

13. Department of Defense, *Nuclear Posture Review*, February 2018, p. 21.

14. United States Computer Emergency Readiness Team, "Russian Government Cyber Activity Targeting Energy and Other Critical Infrastructure Sectors," March 15, 2018 (www.us-cert.gov/ncas/alerts/TA18-074A).

15. John R. Harvey, "Commentary: Negating North Korea's Nukes," *DefenseNews*, February 15, 2016 (www.defensenews.com/story/defense/commentary/2016/02/15/commentary -negating-north-koreas-nukes/80189872/); Vince A. Manzo and John K. Warden, "The Least Bad Option: Damage Limitation and U.S. Deterrence Strategy toward North Korea," *Texas National Security Review* Policy Roundtable, February 7, 2018 (https://tnsr.org /roundtable/policy-roundtable-good-choices-comes-north-korea/#essay6).

16. Long, *Deterrence from Cold War to Long War*; Joshua Rovner, "AirSea Battle and Escalation Risks," Working Paper (University of California Institute on Global Conflict and Cooperation, 2012), pp. 1–5; C. Talmadge, "Would China Go Nuclear? Assessing the Risk of Chinese Nuclear Escalation in a Conventional War with the United States," *International Security* 41, no. 4 (2017), pp. 50–92.

17. Barry Posen, *Inadvertent Escalation: Conventional War and Nuclear Risks* (Cornell University Press, 1991), esp. chap. 4.

18. Bruce G. Blair, *The Logic of Accidental Nuclear War* (Brookings Institution Press, 1993), pp. 127–28.

19. Harvey, "Commentary: Negating North Korea's Nukes."

20. NSA, "Policy Guidance for the Employment of Nuclear Weapons."

21. Jon Lindsay, "Stuxnet and the Limits of Cyberwarfare," *Security Studies* 22 (2013), pp. 365–404.

22. Mandiant, "APT1: Exposing One of China's Cyber Espionage Units" (http://intelreport.mandiant.com/Mandiant_APT1_Report.pdf).

23. Benjamin B. Fischer, "CANOPY WING: The U.S. War Plan That Gave the East Germans Goose Bumps," *International Journal of Intelligence and Counterintelligence* 27, no. 3 (2014), pp. 431–64; F. Kaplan, *Dark Territory: The Secret History of Cyber War* (New York: Simon & Schuster, 2016), pp. 12–20.

24. Jason Richards, "Denial-of-Service: The Estonian Cyberwar and Its Implications for U.S. National Security," *George Washington University International Affairs Review* 18 (2009) (www.iar-gwu.org/node/65); Jason Healey, ed., *A Fierce Domain: Conflict in Cyberspace, 1986 to 2012* (Washington: Cyber Conflict Studies Association, 2013).

25. Michael J. Assante, Tim Conway, and Robert M. Lee, "German Steel Mill Cyber Attack," SANS Industrial Control System, 2014 (https://ics.sans.org/media/ICS-CPPE -case-Study-2-German-Steelworks_Facility.pdf).

26. Michael B. Kelley, "The Sony Hack Wrecked A LOT of Equipment," *Business Insider*, January 4, 2015 (www.businessinsider.com/we-now-have-an-idea-of-the-sony-hacks -destruction-2015-1).

27. Erik Gartzke and Jon Lindsay, "Weaving Tangled Webs: Offense, Defense, and Deception in Cyberspace," *Security Studies* 24 (2015), pp. 316–48.

28. See overview of GPS control and related topics in "Official U.S. Government Information about the Global Positioning System (GPS) and Related Topics" (www.gps .gov/systems/gps/control/).

29. Benjamin Edelman and Jonathan Zittrain, "Empirical Analysis of Internet Filtering in China," Berkman Center for Internet & Society (http://cyber.law.harvard.edu/filtering /china/appendix-tech.html).

30. Kevin N. Lewis, "Getting More Deterrence out of Deliberate Capability Revelation" (Santa Monica, Calif.: RAND, 1989); Brendan Green and Austin Long, "The Role of Clandestine Capabilities in Deterrence: Theory and Practice," U.S. Naval Postgraduate School (NPS) Center on Contemporary Conflict (CCC), Project on Advanced Systems and Concepts for Countering WMD (PASCC), Grant N00244-16-1-0032, September 2017.

31. Marshall Michel, *Clashes: Air Combat over North Vietnam, 1965–1972* (Annapolis, Md.: Naval Institute Press, 1997), p. 181; Robert Hanyok, *Spartans in Darkness: American SIGINT and the Indochina War, 1945–1975* (Ft. Meade, Md.: Center for Cryptologic History, 2002), pp. 255–58.

32. Russell E. Dougherty, "The Psychological Climate of Nuclear Command," in Carter, Steinbruner, and Zraket, *Managing Nuclear Operations*, p. 412.

33. Jeffrey Richelson, "Dilemmas in Counterpower Targeting," *Comparative Strategy* 2, no. 3 (January 1980), pp. 164–65.

34. For an overview of vulnerability, payload, and access requirements, see Herbert Lin, "Offensive Cyber Operations and the Use of Force," *Journal of National Security Law and Policy* 4, no. 1 (2010), pp. 63–86.

35. Author's conversation with a senior adviser to U.S. Cyber Command, March 2016.

36. Jeremy Hsu, "Why the NSA's Spying on Offline Computers Is Less Scary Than Mass Surveillance," *IEEE Spectrum*, January 20, 2014 (http://spectrum.ieee.org/tech -talk/telecom/wireless/why-the-nsa-spying-on-offline-computers-is-less-scary-than -mass-surveillance).

37. Sydney J. Freedberg Jr., "Wireless Hacking in Flight: Air Force Demos Cyber EC-130," *Breaking Defense*, September 15, 2015 (http://breakingdefense.com/2015/09/wireless -hacking-in-flight-air-force-demos-cyber-ec-130/).

38. Brandon Shapiro, "Acquire, Assess, Exploit," *Airman Magazine*, November 21, 2016 (www.nasic.af.mil/News/ArticleDisplay/tabid/1356/Article/1010245/acquire-assess -exploit.aspx).

39. John Barron, *MiG Pilot: The Final Escape of Lieutenant Belenko* (New York: McGraw-Hill, 1980).

40. David Hoffman, *The Billion Dollar Spy: A True Story of Cold War Espionage and Betrayal* (New York: Doubleday, 2015). For a contrary argument on the importance of Tolkachev, see Benjamin B. Fischer, "The Spy Who Came in for the Gold: A Skeptical View of the GTVANQUISH Case," *Journal of Intelligence History* 8, no. 1 (Summer 2008), pp. 29–54.

41. "Topol-M," *Jane's Strategic Weapons Systems*, November 2, 2016.

42. An overview and critique of the offense-defense literature in political science can be found in K. Lieber, *War and the Engineers: The Primacy of Politics over Technology* (Cornell University Press, 2005); and Stephen Biddle, "Rebuilding the Foundations of Offense-Defense Theory," *Journal of Politics* 63, no. 3 (2001), pp. 741–74. See also Rebecca Slayton, "What Is the Cyber Offense-Defense Balance? Conceptions, Causes, and Assessment," *International Security* 41, no. 3 (2017), pp. 44–71.

43. Kello, "The Meaning of the Cyber Revolution."

44. Gartzke and Lindsay, "Weaving Tangled Webs."

45. Thomas Rid, "Cyber War Will Not Take Place," *Journal of Strategic Studies* 35, no. 1 (2012), pp. 5–32.

46. "Compass Call," *Jane's C4ISR & Mission Systems: Air*, May 17, 2016.

47. Thanks to Herbert Lin for helping me understand this key difference in terminology across communities.

48. Defense Science Board, "Resilient Military Systems and the Advanced Cyber Threat," January 2013, p. 1 (http://www.dtic.mil/docs/citations/ADA569975).

49. Ibid., p. 2.

50. As Charles Glaser and Chaim Kaufmann characterize it, the offense–defense balance is "the ratio of the cost of the forces that the attacker requires to take territory to the

cost of the defender's forces." See Chaim Kaufmann and Charles Glaser, "What Is the Offense-Defense Balance and Can We Measure It?," *International Security* 22 (1998), p. 46.

51. Defense Science Board, "Resilient Military Systems," chap. 8; quotation on p. 22.

52. Ibid., p. 64.

53. Biddle, "Rebuilding the Foundations of Offense-Defense Theory."

54. Richard B. Gasparre, "The Israeli 'E-tack' on Syria—Part II," *Air Force Technology*, March 10, 2008 (www.airforce-technology.com/features/feature1669/); United States Air Force, "Project Suter," n.d. (PowerPoint briefing in the author's possession).

55. Eric Schmitt and Thom Shanker, "U.S. Debated Cyberwarfare in Attack Plan on Libya," *New York Times*, October 18, 2011.

56. Jim Finkle, "Bangladesh Bank Hackers Compromised SWIFT Software, Warning Issued," Reuters, April 24, 2016 (www.reuters.com/article/us-usa-nyfed-bangladesh -malware-exclusiv-idUSKCN0XM0DR).

57. USSTRATCOM Global Operations Center Fact Sheet (www.stratcom.mil /factsheets/3/Global_Operations_Center/printable/).

58. Jamil Anderlini and Tom Mitchell, "Top China Defector Passes Secrets to U.S.," *Financial Times*, February 4, 2016 (https://www.ft.com/content/4e900936-cb20-11e5-a8ef -ea66e967dd44).

59. Desmond Ball, "The Development of the SIOP, 1960–1983," in *Strategic Nuclear Targeting*, edited by Desmond Ball and Jeffrey Richelson (Cornell University Press, 1986).

60. Department of Defense, *Nuclear Matters Handbook 2016*, chap. 6 (www.acq.osd.mil /ncbdp/nm/NMHB/chapters/chapter_6.htm).

61. John C. Toomay, "Warning and Assessment Sensors," in Carter, Steinbruner, and Zraket, *Managing Nuclear Operations*, pp. 282–321.

62. United States Air Force, "USCYBERCOMMAND Cyber Mission Force," n.d. (PowerPoint briefing in the author's possession).

63. On TS/SCI IP, see TS/SCI IP Data, Defense Information Systems Agency (www .disa.mil/Network-Services/Data/TS-SCI-IP).

64. Defense Intelligence Agency, *Communiqué* 16 (2004), p. 4 (https://issuu.com /nationalsecurityarchive/docs/communique-2004-december).

65. David E. Sanger and Eric Schmitt, "Russian Ships Near Data Cables Are Too Close for U.S. Comfort," *New York Times*, October 25, 2015.

66. Elbridge Colby, *From Sanctuary to Battlefield: A Framework for a U.S. Defense and Deterrence Strategy for Space* (Washington: Center for New American Security, 2016).

67. This same logic holds even if C3 is conducted over other classified networks such as the National Security Agency's NSANet or the Joint Staff–sponsored Planning and Decision Aid System (PDAS) (http://comptroller.defense.gov/Portals/45/Documents/defbudget /fy2009/budget_justification/pdfs/01_Operation_and_Maintenance/O_M_VOL_1 _PARTS/TJS%2009PB%20OP-5.pdf).

68. Steinbruner, "National Security and the Concept of Strategic Stability"; J. Snyder, *The Ideology of the Offensive: Military Decision-Making and the Disasters of 1914* (Cornell University Press, 1984).

69. Kevin McCaney, "IARPA Wants an Early Warning System for Cyber Attacks," *Defense Systems*, July 24, 2015 (https://defensesystems.com/articles/2015/07/24/iarpa -cause-cyber-early-warning-system.aspx).

70. Gartzke and Lindsay, "Weaving Tangled Webs."

71. Gasparre, "The Israeli 'E-tack' on Syria."

72. See Catherine Kelleher, "NATO Nuclear Operations," in Carter, Steinbruner, and Zraket, *Managing Nuclear Operations*, pp. 445–69.

73. Ibid., pp. 450 and 457–64.

74. See remarks by Vice Chief of Naval Operations Admiral Michelle Howard in Scott Maucione, "Cyber Offensive Weapons Pits Strategic vs. Tactical," Federal News Radio, September 25, 2015 (http://federalnewsradio.com/defense/2015/09/top-naval-official -will-take-presidents-permission-use-offensive-cyber-weapon/); J. Lewis, "The Role of Offensive Cyber Operations in NATO's Collective Defence," Tallinn Paper 8 (Tallinn, Estonia: NATO Cooperative Cyber Defence Centre of Excellence, 2015).

75. *Department of Defense Cyber Strategy* (April 2015) (www.defense.gov/Portals/1 /features/2015/0415_cyber-strategy/Final_2015_DoD_CYBER_STRATEGY_for _web.pdf).

76. U.S. Naval War College Public Affairs, "Naval War College Report Reveals New Joint Defense Needs," March 10, 2015 (www.navy.mil/submit/display.asp?story_id =85958); Ben FitzGerald and Parker Wright, *Digital Theaters: Decentralizing Cyber Command and Control* (Washington: Center for New American Security, 2014).

77. Jim Garamone, "Air Force, Army Developing Multidomain Doctrine," U.S. Department of Defense, January 25, 2018 (www.defense.gov/News/Article/Article/1424263 /air-force-army-developing-multidomain-doctrine/).

78. Earl C. Ravenal, "Counterforce and Alliance: The Ultimate Connection," *International Security* 6, no. 4 (1982), pp. 26–43.

79. Hans M. Kristensen, "Obama and the Nuclear War Plan," *Federation of the American Scientists Issue Brief*, February 2010 (https://fas.org/programs/ssp/nukes/publications1 /WarPlanIssueBrief2010.pdf).

6

Second Acts in Cyberspace

MARTIN C. LIBICKI

Although the effects of almost all weapons depend on the characteristics of the target, this is particularly so for the weapons of cyberwar. A piece of malware that brings one system down may have absolutely no effect on another. The difference between the two may be a simple as which patch version of a piece of software each system runs.

Were systems immutable, this facet of cyberwar would be of interest to cyber targeters but not to planners. The former would examine particular targets for particular weaknesses and then attack them. In so doing they would act like air targeters that examine imagery for targets and electronic orders of battle for access and egress routes and then design attacks to maximize return and minimize risk.

But computer systems *are* mutable; indeed, when people say that cyberspace is the only man-made medium, they are also saying that it is the only man-alterable medium. Alteration can take place rapidly. If the patch level of a system determines a target's susceptibility to attack, that target may transition from vulnerability (to a particular attack) to invulnerability in, literally, minutes.

The ability of targets to alter—which is largely to say reduce—their vulnerability to a cyberattack after having experienced one has broader implications. First, knowing a target's abilities helps the attacker determine the returns to offensive cyberwar capabilities over the course of a campaign. It thus influences what kind of resources can be cost-effectively invested in the campaign and the extent to which state strategies should rely on its attacks working. Second, a target's abilities will shape how cyberattacks should be used. Granted, some attackers may satisfy their goals with a single attack; others, not. The latter will be interested in inhibiting the process by which targets, having been infected once, immunize their systems against repeated attack. They should understand which targets can be repeatedly attacked and how to shape attacks so that they can attack again if they have to.

The process of adjustment may arise from the target's realization that many of its systems are more vulnerable than they should be (it may also realize that many of its systems are extravagantly protected, but that insight is apt to produce less change). The target will respond to this realization in one of two ways. One, it will reassess its rational pre-attack calculations of the vulnerability of its system. Two, it will reassess the importance of attending to cybersecurity if previously other needs dominated its attention.

Either way, tightening up is in order. Reducing its vulnerabilities to future cyberattacks entails actions by the target that span the spectrum from tactical, local, and short-term to strategic, global, and long-term. An example of a tactical fix is to install a patch to the system that was attacked. Further along the spectrum, all systems will need to be patched. Then might come the installation of cybersecurity tools. Yet further along is reviewing which people or processes can access which services, increasing user education, monitoring what users do more closely, and gaining a capacity for faster response. The more strategic options may include hardware fixes (for example, disconnecting emitter and transmission devices), architectural alterations, network reconfigurations, limits on what systems are exposed to (for example, air-gapping), and redteaming.[1] And that is just a partial list.

To be fair, not all of the adjustments a target makes are bad for the attacker. Indeed, forcing adjustments to be made could be the point of the cyberattack. Consider Stuxnet. Its immediate effect was the destruction (or at least premature retirement) of roughly one thousand centrifuges.[2] But its longer-term effect may have been to make Iran wary of adding centrifuges to its program until it could assure itself the risk from future cyberattacks was minimized. The latter created an eighteen-month pause in the buildup of centrifuges,[3] a period during which Iran could have added several thousand centrifuges were it not inhibited by fears that Stuxnet could have further surprises in store, or that future Stuxnet-like attacks would not frustrate their efforts. The indirect effects of Stuxnet are comparable to or may have been even stronger than its direct effects (a lot depends on what Iran would have otherwise done). A similar adjustment was made by Iraqi forces in the first Gulf War when their fiber-optic lines were destroyed and they reverted to over-the-air communications that were easier to intercept. Analogously, the victim of a cyberattack may abandon a secure communications mode that is prey to disruption in favor of a more reliable mode that is easier to intercept.

Correspondingly, part of a cyberattack strategy may be to use the fear of a repeat attack to drive adversaries to adopt counterproductive behaviors, such as not trusting the information they see or the people they deal with. If the target has to check everything, then its OODA (observe-orient-decide-act) loops will run more slowly and potentially give the attacker a decisive edge in some situations. Similarly, if cyberattacks persuade their targets to abjure digitization, or at least networked computers—and if they are worse off for having done so—then attackers gain *because* adjustment is possible. Indeed, attackers who understand that their opponents view technology with a gimlet eye may deliberately want to induce a strong immune response in the hope that anaphylaxis (a life-threatening allergic reaction) will yield more benefits than the original disease would have.

Even when operating against a rational opponent (one that will never consciously adopt policies that make it worse off), attackers can take heart that an opponent's postattack adjustments to systems in order to prevent another, though rational, can be costly. By forcing the adversary to take pains when it was otherwise complacent, an attack can introduce fog and friction into the adversary's operations. Thus, well after the initial cyberattacks have come and gone, they may keep on giving, albeit not as much as if the target had made no adjustments at all. The imposition of fog and friction is a consolation prize.

Two caveats merit note. First, determining the costs (in terms of reduced military efficiency) borne by the target in the process of adjustment is likely to be no better than guesswork on the part of the attacker. Second, military communities are not always satisfied by actions that impose long-term costs on the adversary but render themselves largely irrelevant and thus subject to reassignment while the conflict is still going on.

Let us now discuss the factors that should be correlated with a faster adjustment response by the target. "Faster" refers to the time it takes the target to significantly fix and then harden a system so as to make future cyberattack attempts less successful, or at least far costlier for the attackers. It does *not* refer exclusively to the time required to restore a crippled system to service, or restore confidence in data that had been corrupted. If service is restored and even if the malware is eliminated, but nothing else changes, then the underlying susceptibility of the system to reattack has not changed either.

Furthermore, adjustment is usually not an event but a multi-step process. A target may make superficial adjustments in the hope that it has warded off further attacks and then find that attackers have other ways in: for instance, it may patch a system and then fall victim to another attack because it used software with multiple, seemingly endless, vulnerabilities (the Java client, for instance, had such a bad reputation at one point that the Department of Homeland Security recommended users uninstall it).[4] The next step may be to eliminate such software; this will work until other product vulnerabilities are exploited. The target may then have to make more profound adjustments, such as isolating itself or white-listing inputs (meaning only those known not to be troublesome are allowed in). These more profound adjustments are in turn more expensive, and, as noted, some of them may simply not have been worth making. The trade-offs associated with increasing a system's cybersecurity echo those of a system's development: you can have fast, good, or cheap—pick two.[5]

The preceding argument can be illustrated in three steps. I first describe an adjustment process. Next I look at factors that may explain why one target adjusts more quickly or more completely than another. I then discuss how an attacker might shape its cyberattacks to suppress the target's adjustment process.

A Heuristic Adjustment Process

A heuristic adjustment process is useful for showing what factors may predispose targets to react more or less rapidly to cyberattacks.

Adjustment begins with the recognition that a system is not performing as it should. In some cases this is obvious: systems stop working or produce obvious garbage. In other cases the loss of performance is subtle or intermittent; it can be hard to detect or discern when a system is operating at the edge of its performance envelope. If corruption is involved, someone has to notice a variation between the information (or services) people expect and what they actually get (or detection may be as simple as results being implausible or contradicting other sources). If the problem is that information is leaking (technically not a cyberattack, but something that also merits a response), there has to be some evidence of a leak: for example, sensitive information is found in the wrong hands, information is being directed to an unauthorized recipient, or it is otherwise difficult to explain certain behaviors (such as foes appearing to act with superior knowledge).

Next, the cause of the malfunction has to be correctly identified—or at least the possibility that a cyberattack *could* be a cause has to be recognized. In the United States (and in developed economies in general) causes of system malfunction are usually identified correctly within hours or days. Countries with poorer access to technical resources (Iran under boycott, for example) may have a harder time isolating or characterizing faults. In war, the malfunctioning system may be destroyed if the induced malfunction impedes mobility or creates a tell-tale signature. This step is not absolutely necessary to produce a response; military users may adjust by deciding that their information systems are undependable and looking elsewhere to inform their decisions more reliably. As a result, they ignore what the systems are telling them, disconnect them from process controls, or revert to less advanced systems that have worked in the past.[6] Although these are all adjustments that can modulate the impact of a cyberattack, they may end up hindering military operations more than a focused fix might have.

Having understood the nature of the problem, a critical step is to identify the weaknesses in the target system that allowed the cyberattack. Doing so requires a willingness and ability to trace the attack back, often to a specific access point that should have stopped the intrusion (or malware or rogue commands or . . .) but failed to. Done well, a systemic analysis will rarely conclude that the mistake was singular. Sophisticated systems are built to avoid single points of failure, and typically, many things have to fail for a cyberattack to succeed (for example, not only was the perimeter penetrated, but the software used to prevent a single infection from ruining a process was inadequate). In many cases, the true failure arises when the set of assumptions that undergird the security model were violated and thereby proven faulty.[7]

Although understanding the problem should lead to a fix, some fixes are more easily achieved than others. In some cases, access controls have to be instituted, which implies that system administrators know how to set them. In other cases, software has to be rewritten. Because most software is packaged, unless a fix is built into existing resources (e.g., a patch can be applied, a security setting can be changed), the manufacturer has to be persuaded to put it in, and expeditiously. A meta-requirement is that managers (superior officers) have to support the effort. At a minimum, detection, diagnosis, characterization, and forensics are not free. But the fix itself may be far costlier in terms of money (the cost to replace software or hardware) or efficiency (e.g., lost from limiting access, forbidding certain processes, or cutting down on exposure). Where security is a trade-off for convenience and usability,[8] it is not always obvious that security will or even should win.

In many cases, the adjustment process culminates when these changes are promulgated throughout the target's organization. A victim may detect an attack, fix the problem, and itself be more secure against a repeated attempt, but if it keeps the attack and its responses quiet, others in its organization will have learned nothing and will therefore be as vulnerable as they were before the attack. Information-sharing habits within an organization therefore determine how systemically it can react to attack. Note that a country's national security establishment may be composed of competing organizations that do not communicate well among themselves (intelligence communities have a reputation for being tight-lipped). An organization may also share information internally by sharing it externally: for example, a software vulnerability that allowed an attack is reported to its manufacturer and the broader lessons learned are communicated to the public. Everyone becomes correspondingly more secure, including organizations that work for the military that has been attacked.

Let us now discuss characteristics of the target that might reasonably be associated with how quickly or slowly the target responds.

Why a Target's Response May Be Slow

If an attacker wants to guess how long a target will be susceptible to cyberattacks, particularly when the source of the relevant vulnerabilities is structural rather than one-off, it may want to take the following characteristics of the target into account.

Organizational Culture
This section discusses how and why an organization's culture affects its tendency to respond to cyberattacks with alacrity and fundamental changes (when warranted).

First, the organization has to take cybersecurity seriously enough to realize where cybersecurity failures can lead to shortfalls in military effectiveness. This means it must invest sufficiently in competent system administrators (sysadmins). They, in turn, have to be empowered to tell users, even powerful ones, what they cannot do. In some cases sysadmins have to be able to shut down networks. The U.S. cyberwar community has been arguing, with some success, that cybersecurity is the responsibility of the unit commander, not the responsibility of those who provision systems; commanders who accept such a responsibility are apt to make intelligent adjustments in the face of cyberattack.[9] That noted, some measures to increase security, such as the enforced use of encrypted communications or reductions in user access to sensitive information, can hamper operational effectiveness. When that happens, commanders need to know enough about cybersecurity to distinguish the need-to-have from the nice-to-have.

Second, organizations should maintain an ability to carry out objective fault-finding, even if the results are disturbing. An important question for an organization that has been hacked is whether to respond to an incident with more and better cybersecurity tools or by changing work patterns. The first, although expensive, is less disruptive and consistent with the belief that the cure for bad technology is more and better technology. The second not only gets in the way of doing work but requires accepting when technology can sometimes go too far (or at least get ahead of its ability to be protected). Which of the two approaches is correct will vary by context, but the ability to address such questions with an open mind allows fundamental adjustments.

Third, the organization has to reward truth-telling. Organizations that shoot the messenger encourage cover-ups. People who work in organizations that concentrate on fault-finding, especially if the fault-finding is incompetent or corrupt, will find ways to blame others, even if so doing makes it harder to find, isolate, and characterize faults themselves[10] (this is why it helps that the National Safety Transportation Board abjures fault-finding when studying accidents).[11] It is harder (but alas, not impossible) to hide consequential mistakes in the United States and other Western societies than in authoritarian ones; the plethora of investigations and reports makes Western societies seem vulnerable but contributes to their resiliency.

Fourth, an organization must have the kind of command and control that makes it clear whose responsibility it is to fix which problems.

Fifth, an organization that shares and accepts information widely is more likely to react quickly and correctly to incidents than one that does not. As with medicine and aircraft safety, progress in cybersecurity is a collective learning activity.

Exactly what predisposes an organization to be security-conscious, objective, open, and sharing is a broad topic that goes well beyond cybersecurity. Among the influences are national characteristics, the nature of the ruling regime, the history of the organization (for example, what lessons it has drawn from previous shocks), the character of its leaders, its standard operational procedures, its institutional constraints, its relationships with sister institutions, and the incentives under which it operates. Sometimes, past behavior under the stress of similar events may provide a clue to future behavior. The particular context of combat during which a cyberattack takes place also matters. But these factors are just clues to deciphering an organization's behavior. Finally, because cyberattacks have, so far, been rare, even an organization that knows itself very well may not be able to predict how well it will respond to a cyberattack. By contrast, instances of systems being compromised are common, but if organizations do not find the attacks particularly dangerous or costly, they may not make fundamental adjustments in their aftermath.

Characteristics of an Attacked System

Sometimes adjustments are slow because of features particular to the affected system. For example:

- A system has to be continuously available; it is both critical and unique. Taking a system offline for any nontrivial length of time (especially if others can tell it has been withdrawn) may lead to a systemic operational vulnerability that could spell military disaster.[12] This effect is exacerbated if there is continuous military pressure on the target. Only minor fixes can be done in short intervals.

- Fundamental changes in the affected system require substantial retraining by users lest military effectiveness drop sharply and there is simply no time to conduct training while conflict rages.

- The system is too isolated to be on a patch distribution network (but not so isolated as to be invulnerable: for example, it is wireless-accessible but not internet-connected).

- The faults are in hardware or in parts of software that are not easily accessible because they cannot be reprogrammed in situ. A vulnerability in embedded hardware may be impossible to fix without a replacement part, which is not as easily available as a software patch can be, and must anyway be shipped out to the field to be installed—and sometimes cannot be installed until the affected system is returned to depot-level maintenance. The alternative strategy of filtering out troubling classes of inputs, including those known to trigger vulnerabilities, will not work easily if communications among systems are encrypted (as they should be) but there is no way to insert the filter between the decryption module and the rest of the system.

- The best adjustments are known to create problems of their own; for example, they require the use of digital signatures, but inexperience with cryptography leads too many messages to be improperly rejected when validation tests are failed.

Access to the Rest of the World

When it comes to detecting and fixing specific vulnerabilities (a consideration at the tactical end of the spectrum), the superior access that U.S. and allied forces have to the U.S. software and cybersecurity base may matter. Outsiders can provide a great deal of assistance in the identification and remediation of vulnerabilities that allow cyberattacks. Iran provides the clearest case. Stuxnet was found only after an infected computer was sent to Belarus for analysis. Flame was detected by Kaspersky, which the United Nations International Telecommunications Union hired to take a look at Iran's refinery.[13]

Issues of access may be particularly acute with commercial software. These days, U.S. companies (as well as U.S.-based foundations) account for well over 90 percent of all commercial software and a like percentage of all exploitable software vulnerabilities.[14] It is plausible that a vulnerability in U.S. software that is common on U.S. systems would be patched with greater alacrity than a vulnerability in software that is common on adversary systems but not common on software used by U.S. and allied forces.

But although there is a built-in U.S. advantage, its extent is unclear. First, although outside cybersecurity companies are understandably reluctant to enter war zones, in cyberspace most problems can be sent to them for solution rather than their having to go to where it has occurred (for insurgencies there may not be a war zone, or at any rate a zone in constant danger). I say "most" problems because the problem may be in hardware, in how it is physically configured or in its radio-frequency parameters, all of which may have to be measured on site; or the problem may require the victim to extract bits from hardware, not all of it disk drives. The ability to ship information abroad depends on communications channels, which are not always available in wartime.

Furthermore, there are large pools of expertise that cannot necessarily be counted on to tilt in the U.S. direction, particularly if the United States is criticized for having carried out cyberattacks *and* the target is not at war with the United States. Almost all relevant U.S. companies are multinationals that make a point of not being seen as beholden to the U.S. government, in particular after the Edward Snowden stories broke revealing National Security Agency surveillance programs. They portray themselves as being in favor of cybersecurity in general and thus working for everyone; thus they would have a difficult time appearing to be on the side of attackers and against defenders. Although they probably could not be seen overtly aiding rogue regimes, they could easily justify issuing patches for vulnerabilities that were reported only by regimes on the grounds that a vulnerability for one is a vulnerability for all (Microsoft patched all four zero-days found in Stuxnet code by the end of 2010).

A similar logic prevails when companies decide whom to offer their cybersecurity services to. Because the geographic distribution of companies that specialize in cybersecurity is wider than that of those who produce commercial software (the latter, as noted, being overwhelmingly U.S.-based), patriotism is even less likely to be a factor in their deciding whom to help. An Israeli firm might be highly unlikely to assist Iran in a standoff with the United States, but could decide to help China if it were subject to a cyberattack during a confrontation over the South China Sea. Indeed, U.S. opposition may be less of a factor in denying help to rogue regimes than the rogue regimes themselves, who might not trust outsiders from the United States or U.S. allies to examine, much less manipulate, their defense systems.

There is a belief that openness means faster adaptation. But a converse argument is that those who cannot rely on the outside world and must therefore develop their own systems have reason to keep their designs compact (code expansiveness arises from wanting to accommodate unforeseen options). Compact systems have a smaller attack surface. Their builders are forced to understand every facet of the design and can therefore determine quickly where to make the trade-offs between cybersecurity on the one hand and convenience and usability on the other hand. By contrast, most commercial applications are built atop but only use a fraction of the capabilities resident in general-purpose hardware and operating systems; yet these unused capabilities are often where vulnerabilities reside (in large part because developers do not invoke these capabilities and thus rarely know how they would work inside their program). Analogously, systems acquired from or maintained by contractors (who then flee under the pressure of war) are difficult to alter with any confidence and may have to remain vulnerable because they lack support.

But the converse has its own converse. Few people build complex systems from scratch anymore. Iran's centrifuges were built atop gray- and black-market components of dubious provenance. And then there is a corollary of Kerckhoff's principle: the more widely a piece of software is used and hence reviewed, the greater the likelihood that any vulnerability it has will have been detected and purged.[15]

Ways to Slow a Target's Response

Lockheed's cyber kill-chain work posits that attackers must do six things to succeed; thus effective cyber defenses are possible even if only one of them is disrupted.[16] This chapter argues that those who would immunize their systems against further attack have to go through a stepwise process. In the same spirit, disrupting or short-circuiting such processes can retard immunization. Selecting or shaping attacks accordingly might increase the odds that further attacks on a target will succeed. (Note that if the point of the attacks *is* to induce overreaction, then—apart from techniques that mask pre-attack indicators to prevent premature detonation—the point is to do the opposite of what is recommended here.)

So, here are some options.

1. *Choose targets carefully.* Even if attackers cannot inhibit any target's adjustment to an attack, concentrating on targets that react slowly means that any one attack method will enjoy greater reusability.

Granted, if the many potential cyberattack targets of the other side are so insulated from one another that their sysadmins share nothing, then differentiating among targets would have little point. Organizations that respond slowly or poorly can be attacked repeatedly; and the rest cannot be, regardless of the order in which they are hit. Similarly, there is little point to attacking equipment whose fix requires new or modified hardware *rather than or before* attacking a system whose faults can be fixed through a patch. One might as well attack both. Concentrating on the former would have no influence on the susceptibility of the latter.

But because people *do* talk across organizations and even in public, an attack on an alert organization may inform their less-alert colleagues. But a cyberattack on those that generate a weak response to an attack or those who keep such unfortunate events to themselves will not inform those who can generate a strong response. Thus it pays to attack first those unlikely to detect or diagnose an attack, or who cannot discern the vulnerability from the diagnosis, or who are unlikely to communicate their experiences credibly to others. Those who are yet to be attacked could still be vulnerable even after the first wave hits.

A variant on choosing targets carefully is mating attacks to their targets carefully. For instance, if an organization is reluctant to have its defenses exposed as weak, it may cover up the attack. The more embarrassing an attack, the greater the tendency to cover up (Sony's cybersecurity provider, FireEye, was at pains to point out how sophisticated Sony's foes were).[17]

2. *Keep up the military pressure.* Systems that cannot be withdrawn for repair stay broken longer.

Obviously, if a cyberattack has disabled the system completely, it might as well be withdrawn (although physically withdrawing the system from the battlefield may itself create risks in transit). However, partial disability, intermittent faults, and subtle corruption may mean that the system is partially usable and hence may be kept around even if crippled. Systems that cannot be withdrawn for patching stay vulnerable longer. Thus continued military pressure creates, among defenders, a difficult choice between risking harm from cyberattack if they remain in the battle and receiving less military support if they withdraw their system or take it offline.

Note that these considerations may also apply to physical attacks. Keeping up the pressure requires that kinetic warriors shape their actions to meet the needs of cyber warriors; this implies a close level of cooperation across the boundary lines between regular forces and cyber forces (whereas for a physical attack, the two may be the same or closely aligned organizations).

3. *Limit the size and scope of the cyberattack.* The less obvious an attack's effects are, the less likely it will be attended to, particularly when there is competition for the attention of sysadmins (who are, for example, coping with crippled hardware in battle). This strategy requires deliberately choos-

ing to go for smaller effects so that those effects are available longer. An attack with small effects may not get the attention it deserves from the target, especially if no one sees the small effects as illustrating that the attacker could use the same methods to implement a large attack. Similarly, an attack that causes intermittent disruptions might be ignored (or the disruptions ascribed to other causes), particularly if the disruptions do not readily present themselves for diagnosis. Subtle corruption attacks, those that leave most data or instructions intact, may escape notice or diagnosis, leaving the target to accept false data as real. In this case, perhaps it never makes adjustments.

Other methods can be used to limit the odds that an attack will be revealed. Limiting the tendency of malware to signal its presence to a command and control center reduces the odds that unusual activity will be detected and also provides less material with which to characterize the attack.

Another prudent move is to exploit a vulnerability that is particular to the target rather than one that is more widespread. Thus when the target fixes the exposed vulnerability, it does not give other targets a chance to fix their own vulnerabilities, which are different. A close variant is to focus on vulnerabilities that occur in the management of systems (such as network configuration) in ways that allow others to convince themselves that the fault is the victim's and that such vulnerabilities are not present in their own organizations (even if without a painstaking scrub of the network, such self-assurance is often unwarranted).

Similarly, for an attack method that uses malware, the attacker should exercise discipline in designing the malware to avoid its endless replication from one system to another. Taking the requisite pains will prevent collateral damage and limit the number of sysadmins who might stumble across the malware and broadcast their findings to potential targets (including the one against whom the malware was aimed).

4. *Use penetration methods that are difficult to find.* Part of this art is to use entry points that are difficult to trace. A patient attack might have compromised the target system well before effects are needed, so long ago that there are no logs of the original entry. In that case it would be difficult to determine what vulnerability in the system permitted the initial compromise (with ever-cheaper storage, keeping logs forever is becoming best practice, but not everyone does so).

A similarly frustrating way to enter networks is to use radio-frequency (RF) links from beyond a network's normal RF range (for example, insertion platforms with powerful transmitters and antennas). The target, having convinced itself that it has physically secured everything within range, will be confused; if it concludes correctly that it was hacked by something beyond that range, it may conclude that it must scan out further along all dimensions for suspicious emitters, abandon all RF links, install link-based encryption, or white-list all inputs.

Another way to discourage a target's understanding of the attack is to destroy the evidence, perhaps by destroying the hardware whose software was exploited. Attacks on missile guidance systems, for instance, are difficult to deconstruct if they can be detected only by making inferences from a missile's failure to perform well (as well as perhaps from its telemetry). Destructive attacks on industrial facilities may also destroy evidence. But these may not work reliably in circumstances where the most efficient attack campaign does not destroy things (for example, because instant destruction indicates a more serious fault than does accelerated wear and tear of the sort that plagued the Natanz centrifuges). Attacks rarely spread from hardware to hardware; they are more likely to spread through networks and touch systems whose existence is not obvious or that lack the ability to destroy their own records.

5. *Use deception and distraction.* An example of a deceptive attack is one that appears to exploit one vulnerability when it actually exploits another. Since multi-vulnerability attacks are rare, the obvious place for a victim to look is at its weakest point. If that is fixed and seems to stop the problem (for example, because the attacker quits in frustration), the victim will be less inclined to look for other vulnerabilities that might explain the source of attack. The drawback to this approach is that it requires the attacker to find two vulnerabilities. It also assumes that the target does not respond to the attack by doing a thorough investigation that discovers the second (and presumably more valuable) vulnerability. Stuxnet's method of sending recorded data back to operators to convince them that all was well is an example of this type of deceptive tactic.

Distraction can be used to delay or misdirect adjustments, particularly the more fundamental ones. Heavy jamming by an attacker, for instance, can complicate the victim's testing of RF links for possible entryways. Indications that insiders were recruited to open cybersecurity breaches can ignite reprisals against managers when the more technical features of a system may have been responsible; conversely, hints of fundamental architectural weaknesses can mask the exploitation of witting employees. Persuading foes that their cybersecurity problems arise from having alliances could harm their alliances' cohesion.

6. *Persuade third parties not to help.* As noted, third parties can help the victims of a cyberattack respond to an attack. Conversely, anything that inhibits third parties from offering assistance may lead to a slow or misguided adjustment. Persuasion—appealing to patriotism or demonizing the target—may work on third parties. A credible threat to expose—or worse, impose sanctions on—such assistance can add pressure. This strategy must be approached very carefully. The commercial companies that the United States might want to pressure are the very ones whose cooperation is needed for its own defensive efforts. Going public with pressure may backfire if companies feel that they need to decline to cooperate to assure customers in potentially hostile countries (such as China) that they stand behind the security of their products. Furthermore, although a company might avoid visibly helping others, it has less control over what its employees do on their own time. Many cybersecurity problems, if cleansed of identifying attributes, can be circulated for analysis, perhaps crowdsourced, without revealing that the problems are those of U.S. adversaries and have arisen from U.S. attacks.

Conclusion

Adversaries that suffer cyberattacks will adjust, but how quickly or how thoroughly is uncertain. A lot depends on their circumstances, as well as on the strategies that cyber attackers employ to inhibit their targets' immune responses.

Cyber warriors who wish to maintain their relevance for future military campaigns (rather than lose their usefulness after a first strike) need to understand how adversaries are likely to react. Indeed, if cyber warriors are to fulfill their *defensive* roles, they should try to understand how their own non-cyber colleagues are apt to react and to use those lessons learned to better secure their own systems.

Despite the plethora of cyber intrusions to date, few have been so grievous as to allow today's peacetime reactions to predict tomorrow's crisis or conflict reactions. Networks that suffered only leaked information may not necessarily be taken down for an extended period while infections are cleaned out and the cleanliness painstakingly ascertained.[18] Sysadmins often respond to nonexistential cyberattacks by attempting to change user behavior (for example, through refresher awareness courses) and adding cybersecurity software (to detect intrusions) but otherwise leaving the basic architecture and access rules untouched. Military users that respond in the same way will leave themselves open to further attack.

Nevertheless, it is worthwhile to understand how potential targets might react to an attack. A first guess may come from gauging how one's own forces react to a cyberattack (taking due account of unique elements of U.S. military culture, and the private commercial assistance available to U.S. forces that may be unavailable to U.S. adversaries). Modeling a logical decision process, one that reflects known pathologies of potential adversaries, may provide another perspective. Historical analogies may provide an insight or two. In any case, U.S. Cyber Command needs to develop a body of research and exploration that acknowledges the potential of its targets to learn. Doing so will help U.S. Cyber Command figure out how to make adversaries learn slowly, incompletely, incorrectly, or not at all.

Notes

1. On the latter, see, for instance, Micah Zenko, *Red Team: How to Succeed by Thinking Like the Enemy* (New York: Basic Books, 2015).

2. David Albright, Paul Brannan, and Christina Walrond, *Did Stuxnet Take Out 1,000 Centrifuges at the Natanz Enrichment Plant?*, Institute for Science and International Security Report, December 22, 2010 (http://isis-online.org/uploads/isis-reports/documents /stuxnet_FEP_22Dec2010.pdf).

3. Wisconsin Project on Nuclear Arms Control, "Iran's Nuclear Timetable," November 18, 2015 (www.iranwatch.org/our-publications/articles-reports/irans-nuclear-time table).

4. Nicole Perlroth, "Serious Flaw in Java Software Is Found, Then Patched," *Bits* (blog), *New York Times*, January 13, 2013 (http://bits.blogs.nytimes.com/2013/01/13/u -s-agency-warns-of-java-software-problem/).

5. The insight goes back decades; for an example, see Carl Chatfield and Timothy Johnson, "A Short Course in Project Management," 2007 (https://support.office.com/en -us/article/A-short-course-in-project-management-19cfed57-2f85-4a44-aadc -df8482d92688).

6. For an example of a downward adjustment (admittedly one taken *before* GPS has been attacked), see Tim Prudente, "Seeing Stars, Again: Naval Academy Reinstates Celestial Navigation," *Capital Gazette*, October 12, 2015 (www.capitalgazette.com/news/naval _academy/ph-ac-cn-celestial-navigation-1014-20151009-story.html).

7. See, for instance, Joan Feigenbaum, "Towards Realistic Assumptions, Models, and Goals for Security Research," White Paper for NSF Workshop, January 18, 2002 (www .cs.yale.edu/homes/jf/NSF-Security-WP.pdf).

8. See, for instance, Catherine Weir and others, "User Perceptions of Security, Convenience and Usability for ebanking Authentication Tokens," *Computers and Security* 28, nos. 1–2 (2009), pp. 47–62.

9. James Winnefeld, Christopher Kirchhoff, and David Upton, "Cybersecurity's Human Factor: Lessons from the Pentagon," *Harvard Business Review*, September 2015 (https://hbr.org/2015/09/cybersecuritys-human-factor-lessons-from-the-pentagon).

10. See, for instance, Amy Edmondson, "Strategies for Learning from Failure," *Harvard Business Review*, April 2011 (https://hbr.org/2011/04/strategies-for-learning -from-failure).

11. Robert Sumwalt and Sean Dalton, "The NTSB's Role in Aviation Security," March 18, 2015 (www.ntsb.gov/news/speeches/rsumwalt/Documents/Sumwalt_141020 .pdf).

12. As the head of NSA's Tailored Access Organization explains, this is particularly so if repairs require removing user-installed authentication mechanisms so that vendors can remotely access the module at fault. Agile hackers can use the interval to compromise the system. See Kim Zetter, "NSA Hacker Chief Explains How to Keep Him out of Your System," *Wired*, January 28, 2016.

13. Kaspersky Lab, "Kaspersky Lab and ITU Research Reveals New Advanced Cyber Threat," May 28, 2012 (https://usa.kaspersky.com/about/press-releases/2012_kaspersky -lab-and-itu-research-reveals-new-advanced-cyber-threat).

14. See Stefan Frei, *The Known Unknowns*, NSS Labs, 2013 (www.nsslabs.com/reports /known-unknowns-0). Figure 4 indicates that among the "software vendors for which VCP and ZDI purchased vulnerabilities in the last ten years," the highest-ranking foreign company was #19.

15. See for instance Bruce Schneier's argument in his essay "Secrecy, Security, and Obscurity," *Schneier on Security*, May 15, 2002 (www.schneier.com/crypto-gram/archives /2002/0515.html).

16. Eric M. Hutchins, Michael J. Cloppert, and Rohan M. Amin, "Intelligence-Driven Computer Network Defense Informed by Analysis of Adversary Campaigns and Intrusion Kill Chains" (Lockheed Martin, 2010) (www.lockheedmartin.com/content /dam/lockheed/data/corporate/documents/LM-White-Paper-Intel-Driven-Defense .pdf).

17. FireEye cited Joseph Demarest Jr., assistant director of the FBI's cyber division, who told a hearing of the Senate Committee on Banking, Housing and Urban Affairs that "the malware that was used would have slipped—probably have gotten past—90 percent of Net defenses that are out there today in private industry," and perhaps even the government. Reported by CBS News in "Hacking after Sony: What Companies Need to Know," December 15, 2014 (www.cbsnews.com/news/hacking-after-sony-what-companies-need -to-know/).

18. "In 2007, the Department of Commerce had to take the Bureau of Industrial Security's networks offline for several months because its networks were hacked by unknown foreign intruders." See Center for Strategic and International Studies, "Significant Cyber Incidents since 2006" (Washington, 2018) (https://csis-prod.s3.amazonaws.com/s3fs -public/180213_Significant_Cyber_Events_List.pdf).

7

Hacking a Nation's Missile Development Program

HERBERT LIN

In March and April 2017, the *New York Times* published a number of articles describing U.S. efforts regarding "left-of-launch" ballistic missile defense targeting North Korea's program.[1] "Left-of-launch" missile defense refers to attempts to compromise a missile before it launches by one of three means: a kinetic attack that destroys the missile before it is launched; a compromised missile that destroys itself shortly after launch in the boost phase; or a compromise affecting the navigation system that causes the missile to land far away from its intended target. Successful left-of-launch missile defense eliminates the need to intercept the missile after it launches and avoids the difficulties of in-flight missile intercepts. But left-of-launch missile defense is itself both technically difficult and fraught with uncertainty. It also raises important legal and ethical questions about the propriety of interfering in a sovereign nation's missile development activity, or, in the case of an

I gratefully acknowledge the contributions of Max Smeets, Tom Berson, David Elliott, Nelson Hansen, David Wright, and Amy Zegart in the writing of this chapter. Any remaining errors are my responsibility alone.

operational missile, of making what amounts to a pre-emptive strike before an adversary launches an attack.

The articles in the *New York Times* focused on nonkinetic methods of compromising a missile before launch. The authors noted that the frequency of failed tests of the North Korean Musudan ballistic missile was unusually high: seven out of its eight tests failed in 2016—a failure rate of 88 percent, compared to the failure rate of most missile development tests: 5–10 percent.[2] On that basis, *New York Times* reporters David Sanger and William Broad began an investigation in which they concluded that the United States had been conducting a cyber-based program to sabotage the North Korean missile development program.

The *New York Times* articles on this subject contained little technical detail about the workings of the covert program that was the subject of Sanger and Broad's investigation. And this chapter does not make any claims about a covert program that may—or may not—have been proposed or carried out. Instead it provides what might be called informed speculation on how a long-range missile development program of a small, authoritarian, and relatively impoverished and isolated nation might be compromised by cyber (and other) means. In other words, this chapter does not address anything specific that is known to be happening but rather focuses on what might be possible within the limits of known technology and techniques.

Missiles in Development and in Production and Deployment

The phrase "it's not rocket science" is used to mean that a task is easy to perform or to understand, so something that *is* rocket science is understood to be hard. Although rudimentary rockets and missiles have been available for nearly a millennium,[3] building long-range missiles that can work reliably and deliver payloads weighing hundreds of kilograms over a range of thousands of kilometers accurately really is "rocket science" that pushes the practical performance boundaries of well-known principles of science and engineering.[4]

A modern missile is a complex device, with many interconnected systems whose operation must be intricately synchronized. Every missile launch unfolds differently on the inside—because of differences in launch location, missile target, wind conditions, and so on; the precise amounts of fuel injected; the detailed timeline of when valves open and close; and the precise directions in which nozzles swivel. Most launches are determined on the basis of input from human launch controllers (for example, desired target, trajectory) into the missile's computer, and data from on-board sensors that monitor the operation of various missile subsystems. During flight a variety of programmable microprocessors receive data in real time and in turn direct missile subsystems to take appropriate action.

Missiles in Development vs. Missiles for Operational Use

A second key point about missile programs—which is also true for the life cycle of many technologically complex systems—is the difference between prototyping and production. A nation undertaking a missile development program aspires to acquire many missiles, not just one. But it is a long way from manufacturing a few missiles by hand to assembling many missiles on a production line. For two reasons, initial prototypes of a missile are usually less reliable than production versions.

First, a missile is sufficiently complex that testing is often necessary to work out the kinks in its design. Testing provides new information for missile engineers, who gain experience from each launch and incorporate what they have learned into subsequent missile builds.

Second, artisanal prototypes that are put together by hand are often less reliable than those that come from assembly line production. Moving from prototype to production requires codifying what is often called tacit knowledge—knowledge that resides in the intuitions, hunches, and insights of the technicians and engineers that assemble prototypes. In the prototyping stage, the blueprints of a missile would normally be insufficient by themselves to guide the construction of reliable missiles. By analogy, it is well known that most scientific research laboratories have people—usually experienced technicians—who know much more than what is written up in any journal article and who are often the only ones who can make complex experiments work properly.

Missiles in development and missiles in production for operational use have fundamentally different purposes. The complexity of a modern missile is such that missile testing is essential for any missile development program that seeks to build reliable weapons.[5] Missiles in development—in what might be regarded as the prototyping stage—are intended to provide information about the internal operation of the missile before, during, and after the launch. The engineers and technicians learn as they receive feedback from a prototype about which design features do and do not work, and they change the design in the next iteration to improve the missile's performance. By contrast, missiles in production are intended to accomplish a mission, such as delivering a warhead to a specific location on earth or putting a satellite into orbit; their primary purpose is not to provide engineering feedback.

The requirement for a prototype missile to provide feedback means that prototype missiles are usually more heavily instrumented than production missiles. For example, a prototype missile usually has telemetry to report what is going on inside the missile to the engineers on the ground: sensors that collect data and radio transmitters that send the data back to the ground. Sensors report to ground, seaborne, or airborne telemetry stations parameters such as the pressures and flow rates in fuel lines, temperatures in the burn chamber, and nozzle azimuth. Such information is needed mostly during the development phase and during batch tests, when engineers will use it to improve missile performance and determine if the missile functions as designed. But none of this information is needed in an operational missile, which only needs to deliver its payload to the target.[6]

Another example of a difference between prototype and production missiles is that the former usually require mechanisms to provide for range safety. Because prototype missiles are comparatively unreliable, they sometimes go off course. Thus ground controllers need a way to destroy a prototype missile in flight before it can do serious damage on the ground.

A third example is that because software systems in development undergo many changes, engineers sometimes install "back doors" in prototype missiles that facilitate easier access to the code so that they can bypass the (time-consuming) security protocols that would otherwise be necessary. Back doors are supposed to be removed before the system enters operational use, but owing to human or organizational error they may not be. "Left-over" back doors can then be used by adversaries to enter the system.

In practice, missiles in development often have more system entry points than missiles being produced for operational use, which make prototype missiles easier to compromise clandestinely. Any failure could be interpreted as the result of not-uncommon problems that typically affect missiles in the prototype stage, when in fact the failure could be the result of sabotage.

Possible Opportunities for Sabotage of a Missile Development Program

There are many possible opportunities for compromising a missile in a way that increases the likelihood of a failure in some part of its trajectory. A compromise of the most severe type could cause the missile to fail at launch or during powered flight. A lesser failure could interfere with the guidance system so the missile misses its target. A failure of the telemetry system could cause it to send false data to the engineers and prevent them from reconstructing the launch.

Supply Chain

A missile is assembled from a large number of parts and subassemblies, all of which present opportunities for intervention.

One obvious cyber-intervention point is the electronic subsystem in the missile. For example, the missile guidance system may use inertial navigation (gyroscopes) or a GPS tracker as the source of position and velocity information during the boost phase of a launch. Microprocessors in the guidance system use this information to calculate the changes in thrust direction and magnitude to aim the missile at its target. In a liquid-fueled missile, microprocessors control fuel flow through a variety of pumps and valves. In modern missiles, microprocessors control the servo motors that direct the missile engine's thrust in one direction or another.

The ubiquitous use of microprocessors in missile electronics provides many opportunities for hacking. Moreover, microprocessor-controlled systems must operate in real time—valves and servo motors must operate within the boundaries of physical timelines determined by actual operation of the missile. As a general rule, real-time programming calls for synchronizing the operation of the microprocessor with external events and hence is much more difficult than programming that does not have to meet real-time requirements. A servo motor that actuates a tenth of a second too early may cause a missile to go significantly off course; a valve that closes a half second too late may cause a fuel line to rupture. And such delays or advances may have nothing to do with the programming of the real-time microprocessor per se; instead they happen because another subsystem in the missile failed to operate on time or because something unexpected happened on the missile's trajectory.

Such sensitivities mean real-time programming is already more difficult to debug and fix, even outside of an adversarial environment. Add a hacker who introduces subtle errors into the programming, and identification of the hacker's handiwork as a malicious act becomes even more difficult because observed errors may well have occurred in the hacker's absence.

Cyberattacks can also be used to compromise other aspects of missile assembly that are controlled by computer. One example is materials produced that do not live up to minimum performance specifications because of cyber-induced corruption of the materials production process. For example, the metal used in the rocket nozzle must be able to withstand certain temperatures for a certain period of time; substandard materials may lead to the engine exhaust burning through during boost phase. The metal used in the missile skin must be able to withstand certain mechanical stresses; if the metal delivered is slightly substandard, the missile skin could fail during launch. (Note also that the stresses on a missile are different in different trajectories because it flies through different amounts of atmosphere. Changing the trajectory from a minimum-energy trajectory to a lofted or a depressed trajectory may change the mechanical stresses on a missile and thus on the skin. Thus a missile launch might succeed with one kind of trajectory and fail with a different kind.)[7]

Similarly, parts or subassemblies may not live up to minimum performance specifications. Fuel lines in a missile must be able to withstand certain pressures and vibrations for certain periods of time as they deliver fuel or oxidizer to the missile engine's combustion chamber. If the fuel line delivered is slightly substandard because of a faulty fabrication process, it could blow out during launch.

In examples such as these, it may be possible to sabotage elements of a missile in such a way that they pass in testing but fail in operation. Consider a subassembly that must operate for three minutes during a launch. At first glance, it might seem appropriate to test the subassembly for three minutes before it is integrated into the missile. But after such a test, the subassembly would have to operate an additional three minutes—that is, it would have to be designed to operate for a total of six minutes. Given that missiles operate at the boundaries of performance, the penalties for overengineering the subassembly (that is, making it better than it needs to be) could be prohibitive.[8]

So there is a significant possibility that any test would not test the subassembly to its full performance requirement. Assume it is known that the subassembly will be tested for one minute; if the compromised subassembly needs to perform for ninety seconds, the subassembly could pass the test but fail in operation.

The fuels used by the missile could also be compromised. A small amount of contamination added to a computer-controlled fuel supply might enable it to pass a short fuel combustion test but not be adequate for an actual launch. Additional opportunities for compromise are available in a solid-fuel missile, in which the solid fuel mass must be relatively uniform throughout to ensure proper burning. The solid fuel mass is formed by pouring thick liquid fuel that then hardens (cures) into a uniform mass. If the pouring results in a lack of uniformity in the mold (for example, some parts of the mold are significant less dense than others), the burn of the fuel could be compromised during launch in a way that causes the launch to fail.[9]

The supply chain could also be attacked by exploiting engineering tolerances in parts fabrication. The specification of a part may call for it to be 1 centimeter (cm) long, plus or minus 0.001 cm; the latter portion of the specification is the allowable tolerance. As long as the part is between 1.001 cm and 0.999 cm, the part is deemed acceptable for use.

For randomly chosen parts, it is expected that some are a little over and others a little under, but all are within tolerance—in such a situation, fabrication errors, which are usually assumed to follow a normal distribution,[10] tend to cancel each other out. But imagine a situation in which a computer-controlled fabrication process with a different error distribution—perhaps still normal but with the mean centered on the high side of the tolerance envelope—that is, between 1.000 and 1.001 cm. Individual parts would pass inspection, but the entire assembly would not have the benefit of random errors being canceled. For some types of assembly the tolerance accumulation from the use of multiple parts is entirely acceptable; for others it is not, and the latter types of assembly may be more likely to fail in operation.

This discussion points to a variety of potential intervention points in the supply chain of a missile development or production program. But actual intervention requires access to the relevant intervention point. For example, an insider might be persuaded or given an incentive to help, or tricked into helping. An insider might be bribed to take some action—change a specification here, insert a USB drive there, write malicious code, provide information to help plan a later intervention (for example, by altering the signal data that would trigger the command self-destruct subsystem), leave a door unlocked on a certain day, provide a password. The insider might be coerced to help—for example, by a threat to kill his family, to denounce him to the host government, or to release falsified documents about him that contain incriminating claims. Or the insider could be unwitting, as in the case of someone who is tricked into inserting a poisoned CD into an optical disk drive that then runs a malware program.

In addition, the parts, subassemblies, and materials that are assembled into a missile are themselves produced or fabricated in factories with computer-controlled production or fabrication machinery that could be exploited if the cybersecurity posture of those factories were not as robust as those of the importing nation. A cyberattack on such factories would be analogous to the 2013 data breach at Target in which attackers targeted an HVAC vendor connected to Target's data systems to gain access to those systems.[11]

Parts, materials, and subassemblies that are fabricated indigenously are vulnerable to compromise, but in practice it is difficult to do so in authoritarian nations that are closed to foreign visitors and thus more difficult places to embed or recruit a saboteur. The activities described here are usually more easily conducted when the factories and fabrication facilities involved are located abroad. There the less stringent controls and oversight than those located domestically provide more opportunities for compromise.

Missile components must also be transported from the foreign facility to the host nation. While a missile element is in transport to the host nation, it can be interdicted. Cargo arriving by sea can be intercepted on the high seas—a cargo ship may be stopped, a team of special operations forces (SOF) may board and blindfold the crew while the SOF personnel go to certain containers on the ship and do interesting things inside for several hours. Upon arrival at a port, the crew has little incentive to report what happened, likely because they have been cautioned under threat of severe penalty to keep quiet.[12] And with good intelligence it is possible that the SOF personnel are able to identify the specific containers in which missile elements are being transported and make hard-to-detect modifications to those elements.[13]

Launch Preparation and Launch Sequence

Missiles usually require a significant amount of preparation before launch. Some of the tasks associated with launch preparation include selection of the missile's target and trajectory (flight path), fueling the missile (if liquid-fueled), and a variety of last-minute checks on missile subsystems. All of these tasks provide opportunities for compromise or interference.

For example, inputting missile flight parameters (the most important of which are the location of the target and the location of the missile at launch) is almost certain to require entering those parameters at a computer keyboard or on a CD or thumb drive. But it is possible for the path from keyboard entry to the flight-control computers on the missile to be interrupted and the data altered. The keyboard itself could be compromised and pass along data that differ from what was input.[14] The computer to which the keyboard is attached could alter flight parameter data before passing it on while still displaying the data entered by the operator (so that the operator would not know that his input was being altered). It may even be possible to alter missile flight parameters after launch.

A liquid-fueled missile must be fueled shortly before launch. Missile fuels are volatile liquids that must be handled very carefully. If fueling is accomplished by keying commands into a computer, consider the possibility of instructing the computer to load too little fuel (so that the missile would not have the proper range) or too much fuel (perhaps causing an overflow of toxic fuels outside the missile fuel tanks).

Compromising the last-minute checks on missile subsystems is an easy way to delay launches. If launch controllers receive data from these subsystems indicating a problem, they are likely to delay the launch, especially if the launch in question is part of a development program. Pre-launch, an important goal of the attacker is to use malware to convince launch controllers that problems exist when in fact they do not.

If a test involves a mobile missile, the missile's transporter erector launcher (TEL) is responsible for moving the missile from a horizontal position to a vertical one for launch. If the TEL is a modern one, the erecting mechanism may be computer-controlled, and it may be possible to move the erecting mechanism in a manner that damages it or even topples the missile. A properly designed TEL will have physical interlocks that prevent unsafe motion regardless of what an operator directs, but the TEL may not have been properly designed.

After the missile is in firing position, the missile undergoes a timed launch sequence in which a number of events occur.

For example, power supplies in the missile must be turned on to energize components in the missile—sensors, actuators, electronic instruments, and components. The switchover from ground/TEL power supplies to internal power supplies typically occurs just before launch. Internal power supplies usually have a limited operating life—it is wasteful from an engineering standpoint to design a power supply to last much longer than the period in which it needs to operate. Limited operating life means that turning on the power supply too early may cause it to fail prematurely. Thus one way of interfering with the launch sequence is to interfere with missile power supplies.

Guidance systems must be warmed up. For example, mechanical gyroscopes have spinning elements while in operation. Before the launch actually occurs, the spinning elements must go from a standstill to spinning stably at operating speed. As with a power supply, the operating life of a gyroscope is often limited, so if it can be turned on earlier than it is supposed to be, it may fail while it is still necessary. Another possibility is to rapidly cycle the power to the gyroscope, an action that may disrupt its internal electronics. In addition, the guidance system must know where the missile is at launch because errors in the launch position translate into errors in the missile's trajectory. Entering launch position information again presents opportunities for useful cyber manipulation of the data.

Actuators are often tested immediately before launch. For example, the missile's nozzle is swiveled using actuators that push it in the desired direction. Pumps inside the missile must operate to deliver fuel from tanks to the engine combustion chamber. Clamps must open to release the missile after ignition. Reported problems in any of these systems may delay the launch.

Post-Launch

Once the missile is launched and leaves the earth, there are many other opportunities for externally introduced cyber-enabled malfunctions to cause failure. A missile is largely a collection of cyber-physical systems, and the logic of cyberattacks post-launch is to hack the cyber part and thereby cause malfunction in the physical part even if it passed all earlier tests. In post-launch, the attacker will seek to cause failures in the missile while concealing data that might help engineers on the ground understand those failures. An attacker could:

- Disrupt the power supplies. Malware introduced into the processors controlling power supplies could disrupt the power to key circuits and thus cause those circuits to malfunction.

- Hack the pumps delivering fuel and oxidizer to the engine combustion chamber. Altering this balance would affect the temperature of the exhaust; if it is too hot, the exhaust could burn through the nozzle.

- Manipulate pressures in fuel lines. Excessive pressure can rupture a fuel line. Insufficient pressure can cause it to collapse.

- Delay or advance commands directing the gimbals that control nozzle orientation. If the nozzle is not moved at the proper time, the missile may go off course momentarily. Similarly, a command to freeze the nozzle in place could result in an unsteerable missile.

Another potential vulnerability is telemetry. As noted earlier, telemetry is the mechanism by which ground controllers receive information about what the missile is doing. Without telemetry data, engineers would not learn much about how the internal machinery is malfunctioning.

Interfering with telemetry can be accomplished in several ways. One simple method for interfering with telemetry is to jam it at the ground receiver. Telemetry is based on radio transmissions, and jamming overwhelms the receiver with so much noise that it cannot pick out the telemetry data contained in an artificially massive signal. In principle, it is possible to corrupt the data being fed by the missile into the telemetry stream back to the ground. In this case, corruption is made possible by malware operating on board the missile to manipulate data from the sensors.

A complementary method is to insert a false radio signal into the telemetry receivers from outside the missile. Various techniques could be tried, and their likelihood of success will vary with the circumstances (for example, the location of the missile launch must be known, and that knowledge may be difficult to obtain if the missile is being launched from a mobile launcher), but all such methods require assets in the proper locations to transmit the false signals, such as an airplane (piloted or unpiloted) configured for electronic warfare that is flying a safe distance away from the launch site. The ability to position assets in turn requires some advance knowledge of when the missile launch will occur because it is not feasible to station such assets in the air continuously. A last caution on interfering with telemetry from missile to ground is that encrypted telemetry is more difficult to spoof but is still subject to jamming.

Yet another possible point of interference with telemetry is wherever the storage and processing of such information takes place. One might imagine cyberattacks that alter information collected on current and past tests or compromise the programs used to analyze telemetry information. (In such instances, insider access would almost certainly be required.)

The technique of an attacker to insert his own data stream into an adversary's radio receivers may be useful when the missile's guidance system depends on external commands or data. For example, early U.S. ICBMs, such as the Atlas, were guided from the ground. Its position and velocity were tracked after launch, and if it was going in the wrong direction ground controllers would send a signal to the missile to correct its course.[15] That signal would be captured by a receiver on the missile and converted into instructions to move the nozzle appropriately.

That kind of missile guidance eliminates the need to develop self-contained guidance systems, which are technically much more sophisticated. But ground-based missile guidance has a major vulnerability: if the commands from the ground are spoofed, the missile can be diverted from its planned trajectory. For that reason U.S. ballistic missiles no longer use ground-based guidance.

The infrastructure needed to support interference with ground-based missile guidance is likely to be less complex than that needed for spoofing telemetry from missile to ground. The reason is that one might plausibly expect a ground-based infrastructure for receiving signals from a missile in flight to be directionally sensitive—that is, it would tend to reject signals that come from a direction where the missile is not located. But directionally sensitive receivers on a missile presume an ability to control the orientation of the missile, which is a technically demanding task.

Finally, consider range safety issues. In any missile development program there is a chance that a launched missile will go awry. A missile that goes significantly off course, for whatever reason, should be destroyed in flight because of the damage it may cause if it lands in the wrong place. Admittedly, range safety considerations may be less worrisome for some nations than for others (for example, an authoritarian regime may care much less about a missile gone awry landing on its own territory simply because its citizens will not be inclined to sue their government for damages),[16] but all nations are likely to have some range safety concerns.

If they do, a self-destruct mechanism will be built into the missile, and it will be activated by a ground controller, if necessary. The command link between ground and missile can, in principle, be compromised. During a missile development program, an attacker with access to the self-destruct mechanism can impede development.

A second reason for installing a self-destruct package into a test launch is to prevent it from falling into foreign hands after its mission is completed, thereby depriving others of intelligence that could be derived from an intact first or second stage that might otherwise be recovered from the sea. As the stage is falling to the water, an on-board sensor (for example, a sensor that measures atmospheric pressure) triggers the self-destruct mechanism and destroys the stage. Thus any spoofing data received by the sensor could cause premature detonation (before the spent stage separates) and thus destruction of the entire missile.

Blowback Considerations

In conducting cyberattacks, concerns are often raised about blowback—negative effects on the attacker (or other parties friendly to the attacker) that result directly from the fact of the initial attack.

One common concern is that the cyber weapons used will inadvertently disrupt systems that are not its target. The risks of an escape from the target environment are of course significantly diminished if the target environment is isolated from the rest of the world. In addition, careful design of the weapons used for an attack, coupled with high-quality intelligence, can limit its effects to the targeted system.[17]

A second concern is that an adversary will be able to repurpose the code that was used in the initial attack, and perhaps turn it against systems or infrastructure that the attacker holds dear. For example, could cyber weapons hypothetically used against North Korean missiles be turned against U.S. missiles? Unlikely, because U.S. missiles and North Korean missiles have entirely different designs and use different components.[18]

A third concern is that manipulation of a missile's trajectory might send it off course and toward friendly territory—in the case of North Korea, toward the territory of its allies. But even if the attackers sent the missile into a circular path and it came down in North Korean territory, the North Korean government might well blame the "attack" on a foreign government.

Possible Utility against Operational Missiles

Any discussion of hacking a missile development program understandably raises questions about its efficacy against operational or production missiles. For example, how and to what extent, if any, could the cyber tools and weapons developed to disrupt and sabotage missiles in their development stage be useful in left-of-launch ballistic missile defense (BMD) scenarios against operational missiles launched in anger?

It is important to distinguish between the general applicability of an approach and its actual operational utility in any specific instance. Unlike kinetic weapons, the efficacy of a cyber weapon is a strong function of the target's characteristics.[19] While kinetic interceptors can be expected to kill missiles that they hit, a cyber weapon specifically designed to work against missile A is unlikely to work against missile B without significant modification if A and B are different missile types. As an example, solid-fuel missiles are considerably simpler than liquid-fuel missiles and thus present fewer opportunities for a cyberattack targeted on the missile's propulsion systems.

Prototype missiles and production missiles based on those prototypes could reasonably be expected to have many similarities. To the extent that this is so, the same tools and weapons may indeed work against operational missiles. But they are also different in a variety of ways. For example and as noted earlier, operational missiles do not have self-destruct mechanisms or carry telemetry transmitters, so any cyber weapon that depends on the availability of such a mechanism will be ineffective against an operational missile even if it was useful against a missile in development. Prototype missiles also have a variety of sensors and other apparatuses to support telemetry to the ground, and if access through the telemetry infrastructure is used to gain remote entry to other parts of the missile, removal of that infrastructure will have consequences for left-of-launch BMD success in operational scenarios.

A second consideration is that prototype missiles in development are usually fired on a more relaxed timeline than an operational missile. The launch of a missile in development can be paused to provide some time for investigating any problems that appear in the launch sequence and countdown. Not so with an operational missile, whose launch is almost certainly intended to be synchronized with activities in a broader military campaign. Thus the timeline on which an attacker might compromise a launch sequence is similarly constrained and therefore harder to execute.

All of these factors reduce the likelihood that cyberattacks on operational missiles will be as successful as those on prototype missiles. On the other hand, in operational use it is likely that the top leadership of the nation rather than the local commander would order the launch of a nuclear-tipped missile. That order would have to be transmitted to the launch site, and a cyberattack could, in principle, interfere with such an order.

On balance, it is this author's judgment that a cyber-enabled left-of-launch BMD in an operational scenario is less likely to be successful than a cyber-enabled campaign to disrupt a missile development program. However, even if this judgment is inaccurate, the party whose missiles are being targeted may nevertheless believe it poses a threat to its missiles. Further, other third-party nations may become concerned about the threat that cyber weapons pose to their own missile systems. Such considerations attend to the deployment of any BMD system, including cyber-based systems.

These considerations point to possibly destabilizing effects of certain BMD deployments. But cyber-based BMD is unique: while the scope and scale (and thus the potency) of a kinetic BMD capability can be ascertained to a certain extent by counting the number of interceptors on station and measuring the power of the radars involved, there are no such parameters to be observed with cyber-based BMD weapons. Thus the party whose missiles are being targeted by cyber means has no way to estimate the threat and what would be needed to defend against it—a situation that lends itself to extreme worst-case analysis.

Strategic and Policy Considerations in Cyber Campaigns against Missile Development Programs

A first strategic consideration is that, in a development program, failures in missile launches are to be expected,[20] and a failure caused by a cyberattack is likely to be indistinguishable from one that results from the usual glitches and problems of missiles in development. Indeed, it is this fact that makes targeting a missile development program desirable. Distinguishing between the two might be possible given a detailed forensic analysis, but given that a missile test success or failure results in the destruction of the missile, detailed forensics are mostly limited to what one can derive from telemetry data (and subtle cyberattacks against the integrity of telemetry data might not be detected by examiners). Thus a higher-than-expected failure rate in a missile development program may be the result of sloppy construction processes, design flaws in the missile's design, or a successful cyber campaign.[21]

A second consideration is that sustaining a cyber campaign over an extended period of time (perhaps years) will be difficult. Over time, the effectiveness of a cyber campaign may well degrade as the adversary's technologies advance and as its cyber defensive efforts improve; other methods to suppress a missile development program, such as diplomacy, would be necessary in the long run, and in the worst case destruction of the missile after launch using the more traditional technologies of ballistic missile defense. A further twist on the improvement of defenses against a cyber campaign for sabotage of a development program is that improved defenses may also help defend operational missiles against cyberattack; such missiles of course pose more of a threat because they will be armed and they will operate more reliably in the face of a cyberattack.

A third consideration is that a cyber campaign may have psychological and political impact as well as practical impact. If program scientists and engineers are experiencing failures that they believe to be their own fault, they may lose confidence or proceed more carefully and deliberately. Political leaders might fault them as well, believing them to be incompetent and either pressuring them or replacing them with others, or believing them to be traitors.[22] Such impacts are likely to delay the program even more than might be expected from the technical failures alone.[23]

Fourth, cyber campaigns require access to the targeted systems; without access, failure is essentially assured. Closed societies are, by definition, more difficult to penetrate than open societies, and access in closed societies is more difficult to obtain. Thus fewer access paths are available. Access in North Korea—to factories in the supply chain or to the launch control center managing a test launch and to all other points in between—is particularly problematic given that online access in North Korea is limited to an intranet that is not connected to the broader internet.[24] And of course, North Korean authorities—knowing the importance of denying access to adversaries to potential points of compromise—would go out of their way to protect those points from outside interference. Thus access to North Korean systems—especially military systems—will rely on errors in operational security practices on the part of North Korean personnel, insiders that have been compromised, or clandestinely conducted physical operations to create or exploit access points unprotected by the authorities.

A fifth and related consideration is that, as Chris Inglis notes in chapter 2, highly targeted cyberattacks require a high degree of intelligence information about the target (the missile), information that is detailed, accurate, and timely. Without adequate intelligence, tools developed for action against a target with a certain set of characteristics may be deployed against a target with a different set of characteristics—and fail to achieve the objectives of the attacker. And in a development program it is likely that the design of the missile will be changing; indeed, the point of a development program is to make sure the missile performs as planned and make updates as needed.

An important corollary of this consideration is that tools developed for action against one missile type may be entirely ineffective against a different missile type. For example, cyber weapons aimed at crippling key components in a liquid-fueled missile will be ineffective against a solid-fueled missile. If the adversary shifts resources to developing a different type of missile (perhaps because a cyber campaign against the original missile type was successful), a largely new set of cyber weapons and capabilities may need to be developed, and a new cyber campaign based on the new set might not be as successful.

As for policy, the success of a cyber campaign against a nation's missile development program will be greatly enhanced by keeping it secret. The campaign's effects would be obvious (more missile failures), but the cause would not be. Thus a U.S. activity intended to disrupt the missile development program of another nation would almost certainly fall under the auspices of what the U.S. Code (50 U.S. Code § 3093) defines as covert action—that is, "an activity or activities of the United States Government to influence political, economic, or military conditions abroad, where it is intended that the role of the United States Government will not be apparent or acknowledged publicly." Such action must support "identifiable foreign policy objectives of the United States" and be reported to appropriate individuals in the U.S. Congress. Covert action must not violate the Constitution or any statute of the United States, nor influence United States political processes, public opinion, policies, or media. Note, however, that the U.S. definition of covert action does not prohibit violations of international law; in fact, a number of U.S. covert actions have reportedly violated national sovereignty in the past.[25]

Also relevant for policy is that if the previous judgment is correct (regarding the greater likelihood of success for cyber campaigns against a development program than against operational scenarios), policymakers have only a limited amount of time to decide to deploy such campaigns and for such campaigns to be effective. For example, the North Korean Hwasong-15 missile is an intercontinental ballistic missile (ICBM) that is apparently capable of carrying a nuclear payload to any target in the United States. It was last tested (as of this writing) on November 28, 2017, and the open-source website 38 North suggests that only a few more tests would be needed to establish if low confidence in the missile's reliability is acceptable; two or three additional test firings may be all that is required before Kim Jong Un declares the Hwasong-15 combat-ready.[26]

Finally, it should be noted that cyber campaigns against the missile development programs of other nations have their counterpart in U.S. concerns about the cyber threats against U.S. strategic systems.[27] That is, other nations may well be considering or conducting cyber campaigns targeting U.S. missile development programs (and U.S. operational capabilities as well), and a good U.S. response to such campaigns has yet to be formulated.[28]

Conclusion

This survey of possible approaches to hacking a missile development program can be regarded as an informed speculative case study in the utility of offensive cyber capabilities and related techniques. On one hand, cyber weapons are not magical tools that can be deployed at will and used with certain effect. Their success depends on adequate access and intelligence information, both of which must be acquired long prior to activation of these weapons and maintained until the weapons are used and afterward. On the other hand, cyber weapons can also buy time for policymakers who are faced with the need for immediate action—time that can be used to put into place other measures that might be more useful over the long term. "Kicking the can down the road" and deferring or postponing a day of reckoning can have value even if no decisive or final solutions are available at the moment of can-kicking. But in the long term, the utility of a deferral strategy depends on taking policy actions in the time thereby made available.

Notes

1. William J. Broad and David E. Sanger, "U.S. Strategy to Hobble North Korea Was Hidden in Plain Sight," *New York Times,* March 4, 2017; David E. Sanger and William J. Broad, "Trump Inherits a Secret Cyberwar against North Korean Missiles," *New York Times,* March 4, 2017; David E. Sanger and William J. Broad, "Hand of U.S. Leaves North Korea's Missile Program Shaken," *New York Times,* April 18, 2017.

2. Sanger and Broad, "Hand of U.S. Leaves North Korea's Missile Program Shaken."

3. The first reports of gunpowder-propelled rockets originate in China during the Sung Dynasty (960–1279 AD), likely in the second half. See Frank Winter and Michael Neufeld, *The First Fireworks: Origins of the Rocket,* Smithsonian National Air and Space Museum, July 3, 2013 (https://airandspace.si.edu/stories/editorial/first-fireworks-origins-rocket).

4. As an example of "pushing the performance boundaries," consider that rocket launches to place satellites in orbit often take advantage of the rotational motion of the earth to increase their payload lift capacity. Launching the missile in an easterly direction and close to the equator gives the missile a free "boost" from the earth's rotation. Such launches are especially important for nations that are inexperienced in space, though all nations do so to obtain the free boost.

5. The same is not true of all nuclear weapons, which, depending on design, can be built to work with high reliability without testing. Consider that even the Hiroshima bomb

exploded in 1945 was of a design that had never been tested; in fact, it was chosen because the scientists of the Manhattan Project had a great deal of confidence that its very simple design would work.

6. It may be that operational missiles also have telemetry and range safety mechanisms, but that these mechanisms are simply turned off when the missiles are placed in operation. If such an arrangement is in place, an operational missile selected for testing (for example, after a number of years sitting in a silo) can be essentially identical to all of the other missiles not selected for testing, since the telemetry mechanisms necessary to supply performance information and to ensure range safety would not have to be integrated into the missile at the time of testing. Testing for reliability is then a simple matter of removing a missile from operational status, turning on the instrumentation circuitry, and launching the missile; reinstallation of the instrumentation circuitry would not be necessary in the test missile.

7. For a discussion of stresses on a missile in flight depending on trajectory, see Lisbeth Gronlund and David C. Wright, "Depressed Trajectory SLBMs: A Technical Evaluation and Arms Control Possibilities," *Science & Global Security* 3 (1992), pp. 101–59 (www .scienceandglobalsecurity.org/archive/sgs03gronlund.pdf). Gronlund and Wright conclude that some kinds of depressed trajectories do significantly increase stresses on a missile body and others do not. However, the latter require a missile to have a greater motor gimballing capability that enables it to make sharper turns during the boost phase.

8. Random sampling of identical components is one obvious way to deal with this problem; an untested component presumed to be identical to the ones that were tested can be used in the missile. However, if components are scarce and difficult to procure (as they may well be for an impoverished nation seeking to develop missiles), such a procedure is less feasible.

9. In practice, factories that produce fuels indigenously are less vulnerable to compromise. Moreover, fuels are usually produced in bulk, meaning that fuels used in the ground testing of engines are likely to be identical to the fuels used in missiles that are launched. Tampering with the composition of fuel that will only be used in a missile to be launched would thus have to occur after the point at which the fuels have been produced; such tampering is much harder than tampering with the manufacturing process.

10. Fritz Scholz, *Tolerance Stack Analysis Methods*, Boeing Information & Support Services, December 1995 (www.stat.washington.edu/people/fritz/Reports/isstech-95-030.pdf).

11. Xiaokui Shu and others, "Breaking the Target: An Analysis of Target Data Breach and Lessons Learned." Arxiv.org, January 18, 2017 (https://arxiv.org/pdf/1701.04940.pdf).

12. For very sensitive shipments, someone whose job it is to report possible tampering may accompany the shipment. Whether such a person can be compromised is open to question, but not all sensitive shipments will have someone accompanying them.

13. In 2013, *Der Spiegel* reported that the National Security Agency sometimes intercepted computer-related equipment being delivered to specific purchasers to install its own software or hardware modifications that would subsequently give it access. See "Documents Reveal Top NSA Hacking Unit," *Der Spiegel*, December 29, 2013 (www .spiegel.de/international/world/the-nsa-uses-powerful-toolbox-in-effort-to-spy-on -global-networks-a-940969-3.html).

14. As an example that works only on a PC, a person who uses Microsoft's Word to type the text string "=rand.old()" and then immediately presses "Enter" will see that the program inserts nine iterations of the text "The quick brown fox jumps over the lazy dog" and deletes the string that was just typed ("=rand.old()").

15. See, for example, Air Force Space and Missile Museum, "Atlas Radio Guidance System" (http://afspacemuseum.org/displays/AtlasGuidance/).

16. As an illustration of North Korea's possible stance toward regarding range safety, consider that the International Civil Aviation Organization has criticized North Korea for failure to give notice of its ballistic missile testing to commercial air traffic. Allison Lampert, "U.N. Aviation Agency Not Eyeing 'No-Fly' Zone around North Korea: Sources," Reuters, December 7, 2017 (www.reuters.com/article/us-un-icao-northkorea/u-n-aviation -agency-not-eyeing-no-fly-zone-around-north-korea-sources-idUSKBN1E135H). A second and more telling example is the accidental impact of a North Korean missile being tested in April 2017; failing shortly after launch, the missile crashed in the North Korean city of Tokchon, damaging a complex of buildings. Ankit Panda and Dave Schmerler, "When a North Korean Missile Accidentally Hit a North Korean City," *The Diplomat*, January 3, 2018 (https://thediplomat.com/2018/01/when-a-north-korean-missile-accidentally-hit-a -north-korean-city/).

17. See Steven M. Bellovin, Susan Landau, and Herbert Lin, "Limiting the Undesired Impact of Cyber Weapons: Technical Requirements and Policy Implications," chapter 11 in this volume.

18. Ibid.

19. See section 2.3.5 in National Research Council, *Technology, Policy, Law, and Ethics Regarding U.S. Acquisition and Use of Cyberattack Capabilities*, edited by William Owens, Kenneth Dam, and Herbert Lin (Washington: National Academies Press, 2009) (https://doi.org/10.17226/12651).

20. For example, ten of the twenty-four launchings of the Atlas ICBM before its first operational deployment resulted in failure. Raw data available at http://planet4589.org /space/lvdb/launch/Atlas; more easily readable data table found at https://en.wikipedia .org/wiki/List_of_Atlas_launches_(1957%E2%80%931959). The Atlas D was the first operational missile of the U.S. Air Force (www.astronautix.com/a/atlas.html).

21. According to the *New York Times*, the North Korean Musudan missile had an overall failure rate of 88 percent; the failure rate of the R-27 "Zyb" ballistic missile on which it was based was only 13 percent. See David E. Sanger and William Broad, "Downing North Korean Missiles Is Hard. So the U.S. Is Experimenting," *New York Times*, November 16, 2017. See also John Schilling, "Three (or Four) Strikes for the Musudan?," *38 North*, June 1, 2016 (www.38north.org/2016/06/jschilling060115/). On the other hand, modifications to the original Zyb design were substantial, including a lengthened missile body and the addition of grid fins. See Ralph Savelsberg and James Kiessling, "North Korea's Musudan Missile: A Performance Assessment," *38 North*, December 20, 2016 (www.38north.org/2016 /12/musudan122016/). So it is entirely possible that even in the absence of a cyber campaign against the Musudan development program, a failure rate higher than that of the Zyb would have been seen.

22. Dagyum Ji, "Kim Jong Un to Investigate Espionage Linked to Failed Missile Launch: Report," *NK News*, October 28, 2016 (www.nknews.org/2016/10/kim-jong -un-to-investigate-espionage-linked-to-failed-missile-launch-report/).

23. In the wake of the Stuxnet attack on Iranian centrifuges, such psychological and political effects were reported on the Iranian nuclear program to refine U-235. See Yossi Melman, "Israel's Rash Behavior Blew Operation to Sabotage Iran's Computers, U.S. Officials Say," *Jerusalem Post*, February 16, 2016 (www.jpost.com/Middle-East/Iran /Israels-rash-behavior-blew-operation-to-sabotage-Irans-computers-US-officials-say -444970).

24. Andy Greenberg, "Hacking North Korea Is Easy. Its Nukes? Not So Much," *Wired*, October 10, 2017 (www.wired.com/story/cyberattack-north-korea-nukes/).

25. For example, in an interview on PBS in May 2011, Leon Panetta, then director of the Central Intelligence Agency, acknowledged that the raid into Pakistan that killed Osama Bin Laden was a covert operation. See "CIA Chief Panetta: Obama Made 'Gutsy' Decision on Bin Laden Raid," PBS, May 3, 2011 (www.pbs.org/newshour/show/cia-chief -panetta-obama-made-gutsy-decision-on-bin-laden-raid). If Pakistan had not given permission for the raid, the Bin Laden raid would have clearly violated Pakistani sover-eignty (albeit for good reasons), and it is difficult to imagine that a covert action cyber campaign against another nation's missile development program would not do the same.

26. Michael Elleman, "The New Hwasong-15 ICBM: A Significant Improvement That May Be Ready as Early as 2018," *38 North*, November 30, 2017 (www.38north.org /2017/11/melleman113017/).

27. Defense Science Board, *Resilient Military Systems and the Advanced Cyber Threat* (Department of Defense, 2013) (www.dtic.mil/docs/citations/ADA569975).

28. Page Stoutland and Samantha Pitts-Kiefer, *Nuclear Weapons in the New Cyber Age: Report of the Cyber-Nuclear Weapons Study Group*, Nuclear Threat Initiative, Washington, September 2018.

8

The Cartwright Conjecture

The Deterrent Value and Escalatory Risk of
Fearsome Cyber Capabilities

JASON HEALEY

> We've got to talk about our offensive capabilities . . . to
> make them credible so that people know there's a penalty
> [for attacking the United States].
>
> —General James Cartwright, USMC, retired, 2011

Many advocates of cyber deterrence argue that the United States needs both fearsome cyber capabilities and assurance that America's adversaries know about them. This opinion might be called the Cartwright Conjecture, as expressed by General James Cartwright in this chapter's epigraph. I've heard very senior national security and cyber experts express relief that China believes the United States is "ten feet tall" in cyberspace because it has led China to be fearful and deterred, perhaps causing them to show

The author wishes to acknowledge the feedback provided by colleagues at workshops held at the Hoover Institution at Stanford University and at the School of International and Public Affairs at Columbia University. Nicole Softness provided research and editorial help. This work was supported by the Carnegie Corporation of New York and the Office Naval Research under the OSD Minerva program, grant number N00014-17-1-2423.

more restraint in their cyber operations than they otherwise might. Having fearsome capabilities, in this view, leads to better national security outcomes.

This view of the deterrent effect of U.S. cyber capabilities is mainstream in Washington, D.C., yet rarely put to the test. Stated more formally, the hypothesis of those who support the Cartwright Conjecture might be that adversaries who become aware of U.S. cyber capabilities will in turn restrain their own cyber operations.

Evidence to support this hypothesis is surprisingly thin. The case studies hint that, rather than being restrained in the face of cyber capabilities, states instead ramp up their own cyber capabilities and operations. Not least because cyber capabilities have most often been revealed through actual use, nations are not cowed but rather counterattack. Thus, if cyber conflict is more escalatory than many experts realize, a policy of deterrence built on fearsome capabilities is likely a significant miscalculation.

The Case for Being Feared

This chapter is not a comprehensive assessment of cyber deterrence, but rather an assessment of one view among policymakers. Still, a summary of the topic is a useful place to start. After all, having fearsome capabilities is not the only kind of deterrence.

The White House policy (during the Obama administration) on the topic features *deterrence by denial*: "There should be certainty about the fact that, even in the face of sophisticated cyber threats, the United States can maintain robust defenses, ensure resilient networks and systems, and implement a robust response capability that can project power and secure U.S. interests."[1] Adversaries would decide not to conduct significant cyberattacks because such attacks would not be likely to lead to positive and meaningful strategic outcomes.[2] Denying benefits is often the preferred kind of deterrence because it is useful against a range of adversaries and attack types, and is even useful against many kinds of accidental failures. Moreover, deterrence by denial is usually defensive in nature and therefore not escalatory.

But such powerful defense and resilience is difficult in cyber conflict, as the offense tends to have so many tactical advantages over the defense. Accordingly, it is not just General Cartwright who recommends *deterrence by punishment* or *by cost imposition*. The White House policy is clear that the United States is pursuing measures to both "threaten and carry out actions to inflict penalties and costs against adversaries that choose to conduct cyber attacks or other malicious cyber activity" against the nation through economic costs, such as sanctions, law enforcement, and military options.[3] A Defense Science Board task force, of which the author was a member, completed a report on cyber deterrence, including recommendations for both denial and cost imposition.[4] To these mechanisms Joseph Nye has added entanglement and normative taboos.[5] More recently, Michael Fischerkeller and Richard Harknett have convincingly argued that deterrence is the wrong model, since adversaries are in constant contact with each other, though they also argue explicitly for a "capabilities-based *strategy*" that "would focus less on who might threaten the United States or where it might be threatened, and more on what the United States wants to be able to do in cyberspace."[6]

For many hawks, cyber deterrence means no less than striking back in equal (or greater) measure. That view is increasingly common in Washington, especially after highly emotional incidents, such as the 2015 intrusion on the database of the Office of Personnel Management (OPM), that are evocative for many policymakers. Lawmakers such as U.S. Representative Ed Royce, chairman of the House Committee on Foreign Affairs, have asked "Why aren't we hitting back?" when "our country is taking body blow after body blow in cyberspace."[7] U.S. Representatives Adam Schiff and Peter King, both with intelligence oversight responsibilities, have insisted that "we need to figure out when we're going on an offensive" with disruptive operations in response to the OPM and other cases of Chinese espionage.[8]

The Cartwright Conjecture is not about hacking back, but about talking up a fearsome enough set of capabilities that using them becomes less necessary. It is perhaps less a specific deterrence strategy or theory than a mindset or presumption about how the dynamics of cyber deterrence work: the bigger your hammer and the more others are aware of it, the less you have to swing it.

Deterrence is much more nuanced than this, of course. Decades of research and military and academic analyses—including those on the value of brandishing weapons—have been conducted by strategists and analysts such as Bernard Brodie, Tom Schelling, and Herman Kahn.[9] General Cartwright and Admiral Michael Rogers, the second head of U.S. Cyber Command and the National Security Agency, are certainly familiar with this larger body of work, however both also sometimes focus specifically on the deterrent value of publicly known and fearsome capabilities to "increase our *capacity* on the offensive side to get to that point of deterrence" or "to demonstrat[e] the ability to impose costs on the adversary."[10] Let us then pull on this thread to see where it leads.

For deterrence to be strongly "capabilities based" it must be:

1. rooted in cyber operational capabilities, either general or specific, technical or organizational;

2. separate from any specific red line (this is not a necessity, but does clarify the effect is specific to the capability itself);

3. known by or communicated to adversaries, as with traditional deterrence; and

4. intended to cause restraint in adversaries and reduce their inclination to pursue aggressive actions.

No one, and certainly not General Cartwright or Admiral Rogers, is arguing that deterrence can be accomplished on the basis of just these four points. However, these can help us think more deeply about how capabilities affect deterrence. These points lead to several overlapping archetypes of deterrence: a loud shout, a loud organization, a quiet threat, and a symmetric counter.

A *loud shout* is the classic capabilities-based deterrence achieved by brandishing a cyber capability, the online equivalent of a Bikini Atoll test, meant to scare current and potential adversaries (and reassure friends). For example, to demonstrate resolve and an ability to deliver punishment, a nation might shut off the street lights in an adversary's capital or disrupt a water treatment plant or the nation's internet backbone. An obvious difference between a nuclear and a cyber demonstration is that because all internet infrastructure and systems are owned by someone, it might be hard to conduct a convincing demonstration test on, for example, a deserted island. Some tests may experiment on friendly systems, but such tests do not replicate the threat of conducting intrusions and disruptions on an adversary's systems. Indeed, the loudest shout should send a clear signal, not just to the adversary's leadership, but even to its population. It should be unambiguous that it was a deliberate demonstration, not a failure, and that worse could be coming if the issue at hand is not settled in way that is satisfactory to the attacking state. Some shouts might be meant for an audience in several states, an update to the classic "our words are backed with nuclear weapons."

A loud shout in cyberspace has been considered difficult, since revealing a cyber capability provides the target with suggestions for how to defeat it. Martin Libicki and others have highlighted the many difficulties involved in basing deterrence (or coercion) on particularly threatening capabilities, not least that "brandishing a cyberwar capability, particularly if specific, makes it harder to use such a capability because brandishing is likely to persuade the target to redouble its efforts to find or route around the exploited flaw."[11] There are, he points out, no May Day parades to flaunt capability. Nor, in another frequent analogy, are there mushroom clouds over Bikini Atoll.

In practice, however, the loudest shouts have not been targeted and deliberate attacks, but actual espionage and disruption campaigns that have made the public aware of capabilities, such as Stuxnet, as the case studies in the following section will show. These were not brandished specifically, and indeed the states that conducted them often wish they would have remained hidden, but they still count as shouting because they reveal a state's true capabilities. They are seen not just by a particular adversary, but by all who are paying attention.

A *loud organization* sends the signal that a shout does not need to be technical; states watch for many signals to gauge the capability of other states, including the size and strength of their cyber offense and intelligence organizations. This is the cyber May Day parade, a threatening capability advertised to all potential adversaries. In international relations scholarship, it is "swaggering," by "displaying one's military might at military exercises and national demonstrations and buying or building the era's most prestigious weapons."[12]

A large and well-funded organization can both develop fearsome technical capabilities and employ many of them at the same time, at the right time and place. And it can have a "deep magazine" to continue doing so long after less well-resourced organizations run out of smash. Such things are hard to know with precision but can be guessed at from the overall level of resources possessed by the organization. This information can be learned from both newspapers and secret reports.

Based on a Cold War analogy, Admiral Rogers makes a related argument that cyber-organizational capabilities themselves enhance crisis stability:

> We rapidly learned that we needed a nuclear force that was deployed across the three legs of the triad and underpinned by robust command and control mechanisms, far-reaching intelligence, and policy

structures including a declared deterrence posture. Building these nuclear forces and the policy and support structures around them took time and did not cause a nuclear war or make the world less safe. On the contrary, it made deterrence predictable, helped to lower tensions, and ultimately facilitated arms control negotiations.[13]

A "quiet threat" by comparison is not a pound of brandishing but an ounce of signaling so that adversaries know something they value is at risk. The threat might be made explicitly or subtly brandished, but it need not be made if the defenders believe the adversary understands the danger. However, to be most effective, the capability backing the threat should already be emplaced in the defender's systems, rather than just kept on the shelf, such as Russian intrusions into electrical grids (see later discussion).

On the U.S. side, Cyber Command is pursuing brush-back pitches for circumstances in which "you definitely want to be louder, where attribution is important to you and you actually want the adversary to know" that the effect was caused by the U.S. military.[14] However, because cyber capabilities mesh so well with other kinds of power, the quiet threat might be based on an earlier successful cyberattack. For example, it is easy to imagine the Chinese quietly threatening U.S. policymakers with a mass or selective release of personal information from the OPM data breaches.

A "symmetric counter" is a capability developed to match a similar capability known or suspected to be in the arsenal of another state, or it is holding a target that is similar in function and perceived value. If a state believes another is conducting intrusions into its electrical grid in order to hold it at risk for a future attack, then developing similar capabilities against the adversary's grid would be a version of capability-based deterrence, if properly signaled to the other side. Although such a tactic may be more tied to a specific red line than the other archetypes ("don't mess with our electrical grid or you'll suffer too"), it is worth including here because the deterrent threat is so closely tied to an actual capability.

If the Cartwright Conjecture is broadly accurate, the loud-shout and loud-organization models could be very stabilizing, providing broad deterrence because their capabilities are known to all adversaries. The other two, quiet threat and symmetric counter, are tailored to specific adversaries and probably to specific red lines, making them less capabilities-based than capabilities-*enabled*. These last two broadly map to Fischerkeller and

Harknett's concept of constant contact, capabilities that open opportunities while grappling with adversaries.

What can the actual evidence of history do to illustrate whether capabilities are likely to encourage restraint?

Actual Results of Being Feared

There is certainly a case to be made that being feared for one's cyber capabilities causes adversaries to back down and thus reduces tensions. But there has been almost no research on whether this actually happens, despite a history of thirty years of cyber conflict.

The case studies that can be drawn on are as obvious as they are messy. The relevant capabilities have been revealed through their actual use in espionage and disruptive attacks (and were not specifically conducted with deterrence in mind). Much of the information remains classified, or otherwise hidden, and none of the capabilities were revealed for specific deterrence purposes. Despite these and other limitations, the case studies do suggest important lessons.

Let us quickly dispense with the least useful case: *North Korea*. After North Korea savaged Sony Motion Pictures with an attack in 2014 and launched the WannaCry ransomware attack that spread around the world in 2017, the White House had few response options of any kind to deter the North Koreans, and practically no cyber options.[15] A nation with so little dependence on cyberspace has little reason to fear an adversary's capabilities.

Because there is information about the outbound as well as the inbound fire, perhaps the most promising case study involves *Iran* on one side and the United States and Israel on the other. The opening act appears to be the 2008 U.S.-Israeli Stuxnet attack against Iranian uranium enrichment capability. This destroyed perhaps 1,000 centrifuges.[16] It is still perhaps the ultimate embodiment of the Cartwright Conjecture: incredibly complex, highly engineered, and guided by exquisite intelligence. Though originally deployed as a sabotage capability, it was later repurposed as a deterrent "loud shout" because the story may have been leaked in part specifically to aid U.S. cyber deterrence, to make the nation's cyber forces seem particularly capable and fearsome. Indeed, "no state where news about Stuxnet has penetrated can seriously believe the United States lacks offensive cyberattack capabilities" (or the willingness to use them).[17] If there is evidence to support the conjecture, it would be expected here.

But despite being on the end of such a fear-inducing cyber weapon, the Iranians did not back down; instead they accelerated development of their own capabilities. According to the four-star general then overseeing U.S. Air Force cyber operations, the Iranian response to Stuxnet meant, "They are going to be a force to be reckoned with."[18] Likewise, *Forbes* reported that "U.S. researchers have repeatedly claimed the Middle Eastern nation has expanded its cyber divisions at a startling pace since the uncloaking of Stuxnet."[19] Even worse for the conjecture, Iran did not just create new cyber capabilities, but used them to counterattack the U.S. financial sector, "most likely in retaliation for economic sanctions and online attacks by the United States."[20]

These back-and-forth attacks by both sides continued for years. The next significant cycle started in April 2012, when a damaging "Wiper" worm forced Iran to take some oil wells offline and wiped the hard drives of computers in its energy sector.[21] The attack was most likely the work of Israel, which was keen to disrupt the Iranian economy. The Iranian response was symmetrical, with a nearly identical wiper attack, called Shamoon, which disrupted 30,000 computers at Saudi Aramco and more a few days later at RasGas.[22] Instead of recognizing that the Iranian attacks were a response to an earlier attack against it, the U.S. defense secretary, Leon Panetta, instead called them "a significant escalation of the cyber threat [that] have renewed concerns about still more destructive scenarios that could unfold."[23] Later attacks by Iran targeted U.S. financial companies and a major casino.[24] These attacks were then used in speeches and testimony to push for increasing U.S. capabilities.

The evidence again does not support the Cartwright Conjecture. We cannot know if any nation's responses might have been worse but for their adversary's capabilities. There is no evidence for that, while there is certainly the sense that both sides were egged on by each other's capabilities.

The case of China is just as instructive. Because so little is known about U.S. cyber operations against China, it is hard to know whether they have been moderated by China's own capability. We know much more about Chinese operations against the United States (and nearly all others), and there is little evidence that China was much deterred by U.S. capabilities in its decades-long campaign of commercial espionage or disruptive attacks such as the "Great Cannon."[25]

Rather, China has long claimed to be itself a victim of U.S. cyber operations, claims that gained in credibility after the revelations by Edward

Snowden about U.S. espionage and cyberattack capabilities and operations, which seem to have driven some Chinese actions. According to Adam Segal, the China cyber expert at the Council on Foreign Relations, the Chinese frequently see even routine or benign U.S. actions as swaggering meant to cow Beijing:

> The widespread interpretation of the release of the 2015 version of the DoD's cybersecurity strategy in the Chinese press, for example, was that it signaled a significant bolstering of offensive capabilities directed at China [and] "will further escalate tensions and trigger an arms race." . . . Chinese analysts often interpret U.S. openness as being as much about deterrence as reassurance. From the Chinese perspective, the stronger party often uses transparency to deter and threaten the weaker party by showing its superior capabilities.[26]

China seems to see these developments as a U.S. "loud organization" aimed in part at them. Yet if even *transparency* measures are seen as escalatory, then the United States' purposeful development of more fearsome cyber capabilities (and its conduct of espionage operations) could add further insult and be more escalatory than anticipated. Future research might examine if nations with weak offensive cyber capabilities (say Japan) received significantly more espionage and disruptive attacks than better-armed powers like the United States or Australia. At first blush, this seems unlikely, or if they have there has been a muted effect.

As with Iran, we cannot know if the situation might not be far graver but for some hidden cyber deterrence. But there is little serious evidence of a dynamic of deterrence; instead there are hints of the opposite—that U.S. capabilities egged on the Chinese.

There is increasingly useful evidence, paid for at too high a price, on the case of Russia. Mutual restraint and careful tradecraft were the norm until the 2014 annexation of Crimea from Ukraine, when Russian behavior online (as in the real world) became far more aggressive, with extensive intrusions into the White House,[27] Joint Chiefs of Staff,[28] and Department of State.[29] When discovered, the Russians no longer backed off but fought hard to keep their access. The Russian government also seems to be behind some of the more dangerous campaigns of malicious software, Black Energy and Havex, which have gained access to Western energy targets and disrupted the Ukrainian electricity grid.[30]

Russia, in interventions almost certainly approved by President Vladimir Putin himself, interfered in the 2016 U.S. elections, perhaps in response to Putin's perception that the release of the "Panama Papers" (containing financial records from offshore accounts) was a U.S. covert action (perhaps a loud shout) to expose Russian corruption or for perceived encouragement by the U.S. government of Russian election protests.[31] The U.S. response to this election meddling was weak, apparently constrained by the Obama administration's concern about being construed as partisan. However, the options to directly counter Putin, "to raise the cost in a manner Putin recognized," were scrapped specifically because senior leaders were concerned the conflict might escalate, and specifically that "Russia might respond with cyberattacks against America's critical infrastructure—and possibly shut down the electrical grid."[32]

There are several key takeaways. First, the dynamics cannot be fully understood, no matter how cleanly explanations like this describe the situation. The bulk of evidence only reveals what the Russians have been doing to others; U.S. cyber activity against Russia remains classified (or rather, not yet leaked). When this information is more publicly available—revealing, for example, whether the Panama Papers release was in fact a U.S. covert action—our understanding of the conflict dynamics may change significantly.

Second, the dynamics of Russia's post-Crimea aggression seem to more clearly illustrate tit-for-tat escalation, not deterrence. U.S. capabilities and operations in part *induced* the Russians' actions rather than suppressing them: "The Russians' heightened belligerence is aimed not just at collecting intelligence, but also confronting the United States," said one former senior administration official. "They're sending a message that we have capabilities and that you are not the only player in town," said the official.[33]

The escalatory dynamic would seem to be reinforced if indeed Putin implicitly or explicitly approved U.S. election interference as a like-for-like response to the release of the Panama Papers and interference in his own domestic politics.

Last, the Russia election interference provides proof of the existence of capabilities-based deterrence: the "quiet threat" of Russian capabilities implanted in U.S. critical infrastructure. This was in fact, a classic case of capabilities-based deterrence, meeting all four of the previously stated factors: a general or specific cyber capability, separate from any specific red line, which is known to the adversary, and has the effect of causing restraint.

Assessing the Cartwright Conjecture

Though the evidence is limited, these cases provide important insight. It is clear that one state's cyber capabilities can have some general deterrent effect, or at least lead to restraint on the part of the target. Beyond that, there is only partial evidence that a public policy stance of having strong cyber capabilities does anything to deter adversary nation-states and ample evidence of the counterargument: that capabilities beget capabilities, operations beget operations. General Cartwright's conjecture—that demonstrated capabilities *themselves* ought to have some deterrent effect—is certainly not confirmed and is in some cases specifically refuted. But the single exception is a doozy.

The first lesson of history is that, at the high end, cyber deterrence seems to be alive and well. Nations have proved just as unwilling to launch a strategic attack in cyberspace as they have in the air, on land, at sea, or in space. The new norm is same as the old norm.[34] The most cyber-capable nations (including the United States, China, and Russia) have stayed well under the threshold of strategic cyberwarfare, as no one has yet died from a cyberattack and none have suffered effects truly akin to those caused by kinetic military warfare. Below that threshold the gloves are largely off, and nations have been more than happy to spy with few limits and to disrupt noncritical systems. It is certainly possible that cyber capabilities have reinforced this threshold, but so have nuclear and conventional forces, entanglement, and other more traditional factors.

Below the threshold of death and destruction, there is ample evidence that the Iranians, Chinese, and Russians saw U.S. cyber organizations, capabilities, and operations as a challenge to be risen to, not one from which to back away. Indeed, the positive feedback of tit-for-tat may be the dominant dynamic of gray-zone cyber conflict. At best, fear of U.S. cyber capabilities may have led to short-term tamping down of adversary operations until they were able to compete on more equal terms. Given the low cost of developing cyber capabilities, in comparison with the cost of developing more traditional military options, it did not take long for other countries to join the fray. In particular, both Iran and North Korea increased their relative capability far more quickly than many analysts expected. This speed of convergence in capabilities may mean that any equivalent of the "missile gap" or "bomber gap" can be promptly closed, making U.S. military goals of "cyberspace superiority" futile.[35] When it is easy to close gaps, swaggering is counterproductive.

The tit-for-tat effects can explain only a small amount of the overall dynamic because the behavior of the protagonists is driven by deeper motivations. Iran is a revolutionary power surrounded by perceived enemies; China has felt behind the West since the "unequal treaties" of the 1800s and justified in using any means to catch up; Russia seeks to restore lost prestige and power; and the United States was able to act unilaterally both to protect its own interests and global stability.

Still, after being on the losing end of a cyber engagement (or even seeing others lose), nations seem likely to either accelerate their own capabilities or counterattack, or both. There are certainly other drivers: "They may be responding similarly to technological opportunities, domestic politics, or bureaucratic bargaining, not racing against each other." Yet in the cases of Iran, China, and Russia we have supporting evidence that prior U.S. behavior mattered. The United States often in turn responded to adversary reactions by pursuing further capabilities, a positive feedback loop of "circular causation."[36] If a state causes fear, it may lead to worse real-world outcomes: more attacks from a more capable adversary. This effect might be even worse if a nation pursued, as cyber hawks espouse, a specific policy to be feared.

However, in the most critical case, the Cartwright Conjecture seems to strongly hold: Russian malware in U.S. critical infrastructure specifically moderated the U.S. response to election interference. Though only a single, recent case, it does clarify several dynamics. First, it is oversimplifying to assume that using a capability means that it is taken off the table, a key argument against capabilities-based deterrence. Revealing a capability only weakens it if the underlying vulnerability gets fixed, an assumption that often does not hold for busy cyber defenders. The Russian malware inserted in Western energy grids, Black Energy and Havex, had been in use for several years yet was still effective. Second, the Russian capabilities did not have to be as splashily brandished as a "cyber Bikini Atoll." They were not developed or deployed as part of a deliberate operation to provide a deterrence threat in support of the election interference. It was sufficient that they were appreciated by the defender's decision makers and included in their calculus.

Third, the capability was not known abstractly by the U.S. decision makers; it had actually been implanted by Russia in some of the nation's most sensitive networks in U.S. critical infrastructure. This made the looming threat far more concrete, not "the Russians are ten feet tall" but "if we don't calibrate our response correctly, the impact could immediately be felt in specific plants in our electrical grid."

This is the most important point. Flexing, it turns out, is cheap. Only deep penetrations of adversaries' critical networks may be enough. The Cartwright Conjecture has far deeper implications if it is not enough just "to talk about our offensive capabilities . . . to make them credible" but instead necessary to gain access to the most sensitive networks of an adversary and hold them at risk indefinitely. If an adversary city or intercontinental ballistic missile is "held at risk" with nuclear weapons, it means they are in the crosshairs of specific warheads on delivery systems that are likely to reach them. There was of course a non-negligible risk of escalation and miscalculation, a problem addressed by some of the best strategists and technologists of the day. If capabilities-based deterrence does indeed depend strongly on covert implantation of weapons that can be detonated by a simple order, then it seems likely to be far more open to escalation and miscalculation. This "environment of constant contact," of "persistent engagement" between adversary cyber forces, is a far cry from merely talking about, or even brandishing, capabilities.[37]

Such operations are not properly thought of as deterrence, or even coercion, but as gray-zone warfighting, battling to control the other's key terrain so one's own artillery will command the high ground. Pursing persistent engagement also means preventing adversaries from gaining a perch on your high ground, what one former NSA and CIA director, General Michael Hayden, calls, "'counter battery' or 'suppressive' fires . . . using your offensive power to reduce his offensive capacity."[38] Such operations are not "deterrence" but rather winning, superiority, or supremacy. When adversary cyber forces are persistently engaged, there will not be many obvious firebreaks, a "readily identifiable boundary, or 'pause,' at which to limit the escalation of conflict."[39] Such fights can last far longer than originally planned and develop in directions that are unexpected by those involved.

Not Deterrence but Tit-for-Tat

The United States has spent billions of dollars to develop cyber organizations and capabilities, in part hoping these would be fearsome enough to intimidate adversaries. Why has more traditional cyber deterrence seemingly caused more reaction than restraint? Certainly the famous claim that it is difficult to attribute cyberattacks falls flat: neither Iran nor the United States had much doubt about whom its adversary was.

It is also likely that the U.S. cyber community is misreading the stabilizing impact of organizational capability. As quoted earlier, Admiral Rogers argued that building warfighting "nuclear forces and the policy and support structures" made deterrence "predictable," decreasing tensions and making crises less likely, and that cyber operations could do that as well. Perhaps, but the nuclear standoff was not as stable as Admiral Rogers proposes, if one considers the existential scares caused by the Cuban Missile Crisis in 1962 and the Able Archer wargame and Soviet false alarm that warned of incoming U.S. missiles in 1983.[40]

More crucially, nuclear weapons were never actually used during the Cold War and in fact were seen by many, on both sides of the Iron Curtain, as being unusable. Cyber capabilities, by comparison, are used all the time, up to and including in disruptive attacks against critical infrastructure. All major nations regularly engage in widespread intelligence collection through cyberspace, and such operations are often difficult to distinguish from preparation for attacks. As revealed by Edward Snowden, the United States possesses and uses such capabilities, with perhaps greater frequency and skill than anyone else in the world. In cyberspace, Russia, China, and Iran may all feel they are the aggrieved party. Assuming that because organizations underpinned stability in a bipolar nuclear standoff they will do so in cyberspace is to misapply lessons to a domain with completely different dynamics.

U.S. officials may be further misreading the dynamics (or even believing their own script) that the United States is primarily a victim, not a protagonist in its own right. For example, one "former cyberintelligence official" was quoted after the leak of U.S. hacking tools, "We're getting trounced in an information war we didn't ask for."[41] Putin, rightly or wrongly, believes he is beating us at our own game.

Or perhaps the United States has not developed fearsome enough capabilities or struck back hard enough to deter. This cannot be disproven but does ignore the many times such actions induced the opposite response. With Russia, for example, how far does the United States need to escalate to get Putin to back down? What kind of fearsome capabilities would be enough? And why would we think his pain threshold is suddenly lower than ours? If we gain awesome leverage over him, what is to keep him from doubling down against us? Any actions to deter must exceed his threshold for pain or only lead to worse pain in retaliation. There are easy answers here, but none that seem remotely credible in today's political environment, at least against Russia.

Together these points highlight a critical but overlooked element of escalatory dynamics: deterrence works very differently if your adversary is certain it is striking back, not first. This situation is not new to cyberspace, as noted by Richard Betts: "Deterrence is less reliable when both sides in a conflict see each other as the aggressor. . . . The side that we want to deter may see itself as trying to deter us. These situations are ripe for miscalculation."[42]

This idea is similar to Libicki's reference to an "effect opposite to the one intended," where brandishing capabilities leads not to deterrence but to escalation. Perhaps the most common form of such miscalculation is a classic security dilemma.[43] Adversaries see each other building and using cyber capabilities and instead enter a spiral of escalation. Still, this escalation is quite rational. Each adversary perceives (perhaps correctly) the buildup to be directed at it and invests ever more in building capabilities that will help it catch up. Every new headline—about China's cyber espionage, U.S. cyber organizations' capability and surveillance, Russia's use of cyber means to bully its neighbors—just escalates the spiral higher and higher.

This spiral of escalation is fed by both emotion and the unique dynamics of cyberspace. What if seeing cyber capabilities, especially if you are their target, leads not to fear but to anger? After all, anger often leads to optimistic judgments such as those about the value of retaliating.[44] This optimism bias feeds the natural tendency of national security hawks, whose "preference for military action over diplomacy is often built upon the assumption that victory will come swiftly and easily."[45]

Getting "just enough" fear is a hard effect to calibrate in the best of times, especially in a new and poorly understood area like cyber conflict. Brandishing cyber capabilities to deliberately induce fear in the leaders of another state may overshoot that target and cause anger and a "damaging sense of paranoia" instead, feeding the adversary's own hawks.[46] Moreover, "conflict often hardens attitudes and drives people to extreme positions."[47]

In addition, nations (especially the United States) would likely never accept significant restrictions on collecting traditional political-military intelligence using cyber means. But the same accesses used for collection purposes may, in perception or in fact, allow for destructive attacks. So insistence on nearly unrestricted rights to conduct online espionage may undermine the very stability this intelligence is meant to support. If a U.S. adversary feels it has complied with a demand to back away from a red line, even purely intelligence-gathering intrusions to confirm that fact may cause the adversary to believe it is still being punished or give its hawks justification to conduct their own "constant contact" to disrupt U.S. espionage.

This scenario is particularly germane to Iran and the United States. Even if either side backed off, could either be sure that continuing intrusions for intelligence-gathering purposes (including those to confirm the deal) were not meant to lay the groundwork for future attacks? Could Iran be sure it would not later be sucker-punched by Israel?

This argument is not to make any *moral* equivalence between the operations of the United States and its adversaries. But there may be a *functional* equivalence of operations that feeds the same escalatory dynamics. Leaders who believe this is "just how the intelligence game is played" or rely on nuclear analogies are likely to be miscalculating the reaction from adversaries. A specific policy to be feared might only swirl the spiral of escalation faster and higher, and of course be more expensive to implement.

In the end, it seems the only way to successfully deter is to have the most audacity, the most willingness to penetrate the most sensitive networks of adversaries and use them, if needed. This is a dangerous game. Given the divisions in Washington, it is not clear it is one we are prepared to win, at least with Russia.

Policy Implications

President Obama warned China and Russia to accept limits: "We can choose to make this an area of competition, which I guarantee you we'll win if we have to."[48] Looking back on that comment, it is hard not to imagine the narrator's voice saying: "We did not win." Deterrence rooted in *general* organizational and technical capability—a strong cyber organization or national cyber capabilities that are publicly demonstrated (especially through actual use)—so far seems counterproductive. In these cases of the "loud shout" and "loud organization," the signal most likely to be transmitted is not "back away" but "bring it on," a boastfulness to be emulated.

Capabilities-based deterrence seems most likely to succeed when it is tailored and targeted, a quiet and focused implantation of capabilities into specific infrastructure of a specific adversary nation, in archetypes of the "quiet word" and "symmetric counter." The most obvious effort to do this was the Obama administration's failed attempt to calibrate a response that would be just bad enough to get Putin to back off but not so serious that he would be motivated to shut down parts of the U.S. electrical grid. It is not clear there is enough consensus in Washington to implant sufficient capabilities, and threaten to use them, to get Putin to back down. It is even less obvious that the conditions for targeted deterrence exist with other adversaries, especially Iran or North Korea. The leaders of those nations (or their often semi-independent security structures) may not respect strength but seek to match and overturn it. After all, it could be other parts of the regime, not they, who take the punch. Still, the ability for the United States to make a symmetric deterrence threat gives the president tools to respond earlier and at lower levels of violence, though with a higher chance for miscalculation. Unfortunately, there is no obvious way to know how much is enough, unlike when one is counting bombers, missiles, warheads, or fissile material. There is no upper bound to fearsome capabilities, no threshold above which there is "too much."

With nations in a state of persistently contesting each other, the relevance of classic deterrence models drop away compared to warfighting, crisis stability, and escalation control. Yet the conversation on deterrence has sucked all the air from the room, distracting from the more critical problem of ensuring that conflicts do not spiral out of control. Indeed, in many discussions with colleagues and current and former policymakers, I realized that when they said they wanted "deterrence" it was clear they meant "supremacy" or "superiority": they wanted the adversary to show restraint in response to U.S. power and interests, but did not want U.S. operations to change. This may be a valid national security goal, but even if it could be achieved given the dynamics of cyberspace it would be destabilizing in the medium term. Since the technology-dependent United States has so much more to lose in a cyber conflict, stability needs to be the overall goal, with deterrence as one possible way to achieve it.

Having an end goal of stability, rather than deterrence, seems far more important given the Russian success in inducing U.S. restraint. It seems that audacity is more valuable than having advanced capabilities. If lessons can be drawn from this case, it is that capabilities cannot stay on the shelf but must be pushed deeper into the most sensitive networks of an adversary. They should know they are there and that you might, at a time of your own choosing, elect to detonate them. If this is deterrence, it is on a hair trigger. If both nations, or rather all nations that are cyber powers, pursue this strategy without focusing on the overall stability of the situation, it will destabilize, possibly explosively.

U.S. Cyber Command and others advocating to "defend forward" and "persistently contest malicious cyber activities"[49] must remember that, in a complex and interconnected system like the internet, "we can never merely do one thing" as "not only can actions call up counteractions, but multiple parties and stages permit many paths to unanticipated consequences."[50] Just as capabilities-based deterrence may have helped increase, not decrease, the intensity of competition, so may the cyber forces of nuclear-armed states grappling in a decades-long match with no obvious firebreaks or off-ramps.

And of course cyber is not a closed game. With a general goal to cause fear in adversaries, the United States is likely to cause fear in all, not least its own citizens and allies if the past decade is any guide. It could confuse those who thought the United States wanted a peaceful, free, and open internet, as well as disillusion digital natives who might otherwise be swayed by this once-in-a-century soft-power opportunity to showcase American internet-based values. To create fear, the United States will likely have to continue to co-opt or coerce information technology companies, weaponize their technologies, and conduct widespread monitoring on or through their networks. This outcome would be far more burdensome on the United States and Europe, whose economies are heavily dependent on the internet and whose governments are pushing for an open and secure global internet, than it would be for China, Russia, Iran, or North Korea.

A final implication for policymakers (and other cyber-conflict researchers) is to continue to seek evidence of the effectiveness and efficiency of public policy options. In conducting the research for this chapter, I asked colleagues, "What evidence is there that being feared leads to better national security outcomes?" I received a range of responses. Some veered away from evidence toward theory, such as the "dialectical theory of stability." Others responded that it is difficult to prove that deterrence works, even if it is possible the evidence might at least disprove the negative, that capabilities are escalatory. Since much of the information that might answer this question is classified, it was suggested that we ought to defer to those with clearances to ask and answer such questions, and that "even asking for evidence-based proof that cyber deterrence works" might be a request that is impossible to fulfill.

But don't advocates of cyber deterrence need evidence to show that cyber deterrence works the way they think it does and not in some other way? No, for some reason, the weight of evidence seems to be required in one direction only, against the hawkish, traditional position. But in my view, the *actual behavior* of states, not theory or dogma, should be central to all research on deterrence, or any other dynamics of cyber conflict. Whenever a theorist or a practitioner proposes a course of action, others should always ask, "Why do you think it works that way? What's your evidence?" The work by

Michael Fischerkeller and Richard Harknett to introduce the dynamics of "constant contact" is a strong start.[51]

Together, these arguments lead me to make several specific recommendations: (1) increase research into the escalatory or stabilizing impacts of constant contact; (2) begin to steer policies in these directions and away from interwar deterrence; (3) when analyzing and proposing policies, seek more evidence of how states actually respond; and (4) always ask when proposing a policy, "What then? What happens next, and after that, and after that?"

In conclusion, as Betts noted in regard to stopping Iran from getting a nuclear bomb: "Hawks who think of themselves as stalwart, steely-eyed and far-seeing have regarded . . . obstacles as challenges to be overcome or disregard in order to do what is necessary. . . . [But] the military option that is possible would be ineffective, while the one that would be effective is not possible."[52]

In cyberspace, those who are angry at repeated Chinese, Iranian, or Russian intrusions often see similar obstacles to charging forward with their preferred policies of fearsome cyber capabilities to push deterrence. But the foremost obstacle is that there is little evidence so far that organizational and technical capabilities actually succeed in getting U.S. adversaries to back down; and there is growing evidence that they achieve the opposite. Perhaps it is true that you cannot prove that deterrence is working; but you can certainly see if it isn't.

Cyber conflict is relatively new and the dynamics still relatively unknown. Any act of cyber deterrence is best thought of as an experiment. Some will work, some will not. The best hope is to think, act, and then watch and learn, as with any experiment.

Notes

Epigraph: Andrea Shalal-Ese, "Ex-U.S. General Urges Frank Talk on Cyber Weapons," Reuters, November 6, 2011. (www.reuters.com/article/us-cyber-cartwright-idUSTRE7 A514C20111106).

1. White House, *Report on Cyber Deterrence Policy,* 2015 (http://1yxsm73j7aop3quc9y5ifaw3 .wpengine.netdna-cdn.com/wp-content/uploads/2015/12/Report-on-Cyber-Deterrence -Policy-Final.pdf).

2. This chapter focuses on cyber deterrence against state adversaries for national security purposes, not deterrence of cyber crimes, especially those by nonstate actors. It is worth noting that, for those purposes, "the threat of legal sanctions is the most useful leverage for instrumental crimes [that is, those meant to achieve explicit future goals] by

individuals with low commitment to a criminal lifestyle. In contrast, expressive crimes [unplanned acts of anger or frustration] are regarded as 'undeterrable' actions. . . . Furthermore, expressive computer crimes are substantially more undeterrable in cases where companies are reluctant to bring in law enforcement agencies." Merrill Warkentin, Joshua Regan, and Amin Kosseim, "Toward Cognitive Immunization of Potential Criminals against Cyberterrorism," Proceedings of the 11th Annual Symposium on Information Assurance, Albany, N.Y., June 8–9, 2016.

3. White House, *Report on Cyber Deterrence Policy*, 2015.

4. Department of Defense, *Final Report of the Defense Science Board Task Force on Cyber Deterrence*, 2017 (www.acq.osd.mil/dsb/reports/2010s/DSB-CyberDeterrenceReport_02 -28-17_Final.pdf).

5. Joseph Nye, "Deterrence and Dissuasion in Cyberspace," *International Security* (Winter 2016/17) (www.belfercenter.org/publication/deterrence-and-dissuasion-cyberspace).

6. Michael Fischerkeller and Richard Harknett, "Deterrence Is Not a Credible Strategy for Cyberspace," *Science Direct* 61, no. 3 (2017), pp. 381–93 (www.sciencedirect .com/science/article/pii/S0030438717300431); emphasis added.

7. Zach Noble, "Time to Consider the 'Hack-Back' Strategy?," *FCW Magazine*, September 30, 2015 (https://fcw.com/articles/2015/09/30/hack-back-strategy.aspx).

8. Associated Press, "Schiff, King Call on Obama to Be Aggressive in Cyberwar, after Purported China Hacking," Fox News, June 7, 2015 (www.foxnews.com/politics/2015/06 /07/schiff-king-call-on-obama-to-be-aggressive-in-cyber-war-after-purported-china.html).

9. For an overview of the early nuclear strategists and their work, see Fred Kaplan, *The Wizards of Armageddon* (1983; reprint, Palo Alto, Calif.: Stanford University Press, 1991).

10. Ellen Nakashima, "Cyber Chief: Efforts to Deter Attacks against the U.S. Are Not Working," *Washington Post*, March 19, 2015; Senate Committee on Armed Services, Advance Questions for Vice Admiral Michael S. Rogers, USN, Nominee for Commander, United States Cyber Command, March 11, 2014 (www.armed-services.senate .gov/imo/media/doc/Rogers_03-11-14.pdf).

11. Martin Libicki, "Brandishing Cyberattack Capabilities" (Santa Monica, Calif.: RAND, 2013), p. x (www.rand.org/content/dam/rand/pubs/research_reports/RR100 /RR175/RAND_RR175.pdf).

12. Robert J. Art, "The Political Uses of Force: The Four Functions of Force," in *International Politics: Enduring Concepts and Contemporary Issues*, edited by Robert J. Art and Robert Jervis (New York: Pearson/Longman, 2009), pp. 164–71.

13. Senate Committee on Armed Services, Statement of Admiral Michael S. Rogers before the Senate Committee on Armed Services, March 19, 2015 (https://fas.org/irp /congress/2015_hr/031915rogers.pdf).

14. Chris Bing, "U.S. Cyber Command Director: We Want 'Loud,' Offensive Cyber Tools," *FedScoop*, August 2016 (www.fedscoop.com/us-cyber-command-offensive-cyber security-nsa-august-2016/). U.S. Cyber Command is calling these "loud" capabilities, but they usually want the effect known only to the particular adversary, not to the entire world; these are not Bikini Atoll loud.

15. David E. Sanger and Nicole Perlroth, "U.S. Said to Find North Korea Ordered Cyberattack on Sony," *New York Times*, December 17, 2014; E. Nakashima and P. Rucker, "U.S. Declares North Korea Carried Out Massive WannaCry Cyberattack," *Washington Post*, December 19, 2017.

16. David E. Sanger, "Obama Order Sped Up Wave of Cyberattacks against Iran," *New York Times*, June 1, 2012.

17. Libicki, "Brandishing Cyberattack Capabilities," p. 2.

18. Andrea Shalal-Esa, "Iran Strengthened Cyber Capabilities after Stuxnet: U.S. General," Reuters, January 17, 2013 (www.reuters.com/article/us-iran-usa-cyber-idUSBRE90 G1C420130118).

19. Thomas Fox-Brewster, "'Bone-Chilling' Research Suggests Iran Gearing Up to Avenge Stuxnet Hacks," *Forbes*, December 2, 2014.

20. Nicole Perlroth and Quentin Hardy, "Bank Hacking Was the Work of Iranians, Officials Say," *New York Times*, January 9, 2013.

21. Thomas Erdbrink, "Facing Cyberattack, Iranian Officials Disconnect Some Oil Terminals from Internet," *New York Times*, April 24, 2012.

22. Nicole Perlroth, "In Cyberattack on Saudi Firm, U.S. Sees Iran Firing Back," *New York Times*, October 24, 2012.

23. Ellen Nakashima, "Cyberattack on Mideast Energy Firms Was Biggest Yet, Panetta Says," *Washington Post*, October 11, 2012.

24. Department of Justice, "Seven Iranians Working for Islamic Revolutionary Guard Corps–Affiliated Entities Charged for Conducting Coordinated Campaign of Cyber Attacks against U.S. Financial Sector," March 2016 (www.justice.gov/opa/pr/seven -iranians-working-islamic-revolutionary-guard-corps-affiliated-entities-charged).

25. The Great Cannon is capable of manipulating the traffic of "bystander" systems outside China so that these systems conduct a massive DDoS attack. See Bill Marczak and others, "China's Great Cannon," *The Citizen Lab*, April 10, 2015 (https://citizenlab.org /2015/04/chinas-great-cannon).

26. Adam Segal, "What Briefing Chinese Officials on Cyber Really Accomplishes," Council on Foreign Relations, April 7, 2014.

27. Michael Schmidt and David E. Sanger, "Russian Hackers Read Obama's Unclassified Emails, Officials Say," *New York Times*, April 26, 2015.

28. Barbara Starr, "Official: Russia Eyed in Joint Chiefs Email Intrusion," CNN, August 5, 2015 (www.cnn.com/2015/08/05/politics/joint-staff-email-hack-vulnerability/).

29. Evan Perez and Shimon Prokipecz, "Sources: State Dept Hack the 'Worst Ever,'" CNN, March 10, 2015.

30. F-Secure Labs, "The Convergence of Crimeware and APT Attacks," 2014 (www.f -secure.com/documents/996508/1030745/blackenergy_whitepaper.pdf); L. Constantine, "New Havex Malware Variants Target Industrial Control System and SCADA Users," *PCWorld*, June 24, 2014 (www.pcworld.com/article/2367240/new-havex-malware -variants-target-industrial-control-system-and-scada-users.html); Kelly Jackson Higgins, "Lessons from the Ukraine Electric Grid Hack," *Dark Reading*, March 18, 2016 (www.darkreading.com/vulnerabilities—threats/lessons-from-the-ukraine-electric-grid -hack/d/d-id/1324743).

31. Office of the Director of National Intelligence, "Background to 'Assessing Russian Activities and Intentions in Recent U.S. Elections': The Analytic Process and Cyber Incident Attribution," January 2017 (www.dni.gov/files/documents/ICA_2017_01.pdf).

32. David Korn and Michael Ishikof, "Why the Hell Are We Standing Down?," *Mother Jones*, March 9, 2018 (www.motherjones.com/politics/2018/03/why-the-hell-are -we-standing-down/).

33. Ellen Nakashima, "New Details Emerge about 2014 Russian Hack of the State Department: It Was 'Hand to Hand Combat,'" *Washington Post*, April 3, 2017.

34. Jason Healey, "Cyber Deterrence Is Working," *Defense News*, July 30, 2014 (www .atlanticcouncil.org/news/in-the-news/healey-cyber-deterrence-is-working).

35. U.S. Cyber Command Factsheet, "Achieve and Maintain Cyberspace Superiority," February 2018 (www.thecipherbrief.com/wp-content/uploads/2018/02/Cyber-Command -Achieve-and-Maintain-Cyber-Superiority-1.pdf).

36. Robert Jervis, *System Effects: Complexity in Political and Social Life* (Princeton University Press, 2017), pp. 26, 125.

37. Fischerkeller and Harknett, "Deterrence Is Not a Credible Strategy for Cyberspace."

38. Michael Hayden "To Defend against Hostile Nations, America Needs Fierce Cyberpower," *The Hill*, March 12, 2018 (http://thehill.com/opinion/national-security /377876-america-needs-to-step-up-cyber-combat-against-hostile-nations).

39. Michael T. Klare, "Securing the Firebreak," *World Policy Journal* 2, no. 2 (1985), p. 232.

40. For more on Able Archer, see National Security Archive, "The 1983 Warscare Declassified, and for Real" (http://nsarchive.gwu.edu/nukevault/ebb533-The-Able-Ar cher-War-Scare-Declassified-PFIAB-Report-Released/). On the Soviet false alarm that led to an order to launch a retaliatory strike, see Megan Garber, "The Man Who Saved the World by Doing Absolutely Nothing," *The Atlantic*, September 26, 2013 (www .theatlantic.com/technology/archive/2013/09/the-man-who-saved-the-world-by-doing -absolutely-nothing/280050/).

41. Jenna McLaughlin, "Trove of Stolen NSA Data Is 'Devastating' Loss for Intelligence Community," *Foreign Policy*, April 17, 2017 (https://foreignpolicy.com/2017/04/17 /trove-of-stolen-nsa-data-is-devastating-loss-for-intelligence-community/).

42. Richard Betts, *American Force: Dangers, Delusions, and Dilemmas in National Security* (Columbia University Press, 2013), p. 140.

43. See Ben Buchanan, *The Cybersecurity Dilemma: Hacking, Trust, and Fear between Nations* (Oxford University Press, 2017) for an excellent book-length treatment of this topic.

44. Rose McDermott, "The Feeling of Rationality: The Meaning of Neuroscientific Advances for Political Science," *Perspectives on Politics* 2, no. 4 (December 2004), p. 696.

45. Daniel Kahneman and Jonathan Renshon, "Why Hawks Win," *Foreign Policy*, October 13, 2009.

46. Buchanan, *The Cybersecurity Dilemma*, p. 7.

47. Jervis, *System Effects*, p. 52.

48. Obama quoted in David E. Sanger, "Cyberthreat Posed by China and Iran Confounds White House," *New York Times*, September 16, 2015.

49. U.S. Cyber Command Factsheet, "Achieve and Maintain Cyberspace Superiority."

50. Jervis, *System Effects*, pp. 10, 18. "Never merely do one thing" is quoted from Garrett Hardin, "The Cybernetics of Competition," *Perspectives in Biology and Medicine* (Autumn 1963), pp. 79–80.

51. Fischerkeller and Harknett, "Deterrence Is Not a Credible Strategy for Cyberspace."

52. Betts, *American Force*, p. 140.

9

The Cyber Commitment Problem and the Destabilization of Nuclear Deterrence

ERIK GARTZKE *and* JON R. LINDSAY

In March 2017, the *New York Times* reported that the Obama administration initiated, and the Trump administration inherited, a covert action program to "remotely manipulate data inside North Korea's missile systems."[1] Cyber and electronic warfare techniques to sabotage missile components, impair command and control systems, or jam communication signals offer a "left-of-launch" capability to preempt enemy weapons before or shortly after they are launched. Since the beginning of the U.S. program, code-named Nimble Fire, North Korea has suffered numerous unsuccessful tests, including some catastrophic failures. Although it is impossible to rule out accident as the cause of these incidents, it is tempting to suggest that U.S. left-of-launch efforts have been successful.

The authors would like to thank William J. Perry, Scott Sagan, participants of the Stanford Workshop on Strategic Dimensions of Offensive Cyber Operations, and two anonymous reviewers for comments on previous drafts of this chapter. This research was supported by SCPP and a grant from the Department of Defense Minerva Initiative through the Office of Naval Research [N00014-14-1-0071].

As reported, the United States used such techniques to interfere with North Korean missile tests, but in principle the same methods could be used to disrupt an actual wartime launch. Left-of-launch cyberattacks could complement kinetic counterforce missile strikes to neutralize a North Korean missile before it departed its launch pad. This is an attractive military alternative to ballistic missile defense systems like Terminal High Altitude Air Defense (THAAD), the Aegis Ballistic Missile Defense System deployed on warships and Aegis Ashore batteries, and the Ground-based Midcourse Defense system. President Trump claimed in October 2017, "We have missiles that can knock out a missile in the air 97 percent of the time, and if you send two of them, it's going to get knocked down," but he wildly exaggerates the testing success rate under even controlled peacetime conditions.[2] Ballistic missile defense systems must solve a very difficult physics problem, described as "hitting a bullet with a bullet," and be able to differentiate decoys from real weapons amidst the "fog of war" encountered in combat conditions. Given that even a single North Korean missile might destroy an entire city (in South Korea, Japan, Guam, Hawaii, Alaska, or California), the prospects of relying completely on right-of-launch missile defense are not reassuring. The United States is thus investigating numerous alternatives, including using drones to intercept missiles after launch and cyberwarfare to disrupt command and control before launch.[3]

A U.S. Joint Chiefs of Staff paper from 2013 clearly states the military rationale for preemption:

> If deterrence fails, neutralizing an adversary's offensive air and missile assets prior to use continues to be the preferred method to negate them, and with the increasing growth in numbers, is the only practical means to defeat large inventories. . . . Initial offensive operations should place a priority on attacking air and missile systems and their supporting command and control structures, employing all means.[4]

Malware and jamming means do indeed seem desirable "if deterrence fails," especially since relying totally on ballistic missile defense systems to "hit a bullet with a bullet" is risky. While the technology here is new, the counterforce concept is not. The electronic attack and offensive cyber operations tested as part of the Nimble Fire program are updated analogues of Cold War programs like Canopy Wing that targeted Soviet nuclear command and control. The U.S. military has a long history of developing targeting capabilities to "find, fix, and finish" enemy missile systems, even as deterrence theorists have long warned that counterforce strategies can undermine the stability of deterrence.[5]

Unfortunately, as we shall argue, deterrence failure becomes even more likely when one side depends on covert counterforce capabilities to preempt the other side's nuclear deterrent. Left-of-launch cyber operations are just such a capability. Moreover, strategic instability is greatest in confrontations between asymmetric nuclear powers, where only the stronger side has effective covert cyber counterforce capabilities. This is, more or less, the situation with the United States and North Korea. In the language of game theory, the ability to win the warfighting subgame of the deterrence game makes playing the nuclear subgame more likely. Covert cyber operations targeting nuclear weapons are strategically destabilizing. There are both historical and theoretical reasons for taking seriously the effects of cyberattacks on nuclear systems, and we should expect the risk of destabilization to vary with the relative cyber capabilities of the actors in a crisis interaction.

This chapter proceeds in four parts. First we discuss the vulnerability of nuclear weaponry to cyberattack, drawing on historical cases where possible. Second we contrast the informational characteristics of nuclear deterrence and cyber operations. Third we analyze the implications of combining these two domains for strategic stability. We close with policy recommendations.

The Vulnerability of Nuclear Command and Control

In the 1983 movie *WarGames*, a teenager played by Matthew Broderick hacks into the North American Air Defense Command (NORAD) and almost triggers World War III. After a screening of the film, President Ronald Reagan allegedly asked his staff, "Could something like this really happen?" The chairman of the Joint Chiefs of Staff replied, "Mr. President, the problem is much worse than you think." The National Security Agency (NSA) had been hacking Russian and Chinese communications for years, but the burgeoning personal computer revolution was creating serious vulnerabilities for the United States too. Reagan directed a series of reviews that culminated in a classified National Security Decision Directive, NSDD-145 entitled "National Policy on Telecommunications and Automated Information Systems Security." Technicians and policymakers slowly came to appreciate the evolving cybersecurity threat to all types of government and civilian systems over the following decades.[6]

In no small irony, the internet itself owes its intellectual origin, in part, to the threat to nuclear systems from large-scale physical attack. A 1962 RAND Corporation report by Paul Baran had considered "the problem of building digital communication networks using links with less than perfect reliability" to enable "stations surviving a physical attack and remaining in electrical connection . . . to operate together as a coherent entity after attack."[7] As a solution, Baran advocated decentralized packet switching protocols, not unlike those realized in the Advanced Research Projects Agency Network (ARPANET) program. The emergence of the internet was the result of many other factors that had nothing to do with managing nuclear operations, notably the meritocratic ideals of 1960s counterculture that contributed to the neglect of security in the internet's founding architecture.[8] It is interesting that the present-day cybersecurity epidemic, which owes its roots in part to fears about nuclear vulnerability, has come full circle to create new fears about nuclear vulnerability.

"There Is a Mistake in the Computer Code"

Nuclear command, control, and communications (NC3) form the nervous system of the nuclear enterprise spanning intelligence and early warning sensors located in orbit and on earth; fixed and mobile command and control centers through which national leadership can order a launch; operational nuclear forces including strategic bombers, land-based intercontinental ballistic missiles (ICBMs), submarine-launched ballistic missiles (SLBMs); and the communication and transportation networks that tie the whole apparatus together.[9] Ideally, NC3 should ensure that nuclear forces will always be available if authorized by the National Command Authority (to enhance deterrence) and never used without authorization (to enhance safety and reassurance). Friendly errors or enemy interference in NC3 can undermine the "always-never" criterion, weakening deterrence.[10]

NC3 has long been recognized as the weakest link in the nuclear enterprise. According to a declassified official history, a Strategic Air Command (SAC) task group in 1979 "reported that tactical warning and communications systems . . . were 'fragile' and susceptible to electronic countermeasures, electromagnetic pulse, and sabotage, which could deny necessary warning and assessment to the National Command Authorities."[11] Two years later the principal deputy under secretary of defense for research and engineering released a broad-based, multiservice report that doubled down on SAC's findings: "The United States could not assure survivability, endurability, or connectivity of the national command authority function" owing to

> major command, control, and communications deficiencies: in tactical warning and attack assessment where existing systems were vulnerable to disruption and destruction from electromagnetic pulse, other high altitude nuclear effects, electronic warfare, sabotage, or physical attack; in decision making where there was inability to assure national command authority survival and connection with the nuclear forces, especially under surprise conditions; and in communications systems, which were susceptible to the same threats above and which could not guarantee availability of even minimum-essential capability during a protracted war.[12]

The nuclear weapons safety literature likewise provides a number of troubling examples of NC3 glitches that illustrate some of the vulnerabilities attackers could, in principle, exploit.[13] The SAC history noted that NORAD has received numerous false launch indications from faulty computer components, loose circuits, and even a nuclear war training tape that was loaded by mistake into a live system that produced erroneous Soviet launch indications.[14] In a 1991 briefing to the U.S. Strategic Command (STRATCOM) commander, a Defense Intelligence Agency staffer confessed, "Sir, I apologize, but we have found a problem with this target. There is a mistake in the computer code. . . . Sir, the error has been there for at least the life of this eighteen-month planning cycle. The nature of the error is such that the target would not have been struck."[15] It would be a difficult operation to intentionally plant undetected errors like this, but the presence of bugs does reveal that such a hack is possible.

"We Don't Know What We Don't Know"

General Robert Kehler, commander of STRATCOM in 2013, stated in testimony before the Senate Armed Services Committee, "We are very concerned with the potential of a cyber-related attack on our nuclear command and control and on the weapons systems themselves."[16] Following many near-misses and self-audits during and after the Cold War, American NC3 has been much improved with the addition of new safeguards and redundancies. As General Kehler pointed out in 2013, "The nuclear deterrent force was designed to operate through the most extreme circumstances we could possibly imagine."[17] Yet vulnerabilities remain. In 2010 the U.S. Air Force lost contact with fifty Minuteman III ICBMs for an hour because of a faulty hardware circuit at a launch control center.[18] If the accident had occurred during a crisis, or the component had been sabotaged, the Air Force would have been unable to launch and unable to detect and cancel unauthorized launch attempts. As Bruce Blair, a former Minuteman missileer points out, during a control center blackout the antennas at unmanned silos and the cables between them provide potential surreptitious access vectors.[19]

The unclassified summary of a 2015 audit of U.S. NC3 stated that "known capability gaps or deficiencies remain."[20] Perhaps more worrisome are the unknown deficiencies. A 2013 Defense Science Board report on military cyber vulnerabilities disclosed that while the "nuclear deterrent is regularly evaluated for reliability and readiness . . . , most of the systems have not been assessed (end-to-end) against a [sophisticated state] cyberattack to understand possible weak spots. A 2007 Air Force study addressed portions of this issue for the ICBM leg of the U.S. triad but was still not a complete assessment against a high-tier threat."[21] If NC3 vulnerabilities are unknown, it is also unknown whether an advanced cyber actor would be able to exploit them. As Kehler notes, "We don't know what we don't know."[22]

Even if NC3 of nuclear forces narrowly conceived are a hard target, cyberattacks on other critical infrastructure before or during a nuclear crisis could complicate or confuse government decision making. General Keith Alexander, director of the NSA, who testified in the same Senate hearing with General Kehler in 2013, stated:

> Our infrastructure that we ride on, the power and the communications grid, are one of the things that is a source of concern. . . . We can go to backup generators and we can have independent routes, but . . . our ability to communicate would be significantly reduced and it would complicate our governance. . . . I think what General Kehler has would be intact . . . [but] the cascading effect . . . in that kind of environment . . . concerns us.[23]

Kehler further emphasized that "there's a continuing need to make sure that we are protected against electromagnetic pulse and any kind of electromagnetic interference."[24]

Many NC3 components are antiquated and hard to upgrade, which is a mixed blessing. Kehler points out, "Much of the nuclear command and control system today is the legacy system that we've had. In some ways that helps us in terms of the cyber threat. In some cases it's point to point, hard-wired, which makes it very difficult for an external cyber threat to emerge."[25] The Government Accountability Office notes that the "Department of Defense uses 8-inch floppy disks in a legacy system that coordinates the operational functions of the nation's nuclear forces."[26] Although these older technologies may limit some forms of remote access, they were developed when security engineering standards were less mature. Upgrades to the digital Strategic Automated Command and Control System have the potential to correct some of these problems, but the changes introduced may themselves create new access vectors and vulnerabilities.[27] Admiral Cecil Haney, Kehler's successor at STRATCOM, highlighted the challenges of NC3 modernization in 2015:

> Assured and reliable NC3 is fundamental to the credibility of our nuclear deterrent. The aging NC3 systems continue to meet their intended purpose, but risk to mission success is increasing as key elements of the system age. The unpredictable challenges posed by today's complex security environment make it increasingly important to optimize our NC3 architecture while leveraging new technologies so that NC3 systems operate together as a core set of survivable and endurable capabilities that underpin a broader, national command and control system.[28]

NC3 vulnerability is also a problem for other nuclear-capable nations. The NC3 of other nuclear powers may even be easier to compromise, especially in the case of new entrants to the nuclear club like North Korea. Moreover, the United States has already demonstrated both the ability and the willingness to infiltrate sensitive foreign nuclear infrastructure through operations like Olympic Games (Stuxnet), although this particular cyberattack targeted Iran's nuclear fuel cycle rather than NC3. It would be surprising to learn that the United States has failed to upgrade its Cold War NC3 attack plans to include offensive cyber operations (OCO) against a wide variety of near-peer and nuclear-capable national targets.

Covert Counterforce before Offensive Cyber Operations

NC3 counterforce long predates the use of OCO. The United States included NC3 attacks in its Cold War counterforce and damage limitation war plans, even as contemporary critics perceived these options to be destabilizing for deterrence.[29] The best-known example of these activities and capabilities is a Special Access Program named Canopy Wing. East German intelligence obtained the highly classified plans from a recruited source in the U.S. Army in Berlin, and the details began to emerge publicly after the Cold War. An East German intelligence officer, Markus Wolf, writes in his memoir that Canopy Wing "listed the types of electronic warfare that would be used to neutralize the Soviet Union and Warsaw Pact's command centers in case of all-out war. It detailed the precise method of depriving the Soviet High Command of its high-frequency communications used to give orders to its armed forces."[30]

It is easy to see why NC3 is such an attractive target in the unlikely event of a nuclear war. If for any reason deterrence fails and the enemy decides to push the nuclear button, it would obviously be better to disable or destroy missiles before they launch than to rely on possibly futile efforts to shoot them down, or to accept the loss of millions of lives. American plans to disable Soviet NC3 with electronic warfare, furthermore, would have been intended to complement plans for decapitating strikes against Soviet nuclear forces.

Temporary disabling of information networks in isolation would fail to achieve any important strategic objective. A blinded adversary would eventually see again and would scramble to reconstitute its ability to launch its weapons, expecting that preemption was inevitable in any case.[31] Reconstitution, moreover, would invalidate much of the intelligence and some of the tradecraft on which the blinding attack relied. Capabilities fielded through Canopy Wing were presumably intended to facilitate a preemptive military strike on Soviet NC3 to disable the ability to retaliate and limit the damage of any retaliatory force that survived the initial attack, given indications that war was imminent. Canopy Wing included:

- "Measures for short-circuiting . . . communications and weapons systems using, among other things, microscopic carbon-fiber particles and chemical weapons";

- "Electronic blocking of communications immediately prior to an attack, thereby rendering a counterattack impossible";

- "Deployment of various weapons systems for instantaneous destruction of command centers, including pin-point targeting with precision-guided weapons to destroy 'hardened bunkers'";

- "Use of deception measures, including the use of computer-simulated voices to override and substitute false commands from ground-control stations to aircraft and from regional command centers to the Soviet submarine fleet";

- ". . . Us[e of] the technical installations of 'Radio Free Europe/Radio Liberty' and 'Voice of America,' as well as the radio communications installations of the U.S. Armed Forces for creating interference and other electronic effects."[32]

Wolf also ran a spy in the U.S. Air Force who disclosed the following:

The Americans had managed to penetrate the [Soviet air base at Eberswalde]'s ground-air communications and were working on a method of blocking orders before they reached the Russian pilots and substituting their own from West Berlin. Had this succeeded, the MiG pilots would have received commands from their American enemy. It sounded like science fiction, but, our experts concluded, it was in no way impossible that they could have pulled off such a trick, given the enormous spending and technical power of U.S. military air research.[33]

Another East German source claimed that Canopy Wing had a $14.5 billion budget for research and operational costs and a staff of 1,570 people, while another claimed that it would take over four years and $65 million to develop "a prototype of a sophisticated electronic system for paralyzing Soviet radio traffic in the high-frequency range."[34] Canopy Wing was clearly not cheap, and even so, it was still just a research and prototyping program. Operationalization of similar capabilities and integration into NATO war plans would have been even more expensive. This is suggestive of the level of effort—organizational as well as technological—required to craft effective offensive cyber operations against NC3.

Preparation comes to naught when sensitive programs are compromised. Canopy Wing posed what we have characterized as the cyber commitment problem, the inability to disclose a warfighting capability for the sake of deterrence without losing it in the process.[35] According to *New York Times* reporting on the counterintelligence investigation of Warrant Officer James Hall, the East German spy in the U.S. Army, "Officials said that one program rendered useless cost hundreds of millions of dollars and was designed to exploit a Soviet communications vulnerability uncovered in the late 1970's."[36] This program was most likely Canopy Wing. Wolf writes, "Once we passed [Hall's documents] on to the Soviets, they were able to install scrambling devices and other countermeasures."[37] It is not unreasonable to conclude that the Soviet deployment of a new NC3 system known as Signal-A to replace Signal-M (most likely the system targeted by Canopy Wing) was motivated in part by Hall's betrayal.[38]

Canopy Wing underscores the potential and limitations of NC3 subversion. Modern cyber methods can potentially perform many of the missions Canopy Wing addressed with electronic warfare and other means, but with even greater stealth and precision. Cyber operations might be able to compromise any part of the NC3 system (early warning, command centers, data transport, operational forces) by blinding sensors, injecting bogus commands or suppressing legitimate ones, monitoring or corrupting data transmissions, or interfering with the reliable launch and guidance of missiles. In practice, the operational feasibility of cyberattack against NC3 or any other target depends on the software and hardware configuration and organizational processes of the target, the intelligence and planning capacity of the attacker, and the ability and willingness of the attacker to take advantage of the effects of a cyberattack.[39] Cyber compromise of NC3 is technically plausible though operationally difficult, a point to which we return in a later section.

To understand which threats are not only technically possible but also probable actual circumstances, we need to address a political logic of cost and benefit.[40] In particular, how is it possible for a crisis to escalate to levels of destruction that are more costly than any conceivable political reward? Canopy Wing highlights some of the strategic dangers of NC3 exploitation. Warsaw Pact observers appear to have been deeply concerned that the program reflected an American willingness to undertake a surprise decapitation attack: it "sent ice-cold shivers down our spines."[41] The Soviets designed a system called Perimeter that, not unlike the doomsday device in *Dr. Strangelove*, was designed to detect a nuclear attack and retaliate automatically, even if cut off from Soviet high command, through an elaborate system of sensors, underground computers, and command missiles to transmit launch codes.[42] Both Canopy Wing and Perimeter show that the United

States and the Soviet Union took nuclear warfighting seriously and were willing to develop secret advantages for such an event. By the same token, they were not able to reveal such plans or capabilities to improve deterrence in order to avoid nuclear war in the first place.

Informational Characteristics of the Cyber and Nuclear Domains

Cyberwarfare is routinely overhyped as a new weapon of mass destruction, but when used in conjunction with actual weapons of mass destruction there are severe and underappreciated dangers. One side of a stylized debate about cybersecurity in international relations argues that offensive advantages in cyberspace empower weaker nations, terrorist cells, or even lone rogue operators to paralyze vital infrastructure.[43] The other side argues that operational difficulties and effective deterrence restrain the severity of a cyber-attack, while governments and cybersecurity firms have a pecuniary interest in exaggerating the threat.[44] Although we have contributed to the skeptical side of this debate in previous research,[45] the same strategic logic that leads us to view cyberwar as a limited political instrument in most situations also causes us to consider the cross-domain combination of cyber and nuclear to be incredibly destabilizing. In a recent Israeli wargame of a regional scenario involving the United States and Russia, one participant remarked on "how quickly localized cyber events can turn dangerously kinetic when leaders are ill-prepared to deal in the cyber domain."[46] Importantly, this sort of catalytic instability arises not from the cyber domain itself but through its interaction with forces and characteristics in other domains (land, sea, air). Further, it arises only in situations where actors possess, and are willing to use, robust traditional military forces to defend their interests.

Classical deterrence theory developed to explain nuclear deterrence with nuclear weapons, but different types of weapons or combinations of operations in different domains can have contrasting effects on deterrence and defense.[47] Nuclear weapons and cyber operations have extremely contrasting strategic characteristics. Theorists and practitioners have stressed the unprecedented destructiveness of nuclear weapons in explaining how nuclear deterrence works, but it is equally, if not more, important for deterrence that capabilities and intentions are clearly communicated. As quickly became apparent, public displays of a nation's nuclear arsenal improved deterrence. At the same time, disclosing details of a nation's nuclear capabilities did not do much to degrade a nation's ability to strike or retaliate (defense against nuclear attack remains extremely difficult). Knowledge of nuclear capabilities is necessary to achieve a deterrent effect.[48] Cyber operations, by contrast, rely on undisclosed vulnerabilities, social engineering, and creative guile to generate indirect effects in the information systems that coordinate military, economic, and social behavior. Disclosure allows the adversary to develop crippling countermeasures, while the imperative to conceal capabilities constrains both the scope of cyber operations and their utility in coercive signaling.[49] The ambiguity, diversity, and confusion associated with cyber operations, which often create only minor and reversible material effects, also contrast with the singular, obvious, and irreversible destructiveness of nuclear weapons.

The basic problem is that nuclear credibility and cyber deception do not mix well. An attacker who hacks an adversary's nuclear command and control apparatus, or even its nuclear weapons, will gain an advantage in warfighting that the attacker cannot reveal, while the adversary will continue to believe it wields a deterrent that may no longer exist. Most analyses of inadvertent escalation from cyber or conventional to nuclear war focus on "use it or lose it" pressures or the "fog of war" created by attacks that become visible to the target.[50] In a U.S.-China conflict scenario, for example, conventional military strikes in conjunction with cyberattacks that blind sensors and confuse decision making could generate incentives for both sides to rush to preempt or escalate.[51] These are plausible concerns, especially when emotionally charged cognitive deviations from rational decision making become salient. From a rationalist perspective, however, the discovery of a cyberattack on command and control systems might also reveal a change in the relative balance of power, which could cause the target to hesitate and consider compromise. Preemptive cyber blinding attacks by the defender could also potentially make traditional offensive operations more difficult, shifting the advantage to defenders, this time causing the attacker to hesitate and consider compromise. In each case, the revelation of information that control systems are less reliable, which thus implies that the expected outcome of conflict will be less favorable, should make conflict initiation less likely. Yet clandestine attacks that remain invisible to the target potentially present an even more insidious threat to crisis stability. Asymmetric information about the balance of power can create rational incentives to escalate to nuclear war.

The Transparency of Nuclear Deterrence

Nuclear weapons have a variety of salient political properties. They are singularly and obviously destructive. They kill in more, and more ghastly, ways than conventional munitions through electromagnetic radiation, blast, firestorms, radioactive fallout, and health effects that linger for years. Bombers, ICBMs, and SLBMs can project warheads globally without significantly mitigating their lethality, steeply attenuating the well-known loss-of-strength gradient.[52] Defense against nuclear attack is very difficult, even with modern ballistic missile defenses, given the speed of incoming warheads and use of decoys; multiple warheads and missile volleys further reduce the probability of perfect interception. If one cannot preemptively destroy all of an enemy's missiles, then there remains an irreducible and enormously consequential chance of getting hit by even a few nuclear weapons. The notion of victory becomes meaningless when one missed missile can incinerate millions of people.

As defense seemed increasingly impractical, early Cold War strategists championed the threat of assured retaliation as the chief mechanism for avoiding war.[53] Political actors have issued threats for millennia, but the advent of nuclear weapons brought deterrence as a strategy to center stage. The Cold War was an intense learning experience for both practitioners and students of international security, rewriting well-worn realities more than once.[54] A key conundrum was the practice of brinkmanship. Adversaries who could not compete by *winning* a nuclear war could still compete by manipulating the *risk* of nuclear annihilation, gambling that an opponent would have the good judgment to back down at some point short of the nuclear brink. Brinkmanship crises—conceptualized as games of chicken where one cannot heighten tensions without increasing the hazard of the mutually undesired outcome—require that decision makers behave irrationally, or possibly that they act randomly, which is difficult to conceptualize in practical terms.[55] The chief concern in historical episodes of chicken, such as the Berlin Crisis and the Cuban Missile Crisis, was not whether a certain level of harm was possible, but whether an adversary was resolved enough to risk nuclear suicide. The logical inconsistency of the need for illogic to win led almost from the beginning of the nuclear era to elaborate deductive contortions.[56]

Both mutually assured destruction (MAD) and successful brinkmanship depend on a less appreciated, but no less fundamental, feature of nuclear weapons: political transparency. Most elements of military power are weakened by disclosure.[57] Military plans are considerably less effective if shared with an enemy. Conventional weapons become less lethal as adversaries learn what different systems can and cannot do, where they are located, how they are operated, and how to devise countermeasures and array defenses to blunt or disarm an attack. In contrast, relatively little reduction in destruction follows from enemy knowledge of nuclear capabilities. For most of the nuclear era, no effective defense existed against a nuclear attack. Even today, with evolving antiballistic missile systems, one ICBM still might get through and annihilate the capital city. Nuclear arsenals are more robust to revelation than many other kinds of military forces, enabling nuclear nations better to advertise the harm they can inflict.

The need for transparency to achieve an effective deterrent is driven home by a critical plot twist in the satirical Cold War drama *Dr. Strangelove*: "The whole point of a Doomsday Machine is lost, if you keep it a secret! Why didn't you tell the world, eh?" During the real Cold War, fortunately, Soviet leaders paraded their nuclear weapons through Red Square for the benefit of foreign military attachés and the international press corps. Satellites photographed missile, bomber, and submarine bases. While other aspects of military affairs on both sides of the Iron Curtain remained closely guarded secrets, the United States and the Soviet Union permitted observers to evaluate their nuclear capabilities. These displays are especially remarkable given the secrecy that pervaded Soviet society. The relative transparency of nuclear arsenals ensured that the superpowers could calculate the risks and consequences of nuclear war within a first-order approximation, which led to a reduction in severe conflict and instability even as political competition in other arenas was fierce.[58]

Recent insights about the causes of war suggest that divergent expectations about the costs and consequences of war are necessary for contests to occur.[59] These insights are associated with rationalist explanations for interstate conflict, including deterrence theory itself. Empirical studies and psychological critiques of the rationality assumption have helped to refine models and bring some circumspection to their application, but the formulation of sound strategy (if not its execution) still requires planners to articulate some rational linkage between policy actions and their desired effect.[60] Many supposedly nonrational factors, moreover, simply manifest as random noise or uncertainty in strategic interaction.

Our focus here is on the effect of uncertainty and ignorance on the ability of states and other actors to bargain in lieu of fighting. Many wars are a product of what adversaries do not know or what they misperceive, whether as a result of bluffing, secrecy, or intrinsic uncertainty.[61] If knowledge of capabilities or resolve is a prerequisite for deterrence, then one reason for deterrence failure is the inability or unwillingness to credibly communicate details of the genuine balance of power, threat or interests. Fighting, conversely, can be understood as a costly process of discovery that informs adversaries of the true status of relative strength and resolve. From this perspective, successful deterrence involves instilling in an adversary perceptions that parallel those likely to result from fighting, but before fighting actually begins. Agreement about the balance of power can enable states to bargain effectively (tacitly or overtly) without needing to fight, forging compromises that each prefers to military confrontation or even to the bulk of possible risky brinkmanship crises.

Despite other drawbacks, nuclear weapons have long been perceived to be stabilizing with respect to rational incentives for war (the risk of nuclear accidents is another matter).[62] If each side has a secure second-strike capability—or even a minimal deterrent that preserves some nonzero chance of launching a few missiles—then each side can expect to gain little and lose much by fighting a nuclear war. Whereas the costs of conventional war can be more mysterious because each side might decide to hold something back and mete out punishment more slowly because of some internal constraint or based on a theory of graduated escalation, even a modest initial nuclear exchange will inevitably be extremely costly. As long as both sides understand this and believe that the adversary understands this as well, then the relationship is stable. Countries engage nuclear powers with considerable deference, especially over issues of fundamental national or international importance. At the same time, nuclear weapons appear to be of limited value in prosecuting aggressive action, especially over issues of secondary or tertiary importance, or in response to aggression from others at lower levels of dispute intensity. Nuclear weapons are best used for signaling a willingness to run serious risks to protect or extort some issue that is considered of vital national interest.

Both superpowers in the Cold War contemplated the warfighting advantages of nuclear weapons quite apart from any deterrent effect these weapons were thought to have. Both the United States and Russia continue to prepare for a possible nuclear war. High-altitude bursts for air defense, electromagnetic pulses for frying electronics, underwater detonations for antisubmarine warfare, hardened target penetration, area denial, and so on have some battlefield utility. Transparency per se is less important than weapon effects for warfighting uses, and revelation can even be deleterious for tactics that depend on stealth and mobility. Even a solitary use of nuclear weapons, however, would constitute a political event. Survivability of the second-strike deterrent can also mitigate against transparency, as in the case of the Soviet Perimeter system, because mobility, concealment, and deception can make it harder for an observer to track and count respective forces from space. Counterforce strategies, platform diversity and mobility, ballistic missile defense systems, and force employment doctrine can all make it more difficult for one or both sides in a crisis to know whether an attack is likely to succeed or fail. The resulting uncertainty affects not only estimates of relative capabilities but also the degree of confidence in retaliation. At the same time, there is reason to believe that platform diversity lowers the risk of nuclear or conventional contests, because increasing the number of types of delivery platforms heightens second-strike survivability without increasing the lethality of an initial strike.[63] While in military terms transparency is not required to use nuclear weapons, stable deterrence benefits to the degree that retaliation can be anticipated, as well as the likelihood that the consequences of a first strike are more costly than any plausible benefit. Cyber operations, by contrast, are neither robust to revelation nor as destructive, except when extended to other domains.

The Secrecy of Cyber Operations

Deterrence (like compellence) uses force or threats of force to *warn* an adversary about the consequences of taking or failing to take an action. By contrast, defense (like conquest) uses force to *win* a contest of strength and change the material distribution of power. Sometimes militaries can alter the distribution of information and power at the same time. Military mobilization in a crisis signifies resolve and displays a credible warning, but it also makes it easier to attack or defend if the warning fails. Persistence in a battle of attrition not only bleeds an adversary but also reveals a willingness to pay a higher price for victory. More often, however, the informational requirements of winning and warning are in tension. Combat performance often hinges on well-kept secrets, feints, and diversions. Military plans and capabilities degrade when revealed. National security involves trade-offs between the goals of preventing war, by advertising capabilities or interests and improving fighting power should war break out, and by concealing capabilities and surprising the enemy.

The need to conceal details of the true balance of power in order to preserve battlefield effectiveness gives rise to the military commitment problem.[64] Japan could not coerce the United States into lifting the oil embargo by revealing the Japanese plan to attack Pearl Harbor because the United States, once advised, could not credibly refrain from reorienting its defenses and dispersing the Pacific Fleet. War resulted not just because of what opponents did not know but because of what they could not tell each other without losing their military advantage. The military benefits of surprise (winning) trumped the diplomatic benefits of coercion (warning).

Cyber operations, whether for disruption or intelligence, are extremely constrained by the military commitment problem. Revelation of a cyber threat in advance that is specific enough to convince a target of the validity of the threat also potentially provides enough information to neutralize it. Stuxnet took years and hundreds of millions of dollars to develop but was patched within weeks of its discovery. The leaks by intelligence contractor Edward Snowden in 2013 negated a whole swath of tradecraft that took the NSA years to develop. States may use other forms of covert action, such as publicly disavowed lethal aid or aerial bombing (for example, President Nixon's Cambodia campaign in 1969), to discretely signal their interests, but such cases can only work to the extent that revelation of operational details fails to disarm rebels or prevent airstrikes.[65]

Cyber operations, especially against NC3, must be conducted in extreme secrecy as a condition of the efficacy of the attack. Cyber tradecraft relies on stealth, stratagem, and deception.[66] Operations tailored to compromise complex remote targets require extensive intelligence, planning and preparation, and testing to be effective. Actions that alert a target of an exploit allow the target to patch, reconfigure, or adopt countermeasures that invalidate the plan. As the Defense Science Board points out, competent network defenders "can also be expected to employ highly-trained system and network administrators, and this operational staff will be equipped with continuously improving network defensive tools and techniques (the same tools we advocate to improve our defenses). Should an adversary discover an implant, it is usually relatively simple to remove or disable. For this reason, offensive cyber will always be a fragile capability."[67]

The world's most advanced cyber powers—the United States, Russia, Israel, China, France, and the United Kingdom—are also nuclear states; recent nuclear states like India, Pakistan, and North Korea also have cyber-warfare programs. NC3 is likely to be an especially well-defended part of their cyber infrastructures. This makes NC3 a hard target for offensive cyber operations, which thus requires the attacker to undertake careful planning, detailed intelligence, and long lead times to avoid compromise. The very sensitivity and difficulty of the target heightens the imperatives for secrecy on cyber operations that successfully undermine NC3 reliability.

Cyberspace is further ill-suited for signaling because cyber operations are complex, esoteric, and hard for commanders and policymakers to understand. Most targeted cyber operations have to be tailored for each unique target (which is always a complex organization, not simply a machine), which is quite unlike a general-purpose munition that can be tested on a range and exercised in peacetime to give commanders confidence. Malware can fail in many ways and produce unintended side effects, as when the Stuxnet code was accidentally released to the public when it caused an Iranian computer to get stuck in a reboot loop. The category of "cyber" includes tremendous diversity: irritant scams, hacktivist and propaganda operations, intelligence collection, critical infrastructure disruption, and so forth. Few intrusions create consequences that rise to the level of attacks carried out by Stuxnet or Black Energy, and even they pale beside the harm imposed by a small war.[68]

Vague threats are less credible because they are indistinguishable from casual bluffing. Ambiguity can be useful for concealing a lack of capability or resolve, allowing an actor to pool with more capable or resolved states and acquire some deterrence success by association. But vagueness and ambiguity work by discounting the costliness of the threat. Nuclear threats, for example, are usually veiled because one cannot credibly threaten nuclear suicide. The consistently ambiguous phrasing of U.S. cyber declaratory policy (for example, "We will respond to cyber-attacks in a manner and at a time and place of our choosing using appropriate instruments of U.S. power.")[69] seeks to operate across domains to mobilize credibility in one area to compensate for a lack of credibility elsewhere, specifically by leveraging the greater robustness to revelation of military capabilities other than cyber.

Cyberspace is most useful for conducting actual operations, but it is not categorically useless for signaling, just as nuclear weapons, which are most useful for signaling, are not categorically useless for warfighting. Ransomware attacks work when the money extorted to unlock the compromised host is priced below the cost of an investigation or replacing the system. The United States probably gained some benefits in general deterrence through the disclosure of Stuxnet and the Snowden leaks (that is, the disclosure may have discouraged the emergence of future challenges rather than immediately deterring a specific challenge). Both revelations compromised tradecraft, but they also advertised that the NSA probably had more exploits and tradecraft where the compromised capability came from. Some cyber operations may actually be hard to mitigate within tactically meaningful timelines (for example, hardware implants installed in hard-to-reach locations). Such operations might be revealed to coerce concessions within the tactical window created by a given operation, if the attacker can coordinate the window with the application of coercion in other domains. As a general rule, however, the cyber domain on its own is better suited for winning than for warning.[70] Cyber and nuclear weapons fall on the extreme opposite ends of this spectrum.

The Cyber Commitment Problem

Cyber penetrations of NC3 can potentially be used in either a preventive or a preemptive role. A *preventive* cyber operation supports a *counterproliferation* strategy to prevent a target state from acquiring a fully functional nuclear deterrent. A *preemptive* operation supports a *counterforce* strategy to attack a fully functional nuclear deterrent before the target can exercise it in war. The ideal preemptive strike disarms the target by preventing it from launching any weapons. More realistic preemptive strikes slow or disrupt some proportion of launches to limit the damage the enemy can inflict. Prevention aims to preclude nuclear crises. Preemption aims to prevail in nuclear crises when they do arise.

The alleged sabotage of North Korean missile tests, discussed at the beginning of this chapter, was a preventive operation. As such it has something in common with the Stuxnet operation to disrupt uranium enrichment in Iran. The covert sabotage of a nuclear program can delay the acquisition of an operational capability by prompting a proliferator to waste valuable time looking for errors or even questioning the competence of its scientists. According to one participant in the Stuxnet operation, "The intent was that the failures should make them feel they were stupid, which is what happened. . . . They overreacted. . . . We soon discovered that they fired people."[71] Yet when mistakes in the Stuxnet code led to the public compromise of the operation, Microsoft and Siemens quickly issued patches to close the vulnerabilities that Stuxnet exploited, and the Iranians cleaned up their systems and redoubled their efforts at enrichment.[72] Stuxnet ultimately failed to halt Iranian counterproliferation, and may have complicated negotiations on the Joint Comprehensive Plan of Action (JCPOA), the U.S.–Iranian nuclear deal that ended Iran's nuclear aspirations, at least for the time being. Public awareness of sabotage could harden the proliferator's resolve by underscoring the fact that the saboteur fears the very deterrent the proliferator hopes to acquire. A tactical success can thereby become politically counterproductive.

Although Stuxnet was purely a counterproliferation operation, left-of-launch attacks can also be used for preemption. Stuxnet attacked the fuel cycle by interfering with the control software operating centrifuge rotors and valves. The Stuxnet virus was designed to slow the rate of enrichment of highly enriched uranium (HEU). Once the Iranians had enough HEU to build a bomb, Stuxnet itself would not be useful in operations against Iranian NC3 or missile systems. The alleged American use of left-of-launch OCO, by contrast, targeted a more mature North Korean deterrent. North Korea had already tested several nuclear devices, and its challenge at that point was to miniaturize a warhead and couple it to a reliable delivery platform. The United States may have used cyber and electronic warfare techniques as a last-ditch effort to disrupt these final proliferation preparations. Yet because these OCO targeted missile operations and not the fuel cycle, they could be used for preemption as well as prevention.

They could, that is, so long as the vulnerabilities exploited for prevention remained open for preemption. When Stuxnet was revealed to the world, the usefulness of that particular code for prevention came to an end. The vulnerabilities it relied on were closed. Years of careful code development, target reconnaissance, and patient preparation by the NSA and U.S. Strategic Command were undone in a matter of weeks. The compromise of Stuxnet only closed down a counterproliferation option for the United States (and Israel). Yet when OCO offers potential for both prevention and preemption, a compromised attack precludes both. There is too little detail in available journalistic accounts to know exactly what OCO was doing in the North Korean case and no mention of the North Korean reaction, but it is reasonable to assume that North Korean scientists launched an investigation to discover the malicious code in their NC3 and redoubled efforts to address existing vulnerabilities. In any event, North Korea is now assessed to have a working strategic deterrent with ICBMs capable of delivering a nuclear weapon to North America.

Counterforce, of course, is not the only alternative to a failed counterproliferation strategy. The other alternative is deterrence. A deterrence strategy should aim to convince the North Koreans that the costs of using nuclear weapons outweigh any conceivable political benefit. Effective deterrence policy should clearly and credibly communicate to the North Korean regime that it will face punishing retaliation for any decision to launch a nuclear attack, thereby making it less likely that the North Koreans would initiate a nuclear crisis in the first place. A deterrence strategy would tolerate North Korean possession of nuclear weapons on the understanding that their only role is to deter an attack on the regime. Despite the declaratory aspirations of American policymakers that a North Korean bomb is unacceptable, the de facto strategic posture of the United States with respect to North Korea has already shifted to deterrence rather than counterproliferation.

The introduction of OCO that can be used for both prevention and preemption in this situation raises several issues that are both interesting from the perspective of rational deterrence theory and troubling from the perspective of deterrence policy. First, to be useful for either prevention or preemption, the preparation of OCO must be protected. If the OCO was revealed, the target could take countermeasures such as patching, network reconfiguration, and other defensive measures. Second, the revelation of OCO for prevention precludes their use for preemption. Whatever damage is done in the name of prevention can eventually be undone by the target, given enough time. The distinction between prevention and preemption implies that the target has plenty of time, since prevention deals only with fears of future capability, not with the threat of imminent attack. When the failure of prevention reveals the possibility of preemption, the target will take countermeasures to undo the attacker's prior preparation. Third, the revelation of OCO for prevention that could have been used for preemption puts the target on notice about the potential risks to its operational systems. Not only will the target redouble its efforts to disarm the OCO threat and improve the survivability of its deterrent, but it will also likely assume that there are still some OCO penetrations it has not yet discovered. One can argue that a reduction in the target's confidence should improve deterrence by making the target less likely to initiate a crisis. However, if the target does initiate a crisis, for whatever reason, it will have done so having already discounted the effects of preemptive OCO—for example, by building in redundant controls and launch systems. Preemption revealed is preemption defeated.

These considerations give rise to what we call *the cyber commitment problem*, an extreme version of the military commitment problem, which, as already discussed, is the inability to threaten to use a capability that can be disarmed through the very act of communicating the threat. A credible threat is one the coercer commits to execute if its demands are not met.[73] Threats without commitment are cheap talk. Threats that require the use of secret capabilities are essentially cheap talk because they cannot be executed once the target understands the nature of the threat. If the coercer makes vague claims about a threat, then the target cannot distinguish the threat from a meaningless bluff. If the coercer makes specific enough threats to be believed, then the target can disarm the threat. The cyber commitment problem implies that OCO can be used for prevention or preemption if and only if the operation is kept secret to protect the preparation on which OCO depends. If the OCO are revealed, either through declaratory statements, inadvertent compromise, or leaks to journalists, then they cannot be used to make specific, credible coercive threats.

Dangerous Complements

Nuclear weapons have been used in anger twice—against the Japanese cities of Hiroshima and Nagasaki—but cyberspace is abused daily. Considered separately, the nuclear domain is stable and the cyber domain is unstable. In combination, the results have ambiguous implications for strategic stability.

The direction of influence between the cyber and nuclear realms depends to a large degree on which domain is the main arena of action. Planning and conducting cyber operations will be bounded by the ability of aggressors to convince themselves that attacks will remain secret, and by the confidence of nuclear nations in their invulnerability. Fears of cross-domain escalation by military and ultimately nuclear means will tend to keep instability in cyberspace bounded. However, if a crisis has already risen to the point where nuclear threats are being seriously considered or made, then NC3 exploitation will be destabilizing. Brinkmanship crises seem to have receded in frequency since the Cold War but may remain more likely than is generally believed. President Vladimir Putin of Russia has insinuated more than once in recent years that his government is willing to use tactical nuclear weapons if necessary to support his policies. President Donald J. Trump of the United States has threatened to "totally destroy" North Korea with "fire and fury" and has threatened Iran with "CONSEQUENCES THE LIKES OF WHICH FEW THROUGHOUT HISTORY HAVE EVER SUFFERED BEFORE" (capitalization in original tweet). A future nuclear crisis has sadly become all too conceivable; moreover, if one should come to pass, it will quite likely have a cyber component.

Nuclear Threats May Deter Cyber Aggression

The nuclear domain can bound the intensity of destruction that a cyber attacker is willing to inflict on an adversary. U.S. declaratory policy states that unacceptable cyberattacks may prompt a military response; although nuclear weapons are not explicitly threatened, neither are they withheld. Nuclear threats have no credibility at the low end, where the bulk of cyberattacks occur. The result is a cross-domain version of the stability-instability paradox, where deterrence works at the high end but is not credible, and thus encourages provocation, at low intensities. Nuclear weapons, and military power generally, create an upper bound on cyber aggression to the degree that retaliation is anticipated and feared.[74]

Cyber Operations May Undermine Nuclear Deterrence

In the other direction, the unstable cyber domain can undermine the stability of nuclear deterrence. Most analysts who argue that the cyber-nuclear combination is a recipe for danger focus on the fog of crisis decision making.[75] Stephen Cimbala points out that today's relatively smaller nuclear arsenals may perversely magnify the attractiveness of NC3 exploitation in a crisis: "Ironically, the downsizing of U.S. and post-Soviet Russian strategic nuclear arsenals since the end of the Cold War, while a positive development from the perspectives of nuclear arms control and nonproliferation, makes the concurrence of cyber and nuclear attack capabilities more alarming."[76] Cimbala focuses mainly on the risks of misperception and miscalculation that emerge when a cyberattack muddies the transparent communication required for opponents to understand one another's interests, red lines, and willingness to use force, and to ensure reliable control over subordinate commanders. Thus a nuclear actor "faced with a sudden burst of holes in its vital warning and response systems might, for example, press the preemption button instead of waiting to ride out the attack and then retaliate."[77]

The outcome of fog-of-decision-making scenarios such as these depends on how humans react to risk and uncertainty, which in turn depends on bounded rationality and organizational frameworks that might confuse rational decision making.[78] These factors exacerbate a hard problem. Yet within a rationalist framework, cyberattacks that have already created their effects need not trigger an escalatory spiral. Being handed a fait accompli may trigger an aggressive reaction, but it is also plausible that the target's awareness that its NC3 has been compromised in some way would help to convey new information that the balance of power is not as favorable as previously thought. This in turn could encourage the target to accommodate, rather than escalate. Defects in rational decision making are a serious concern in any cyber-nuclear scenario, but the situation becomes even more hazardous when there are rational incentives to escalate. Although "known unknowns" can create confusion, to paraphrase former defense secretary Donald Rumsfeld, the "unknown unknowns" may be even more dangerous.

A successful clandestine penetration of NC3 can defeat the informational symmetry that stabilizes nuclear relationships. Nuclear weapons are useful for deterrence because they impose a degree of consensus about the distribution of power—or more precisely, the costs—in a nuclear contest; each side knows the other can inflict an unacceptable level of damage, even if they may disagree about its extent. Cyber operations are attractive precisely because they can secretly revise the distribution of power. NC3 neutralization may be an expensive and rarified capability within reach of only a few states with mature signals intelligence agencies, but it is much cheaper than nuclear attack. Yet the very usefulness of cyber operations for making nuclear warfighting a viable prospect ensures that deterrence failure during brinkmanship crises is more likely in the cyber age.

Nuclear states may initiate crises of risk and resolve to see who will back down first, which is not always clear in advance. Playing a game of chicken appears viable, ironically, because each player understands that a nuclear war would be a disaster for all, and thus all can agree that someone can be expected to swerve. Nuclear deterrence should ultimately make dealing with an adversary diplomatically more attractive than fighting, assuming that bargains are available to states willing to accept compromise rather than annihilation. If, however, only the attacker knows that it has disabled the target's ability to perceive an impending military attack, or to react to one when it is under way, then the two sides will not have a common understanding of the probable outcome of war, even in broad terms.

Consider a brinkmanship crisis between two nuclear states where only one state has successfully penetrated the rival's NC3. The cyber attacker knows that it has a military advantage, but it cannot reveal the advantage to the target, lest the advantage be degraded or removed. The target does not know about this disadvantage, and it cannot be told by the attacker because of the "perishability" of the exploit. The attacker and target have different perceptions of the balance of threat or power. A dangerous competition in risk taking ensues. The attacker knows that it does not need to back down. The target is (mistakenly) confident that it can stand fast and raise the risk of war far beyond what it would be willing to commit to if it understood the true balance of power or nuclear threat. Each side is willing to escalate to create more risk for the other side, making it more likely that one or the other will conclude that deterrence has failed and move into warfighting mode in an attempt to limit the damage that the other can inflict.

The targeted nature and uncertain effects of offensive cyber operations put additional pressure on decision makers. An intrusion is likely to disable only part of the enemy's NC3 architecture, not all of it. Especially in cyber operations, ambitious attacks are less likely to succeed and more likely to be noticed by the target. Thus the target may retain control over some nuclear forces, or conventional forces. The target may be tempted to use some of their remaining capabilities piecemeal to signal a willingness to escalate further, even though its capabilities have been attrited as a result of the cyber operation. The cyber attacker knows, or strongly believes, that it has escalation dominance, but when even a minor demonstration by the target can cause great damage, it is tempting to preempt this move or others like it. This situation would become especially unstable if only second-strike but not primary-strike NC3 were to be affected by a cyberattack. Uncertainty about the efficacy of the clandestine penetration would discount the attacker's confidence in its escalation dominance, with a range of possible outcomes. Sufficient uncertainty would reduce the political impact of the cyberattack to nothing, which would have a stabilizing effect by returning the crisis to the pure nuclear domain. More generally, adding a modicum of uncertainty about cyber effectiveness to a crisis would heighten both actors' risk acceptance while also raising their incentives to preempt as an insurance measure.

Adding allies to the mix introduces additional instability. An ally emboldened by its nuclear umbrella might run provocative risks that it would be much more reluctant to embrace if it were aware that the umbrella was full of holes. Conversely, if the clandestine advantage is held by the state extending the umbrella, allies could become unnerved by the willingness of their defender to run what appear to be outsize risks, oblivious to the reasons for the defender's confidence. The resulting discord in the alliance and incentives for self-protective action would lead to greater uncertainty about the alliance's solidarity.

Cyber Power and Nuclear Stability

Not all crises are the same. Indeed, their very idiosyncrasies create the uncertainties that make bargaining failure more likely.[79] So far our analysis
would be at home in the Cold War, with the additional introduction of the
technological novelty of cyber operations. Yet not every state has the same
cyber capabilities or vulnerabilities. Variation in cyber power relations between two states should be expected to affect the strategic stability of nuclear states.

The so-called second nuclear age differs from superpower rivalry in
important ways.[80] There are fewer warheads in the world, down from a peak
of over seventy thousand in the 1980s to about fifteen thousand today (fewer
than five thousand are deployed), but they are distributed very unevenly.[81]
The United States and Russia have comparably sized arsenals, each with a
fully diversified triad of delivery platforms, while North Korea only has a
few dozen or so bombs (for now) and has only recently demonstrated a work-
able delivery system. China, India, Pakistan, Britain, France, and Israel have
modest arsenals in the range of several dozen to a couple hundred weapons,
but they have very different doctrines, conventional force complements, domestic political institutions, and alliance relationships. Several other states
are latent nuclear powers that already have the capacity to develop the bomb
or could sprint quickly to get it, to include Iran, Saudi Arabia, Japan, and
South Korea. Newer nuclear powers lack the hard-won experience and
shared norms of the Cold War to guide them through future crises. Even
the United States and Russia have much to relearn.

Cyberwarfare capacity also varies considerably across contemporary nuclear nations. The United States, Russia, Israel, and Britain are in the top
tier, able to run sophisticated, persistent, clandestine penetrations. China is
a uniquely active cyber power with an ambitious cyberwarfare doctrine, but
because its operational focus is on economic espionage and political censorship, its tradecraft is less refined and its defenses more porous for military
purposes.[82] France, India, and Pakistan also have active cyberwarfare programs, while North Korea is the least developed cyber nation, depending
on China for its expertise.[83]

It is beyond the scope of this chapter to assess potential crises between
particular countries in detail, and data on nuclear and cyber power for these
countries are shrouded in secrecy. As a way of summing up the arguments
presented here, we offer a few conjectures about how stylized aspects of cyber
power affect the stability of crises through incentives and key aspects of

decision making by each country in the various pairs (dyads) that might actually get into a crisis. We do not stress relative nuclear weapon capabilities on the admittedly strong (and contestable) assumption that nuclear transparency, beyond some minimal number of operational weapons, in the absence of cyber operations, should render nuclear asymmetry irrelevant for crisis bargaining (because both sides should agree about the terrible consequences of full-scale nuclear conflict).[84] Yet where extreme nuclear asymmetry makes contemplation of a disarming first strike by the stronger against the weaker state attractive, the risks of cyber counterforce discussed herein should be even greater. We do not discuss interactions with nonstate actors here because we assume that states are unlikely to give nuclear weapons to nonstate clients,[85] and the development of viable cyber NC3 options requires the skill and resources of state intelligence agencies. We also omit domestic or psychological variables that affect relative power assessments, although these are clearly important. Even if neither India nor Pakistan has a viable cyber-nuclear capability, brinkmanship between them is dangerous for many other reasons—notably, compressed decision timelines, Pakistan's willingness to shoot first, and domestic regime instability. Our focus is on the impact of offensive and defensive cyber power on nuclear deterrence above and beyond all of the other factors that determine real-world outcomes.

There are three important questions to ask about cyber power in this context. First, does the cyber attacker have the organizational capacity, technical expertise, and intelligence support to *compromise* the target's NC3? Can hackers gain access to critical networks, exploit technical vulnerabilities, and confidently execute a payload to disrupt or exploit strategic sensing, command, forces, or transport capacity? The result would be some tangible advantage for warfighting, such as tactical warning or control paralysis, but one that cannot be exercised in bargaining.

Second, is the target able to *detect* the compromise of its NC3? The more complicated and sensitive the target, the more likely cyber attackers are to make a mistake that undermines the intrusion. Attribution is not likely to be difficult given the constricted pool of potential attackers, but at the same time the consequences of misattributing "false flag" operations could be severe.[86] At a minimum, detection is assumed to provide information to the target that the balance of power is perhaps not as favorable as imagined previously. We assume that detection without an actual compromise is possible because of false positives or deceptive information operations designed to create pessimism or paranoia.

TABLE 9-1   Cyber Operations and Crisis Stability

Operation	Not compromised	Compromised
Not detected	Deterrence	War
Detected but not mitigated	Bluff (or Use-Lose)	Coercion (or Use-Lose)
Detected and mitigated	Spiral	Spiral

Third, is the target able to *mitigate* the compromise it detects? Revelation can prompt patching or network reconfiguration to block an attack, but this assumption is not always realistic. The attacker may have multiple pathways open or may have implanted malware that is difficult to remove in a tactically meaningful timeline. In such cases the cyber commitment problem is not absolute, since the discovery of the power to hurt does not automatically disarm it. Successful mitigation in this situation is assumed to restore mutual assessments of the balance of power to what they would have been absent the cyberattack.

Table 9-1 shows how these factors combine to produce different deterrence outcomes in a brinkmanship crisis (often described as a game of chicken). If there is no cyber compromise and the target detects nothing (no false positives), then we have the optimistic ideal case where nuclear transparency affords stable *deterrence* (see column 1 of the table). Transparency about the nuclear balance, including the viability of secure second-strike forces, provides strategic stability. These characteristics would also apply to circumstances in which the target has excellent network defense capabilities and thus the prospect of defense, denial, or deception successfully deters any attempts to penetrate NC3, as occurred during the Cold War (with electronic warfare in lieu of cyber). Likewise, even in the present-day U.S.–Russia dyad, the odds of either side pulling off a successful compromise against a highly capable defender are not favorable. Alternatively, the attack may be deemed risky enough to encourage serious circumspection. However, the existence of Canopy Wing does not encourage optimism in this regard.

Conversely, if there is a compromise that goes undetected, then there is a heightened risk of *war* because of the cyber commitment problem. This outcome may be particularly relevant for highly asymmetric dyads such as the United States and North Korea, where one side has real cyber power but the other side is willing to go to the brink when it believes, falsely, that it has the capability to compel its counterpart to back down. Cyber disruption of NC3 is attractive for damage limitation should deterrence fail, given that the weaker state's diminutive arsenal makes damage limitation by the stronger state more likely to succeed. The dilemma for the stronger state is that the clandestine counterforce hedge, which makes warfighting success more likely, is precisely what makes deterrence more likely to fail. North Korea is highly resolved to stand fast in a nuclear crisis, betting that the United States would not be willing to risk trading San Diego for Seoul so long as Pyongyang retains some nuclear capability. Unit-level factors such as regime security and ideology should be expected to reinforce Pyongyang's resolve. The United States, by contrast, would be highly motivated to preempt North Korea if it felt the combination of OCO attacks on NC3 and preemptive strikes could disarm the threat, but it would not be able to convey this resolve to Pyongyang. Unit-level factors such as President Trump's reputation for bluster followed by backing down would further undercut American credibility in a crisis.

The United States would face similar counterforce dilemmas in other dyads, with China or even Russia, although even a strong cyber power should be more circumspect when confronted by an adversary with a larger and more capable nuclear and conventional arsenal. More complex and cyber-savvy targets, moreover, are more likely to detect a breach in NC3; such detection could lead to more ambiguous outcomes, depending on how the actors cope with risk and uncertainty. Paradoxically, confidence in one's own cybersecurity may be a major contributor to failure; believing one is safe from attack increases the chance that an attack will be successful.

If the successful compromise is detected but not mitigated, then the target learns that the balance of power is not as favorable as thought. This possibility suggests fleeting opportunities for *coercion* by revealing the cyber coup to the target in the midst of a crisis while the cyber attacker maintains or develops a favorable military advantage before the target has the opportunity to reverse or compensate for the NC3 disruption. Recognizing the newly transparent costs of war, a risk-neutral or risk-averse target should prefer compromise. The coercive advantages (deterrence or compellence) of a detected but unmitigated NC3 compromise will likely be fleeting. This suggests a logical possibility to create a window of opportunity for using particular cyber operations that are more robust to revelation as a credible signal of superior capability in the midst of a crisis. It would be important to exploit this fleeting advantage via other credible military threats (such as forces mobilized on visible alert or deployed into the crisis area) before the window closes. The temporal dynamics of temporary windows of vulnerability in a crisis and on the likelihood of future crises after the window closes is a topic for future research.

One side may be able to gain an unearned advantage, an opportunity for coercion via a *bluff*, by the same window-of-opportunity logic. A target concerned about NC3 compromise will probably have a network monitoring system and other protections in place. Defensive systems can produce false positives caused by internal errors or by an attacker's deception operation intended to create paranoia. It is logically possible that some false positives would appear to the target to be difficult to mitigate. In this situation, the target could believe it is at a disadvantage, even though this is not the case. An attacker could also use an initial cyber operation to convince a target that its monitoring system is defective, perhaps leading the target to discount actual evidence of an attack. Either of these gambits would be operationally very difficult to pull off in a real nuclear crisis.

Cyber-nuclear coercion and bluffing strategies are fraught with danger. Detection without mitigation might put a risk-acceptant or loss-averse target into a *use-lose* situation, creating pressures to preempt or escalate.[87] The muddling of decision making heightens the risk of accidents or irrational choices in a crisis scenario. Worry about preemption or accident then heightens the likelihood that the initiator will exercise counterforce options while they remain available. Pressures of this type can be particularly intense if a target's detection is only partial or has not unearthed the full extent of the damage (that is, the target does not realize it has already lost capabilities it hopes to use). Scenarios such as these are usually invoked in analyses of inadvertent escalation.[88] The essential distinction between *use-lose* risks and *war* outcomes in this typology is the target's knowledge of some degree of NC3 compromise. Use-lose and other cognitive pressures can certainly result in nuclear war, since the breakdown of deterrence leads to the release of nuclear weapons, but we distinguish between these outcomes to highlight the different decision-making processes or rational incentives that are in play.

A *spiral* of mistrust may emerge if one side attempts a compromise, which the defender then detects and mitigates. Both sides again have common mutual estimates of the relative balance of power or threat, which superficially resembles the *deterrence* case because the NC3 compromise is negated. Unfortunately, detection of the compromise reveals the intent of the cyber attacker. This in turn is likely to exacerbate other political or psychological factors in the crisis or in the instability ("crisis-proneness") of the broader relationship. The strange logical case where there is no compromise but one is detected *and* mitigated could result from a false positive misperception (including a third-party false flag operation) that could lead to the spiraling of a conflict that never actually occurred.[89] The bluff and coercion outcomes are also likely to encourage spiraling behavior once the fleeting bargaining advantage of the attack dissipates or is dispelled (provided anyone survives the interaction).

The risk of crisis instability is not the same for all dyads. It is harder to compromise the NC3 of strong states because of the redundancy and active defenses in their arsenals; conversely, weaker states should be more vulnerable, so long as they are not so weak that they have no digital NC3 whatsoever. Likewise, strong states are better able to compromise the NC3 of any state because of their greater organizational capacity and expertise in cyber operations. Stable deterrence or MAD is most likely to hold in mutually strong dyads (for example, the United States and the Soviet Union in the Cold War or the United States and Russia today to a lesser extent). Deterrence is slightly less likely in other dyads with rough parity (India-Pakistan), where defensive vulnerabilities create temptations but offensive capabilities may not be sufficient to exploit them. Most states can be expected to refrain from targeting U.S. NC3 given the American reputation for cyber power (a deterrence benefit that has been enhanced by incidents like Stuxnet and the Snowden leaks). The situation is less stable whenever the United States is the attacker. The most dangerous dyad is a stronger state attacking a weaker state (United States vs. North Korea or Israel vs. Iran). Dyads involving strong and middle powers are also dangerous (United States vs. China), but less so given the irreducible risks posed by minimal deterrence postures. The stronger side is tempted to disrupt NC3 as a warfighting hedge in case deterrence breaks down, while the weaker but still formidable side has a reasonable chance at detection. The marginally weaker side may also be tempted to subvert NC3, particularly for espionage or reconnaissance; the stronger side is more likely to detect and correct the intrusion but will have difficulty distinguishing intelligence collection from attack planning.[90] In a brinkmanship crisis between such states, windows for coercion may be available yet fleeting, which produce real risks of spiral and war.

Policy Implications and Conclusion

Offensive cyber operations against nuclear weapons systems raise the risk of nuclear war. They do so because the informational properties of cyber operations and nuclear weapons are extreme complements. Cyber operations rely on hiding information, but nuclear deterrence relies on clear communication. Deception and deterrence are at odds with one another. In a brinkmanship crisis, the former undermines the latter. Nuclear crises were rare events in Cold War history, thankfully. Today, the proliferation and modernization of nuclear weapons and precision targeting capabilities may slightly raise the risk of nuclear crisis.[91] Attacks on NC3 increase the danger of nuclear war slightly further. Cyberwar is not war per se, but in rare circumstances it may make escalation to thermonuclear war more likely.

Skeptics are right to challenge the hype about cyberwar. The term is confusing, and hacking rarely amounts to anything approaching a weapon of mass destruction. Cyberspace is most usefully exploited on the lower end of the conflict spectrum for intelligence and subversion. It is not a substitute for military or economic power but a complement to it. Yet the logic of complementarity poses at least one exception for conflict severity, and it is a big one.

NC3 is a particularly attractive counterforce target because disruption can render the enemy's arsenal less effective without having to destroy individual platforms. Weapons that are never launched do not have to be intercepted by unreliable antiballistic missile systems. Fewer weapons launched may mean fewer cities destroyed. U.S. nuclear strategy in practice has long relied on counterforce capabilities (including Canopy Wing) for both preemption and damage limitation.[92] Deterrence theorists expect counterforce capabilities to undermine the credibility of the adversary's deterrence posture by undermining its reliability, which in turn creates incentives for the adversary to move first in a conflict, knowing that it cannot rely on deterrence.[93] If for some reason deterrence fails, however, countervalue strikes on civilian population centers would be militarily useless and morally odious. Counterforce strikes, by contrast, aim at preemptive disarmament or damage limitation by attacking the enemy's nuclear enterprise. Counterforce capabilities are designed for "winning" a nuclear war once over the brink, but their strategic purpose may still include "warning" if they can somehow be made robust to revelation. During the Cold War, the United States found ways to inform the Soviet Union of its counterforce ability to sink ballistic missile submarines, hit mobile ICBMs, and show off some electronic warfare capabilities without giving away precise details.[94] These demonstrations improved mutual recognition of U.S. advantages and thus led to clearer assessment of the consequences of conflict. But the military commitment problem was real nonetheless, and may be even more difficult today given the sensitivity to compromise of cyber operations relative to the electronic warfare techniques of the Cold

War. The problem is particularly pronounced for cyber disruption of NC3 and similar systems. As one side builds more sophisticated NC3 to improve the possibility for sending credible warnings, the other side engages in cyber operations to improve its capacity for nuclear warfighting. Winning thereby undermines warning.

The prohibitive cost of nuclear war and the relative transparency of the nuclear balance have contributed to seven decades of nuclear peace. If this is to continue, it will be necessary to find ways to maintain transparency. If knowledge of a shift in relative power or threat is concealed, then the deterrent effect of nuclear capabilities will be undermined. This will tend to occur in periods when concern over nuclear attack is heightened, such as in the midst of militarized crises. Yet there is no reason to believe that states will wait for a crisis before seeking to establish advantageous positions in cyberspace. Indeed, given the intricate intelligence and planning required, offensive cyber preparations must of necessity precede overt aggression by months or even years. It is this erosion of the bulwark of deterrence that is most troubling.

What can be done? Arms control agreements to ban cyberattacks on NC3 might seem attractive, but the cyber commitment problem also undermines institutional monitoring and enforcement. Cyberattacks rely on deception, and it is hard to credibly promise not to deceive someone, since a deceiver should be expected to offer such assurances. Even where the United States would benefit from such an agreement by keeping this asymmetric capability out of the hands of other states, it would still have a strong incentive to prepare its own damage limitation options should deterrence fail. Nevertheless, diplomatic initiatives to discuss the dangers of cyber-nuclear interactions with potential opponents should be pursued. Even if cyber-nuclear dangers cannot be eliminated, states should be encouraged to review their NC3 and ensure strict lines of control over any offensive cyber operations at that level.

Classified (and where possible unclassified) studies of the details of NC3 of all nuclear weapons states, to include human, organizational, doctrinal, and technological components, together with wargames employing the scenarios described herein, may help nuclear war planners to think carefully about subverting NC3. Unfortunately the same network reconnaissance operations that can be used to better understand the opponent's NC3 can be misinterpreted as attempts to compromise it.[95] More insidiously, private knowledge can become a source of instability insofar as knowing something about an adversary that improves one's prospects in war increases the incentive to act through force or to exploit windows of opportunity in a crisis that could inadvertently escalate.

Anything that can be done to protect NC3 against cyber intrusion will make the most dangerous possibility of successful but undetected compromises less likely. The Defense Science Board in 2013 recommended "immediate action to assess and assure national leadership that the current U.S. nuclear deterrent is also survivable against the full-spectrum cyber . . . threat."[96] Defense in depth should include redundant communications pathways, error correction channels, isolation of the most critical systems, component heterogeneity rather than a vulnerable software monoculture, and network security monitoring with active defenses (that is, a counterintelligence mindset). Older technologies, ironically, may provide some protection by foiling access by nations that use more modern cyber techniques (Russia reportedly still uses punchcards for parts of its NC3);[97] yet vulnerabilities from an earlier era and inadequate safeguards are also a problem. For defense in depth to translate into deterrence by denial requires the additional step of somehow advertising NC3 redundancy and resilience even in a cyber-degraded environment. Advertising the redundancy of NC3 and active network surveillance for intrusions in peacetime should also be undertaken to discourage the substantial planning and prestaging of cyberattack capabilities that are necessary for attacking NC3.

Cyber disruption of NC3 is a cross-domain deterrence (CDD) problem. CDD might also be part of the solution. As noted earlier, CDD can help to bound the severity of instability in the cyber domain by threatening, implicitly or explicitly, the prospect of military, economic, law enforcement, or diplomatic consequences. Cyberattacks flourish below some credible threshold of deterrence and rapidly tail off above it. CDD may also help in nuclear crises. CDD provides policymakers with options other than nuclear weapons, and perhaps options when NC3 is compromised. A diversity of options provides a variation on Schelling's classic "threat that leaves something to chance." In some dyads, particularly those with highly asymmetric nuclear arsenals and technical capabilities, CDD may provide options for "war" and "coercion" outcomes (in the language of our typology) short of actual nuclear war. CDD does not necessarily improve deterrence and in many ways is predicated on the failure of deterrence, but the broadening of options may lessen the consequences of that failure (that is, if a machine asks, "Do you want to play a game?" it would be helpful to have options available other than "global thermonuclear war"). The implications of choice among an expanded palette of coercive options in an open-ended bargaining scenario is a topic for future research.

Finally, every effort should be made to ensure that senior leaders—the president and the secretary of defense in the United States, the Central Military Commission in China, and their counterparts elsewhere—understand and authorize any cyber operations against any country's NC3 for any reason. Even intrusions focused only on intelligence collection should be reviewed and approved at the highest level. Education is easier said than done given the esoteric technical details involved. Ignorance at the senior level of the implications of compromised NC3 is a major risk factor in a crisis that contributes to false optimism and bad decisions. New technologies of information are, ironically, undermining clear communication.

Notes

1. David E. Sanger and William J. Broad, "Trump Inherits a Secret Cyberwar against North Korean Missiles," *New York Times*, March 4, 2017.

2. Glenn Kessler, "Trump's Claim That a U.S. Interceptor Can Knock Out ICBMs '97 Percent of the Time,'" *Washington Post*, October 13, 2017.

3. David E. Sanger and William J. Broad, "Downing North Korean Missiles Is Hard. So the U.S. Is Experimenting," *New York Times*, November 16, 2017.

4. U.S. Joint Chiefs of Staff, "Joint Integrated Air and Missile Defense: Vision 2020" (December 5, 2013) (www.jcs.mil/Portals/36/Documents/Publications/JointIAMD Vision2020.pdf).

5. Austin Long and Brendan Rittenhouse Green, "Stalking the Secure Second Strike: Intelligence, Counterforce, and Nuclear Strategy," *Journal of Strategic Studies* 38, nos. 1–2 (2014), pp. 38–73; Charles L. Glaser and Steve Fetter, "Should the United States Reject MAD? Damage Limitation and U.S. Nuclear Strategy toward China," *International Security* 41, no. 1 (2016), pp. 49–98 (https://doi.org/10.1162/ISEC_a_00248).

6. Fred Kaplan, "'WarGames' and Cybersecurity's Debt to a Hollywood Hack," *New York Times*, February 19, 2016; Stephanie Ricker Schulte, "'The WarGames Scenario': Regulating Teenagers and Teenaged Technology (1980–1984)," *Television & New Media*, August 19, 2008; Michael Warner, "Cybersecurity: A Pre-History," *Intelligence and National Security* 27, no. 5 (2012), pp. 781–99.

7. Paul Baran, "On Distributed Communications Networks" (Santa Monica, Calif.: RAND, 1962), p. 2.

8. David D. Clark, "A Cloudy Crystal Ball: Visions of the Future" (Paper presented at the 24th Meeting of the Internet Engineering Task Force, Cambridge, Mass., July 17, 1992); Janet Abbate, *Inventing the Internet* (MIT Press, 1999).

9. Ashton B. Carter, John D. Steinbruner, and Charles A. Zraket, *Managing Nuclear Operations* (Brookings Institution Press, 1987); Office of the Deputy Assistant Secretary of Defense for Nuclear Matters, "Nuclear Command and Control System," in *Nuclear Matters Handbook 2015* (U.S. Government Printing Office, 2015), pp. 73–81.

10. Paul J. Bracken, *The Command and Control of Nuclear Forces* (Yale University Press, 1983); Bruce Blair, *Strategic Command and Control* (Brookings Institution Press, 1985).

11. U.S. Joint Chiefs of Staff, "A Historical Study of Strategic Connectivity, 1950–1981," Special Historical Study (Joint Chiefs of Staff, Joint Secretariat, Historical Division, July 1982), p. 30.

12. Ibid., p. 65.

13. Shaun Gregory, *The Hidden Cost of Deterrence: Nuclear Weapons Accidents* (London: Brassey's, 1990); Scott D. Sagan, *The Limits of Safety: Organizations, Accidents, and Nuclear Weapons* (Princeton University Press, 1995); Eric Schlosser, *Command and Control: Nuclear Weapons, the Damascus Accident, and the Illusion of Safety* (New York: Penguin, 2014).

14. U.S. Joint Chiefs of Staff, "A Historical Study of Strategic Connectivity," pp. 44–45.

15. George Lee Butler, *Uncommon Cause: A Life at Odds with Convention*, vol. 2: *The Transformative Years* (Denver: Outskirts Press, 2016), p. 119.

16. "Hearing to Receive Testimony on U.S. Strategic Command and U.S. Cyber Command in Review of the Defense Authorization Request for Fiscal Year 2014 and the Future Years Defense Program," § U.S. Senate Committee on Armed Services (2013), p. 10.

17. Ibid., p. 18.

18. Marc Ambinder, "Failure Shuts Down Squadron of Nuclear Missiles," *The Atlantic*, October 26, 2010.

19. Bruce Blair, "Could Terrorists Launch America's Nuclear Missiles?," *Time*, November 11, 2010.

20. Government Accountability Office, "Nuclear Command, Control, and Communications: Update on DOD's Modernization" (June 15, 2015).

21. Defense Science Board, "Resilient Military Systems and the Advanced Cyber Threat" (January 2013), p. 7.

22. "Hearing to Receive Testimony on U.S. Strategic Command and U.S. Cyber Command," p. 10.

23. Ibid., pp. 11, 18.

24. Ibid., p. 18.

25. Ibid., p. 10.

26. Government Accountability Office, "Information Technology: Federal Agencies Need to Address Aging Legacy Systems" (May 2016).

27. Andrew Futter, "The Double-Edged Sword: U.S. Nuclear Command and Control Modernization," *Bulletin of the Atomic Scientists*, June 29, 2016 (http://thebulletin.org /double-edged-sword-us-nuclear-command-and-control-modernization9593).

28. Cecil Haney, "Department of Defense Press Briefing by Adm. Haney in the Pentagon Briefing Room," March 24, 2015 (www.defense.gov/News/News-Transcripts /Transcript-View/Article/607027).

29. Long and Green, "Stalking the Secure Second Strike."

30. Markus Wolf and Anne McElvoy, *Man without a Face: The Autobiography of Communism's Greatest Spymaster* (New York: PublicAffairs, 1997), pp. 329–30.

31. This is a generic problem of "soft kills." See Erik Gartzke, "The Myth of Cyberwar: Bringing War in Cyberspace Back down to Earth," *International Security* 38, no. 2 (2013), pp. 41–73.

32. Benjamin B. Fischer, "CANOPY WING: The U.S. War Plan That Gave the East Germans Goose Bumps," *International Journal of Intelligence and CounterIntelligence* 27, no. 3 (2014), p. 442.

33. Wolf and McElvoy, *Man without a Face*, p. 331.

34. Fischer, "CANOPY WING," p. 441.

35. Gartzke and Lindsay, "Thermonuclear Cyberwar," p. 41.

36. Stephen Engelberg and Michael Wines, "U.S. Says Soldier Crippled Spy Post Set Up in Berlin," *New York Times*, May 7, 1989.

37. Wolf and McElvoy, *Man without a Face*, p. 330.

38. Fischer, "CANOPY WING," p. 449.

39. William A. Owens, Kenneth W. Dam, and Herbert S. Lin, eds., *Technology, Policy, Law, and Ethics Regarding U.S. Acquisition and Use of Cyberattack Capabilities* (Washington: National Academies Press, 2009); Drew Herrick and Trey Herr, "Combating Complexity: Offensive Cyber Capabilities and Integrated Warfighting" (Paper presented at the 57th Annual Convention of the International Studies Association, Atlanta, 2017).

40. Gartzke, "The Myth of Cyberwar."

41. Fischer, "CANOPY WING," p. 439.

42. David Hoffman, *The Dead Hand: The Untold Story of the Cold War Arms Race and Its Dangerous Legacy* (New York: Random House, 2009), pp. 143–54.

43. Scott Borg, "Economically Complex Cyberattacks," *IEEE Security and Privacy* 3, no. 6 (2005), pp. 64–67; Richard A Clarke and Robert K. Knake, *Cyber War: The Next Threat to National Security and What to Do about It* (New York: Ecco, 2010); Joel Brenner, *America the Vulnerable: Inside the New Threat Matrix of Digital Espionage, Crime, and Warfare* (New York: Penguin, 2011); Lucas Kello, "The Meaning of the Cyber Revolution: Perils to Theory and Statecraft," *International Security* 38, no. 2 (2013), pp. 7–40; Dale Peterson, "Offensive Cyber Weapons: Construction, Development, and Employment," *Journal of Strategic Studies* 36, no. 1 (2013), pp. 120–24.

44. Myriam Dunn Cavelty, "Cyber-Terror—Looming Threat or Phantom Menace? The Framing of the US Cyber-Threat Debate," *Journal of Information Technology & Politics* 4, no. 1 (2008), pp. 19–36; Thomas Rid, "Cyber War Will Not Take Place," *Journal of Strategic Studies* 35, no. 5 (2012), pp. 5–32; Sean Lawson, "Beyond Cyber-Doom: Assessing the Limits of Hypothetical Scenarios in the Framing of Cyber-Threats," *Journal of Information Technology & Politics* 10, no. 1 (2013), pp. 86–103; David C. Benson, "Why the Internet Is Not Increasing Terrorism," *Security Studies* 23, no. 2 (2014), pp. 293–328; Brandon Valeriano and Ryan C. Maness, *Cyber War versus Cyber Realities: Cyber Conflict in the International System* (Oxford University Press, 2015); Erica D. Borghard and Shawn W. Lonergan. "The Logic of Coercion in Cyberspace," *Security Studies* 26, no. 3 (2017), pp. 452–81; Rebecca Slayton, "What Is the Cyber Offense-Defense Balance? Conceptions, Causes, and Assessment." *International Security* 41, no. 3 (2017), pp. 72–109.

45. Gartzke, "The Myth of Cyberwar"; Jon R. Lindsay, "Stuxnet and the Limits of Cyber Warfare," *Security Studies* 22, no. 3 (2013), pp. 365–404; Jon R. Lindsay, "The Impact of China on Cybersecurity: Fiction and Friction," *International Security* 39, no. 3 (2014), pp. 7–47.

46. Barbara Opall-Rome, "Israeli Cyber Game Drags U.S., Russia to Brink of Mideast War," *Defense News*, November 14, 2013 (www.defensenews.com/article/20131115 /C4ISRNET07/311150020/Israeli-Cyber- Game-Drags-US-Russia-Brink-Mideast-War).

47. Jon R. Lindsay and Erik Gartzke, "Cross-Domain Deterrence, from Practice to Theory," in *Cross-Domain Deterrence: Strategy in an Era of Complexity*, edited by Jon R. Lindsay and Erik Gartzke (Oxford University Press, 2019); Shannon Carcelli and Erik Gartzke, "The Diversification of Deterrence: New Data and Novel Realities," *Oxford Research Encyclopedia of Politics* (Oxford University Press, September 2017).

48. Robert Powell, *Nuclear Deterrence Theory: The Search for Credibility* (Cambridge University Press, 1990).

49. Erik Gartzke and Jon R. Lindsay, "Weaving Tangled Webs: Offense, Defense, and Deception in Cyberspace," *Security Studies* 24, no. 2 (2015), pp. 316–48; Jon R. Lindsay, "Tipping the Scales: The Attribution Problem and the Feasibility of Deterrence against Cyber Attack," *Journal of Cybersecurity* 1, no. 1 (2015), pp. 53–67.

50. Barry R. Posen, *Inadvertent Escalation: Conventional War and Nuclear Risks* (Cornell University Press, 1991); Stephen J. Cimbala, "Nuclear Crisis Management and 'Cyberwar': Phishing for Trouble?," *Strategic Studies Quarterly* 5, no. 1 (2011), pp. 117–31.

51. Avery Goldstein, "First Things First: The Pressing Danger of Crisis Instability in U.S.-China Relations," *International Security* 37, no. 4 (2013), pp. 49–89; David C. Gompert and Martin Libicki, "Cyber Warfare and Sino-American Crisis Instability," *Survival* 56, no. 4 (2014), pp. 7–22; Caitlin Talmadge, "Would China Go Nuclear? Assessing the Risk of Chinese Nuclear Escalation in a Conventional War with the United States," *International Security* 41, no. 4 (2017), pp. 50–92.

52. Kenneth Ewart Boulding, *Conflict and Defense: A General Theory* (New York: Harper & Row, 1962).

53. Bernard Brodie and others, *The Absolute Weapon: Atomic Power and World Order* (New York: Harcourt, Brace, 1946); Albert Wohlstetter, "The Delicate Balance of Terror," *Foreign Affairs* 37, no. 2 (1959), pp. 211–34 (https://doi.org/10.2307/20029345); Herman Kahn, *On Thermonuclear War* (Princeton University Press, 1960); Glenn H. Snyder, *Deterrence and Defense: Toward a Theory of National Security* (Princeton University Press, 1961).

54. Marc Trachtenberg, *History and Strategy* (Princeton University Press, 1991); Francis J. Gavin, *Nuclear Statecraft: History and Strategy in America's Atomic Age* (Cornell University Press, 2012); Erik Gartzke and Matthew Kroenig, "Nukes with Numbers: Empirical Research on the Consequences of Nuclear Weapons for International Conflict," *Annual Review of Political Science* 19, no. 1 (2016), pp. 397–412 (https://doi.org/10.1146/annurev-polisci-110113-122130).

55. Robert Powell, "Nuclear Brinkmanship with Two-Sided Incomplete Information," *American Political Science Review* 82, no. 1 (1988), pp. 155–78.

56. Thomas C. Schelling, *The Strategy of Conflict* (Harvard University Press, 1960); Frank Zagare, "Rationality and Deterrence," *World Politics* 42, no. 2 (1990), pp. 238–60; Thomas C. Schelling, *Arms and Influence: With a New Preface and Afterword* (Yale University Press, 2008).

57. Branislav L. Slantchev, "Feigning Weakness," *International Organization* 64, no. 3 (2010), pp. 357–88.

58. Powell, *Nuclear Deterrence Theory*; Robert Powell, "Nuclear Brinkmanship, Limited War, and Military Power," *International Organization* 69, no. 3 (2015), pp. 589–626 (https://doi.org/10.1017/S0020818315000028); Gavin, *Nuclear Statecraft*.

59. Geoffrey Blainey, *Causes of War*, 3rd ed. (New York: Simon & Schuster, 1988); James D. Fearon, "Rationalist Explanations for War," *International Organization* 49, no. 3 (1995), pp. 379–414; Robert Powell, *In the Shadow of Power: States and Strategies in International Politics* (Princeton University Press, 1999); Dan Reiter, "Exploring the Bargaining Model of War," *Perspectives on Politics* 1, no. 1 (2003), pp. 27–43; R. Harrison Wagner, *War and the State: The Theory of International Politics* (University of Michigan Press, 2010).

60. Richard K. Betts, "Is Strategy an Illusion?," *International Security* 25, no. 2 (2000), pp. 5–50; Gartzke and Kroenig, "Nukes with Numbers"; Carcelli and Gartzke, "The Diversification of Deterrence."

61. Erik Gartzke, "War Is in the Error Term," *International Organization* 53, no. 3 (1999), pp. 567–87; Jeffrey M. Kaplow and Erik Gartzke, "Knowing Unknowns: The Ef-

fect of Uncertainty in Interstate Conflict" (Paper presented at the 56th Annual Convention of the International Studies Association, New Orleans, 2015).

62. Scott D. Sagan and Kenneth N. Waltz, *The Spread of Nuclear Weapons: An Enduring Debate*, 3rd ed. (New York: W. W. Norton, 2012).

63. Erik Gartzke, Jeffrey M. Kaplow, and Rupal N. Mehta, "Deterrence and the Structure of Nuclear Forces" (Working Paper, University of California, San Diego, 2017).

64. Erik Gartzke, "War, Bargaining, and the Military Commitment Problem" (Political Economy of Conflict Conference, Yale University, 2001); Robert Powell, "War as a Commitment Problem," *International Organization* 60, no. 1 (2006), pp. 169–203.

65. Austin Carson and Keren Yarhi-Milo, "Covert Communication: The Intelligibility and Credibility of Signaling in Secret," *Security Studies* 26, no. 1 (2017), pp. 124–56.

66. Gartzke and Lindsay, "Weaving Tangled Webs."

67. Defense Science Board, "Resilient Military Systems and the Advanced Cyber Threat," p. 49.

68. Jon R. Lindsay, "Restrained by Design: The Political Economy of Cybersecurity," *Digital Policy, Regulation and Governance* 19, no. 6 (2017), pp. 493–514.

69. Ash Carter, "Remarks by Secretary Carter" (Drell Lecture, Stanford Graduate School of Business, Stanford, California, April 23, 2015) (www.defense.gov/Transcripts /Transcript.aspx?TranscriptID=5621).

70. Jon R. Lindsay and Erik Gartzke, "Coercion through Cyberspace: The Stability-Instability Paradox Revisited," in *Coercion: The Power to Hurt in International Politics*, edited by Kelly M. Greenhill and Peter Krause (Oxford University Press, 2018), pp. 179–203.

71. David E. Sanger, "Obama Ordered Wave of Cyberattacks against Iran," *New York Times*, June 1, 2012.

72. Lindsay, "Stuxnet and the Limits of Cyber Warfare"; Rebecca Slayton, "What Is the Cyber Offense-Defense Balance? Conceptions, Causes, and Assessment," *International Security* 41, no. 3 (2017), pp. 72–109.

73. Schelling, *Arms and Influence*, chap. 2.

74. Elbridge Colby, "Cyberwar and the Nuclear Option," *National Interest*, June 24, 2013; Lindsay, "Tipping the Scales"; Lindsay and Gartzke, "Coercion through Cyberspace."

75. Stephen J. Cimbala, *Nuclear Weapons in the Information Age* (New York: Continuum International Publishing, 2012); Jason Fritz, "Hacking Nuclear Command and Control," Research Paper (Canberra, Australia: International Commission on Nuclear Non-proliferation and Disarmament, July 2009); Andrew Futter, "Hacking the Bomb: Nuclear Weapons in the Cyber Age" (Paper presented at the ISA Annual Conference, New Orleans, 2015).

76. Stephen J. Cimbala, "Nuclear Deterrence and Cyber: The Quest for Concept," *Air & Space Power Journal* 28, no. 2 (2014), pp. 87–107.

77. Cimbala, *Nuclear Weapons in the Information Age*, p. 206.

78. Robert Jervis, Richard Ned Lebow, and Janice Gross Stein, *Psychology and Deterrence* (Johns Hopkins University Press, 1985); J. M. Goldgeier and P. E. Tetlock, "Psychology and International Relations Theory," *Annual Review of Political Science* 4, no. 1 (2001), pp. 67–92; Janice Gross Stein, "The Micro-Foundations of International Relations Theory: Psychology and Behavioral Economics," *International Organization* 71, no. S1 (2017), pp. S249–63.

79. Gartzke, "War Is in the Error Term."

80. Toshi Yoshihara and James R. Holmes, eds., *Strategy in the Second Nuclear Age: Power, Ambition, and the Ultimate Weapon* (Georgetown University Press, 2012).

81. Hans M. Kristensen and Robert S. Norris, "Status of World Nuclear Forces," Federation of American Scientists, 2016 (http://fas.org/issues/nuclear-weapons/status-world-nuclear-forces).

82. Lindsay, "The Impact of China on Cybersecurity."

83. HP Security Research, "Profiling an Enigma: The Mystery of North Korea's Cyber Threat Landscape," HP Security Briefing (Hewlett-Packard Development Company, August 2014).

84. Robert Jervis, *The Illogic of American Nuclear Strategy* (Cornell University Press, 1984); Charles L. Glaser, *Analyzing Strategic Nuclear Policy* (Princeton University Press, 1990); cf. Matthew Kroenig, *The Logic of American Nuclear Strategy: Why Strategic Superiority Matters* (Oxford University Press, 2018).

85. Keir A. Lieber and Daryl G. Press, "Why States Won't Give Nuclear Weapons to Terrorists," *International Security* 38, no. 1 (2013), pp. 80–104.

86. Thomas Rid and Ben Buchanan, "Attributing Cyber Attacks," *Journal of Strategic Studies* 38, nos. 1–2 (2015), pp. 4–37.

87. See Robert Jervis, *The Illogic of American Nuclear Strategy* (Cornell University Press, 1984), for a discussion of use-lose dynamics involving nuclear defense.

88. Posen, *Inadvertent Escalation*; Cimbala, "Nuclear Crisis Management and 'Cyberwar'"; Goldstein, "First Things First"; Gompert and Libicki, "Cyber Warfare and Sino-American Crisis Instability"; Talmadge, "Assessing the Risk of Chinese Nuclear Escalation."

89. Robert Jervis, *Perception and Misperception in International Politics* (Princeton University Press, 1976); Shiping Tang, "The Security Dilemma: A Conceptual Analysis," *Security Studies* 18, no. 3 (2009), pp. 587–623.

90. Ben Buchanan, *The Cybersecurity Dilemma: Hacking, Trust and Fear between Nations* (Oxford University Press, 2017).

91. Keir A. Lieber and Daryl G. Press. "The New Era of Counterforce: Technological Change and the Future of Nuclear Deterrence." *International Security* 41, no. 4 (2017), pp. 9–49.

92. Austin Long, *Deterrence—From Cold War to Long War: Lessons from Six Decades of RAND Research* (Santa Monica, Calif.: RAND, 2008); Long and Green, "Stalking the Secure Second Strike."

93. Jervis, *The Illogic of American Nuclear Strategy*; Stephen Van Evera, *Causes of War: Power and the Roots of Conflict* (Cornell University Press, 1999).

94. Brendan Rittenhouse Green and Austin G. Long. "Signaling with Secrets—Evidence on Soviet Perceptions and Counterforce Developments in the Late Cold War," in *Cross-Domain Deterrence: Strategy in an Era of Complexity*, edited by Jon R. Lindsay and Erik Gartzke (New York: Oxford University Press, 2019).

95. Buchanan, *The Cybersecurity Dilemma*.

96. Defense Science Board, "Resilient Military Systems and the Advanced Cyber Threat," p. 42.

97. Scott Peterson, "Old Weapons, New Terror Worries," *Christian Science Monitor*, April 15, 2004.

10

Cyber Terrorism

Its Effects on Psychological Well-Being,
Public Confidence, and Political Attitudes

MICHAEL L. GROSS, DAPHNA CANETTI,
and DANA R. VASHDI

A primary goal of conventional terrorism is to undermine civilians' resilience by instilling in them a sense of fear and vulnerability that erodes confidence in the ability of the government and law enforcement agencies to protect citizens against future attacks.[1] What about cyber terrorism? Are the psychological ramifications of conventional and cyber terrorism identical? Does the threat of conventional or cyber terrorism affect confidence in government

Research for this chapter was made possible, in part, by grants awarded to Daphna Canetti from the National Institute of Mental Health (R01 MH073687), from the Israel Science Foundation (594/15), and from the United States–Israel Binational Science Foundation (2009460); and to Michael L. Gross from the Israel Science Foundation (156/13). We wish to thank Herb Lin, who organized the conference and provided valuable input during the early stages of this project and to the conference participants who commented on earlier drafts of this study during the workshop. We are further indebted to Sophia Backhaus and Ryan Shandler and for their editorial and research assistance in the preparation of this chapter.

and support for stringent security policies in the same way? To address these questions, we advanced three multiple scenario-based empirical studies to test what might happen when the public experiences cyber terrorism that causes mass casualties or severe economic losses with the avowed goal of undermining the public's morale and its confidence in economic and political institutions.

Our findings from three large studies conducted from 2013 to 2016 suggest that cyber terrorism aggravates stress and anxiety, intensifies feelings of vulnerability, and hardens political attitudes. In these ways, cyber terrorism causes responses similar to those caused by conventional terrorism. These findings highlight the human security dimension of cyber terrorism, which policymakers often neglect as they focus on the national security dimension: the protection of frontiers, critical infrastructures, and military capabilities. Both dimensions are important, and as the threat of cyber terrorism grows, policymakers will have to direct their attention to the emotional distress that cyber terrorism causes just as they strive to bolster deterrent and offensive cyber capabilities. In the sections that follow, we draw out the similarities between the psychology of conventional and cyber terrorism that inform our empirical research, present the details of our findings, and discuss their implications for public policy.

Conventional Terror and Cyber Terror: Mirror Images?

Conventional terrorism employs kinetic means (for example, suicide bombers or improvised explosive devices) and works in many ways. Accompanied by death, injury, and property destruction, terrorism generates fear and anxiety in the target population. Terrorists may therefore use terrorism to demoralize a civilian population to pressure their government to undertake or refrain from a specific policy. Sometimes terrorism is effective. Witness the sudden departure of Spanish troops from Iraq following the terror bombings in Madrid that killed 191 people in 2004. More commonly, however, the civilian population proves exceptionally resilient.[2] Terrorism hardens their hearts as they demand and often receive a forceful response from their government. Armed groups, such as Hamas, may also resort to terrorism to scuttle prospects for peace.[3] Alternatively, terrorism can be theater, specifically designed to seize center stage and provoke a disproportionate response from the government of terror victims with the hopes of turning world opinion. For nearly a decade Israel avoided any massive response to Hamas's crude missile attacks on southern Israel. Although the attacks disrupted everyday life, few people lost their lives. Eventually, though, security concerns and domestic pressure led to a full-scale invasion of the Gaza Strip in 2008 and again in 2014. Apart from achieving a short and fragile ceasefire, Israel faced a storm of international condemnation following the deaths of more than 1,000 Palestinians in each encounter. In this way, terrorism sometimes creates a no-win situation for states.[4] Finally, terrorism may produce relatively few immediate casualties but undermine public confidence more broadly. Airplane hijackings such as those in the United States on September 11, 2001, undermined faith in the air transportation system until governments introduced rigid controls.[5] Generally, however, conventional terrorism does not regularly affect confidence in major government institutions. This is attributable to a "rally 'round the flag" effect and to the growing dependence on government institutions to provide security.[6]

Similar to conventional terrorism, cyber terrorism aims to further the perpetrators' political, religious, or ideological goals by harming civilians physically or psychologically. In contrast to conventional terrorism, cyber terrorism employs malicious computer technology rather than kinetic force. *Cyberwar* uses malware and viruses to disable military targets, while *cyber crime* aims for pecuniary gain or personally motivated harm to others (such as revenge or bullying) unrelated to political conflict. Sometimes these categories overlap and the differences are difficult to discern. Cyber terrorists and nation-states may, like criminals, steal money, data, or identities or, like hacktivists, mount distributed denial of service (DDOS) strikes to shut down major systems. Much depends on the intention and identity of the actors, which are not always known. In the cases described here, Hamas and the hacktivist group Anonymous are the perpetrators, and each publicly announced its intent to terrorize Israeli citizens. In Europe and the United States, attribution may be more difficult as the Islamic State of Iraq and Syria (ISIS) and proxy hacktivists have reason to sometimes conceal their identities. In response, the governments have invested in database security for national information systems at public and private companies by developing compliance policies and engaging in direct investment.[7] By investing in the public and private spheres, cyber-terrorism defense differs from kinetic-terrorism defense, whose measures do not usually engage private industry.

Traditionally, cyber terrorism has not been perceived as a threat to life and limb to the same extent as conventional terrorism. However, recent developments have altered this balance as military cyber-offensive tools have acquired more lethal capacities. Although the act of a cyberattack will not in itself cause physical harm, "the actual use of force is likely to be a far more complex and mediated sequence of causes and consequences that ultimately result in violence and casualties."[8] For example, in May 2017 a global ransomware attack called "WannaCry," which was based on a leaked National Security Agency code, infected hundreds of thousands of computers worldwide and crippled hospital operations in some fifty public hospitals in England.[9] In December 2016 a cyberattack in Ukraine labeled "Crash Override" enabled the remote closure of a central electricity transmission station that provided electricity for one-fifth of the city's power needs, disconnecting hundreds of thousands of homes and businesses from the electric grid.[10] In March 2018, U.S. intelligence sources attributed cyberattacks on American and European nuclear power plants and water and electric systems to state-sponsored Russian hackers.[11] These events reflect a new reality in which physical damage arising from cyber activity is at least technically feasible, even if it is not currently widespread. Fatalities as a second-order consequence of persistent and large-scale cyberattacks "may not be far behind."[12]

The 2017 ransomware attacks that crippled English hospitals and froze the computers of hundreds of thousands of civilians around the world was not a stand-alone event.[13] High-profile ransomware attacks, including the WannaCry and Petya attacks, infected upward of half a million users in more than 150 countries,[14] and almost 47 percent of U.S. companies have reported being targeted by ransomware of other cyber-intrusion methods during a twelve-month period.[15] The development of a multi-billion-dollar ransomware industry has added players to the cyber-offensive field, subjecting millions of civilians to new forms of cyberattack and further obfuscating the difference between cyber terrorism and criminal activity.

Ransomware attacks exploit the principle of anonymity that underlies the internet and takes advantage of the difficulty of attributing attacks to a particular source. Since cyberattacks can be launched from anywhere and sophisticated attackers can hide their identity, attribution is as much an art as a science and relies on variables such as political context, motive, or an assessment of operational capabilities as much as it does on digital clues.[16] Consequently, it is often difficult for authorities, and certainly for civilians, to determine whether an attack has been conducted by countries or criminals, and whether the attack constitutes an act of cyber terrorism or cyber crime. In the case of the 2017 attacks, authorities struggled to determine the source of the attack, and the attack was only formally attributed to the North

Korean government after seven months had passed.[17] This ambiguity was exacerbated by the phenomenon of state actors (most prominently China and Russia) that employ semiprivate proxies to conduct intrusive cyber actions to avoid leaving any digital fingerprints that could lead back to them.[18]

The consequence of this ambiguity is profound. Ransomware is ostensibly a modern form of cyber extortion designed to acquire hard (or crypto) currency. Employed mainly by organized crime in Eastern Europe, its use seems most likely to fall under the category of cyber crime and economic extortion. Yet when employed by government authorities, semiprivate proxies related to governments (as it was during the WannaCry attack), or nonstate actors, it becomes a tool that can threaten lives and property and constitutes cyber terrorism. By locking users out of critical systems the WannaCry attack affected English hospitals, German railways, and government offices in Spain and Russia.[19] These kinds of attacks against critical public infrastructure are reflected in our experimental methodology and represent a new model of cyberattack that clouds the line between terrorism and criminal activity.

As this reality takes hold, new studies are exploring the impact of cyber terrorism on civilians' psychological well-being and political attitudes. A 2015 study showed that simulated cyberattacks (ostensibly launched by Anonymous against phones and computers) resulted in increased stress responses measured by salivary cortisol and anxiety.[20] Other research focused on how exposure to cyber terrorism affects the political preferences of exposed subjects.[21] A third research direction has identified significant psychological effects (anxiety, depression) resulting from even short periods of internet deprivation.[22]

The *Tallinn Manual 2.0 on the International Law Applicable to Cyber Warfare*, for example, describes how cyber operations may rise to the level of an armed attack by threatening widespread loss of life or destruction of property.[23] However, the manual considers operations that block email throughout the country (§92.13), transmit tweets to cause panic by "falsely indicating that a highly contagious and deadly disease is spreading through the population" (§98.3), or comprise "cyber-psychological operations intended solely to undermine confidence in a government" or economy (§69.3) as insufficiently severe to constitute terror. We ask whether current events do not belie this equanimity. Claiming, "The internet does not qualify as an object indispensable to the survival of the civilian population" (§6.5), the framers of the *Tallinn Manual* seem unaware of the effects cyber terrorism may pose.

Indeed, many of the claims in the manual appear to apply an archaic pre-digital standard to cyber considerations. For example, in addressing the nature of cyber interference with physical objects and the widespread damage this can cause, the authors conclude that this would constitute an "attack" only if restoring the functionality of the targeted item would require the replacement of physical components (§92.10). Even the director of the project, Michael Schmitt, noted later that this approach is at odds with the evolving nature of modern cyber functionality, questioning why "a temporary denial of service operation does not qualify [as necessary damage] unless it results in physical damage or injury."[24] While the manual stops short of claiming that common cyber acts could constitute a terror attack, it acknowledges the growing physical threat posed by cyber offensives. The second edition of the manual, published only four years after the first edition, entertains a complex scenario in which a cyberattack is used to "acquire the credentials necessary to access the industrial control system of a nuclear power plant . . . with the intent of threatening to conduct cyber operations against the system in a manner that will cause significant damage or death" (§32.10). This is particularly noteworthy owing to the fact that this scenario did not appear in the first edition and so reflects the growing scope of cyberattacks and the level of physical destruction they can levy.

Just as interesting as what was added is what was removed in the short time between the two editions. The first edition of the manual definitively stated that cyber operations involving or otherwise analogous to economic or political coercion could not constitute prohibited use of force (§11.2). This statement was removed from the second edition, reflecting new equivocation about whether a broad variety of cyberattacks could represent a prohibited use of force with tangible physical manifestations (§69.2).

As cyberattacks grow in frequency and intensity, they push beyond criminal acts. They include concerted attempts to disrupt airport and utility services in Ukraine,[25] perpetrate an electronic Holocaust in Israel, cripple DynDNS (Dynamic Domain Name System) servers across important sectors of the United States, and interfere with and possibly compromise the 2016 U.S. elections. A recent large-scale cyberattack on Germany's government information technology network that lasted several days resulted in a loss of sensitive government information.[26] Although not all the perpetrators or their goals are immediately obvious, they do not appear motivated by monetary gain. Rather it seems that they aim to impair public confidence, disrupt civil society, and seed anxiety and insecurity by crippling digital and financial resources, undermining the institutions of governance, and disrupting social networks. Given the growing threat of cyber terrorism, the question, "How does nonlethal and lethal *cyber* terrorism affect individuals psychologically?" is pressing. In an attempt to shed some light on this question we examined the effects of different kinds of cyberattacks on a person's sense of security and confidence.

Research Design

To evaluate the effects of different kinds of cyberattacks on a person's sense of security and confidence, we used two platforms: experimental manipulations and self-reported past exposure to cyberattacks. Focusing on emotional and political responses to cyberattacks and using original video clips, we conducted three online and panel studies.

Our experimental designs enabled randomization and full control of the research. While online surveys—particularly nonprobability ones—may be slightly skewed toward the younger and the technology savvy, phone surveys tend to include more older respondents, women, and left-leaning individuals. Because we were not conducting a correlational study seeking precise estimates of population values, we followed the recommendations of an AAPOR task force that supports the use of online studies for the purposes described in our studies.[27] Each study received University Institutional Review Board (IRB) approval for research involving human subjects. Following IRB approved-protocols, participants signed a consent form before taking the survey, and we made provisions for psychological support with the survey company if needed. None was requested. Participants were also debriefed and informed after the study that all the scenarios were simulated and not actual attacks.

Study 1 (September 2015) was conducted as an online survey in which Israeli adults were randomly assigned to three treatments, after which they answered a series of psychological and political questions. The control group received no experimental stimulus. In the "high" treatment group, subjects viewed a video clip depicting civilian and military deaths following cyberattacks on missile systems and the electric company. In the "low" treatment group, they viewed a video clip reporting a nonlethal cyberattack accompanied by damage to hardware, loss of data, and theft of funds (the total number of study participants was 1,124). In neither case was the perpetrator identified.

Study 2 (January 2016) was also an online survey. Subjects were randomly assigned to view a news report describing a cyberattack on Israel's water purification network by terrorists, identified as Hamas. The news reports they saw were identical, with the exception of the losses suffered. In one clip, it was reported that two people died and many were injured after terrorists released deadly amounts of chlorine into the water system. In the second clip, it was reported that Hamas retrieved the financial information of the company's customers and successfully transferred substantial funds to its coffers overseas. Alternative manipulations included reports of a conventional terror attack on a water facility; like the cyberattack, it killed two and injured many. A control group (909 participants) viewed a benign clip depicting the dedication of a new water desalinization plant. Immediately after viewing the clip, subjects were asked to report their risk perception, threat perception, and confidence in government and to evaluate offensive cyber policies and cyber-regulation practices.

In study 3, using a two-wave panel design, we administered two surveys to the same panel of 522 experimental subjects ten days apart, leading up to and following Anonymous's well-publicized "electronic Holocaust" campaign against Israel in April 2015. Anonymous's language was belligerent and menacing but did not threaten physical harm. Rather the group warned that "elite cyber squadrons" would "invade and attack your devices and personal data, take down your servers and erase Israel from cyber space."[28] Pre- and postattack questionnaires focused on the emotional and cognitive responses to the attacks and related policy choices, ranging from cyber to kinetic retaliation.

Independent Variables

Type of terrorism was manipulated in studies 1 and 2 by the experimental condition as explained above. In study 1 there were three conditions: (1) control, (2) cyber terrorism (nonlethal attack), and (3) cyber terrorism (lethal attack). In study 2 there was an additional condition, (4) kinetic terrorism.

Previous exposure to a cyberattack was assessed in all three studies by asking subjects four questions on a scale of 1 to 6 regarding the extent to which they, their friends, or their family had suffered harm or loss from a cyberattack. An answer above 3 on any of these questions was regarded as previous exposure.

Dependent Variables

Measures of well-being, stress, and threat perception. In study 1 (unidentified perpetrator) and study 2 (Hamas), we used a four-point scale STAI (state-trait anxiety index).[29] STAI measures two types of anxiety: state (extrinsic) anxiety and trait (intrinsic) anxiety. State anxiety aligns with temporary feelings of fear, nervousness, and discomfort. Trait anxiety aligns with almost daily feelings of stress, worry, and discomfort. The questionnaire includes six items describing various feelings and emotions. The experimental subjects were asked to rate on a scale of 1 to 4 (1 = not at all; 4 = very much so) the extent to which their feelings "at present" (both pre- and postexperimental treatment) correspond to different items. Half of the items represent negative feelings and emotions (for example, I feel upset, I feel nervous) and the other half represent positive feelings and emotions (for example, I feel relaxed, I feel comfortable). Because we were interested in negative affect, we created a variable constituting only the three negative emotions.

In addition to stress, perceptions of threat play a significant role in our understanding of the psychology of terrorism. Perceptions of threat reflect the extent to which thinking about a cyberattack undermines one's sense of personal security. Threat perception is an appraisal of the danger that an outgroup poses to an individual and his or her political community.[30] To gauge threat perception in all three studies we asked, "To what extent do cyberattacks undermine your sense of personal security?" and "To what extent do you feel threatened by cyber terrorism?" (on a scale of 1 to 5).

Measures of public confidence. To assess the effects of cyberattacks, study 2 (Hamas) probed a range of confidence-related questions. First, confidence in government, the army, police, and supreme court were examined, with separate items for each on a scale from 1 = not confident at all to 6 = extremely confident. Following each manipulation, we asked a range of questions about confidence in the government's ability to safeguard information entrusted to government offices: prevent identity and data theft, credit card and bank fraud, and protect critical infrastructure (water, military, transportation, electric) from future attacks (1 = not confident at all; 6 = extremely confident). To add a more precise cyber perspective to the confidence measure, we asked about confidence in a bank, utility company, or health maintenance organization (HMO) that suffered a cyberattack. We also included two behavioral questions that address the public's confidence in government assurances following a cyberattack on the national water supply by posing behavioral choices:

1. "Following a cyberattack on the water system, the authorities advised drinking bottled water. How soon would you drink tap water?"

2. "Following a cyberattack on the water system the authorities suggested waiting three days before showering: After three days, would you [choose one option]?"

After reading each question, subjects were asked to choose one of four modes of behavior that reflect various degrees of compliance (full responses are provided in the results section).

Measures of attitudes toward government policies. In all three studies we asked subjects to consider government surveillance of internet and email communications, government regulation of businesses, and military retaliation in response to cyberattacks. Questions about government surveillance asked whether the government ought to read emails and monitor social networks for security threats. Regulation of the business sector reflected answers to the question, "Should the government require businesses to maintain a mandated level of cybersecurity?" Retaliatory policy offered four options: (1) a limited cyberattack to disable enemy military cyber capabilities (servers, switches, computers, cables); (2) a large-scale cyberattack to disable enemy military and civilian cyber capabilities; (3) a limited conventional attack (missiles or bombs) to disable enemy military cyber capabilities; and (4) a large-scale conventional attack (missiles or bombs) to disable enemy military and civilian cyber capabilities. All questions were rated on a scale of 1 (not at all) to 6 (most definitely).

Measures of risk perception. Following Slovic, we distinguish between risk assessment and risk perception.[31] "Whereas technologically sophisticated analysts employ risk assessment to evaluate hazards, the majority of citizens rely on intuitive judgments typically called risk perceptions."[32] To assess risk perception we posed sixteen questions that asked the experimental subjects in study 2 (Hamas) to assess the risk posed by a cyber terror attack (1 = no risk; 6 = a very high risk). Responses concentrated on four factors: bodily harm (risk of injury or loss of life); material loss (credit card and bank fraud, data theft, theft of confidential medical information); damage to critical infrastructures (transportation, refineries, water), and damage to state facilities (military, stock exchange, government offices). Cronbach's alphas were 0.70, 0.91, 0.81, and 0.94 respectively.

Demographic Variables

We asked respondents about their political orientation on a scale ranging from very right wing to very left wing.

Results

Our findings suggest that the effects of nonlethal and lethal cyber terrorism track those of conventional terrorism. Overall, experimental subjects exhibit marked signs of stress, personal insecurity, and heightened perceptions of cyber threat. Heightened perceptions of threat, in turn, lend support for forceful cyber government policies, a finding consistent with the effects of kinetic terrorism.[33]

Stress and Anxiety

Table 10-1 shows that anxiety increases as attacks become more severe. In comparison with the control group, every form of terrorism, whether cyber or kinetic, lethal or nonlethal, increased people's anxiety and other negative emotions. Conventional (kinetic) terrorism had the greatest effect on all measures of negative affect and anxiety, followed by lethal and nonlethal cyber terrorism. However the effects of lethal and nonlethal cyber terrorism were not statistically distinguishable. Each affected STAI measures similarly, their effects significantly more severe than those seen in the control group. Each kind of cyber terrorism increased people's level of anxiety. As an ongoing feature of Israeli life, conventional terrorist attacks provoke anxiety more readily than cyber terror attacks. Nevertheless, it appears that all remain points on the same terrorist spectrum. Nonlethal cyber terrorism is no exception.

Threat Perception

Both exposure to past cyberattacks and exposure to simulated cyberattacks increased perceptions of threat. As noted earlier, we gauged exposure to past cyberattacks by asking subjects whether they, their friends, or their family had suffered harm or loss from a cyberattack. Eighteen percent of the respondents in study 3 (Anonymous) reported harm or loss from a cyberattack, as did 19 percent in study 2 (Hamas). Among our subjects, perceptions of threat were 3–9 percent stronger among those previously exposed to a cyberattack than among those who were not exposed. The experimental manipulations affected threat perception similarly (table 10-2).

TABLE 10-1   Stress and Anxiety Measures Following a Cyber Terror Attack
Scale: 1–4 (low–high)

	State/Trait Anxiety Measure (STAI)	
Type and outcome of attack presented to each treatment group	Study 1, perpetrator unidentified (n = 1,027)	Study 2, perpetrator Hamas (n = 907)
Control: no terrorism	2.3	2.7
Cyber terrorism, nonlethal: asset and data loss (study 1); disclosure of account information, loss of funds (study 2)	3.5	3.4
Cyber terrorism, lethal: deaths and injuries	3.6	3.6
Conventional (kinetic) terrorism, lethal: deaths and injuries		4.0
Significance	p < .001	p < .001
ANOVA	$F_{2,1035} = 139.65$	$F_{3,942} = 34.23$

In post hoc tests using the Tukey statistic, there is a significant difference in stress and anxiety between all treatment groups except in their response to nonlethal and lethal cyber terrorism, which is not significant for any of the stress and anxiety measures.

Simulated exposure to lethal attacks, whether cyber or kinetic, evoked perceptions of threat 16–22 percent stronger than those unexposed to terrorism in the control group. Among those exposed to nonlethal cyber terrorism, perceptions of threat were 10–17 percent stronger than among those in the control group. These results varied with the nature of the nonlethal cyber terrorism. Perceptions of cyber threat were strongest when nonlethal cyberattacks resulted in the loss of assets and data (study 1, unidentified perpetrator), rather than the loss of money (study 2, Hamas). Whereas loss of data and other digital assets might be irreplaceable or costly to replace, banks and other financial institutions usually reimburse customers for funds lost to hackers. Our results indicate that the fact that the perpetrator was Hamas, a hostile agent that one might expect to induce threat perception, did not change this assessment. Indeed, when nonlethal cyber terrorism is defined in terms of financial loss alone, its effects on threat perception were not statistically different than among those in the control group (see note, table 10-2). Additional data are necessary to substantiate the relationship between perceptions of threat and nonlethal cyber terrorist attacks.

TABLE 10-2   Threat Perception Measures Following Experimental
Cyber Terror Attacks
Scale: 1–5 (low–high)

Type and outcome of attack presented to each treatment group	*Study 1,*[a] *perpetrator unidentified (n = 1,027)*	*Study 2,*[b] *perpetrator Hamas (n = 907)*
Control: no terrorism	2.9	3.1
Cyber terrorism, nonlethal: disclosure of account information and loss of funds		3.4
Cyber terrorism, nonlethal: asset and data loss	3.4	
Cyber terrorism, lethal: deaths and injuries	3.5	3.6
Conventional terrorism, lethal: deaths and injuries		3.8
Significance	p < .001	p < .001
ANOVA	$F_{2,1029} = 21.60$	$F_{3,937} = 11.12$

a. In post hoc tests using the Tukey statistic for the data of study 1, there was no significant difference in the subjects' threat perception in response to nonlethal and lethal cyber terrorism, but both were significantly different from the threat perception of the control group.

b. In post hoc tests using the Tukey statistic for the data of study 2, there was no significant difference between the threat perceptions of the control group and the threat perceptions of those exposed to nonlethal cyber terrorism, no significant difference between the groups exposed to nonlethal and lethal cyber terrorism, and no significant difference between the groups exposed to lethal cyber terrorism and conventional terrorism. The threat perceptions of those exposed to lethal cyber terrorism and conventional terrorism were significantly different from those of the control group, and the threat perceptions of those exposed to conventional terrorism were significantly different from those of the group exposed to nonlethal cyber terrorism.

The data in tables 10-1 and 10-2 clearly suggest that cyberattacks, whether lethal or nonlethal, cause stress, anxiety, and insecurity. In their wake, when cyber terrorism turns deadly, threat perception rises to a level very close to that caused by conventional terrorism. These data demonstrate that cyber terrorism, like conventional terrorism, impairs psychological well-being and increases perceptions of threat. The fear stemming from threat perception may lead to incorrect assessments of risk and risk-averse attitudes that, in turn, reduce confidence in government institutions.

Cyber Terrorism and Public Confidence

Confidence in the government's ability to protect critical infrastructures and data or to prevent a cyberattack did not vary when the manipulations presented increasingly dangerous and life-threatening forms of terrorism. In fact, the slight effect we found (item 4) shows an *increase* in confidence only following a nonlethal cyber terrorist attack (see table 10-3).

To gauge confidence, we posed two other questions:

1. Following a cyberattack on the water system, the authorities advised drinking bottled water. How soon would you drink tap water? ($n = 909$)

Option	Percent
a. When the authorities say it is OK	70
b. Three months after the authorities say it is OK	19
c. One year after the authorities say it is OK	5
d. Never	6

2. Following a cyberattack on the water system the authorities suggested waiting three days before showering: After three days, would you . . . ($n = 909$)

Option	Percent agreeing
a. Shower?	63
b. Wait one week?	24
c. Install a filter that doubled your water bill?	9
d. Install a filter that tripled your water bill?	4

In each case, 30–37 percent of the respondents said they would not trust the authority's instructions. Rather, they preferred to take additional measures to protect themselves. The answers to these two questions were unaffected by the manipulations.

To further investigate the behavioral dimensions of confidence, we asked subjects how they would publicly react to cyber terrorism. Would they be quiescent, or would they take to the streets in a way that might undermine political stability and foment unrest in the way terrorists often hope? Table 10-4 portrays public political behavior in the wake of three kinds of cyber terror attacks: an attack on the national electric company, on a private HMO, and on a private bank. In each case subjects were asked to choose which political action they would be most likely to take.

TABLE 10-3   Confidence Measures, Study 2 (Hamas)
Scale: 1–6 (not confident–extremely confident), *n* = 907

	Condition				
Confidence measure	*Control*	*Cyber terrorism, nonlethal*	*Cyber terrorism, lethal*	*Conventional terrorism*	*Significance / ANOVA*
Confidence in government to protect infrastructures (water, electric, transportation, stock exchange, classified military data)	4.1	4.1	4.2	4.2	NS
Confidence in government to protect personal data	3.6	3.6	3.5	3.5	NS
Confidence in public/ private institutions (army, scientific community, high-tech sector, government, police) to prevent a serious cyber terror attack	4.4	4.6	4.5	4.5	NS
Confidence in those responsible for cybersecurity to know what they are doing	4.8	5.1	5.0	5.0	<.01 / $F_{3,904} = 2.68^a$

a. In post hoc tests using the Tukey statistic, the only significant difference was between the control group and the group presented with a nonlethal cyber terrorism scenario.

Although these questions did not specify whether the attack on the facility was lethal or nonlethal, few people responded that they would be sufficiently riled to take to the streets. A substantial minority (22–30 percent) would complain to the authorities, and some would join a lawsuit (12–18 percent), but few would participate in demonstrations. None of the attacks prompted outrage or lack of confidence in the government. On the contrary, the manipulations prompted support for greater government intervention to

TABLE 10-4   Political Action Following Cyberattack on Selected Facilities
Percent ($n = 907$)

Action	Electric company	HMO	Bank
Complain to the facility	30	25	22
Find a different HMO or bank		7	15
File a lawsuit	12	14	18
Complain to the city	4		
Turn to the press	4	3	3
Participate in a demonstration	14	4	4
File a complaint with the ombudsman		10	7
Complain to the police		12	11
Other or none	37	24	18

ensure security. It is no surprise, then, that confidence in the government is largely unaffected by cyber terrorism and may even increase in its wake.

Cyber Terrorism and Political Attitudes: Security, Civil Liberties, Government Regulation, and Military Retaliation

Confronted with the threat of lethal and nonlethal cyber terrorism, our data suggest that individuals will support strong government measures to police and regulate cyberspace and to respond forcefully to cyberattacks. In all three studies we asked subjects to consider government surveillance of the internet and email communications, government regulation of businesses, and military retaliation in the wake of cyberattacks. These results appear in table 10-5.

Overall, the high percentages of support reflect widespread backing for these policies. Well over 50 percent support government monitoring of emails for suspicious expressions and roughly 50 percent are willing to give up privacy for security and allow the government to monitor social media (Facebook, Twitter). At the same time, 23 percent will permit the government to read emails, a figure that doubles to 46 percent when the perpetrator is Hamas. These numbers are higher than in the United States, where, in a 2015 Pew Research Center survey, 43 percent of the subjects said it is acceptable for the government to monitor the communications of U.S. citizens (in comparison with 48–67 percent in our survey).[34]

TABLE 10-5 Support for Domestic Cyber Policy and for Retaliatory Cyber Policy in Response to a Cyber Terror Attack
Percent who agree, very much agree, or absolutely agree

Policy	Study 1, perpetrator unidentified (%) (n = 1,027)	Study 2, perpetrator Hamas (%) (n = 907)	Study 3, perpetrator Anonymous (%) (n = 522)
Domestic cyber policy			
Surveillance			
Monitor for suspicious expressions		67	54
Read emails		46	23
Monitor Facebook, Twitter		61	48
Regulation of business to maintain cybersecurity	69	62	78
Trade some privacy for security	54	44	
Retaliatory policy			
Cyberattack on military facilities		84	86
Cyberattack on military and civilian facilities		78	69
Conventional attack on military facilities		60	37
Conventional attack on military and civilian facilities		65	31

Looking beyond surveillance to retaliatory policy, we see how military strikes, particularly cybernetic but also kinetic, command significant support from the public. In response to cyber terrorism, the vast majority (69–89 percent) support retaliatory cyberattacks against military and civilian targets, and a significant number (31–65 percent) support conventional kinetic counterattacks. These attitudes remain unstudied in the United States, but there is little doubt that they will play a significant role as public officials and scholars weigh the merit of responding to cyberwar and cyber terrorism with kinetic force.[35]

To explain why individuals hold different attitudes about surveillance and military retaliation, we looked at a number of factors. The experimental manipulations within each study had no direct effect on political attitudes and did not affect the extent to which individuals supported different types of retaliation. That is, support for surveillance, regulation, or military action was not affected by exposure to a simulated cyberattack.[36] Similarly, self-reported exposure to cyberattacks did not affect attitudes toward these policies. Instead, variables that explain greater support for government interference include political and religious conservatism, threat perception, and the identity of the perpetrator. Support from right-wing religious conservatives is consistent with the right's traditional demand for security and their support for the current right-wing government. Among our subjects, the odds that right-wing conservatives would support militant policies were up to two times greater than for those on the left. Beyond the role of political orientation, however, lie the effects of threat perception. As threat perception (in contrast to direct exposure to cyber violence) grows, individuals demand greater security from their government. Here, the odds were 1.3 to 2.2 times greater that individuals with high levels of threat perception will support surveillance, government regulation, and military retaliation than those with lower perceptions of threat.

Our data also suggest that the identity of the perpetrator matters. Note that support for government surveillance and in particular retaliatory *military* strikes, is appreciably greater when the manipulation focused on a known terrorist group, Hamas, (study 2) than on a hacktivist group, Anonymous (study 3). Our question was framed generally and asked whether subjects would support military retaliation following a cyberattack. We did not ask whether they would support an attack against Hamas or Anonymous or their sponsors. Nevertheless, and as table 10-5 demonstrates, subjects participating in the Hamas experiment favored government surveillance far more than those in study 3 (Anonymous) and supported conventional military attacks of either sort (limited or large scale) by a margin of nearly 2 to 1. One reason may be that the manipulation triggered fears of Hamas and burgeoning Islamic radicalism. Another reason may be the recognition that Hamas, like ISIS, has infrastructure and territory that are vulnerable to conventional attack. Because our study found a relationship between threat perceptions and support for surveillance *and* military retaliation, it seems that it is not Hamas's material vulnerability but the fear related to threat perception that better explains why those exposed to Hamas cyber terrorism are more likely to support surveillance and military retaliation than those facing Anonymous. Nevertheless, this may change. In a phenomenon

George Lucas describes as "state-sponsored hacktivism," nations recruit hacktivist groups to mount cyberattacks on their behalf.[37] As this trend continues, fears of such groups may grow accordingly, as might the willingness to retaliate against their sponsors.

Cyber Terrorism and Risk Perception

Risk is a psychological concept that is based on individual perception rather than empirical facts.[38] Researchers of risk perception have long noted that individuals' perceptions of the risk of common hazards[39] or disease[40] are often markedly different from the assessments of experts. For individual nonexperts, personal judgment determines which stimuli are defined as threatening independent of the knowledge of the actual risk.[41] How, then, does the public understand the risk of cyber terrorism? If cyber terrorism, unlike conventional terrorism, disease, or natural disasters, has yet to cause physical harm, there is good reason to suspect that the public does not understand the risk it poses. Experts are themselves divided.[42] Some remain skeptical about the capabilities of terrorist groups or violent hacktivists to mount offensive, catastrophic cyberattacks,[43] while others describe how cyber terrorism may seriously compromise electrical infrastructures,[44] lead to extensive financial loss,[45] disable military defense systems,[46] and, ultimately, undermine conventional and nuclear stability.[47] Divisions among experts might only confound risk perceptions among the lay population. In addition, media reporting on the threat of cyber terrorism is immense and carries an overarching message of concern that affects the perceived risk of cyber terrorism.[48]

In our study, risk perceptions varied with the manipulations of study 2 (Hamas). Those exposed to increasingly severe manipulations assess some cyber threats more severely than the control groups (table 10-6).

These data demonstrate that experimental manipulations exacerbate some assessments of risk related to cyber terrorism. After viewing video clips of cyber or conventional terror attacks with lethal consequences, subjects' perceptions of risk to life, limb, and infrastructure were significantly greater than of those who viewed the more benign clips (rows 3 and 4 in table 10-6). When asked to assess the chances that a cyberattack would cause destruction of critical infrastructure, subjects' average response ranged from 4.4 in the control group to 4.8 in the conventional terrorism group. Similarly, when asked to assess the chances of a cyberattack causing loss of life and limb, the average response ranged from 2.7 in the control group to 3.2 in the conventional

TABLE 10-6   Risk Assessment of Different Types of Cyber Terror Attacks
Perpetrated by Hamas
Scale: 1–6 (very low–very high)

Outcome of attack	Control	Cyber terror, nonlethal	Cyber terror, lethal	Conventional terrorism	Significance / ANOVA	Total average[c]
Theft of data, assets, identity	3.0	3.1	3.1	3.2	NS	3.1
Attack on state facilities: military, stock exchange, government offices	3.7	3.7	3.5	3.8	NS	3.6
Destruction of/ damage to critical infrastructure[a]	4.4	4.7	4.6	4.8	<.001 / $F_{3,907} = 5.9$	4.6
Loss of life or limb[b]	2.7	2.7	3.1	3.2	<.001 / $F_{3,908} = 19.22$	2.9

a. In post hoc tests using the Tukey statistic, there was no significant difference between the nonlethal cyber terrorism group, the lethal cyber terrorism group, and the conventional terrorism group. These three groups were all significantly different from the control group.

b. In post hoc tests using the Tukey statistic, there was no significant difference between the assessments of the control group and the nonlethal cyber terrorism group, and no significant difference between the assessments of the lethal cyber terrorism group and the conventional terrorism group. Significant differences were found between lethal cyber terrorism and the control and nonlethal cyber terrorism, and between the conventional terrorism and the control and nonlethal cyber terrorism.

c. A repeated measures ANOVA with a Greenhouse-Geisser correction was statistically significant ($F2.908, 2640.671 = 904.457, p < .001$). All the mean scores between the all the different categories of risk assessment were significantly different from each other.

terrorism group. On the other hand, the manipulations did not affect the risk associated with data theft or attacks on the stock exchange or government offices (rows 1 and 2). These stayed constant across the manipulations. These attitudes reflect concerns about the future threat of cyber terrorism. The risk associated with identity theft, asset loss, and attacks on government offices is stable, while the risk associated with significant bodily or infrastructural harm is not. Individuals seem to think they understand the risks of nonlethal cyber terrorism but seem unsure about the risks of lethal cyber terrorism when, in fact, our data indicate much the opposite. They underestimate the danger of nonlethal cyber terrorism but often overestimate the danger of lethal terrorism, particularly when the perpetrator is a known terrorist organization. As such, it is important to note that the perception of threat in part contradicts reality. For many subjects, the risk of an attack that destroys or damages critical infrastructure (average response 4.6), which has yet to materialize to any significant degree, is significantly *greater* than the risk of an attack on stock exchanges, government offices, personal computers, banks, and credit cards (average response 3.6) that are clear and present dangers. Although these outcomes might be partially explained by a manipulation that primes subjects for threats to infrastructure, our control group viewed no attack and still assessed some risks at an unrealistically high level. At the same time, the average perception of risk associated with the theft of data, assets, and identity (3.1) was little different from the average perception of risk that a cyberattack would bring death or injury (2.9). Subjects perceive the risk of these hazards equally despite the fact that the former is relatively common and the latter nonexistent.

Discussion: The Psychological Effects of Cyber Terrorism

Our results show that cyber terrorism, even when nonlethal, affects the civilian population in several ways. First, cyber terrorism aggravates anxiety and personal insecurity. Second, lethal and nonlethal terrorism exacerbate perceptions of threat and personal insecurity. Third, many people, particularly those with high levels of threat perception, are willing to support strong government policies. These policies split along two lines and include foreign policy (for example, cyber and kinetic military responses to cyberattacks) and domestic policy (for example, tolerance of government surveillance and control of the internet). As threat perception increases, individuals adopt increasingly stringent political views. Like conventional terrorism, cyber terrorism hardens political attitudes: individuals are willing to exchange civil liberties and privacy for security and to support government surveillance, greater regulation of the internet, and forceful military responses in response to cyberattacks. And while these measures are meant to ensure national security, foreign and domestic policy responses may adversely affect the unfettered discourse necessary for a vibrant and open democratic society.[49]

Nevertheless, cyber terrorism does not significantly undermine confidence in the national government or its institutions any more than conventional terrorism does. This was evident from our confidence measures comparing a control group with those exposed to depictions of conventional and cyber terrorism. As noted at the beginning of this chapter, such broad measures of confidence are not always affected by terrorism or other traumatic events. On the contrary, such events often strengthen public confidence, as occurred in the United States after 9/11.[50] These findings about confidence go hand in hand with demands for greater security. As individuals, particularly those with heightened levels of threat perception, demand more government oversight, they cannot express a lack of confidence in the government without unease. Supporters of intrusive government regulation and surveillance must be confident that the authorities will do their jobs effectively and without abusing the greater authority they now enjoy.

This does not mean governments can remain quiescent. This is true for governments in Israel, whose population was the subject of these studies, and it is just as important for governments in the United States, Europe, and elsewhere. Just as twentieth-century studies of the psychology of terrorism in Israel informed post-9/11 research, the effects of cyber terrorism in Israel are equally relevant. Cyber terrorism is a transnational phenomenon, and we see that agents like Anonymous are equally prepared to disrupt U.S. networks (as they did in Ferguson, Missouri, in 2014) as they are Israeli systems.[51] In fact, the effects of cyber terrorism may prove weaker in Israel than elsewhere as research develops.[52] For Israelis, Hamas is a known quantity, a partner to a long-simmering but, to date, manageable conflict that occasionally erupts into sustained violence. To pursue its goals Hamas must publicize its demands and attacks. Attribution is not an issue. The same is not necessarily true for ISIS and the proxies of hostile nations. Attacks are difficult to attribute with certainty, and hacktivists' motivations are often unknown, thereby allowing foreign governments to conduct offensive cyber operations by proxy. Such attacks trade on uncertainty and disruption that may exacerbate anxiety, threat, and risk perception in many Western nations to a greater extent than has been seen in Israel.

The outsized risk attributed to threats to life, limb, and infrastructure track previous studies that ascribe relatively high levels of risk perception to hazards associated with uncertainty and "dread risk"—that is, events "perceived by lack of control, dread, catastrophic potential and fatal consequences."[53] Sarah Lichtenstein and her colleagues describe how media exposure, particularly sensational media coverage, catastrophic outcomes, and lack of direct experience skew assessments of risk.[54] This skewed sense of risk is reinforced by the mystique associated with cyber operations and the omniscience attributed to its practitioners. Much discussion centers on the "dark web" as a portal, inaccessible to everyday web users, where cyber crime is bought and sold and terrorists lurk.

It is not just the media that embrace the sensationalized coverage associated with cyber terror, but government officials as well. When U.S. senators propose legislation warning that they need to prepare for cyberattacks that will cause "catastrophic economic loss and social havoc,"[55] and senior military officials warn that we are in the midst of a cyberwar that the country is losing[56]—assertions that some consider wildly hyperbolic[57]—it is no wonder that civilians' risk perceptions are skewed.

To some extent, cyber terrorism fits these models. Although there are only hypothetical lines between cyberattacks and mass casualties, the great risk attributable to infrastructure damage and loss of life and limb might be explained by their possible catastrophic effects, the benefits that they provide to attackers (thereby making them a likely target as well as a significant source of concern if threatened), the inability to always identify perpetrators or their motives, and the division of opinion among experts that only exacerbates uncertainty. The role of media coverage remains unstudied but may provide insight into the high risks that many people associate with cyber terrorism. Slovic also reminds us that a kinetic terrorist attack comes with significant "signal value,"[58] the perception that an event will reverberate in the future and generate further death, destruction, and mayhem.[59] The result is to overestimate risk. On the other hand, and in contrast to the studies cited, cyber terrorism has never caused death or injury. As such, cyber risk, with its peculiar counterfactual (if we protect ourselves nothing will continue to happen), is likely to be the next frontier of risk perception theory.

Our data further suggest that threat perception, and not only actual cyber events, drives the cognitive effects of cyber terrorism. In response to the experimental manipulations we conducted, individuals demanded internet surveillance and regulation, as well as forceful military responses to cyberattack; but it seems that many people responded to their fears rather than to specific cyber events. In other words, it does not take exposure to actual events to trigger anxiety; the perception of threat alone can do so. These results are consistent with studies that document how simply raising and lowering terror threat alerts can increase anxiety and depression and foster a willingness to "accept both restrictions on their personal freedoms . . . and violent actions against others."[60] Here, too, there is no actual attack in the offing, only the fear of an attack. The perception of a threat, not an actual attack, is sufficient to unsettle individuals to the extent that many terrorists desire. The implication is that authorities will need to recognize that they cannot reduce fears of cyber terrorism and its pervasive effects by eliminating cyberattacks, and attacks will likely only grow more severe. Rather, policymakers must think about ways to enhance resilience in much the way they have in the context of kinetic terrorism and other disasters.

Conclusion

Enhancing resilience in the face of cyber terrorism will be a key issue as internet access becomes increasingly vulnerable to disconnection following cyberattacks and internal shutdowns. Reflecting our growing dependence on cyber networks, preliminary data suggest that a disruption of internet access alone can generate psychological disquiet and anxiety, even without causing infrastructure harm or threatening mass casualties.[61] A factor contributing to the psychological disquiet caused by disconnection is that people have grown increasingly dependent on internet access to realize basic civil rights and social functions.[62] Digital technology has altered the nature of modern speech and association,[63] mediates political participation,[64] and enables access to information. A 2018 study that quantified the effect of internet deprivation found that internet access was the primary predictor of the ability to realize one's rights to freedom of expression, association, and information.[65] The implications of a finding that internet access is inextricably linked with the realization of basic rights is that internet deprivation caused by cyber terrorism aggravates individual psychological harm and significantly undermines confidence in governmental institutions by preventing citizens from monitoring them. Protecting against cyber disconnection and the concomitant psychological harm is complicated by the fact that internet deprivation can be caused by a variety of mechanisms, including cyber terrorism, government-initiated internet shutdowns, the digital divide, and judicial suspension. As a result, purely technical defensive protocols will be insufficient to defend against terrorist attacks that target internet access. A comprehensive government response to the threat of internet deprivation will require a combination of technical, social, and economic policies to safeguard connectivity, improve risk assessment, and communication, and strengthen resilience.

Notwithstanding the importance of the findings, the present study has certain limitations. First, some of the dependent variables (anxiety, risk and threat perception, political attitudes, behavioral changes) were based on self-reported measures. While self-reporting is an accepted method of collecting data on emotions, cognitive appraisals, and behaviors, future studies could validate these findings by using more objective measures. Second, experiments conducted in a laboratory setting have inherent limitations, and confounding variables may affect the experimental manipulation and influence the observed effects. Specifically, it is hard to tell whether the recorded anxiety and insecurity were caused by the manipulation—that is, the threat of cyber terrorism—or by priming thoughts related to specific perpetrators. It is possible that the threat of the terror group itself activated those feelings and explains the difference between the treatment and control groups. While in study 1 we introduced an unknown perpetrator, and observed that the resulting anxiety and threat perception were similar to those found in the subsequent studies, where the attackers were known, future research may wish to compare responses to known and unknown perpetrators in the same study.

Lessons gleaned from successful (and unsuccessful) efforts to improve disaster preparedness suggest that the government, the private sector, and the academic community should effectively communicate the risks of cyber terrorism and take steps that will help instill effective cybersecurity practices.[66] Furthermore, if individuals feel they can communicate their concerns to their government and that the authorities are attentive (that is, citizens have a sense of political efficacy), then threat perception may be reduced.[67] These efforts are intertwined. Providing cybersecurity depends in part on securing compliance with cybersecurity measures. Compliance, in turn, depends on how accurately the public assesses the risk of cyberattacks and on how successfully government and private agencies communicate cyber risks and the precautions that individuals must take.

To secure computer systems, we draw attention to the many programs in schools and businesses designed to impart the knowledge and skills individuals need to maintain personal cybersecurity. It is our impression that the only current evaluation tool is performative—that is, how well end users master and adopt the necessary skills to protect their online assets (for example, recognizing malware, changing passwords, updating firewalls). To fully assess the benefits of these tools, further research is required to understand how these educational and intervention programs might impart fear- and stress-reducing skills to cope with cyber terrorism and to improve resilience—that is, withstand adverse psychological effects of cyber terrorism, overcome feelings of vulnerability, and regain a sense of control. Experience with kinetic terrorism also points to the benefits of psychological intervention.[68] Mitigating the deleterious effects of cyber terrorism and strengthening resilience may diminish the impact of cyber terrorism and the chance it will spill over into militancy, kinetic war, and protracted conflict.

Notes

1. Samuel J. Sinclair and Daniel Antonius, eds., *The Political Psychology of Terrorism Fears* (Oxford University Press, 2013).

2. Stevan E. Hobfoll and others, "Trajectories of Resilience, Resistance, and Distress during Ongoing Terrorism: The Case of Jews and Arabs in Israel." *Journal of Consulting and Clinical Psychology* 77, no. 1 (2009), p. 138; Fran H. Norris, Melissa Tracy, and Sandro Galea, "Looking for Resilience: Understanding the Longitudinal Trajectories of Responses to Stress." *Social Science & Medicine* 68, no. 12 (2009), pp. 2190–98; Benjamin J. Luft, *We're Not Leaving: 9/11 Responders Tell Their Stories of Courage, Sacrifice, and Renewal* (New York: Greenpoint Press, 2011).

3. Ethan Bueno De Mesquita, "Conciliation, Counterterrorism, and Patterns of Terrorist Violence," *International Organization* 59, no. 1 (2005), pp. 145–76.

4. Michael L. Gross, *The Ethics of Insurgency* (Cambridge University Press, 2015).

5. Jonathan N. Goodrich, "September 11, 2001 Attack on America: A Record of the Immediate Impacts and Reactions in the USA Travel and Tourism Industry," *Tourism Management* 23, no. 6 (2002), pp. 573–80.

6. Karin M. Fierke, "Terrorism and Trust in Northern Ireland," *Critical Studies on Terrorism* 2, no. 3 (2009), pp. 497–511; Kimberly Gross, Paul R. Brewer, and Sean Aday, "Confidence in Government and Emotional Responses to Terrorism after September 11, 2001," *American Politics Research* 37, no. 1 (2009), pp. 107–28; Tom W. Smith, Kenneth A. Rasinski, and Marianna Toce, *America Rebounds: A National Study of Public Response to the September 11th Terrorist Attacks* (University of Chicago, National Opinion Research Center, 2001); Kenneth A. Rasinski and others, *America Recovers: A Follow-up to a National Study of Public Response to the September 11th Terrorist Attacks* (University of Chicago, National Opinion Research Center, 2002); Dag Wollebæk and others, "After Utøya: How a High-Trust Society Reacts to Terror—Trust and Civic Engagement in the Aftermath of July 22," *PS: Political Science & Politics* 45, no. 1 (2012), pp. 32–37. But for contrary data, see Thomas E. Baldwin, Arkalgud Ramaprasad, and Michael E. Samsa, "Understanding Public Confidence in Government to Prevent Terrorist Attacks," *Journal of Homeland Security and Emergency Management* 5, no. 1 (January 2008); M. S. Berry and others, *The Effect of Terrorism on Public Confidence: An Exploratory Study*, ANL/DIS-08/6 (Lemont, Ill.: Argonne National Laboratory, 2008).

7. Jian Hua and Sanjay Bapna, "The Economic Impact of Cyber Terrorism," *Journal of Strategic Information Systems* 22, no. 2 (2013), pp. 175–86.

8. Thomas Rid, "Cyber War Will Not Take Place," *Journal of Strategic Studies* 35, no. 1 (2012), pp. 5–32, quotation on p. 31.

9. See "North Korea 'Directly Responsible' for WannaCry Attack That Paralysed NHS, Says U.S. Homeland Security Chief," *The Independent*, December 19, 2017.

10. See Andy Greenberg, "How an Entire Nation Became Russia's Test Lab for Cyber War," *Wired*, June 20, 2017.

11. See Nicole Perloth and David E. Sanger, "Cyberattacks Put Russian Fingers on the Switch at Power Plants, U.S. Says," *New York Times*, March 15, 2018.

12. Nigel Inkster, "Measuring Military Cyber Power," *Survival* 59, no. 4 (2017), pp. 27–34.

13. "North Korea 'Directly Responsible' for WannaCry Attack."

14. Yellepeddi Vijayalakshmi and others, "Study on Emerging Trends in Malware Variants," *International Journal of Pure and Applied Mathematics* 116, no. 22 (2017), pp. 479–89.

15. See Osterman Survey, "Understanding the Depth of the Ransomware Problem," August 2016 (www.malwarebytes.com/surveys/ransomware/).

16. Thomas Rid and Ben Buchanan, "Attributing Cyber Attacks," *Journal of Strategic Studies* 38, nos. 1–2 (2015), pp. 4–37.

17. See Thomas P. Bossert, "It's Official: North Korea Is behind WannaCry," *Wall Street Journal*, December 18, 2017.

18. See "Hype and Fear," *The Economist*, December 8, 2012.

19. "North Korea 'Directly Responsible' for WannaCry Attack."

20. Daphna Canetti, Michael L. Gross, and I. Waismel-Manor, "Immune from Cyber Fire? The Psychological and Physiological Effects of Cyber War," in *Binary Bullets: The Ethics of Cyberwarfare*, edited by Fritz Allhoff, Adam Henschke, and Bradley Jay Strawser (Oxford Scholarship Online, 2016), pp. 157–76 (DOI:10.1093/acprof:oso/9780190221072 .003.0009).

21. Sophia Backhaus and others, "Terror in the Unknown Space: The Effects of Cyberterrorism on Emotions" (University of Haifa, School of Political Science, March 19, 2018).

22. Constance C. Milbourne and Jeffrey S. Wilkinson, "Chasing Infinity: The Fear of Disconnecting," *American Communication Journal* 17, no. 2 (2015), pp. 1–14; Cecilie Schou Andreassen, "Online Social Network Site Addiction: A Comprehensive Review," *Current Addiction Reports* 2, no. 2 (2015), pp. 175–84; Robert Kraut and Moira Burke, "Internet Use and Psychological Well-Being: Effects of Activity and Audience," *Communications of the ACM* 58, no. 12 (2015), pp. 94–100.

23. Michael N. Schmitt, ed., *Tallinn Manual 2.0 on the International Law Applicable to Cyber Operations* (Cambridge University Press, 2017).

24. Michael N. Schmitt, "Grey Zones in the International Law of Cyberspace," *Yale Journal of International Law* 43, no. 2 (2017) (www.yjil.yale.edu/grey-zones-in-the -international-law-of-cyberspace/).

25. Pavel Polityuk, "Ukraine Sees Russian Hand in Cyber Attacks on Power Grid," Reuters, February 12, 2016 (www.reuters. com/article/us-ukraine-cybersecurity-idUSKC N0VL18E).

26. See Kai Biermann and Ferdinand Otto, "Russische Hackergruppe Snake Soll für Angriff Verantwortlich Sein," *Zeit Online*, March 1, 2018 (www.zeit.de/politik /deutschland/2018-03/cyber-attacke-hackerangriff-parlamentarisches-kontrollgremium -armin-schuster-reaktionen).

27. AAPOR Task Force, "Research Synthesis: AAPOR Report on Online Panels," American Association for Public Opinion Research, *Public Opinion Quarterly* 74, no. 4 (2010), pp. 711–81. See also Mario Callegaro and others, eds., *Online Panel Research: A Data Quality Perspective* (New York: John Wiley & Sons, 2014).

28. Lizzie Deardon, "Anonymous Vows to Wreak 'Electronic Holocaust' on Israel for 'Crimes in the Palestinian Territories,'" *The Independent*, March 31, 2015.

29. Theresa M. Marteau and Hilary Bekker, "The Development of a Six-Item Short-Form of the State Scale of the Spielberger State—Trait Anxiety Inventory (STAI)," *British Journal of Clinical Psychology* 31, no. 3 (1992), pp. 301–06.

30. Daphna Canetti-Nisim, Gal Ariely, and Eran Halperin, "Life, Pocketbook, or Culture: The Role of Perceived Security Threats in Promoting Exclusionist Political Attitudes toward Minorities in Israel," *Political Research Quarterly* 61, no. 1 (2008), pp. 90–103; Daphna Canetti and Miriam Lindner, "Exposure to Political Violence and Political Behavior," in *Psychology of Change: Life Contexts, Experiences, and Identities*, edited by Katherine J. Reynolds and Nyla R. Branscombe (New York: Psychology Press, 2014), pp. 77–94; Rebeca Raijman and Moshe Semyonov, "Perceived Threat and Exclusionary Attitudes towards Foreign Workers in Israel," *Ethnic and Racial Studies* 27, no. 5 (2004), pp. 780–99; Stevan E. Hobfoll and others, "The Association of Exposure, Risk, and Resiliency Factors with PTSD among Jews and Arabs Exposed to Repeated Acts of Terrorism in Israel," *Journal of Traumatic Stress* 21, no. 1 (2008), pp. 9–21; Leonie Huddy and others, "The Consequences of Terrorism: Disentangling the Effects of Personal and National Threat," *Political Psychology* 23, no. 3 (2002), pp. 485–509.

31. Paul Slovic, "Perception of Risk," *Science* 236, no. 4799 (1987), pp. 280–85, quotation on p. 280.

32. Ibid.

33. Darren W. Davis and Brian D. Silver, "Civil Liberties vs. Security: Public Opinion in the Context of the Terrorist Attacks on America," *American Journal of Political Science* 48, no. 1 (2004), pp. 28–46; Agustin Echebarria-Echabe and Emilia Fernández-Guede, "Effects of Terrorism on Attitudes and Ideological Orientation," *European Journal of Social Psychology* 36, no. 2 (2006), pp. 259–65; Anna Getmansky and Thomas Zeitzoff, "Terrorism and Voting: The Effect of Rocket Threat on Voting in Israeli Elections," *American Political Science Review* 108, no. 3 (2014), pp. 588–604; Jennifer S. Lerner and others, "Effects of Fear and Anger on Perceived Risks of Terrorism: A National Field Experiment," *Psychological Science* 14, no. 2 (2003), pp. 144–50.

34. See George Gao, "What Americans Think about NSA Surveillance, National Security and Privacy," *Fact Tank*, May 29, 2015 (www.pewresearch.org/fact-tank/2015/05/29/what-americans-think-about-nsa-surveillance-national-security-and-privacy/).

35. Martin C. Libicki, "From the Tallinn Manual to Las Vegas Rules," in *Cyberspace in Peace and War* (Annapolis, Md.: Naval Institute Press, 2016); Henry Farrell and Charles L. Glaser, "The Role of Effects, Saliencies and Norms in U.S. Cyberwar Doctrine," *Journal of Cybersecurity* 3, no. 1 (2017), pp. 7–17.

36. The exception was in study 1 (unidentified perpetrator), where respondents' willingness to give up privacy increased as the manipulation grew more severe.

37. George Lucas, "State-Sponsored Hacktivism and the Rise of 'Soft' War," in *Soft War: The Ethics of Unarmed Conflict*, edited by Michael L Gross and Tamar Meisels (Cambridge University Press, 2017), p. 77.

38. Paul Slovic and Elke U. Weber, "Perception of Risk Posed by Extreme Events" (paper prepared for the conference "Risk Management Strategies in an Uncertain World," Palisades, N.Y., April 2002).

39. Slovic, "Perception of Risk," pp. 280–85.

40. Sarah Lichtenstein and others, "Judged Frequency of Lethal Events," *Journal of Experimental Psychology: Human Learning and Memory* 4, no. 6 (1978), p. 551.

41. Clinton M. Jenkin, "Risk Perception and Terrorism: Applying the Psychometric Paradigm," *Homeland Security Affairs* 2, no. 2 (2006) (www.hsaj.org/articles/169).

42. Lee Jarvis, Stuart Macdonald, and Lella Nouri, "The Cyberterrorism Threat: Findings from a Survey of Researchers," *Studies in Conflict and Terrorism* 37, no. 1 (2014), pp. 68–90.

43. James Andrew Lewis, *Assessing the Risks of Cyber Terrorism, Cyber War and Other Cyber Threats* (Washington: Center for Strategic and International Studies, 2002); George R. Lucas, *Cyber Warfare* (London: Ashgate, 2015); Brandon Valeriano and Ryan C. Maness, "The Coming Cyberspace: The Normative Argument against Cyberwarfare," *Foreign Affairs*, May 13, 2015 (www.foreignaffairs.com/articles/2015-05-13/coming-cyberpeace).

44. Mission Support Center, "Cyber Threat and Vulnerability Analysis of the U.S. Electric Sector" (Idaho National Laboratory, August 2016) (www.energy.gov/sites/prod/files/2017/01/f34/Cyber%20Threat%20and%20Vulnerability%20Analysis%20of%20the%20U.S.%20Electric%20Sector.pdf).

45. Hua and Bapna, "The Economic Impact of Cyber Terrorism."

46. David Aucsmith, "Disintermediation, Counterinsurgency, and Cyber Defense," chapter 14 in this volume.

47. Erik Gartzke and Jon R. Lindsay, "The Cyber Commitment Problem and the Destabilization of Nuclear Deterrence," chapter 9 in this volume.

48. Lee Jarvis Stuart Macdonald, and Andrew Whiting, "Unpacking Cyberterrorism Discourse: Specificity, Status, and Scale in News Media Constructions of Threat," *European Journal of International Security* 2, no. 1 (2017), pp. 64–87.

49. Michael L. Gross, Daphna Canetti, and Dana R. Vashdi, "The Psychological Effects of Cyber Terrorism," *Bulletin of the Atomic Scientists* 72, no. 5 (2016), pp. 284–91.

50. Gross, Brewer, and Aday, "Confidence in Government"; Rasinski and others, "America Recovers."

51. See D. Kerr, "Ferguson, Mo., Police Site Hit with DDoS Attack," CNET, August 15, 2014 (www.cnet.com/news/st-louis-police-website-suffers-ddos-attack/).

52. Hobfoll and others, "Trajectories of Resilience."

53. Slovic, "Perception of Risk," p. 283.

54. Lichtenstein and others, "Judged Frequency of Lethal Events."

55. Jay Rockefeller and Olympia Snowe, "Now Is the Time to Prepare for Cyberwar," *Wall Street Journal*, April 2, 2010.

56. See Vijayan, "Senators Ramp Up Cyberwar Rhetoric."

57. Rid, "Cyber War Will Not Take Place."

58. Paul Slovic, "The Perception of Risk," in *Scientists Making a Difference*, edited by Robert J. Sternberg, Susan T. Fiske, and Donald J. Foss (Cambridge University Press, 2016), pp. 180–81.

59. Jenkin, "Risk Perception and Terrorism."

60. Rose McDermott and Philip G. Zimbardo, "The Psychological Consequences of Terrorist Alerts," in *Psychology of Terrorism*, edited by B. Bongar and others (Oxford University Press, 2007), pp. 357–70, quotation on p. 362.

61. Milbourne and Wilkinson, "Chasing Infinity"; Andreassen, "Online Social Network Site Addiction"; Kraut and Burke, "Internet Use and Psychological Well-Being."

62. Sara Vissers and Dietlind Stolle, "The Internet and New Modes of Political Participation: Online versus Offline Participation," *Information, Communication & Society* 17, no. 8 (2014), pp. 937–55.

63. Jack M. Balkin, "The Future of Free Expression in a Digital Age," *Pepperdine Law Review* 36 (2008), p. 427.

64. Stephen Coleman and Jay G. Blumler, *The Internet and Democratic Citizenship: Theory, Practice and Policy* (Cambridge University Press, 2009).

65. Ryan Shandler, Daphna Canetti, and Michael L. Gross, "Internet Reliance: A Social and Legal Analysis of Internet Access as an Auxiliary Human Right" (University of Haifa, School of Political Science, March 19, 2018).

66. Margaret M. Barry, Jane Sixsmith, and Jennifer J. Infanti, "A Literature Review on Effective Risk Communication for the Prevention and Control of Communicable Diseases in Europe" (Stockholm: ECDC, 2013); Victoria Basolo and others, "The Effects of Confidence in Government and Information on Perceived and Actual Preparedness for Disasters," *Environment and Behavior* 41, no. 3 (2009), pp. 338–64; George M. Gray and David P. Ropeik, "Dealing with the Dangers of Fear: The Role of Risk Communication," *Health Affairs* 21, no. 6 (2002), pp. 106–16; Baruch Fischhoff and others, "Evaluating the Success of Terror Risk Communications," *Biosecurity and Bioterrorism: Biodefense Strategy, Practice, and Science* 1, no. 4 (2003), pp. 255–58; Michele M. Woodand others, "Communicating Actionable Risk for Terrorism and Other Hazards," *Risk Analysis* 32, no. 4 (2012), pp. 601–15.

67. Daphna Canetti and others, "Political Resources Effect? Evidence from a Longitudinal Study on Exposure to Violence and Psychological Distress in Israel" (University of Haifa, School of Political Science, March 19, 2018).

68. Daphna Canetti and others, "Exposure to Political Violence and Political Extremism," *European Psychologist* 18, no. 4 (2013), pp. 263–72.

11

Limiting the Undesired Impact
of Cyber Weapons

Technical Requirements and Policy Implications

STEVEN M. BELLOVIN, SUSAN LANDAU,
and HERBERT LIN

When new weaponry is initially introduced, it is often accompanied by great fear over its potential for damage. Such has certainly been the case for cyber weapons. In part this is because so many internet attacks have had a damaging effect on a large number of systems. This has given rise to apprehension that cyber weapons are necessarily indiscriminate. The facts do not bear this out. Cyber weapons can be targeted. Indeed, a number of them have already been so. And although cyber weapons are software, and thus replicable, they can be designed to reduce proliferation risks.

Both military commanders and political leaders prefer to have a wide range of options. Decreasing the extent of a weapon's potential damage increases the range of options for how it may be used. When policymakers decide to use weapons, they have certain effects they want the weapons to cause and ancillary effects they wish to avoid. In a military context, the intention is usually to damage designated targets; an undesired effect is causing harm to humans and property that are not among the designated targets. The use of a highly targetable cyber weapon may be as effective against a target as a kinetic weapon, but with significantly less risk of collateral damage.

Excessive damage to unintended targets can be a catalyst for an undesired escalation of conflict. For example, during World War II, German bombers—intending to hit the docks of London—accidentally bombed central London, which Hitler had placed off-limits for the Luftwaffe. In response, the Royal Air Force (RAF) launched a bomber attack against armament factories north of Berlin and Tempelhof Airport in Berlin. However, this attack also hit, accidentally, some residential areas in Berlin. Shortly thereafter, Hitler launched the Blitz against London, apparently in retaliation for the (mistaken) RAF bombing of residential areas in Berlin.[1]

This chapter examines the technical requirements necessary to ensure that cyber weapons are not indiscriminate, and proposes policy guidelines designed to ensure that outcome. We begin by analyzing weapons used in recent targeted cyberattacks in order to draw out the reasons the attacks remained targeted. This analysis illuminates the technical and policy principles that should guide the design of cyber weapons that can be targeted.

It is useful to separate unintended or undesired harm to humans and property into two categories. One category is the unintended or undesired harm that occurs as the direct and immediate result of an attack using a certain cyber weapon. A second category is unintended harm that results from another party's use of a weapon, cyber or otherwise, that is similar in nature to the one that was used in the original attack. (In this context, "similar in nature" means that the weapon employs the same principles of operation to create its damaging effects that the original weapon does.) In other words, concerns often arise about whether A's use of a weapon, cyber or not, in a scenario against B might lead to some adversary (B or a third party C) using that or a similar weapon against persons or property that A does not wish damaged. These concerns are particularly salient when A's use of a weapon is the first time that the weapon has been used. These kinds of challenges are often captured under the rubric of preventing or minimizing the likelihood of proliferation. Preventing or minimizing proliferation may be a sufficiently high policy objective that in some configuration of facts and circumstances it takes precedence over a decision to use a given cyber weapon.

We begin by examining several cyber weapons and discuss what technical means were employed that prevented their spread. We then explore what other considerations must be taken into account to ensure that a cyber weapon stays on target. Finally, we discuss the proliferation of cyber weapons, both the ways in which it can occur and ways that states can work to prevent it.

A note on terminology: for purposes of this chapter, a cyber weapon is a software-based information technology (IT) artifact or tool that can cause destructive, damaging, or degrading effects on the system or network against which it is directed.[2] A cyber weapon has two components: a penetration component and a payload component. The penetration component is the mechanism through which the weapon gains access to the system to be attacked. The payload component is the mechanism that actually accomplishes what the weapon is supposed to do—destroy data, interrupt communications, exfiltrate information, cause computer-controlled centrifuges to speed up, and so on.[3] Penetrations can occur using well-known vulnerabilities, including those for which patches have been released. The vast majority of attacks are accomplished in this way. Some, however, including the sophisticated Stuxnet attack on the Iranian nuclear facility in Natanz, used zero-day vulnerabilities; these are vulnerabilities that are discovered and exploited before being disclosed to the vendor or otherwise publicly disclosed.

We use "target" as a noun to refer to an entity that the attacker wishes to damage, destroy, or disrupt. Any given entity (target) may have multiple computers associated with it, all of which the attacker wishes to damage, destroy, or disrupt. A target might thus be an air defense installation, a corporation, a uranium enrichment facility, or even a nation. In some instances, a given entity may have only one computer associated with it, in which case the term "target" and "computer" can be used interchangeably.

If the payload causes data exfiltration, we call this a cyber exploitation. If the payload causes damage, destruction, degradation, or denial, the use is called a cyberattack.[4]

Inherently Indiscriminate Weapons vs. Targetable Weapons

Weapons that are "inherently indiscriminate" are prohibited as instruments of war. Thus, for example, the U.S. Department of Defense *Law of War Manual* states that "inherently indiscriminate weapons" are "weapons that are incapable of being used in accordance with the principles of distinction and proportionality."[5] U.S. military doctrine explicitly allows offensive operations in cyberspace for damaging or destructive purposes as long as they are conducted in accordance with the laws of war.[6] Thus the doctrine presupposes the existence of cyber weapons that are not "inherently indiscriminate."

Cyber weapons have nonetheless generated great fear. There are multiple reasons for this response. The recent development of computer technology as an instrument of attack readily creates fear, especially in those for whom the technology is far from second nature. The speed with which modern industrialized societies in particular have become dependent on networking technologies has exacerbated this concern.

Early cyber incidents may have contributed to people's concerns as well. Early self-replicating worms and viruses acting against personal computers were indeed designed to spread far and wide.[7] The Morris Incident in 1988 was the first use of an internet worm, though its public impact was limited because the internet was largely unused by the general public at the time.[8] The rapidly spreading worms of the early 2000s had much more impact. For example, in 2003 Blaster affected CSX Railroad's signaling network and interfered with Air Canada's reservation and check-in systems.[9] These attacks were not specifically intended to have these effects; however, they all clogged computers and network links. Had the authors intended these programs to cause such damage, it would have been fair to call their programs cyber weapons and their use indiscriminate. The 1998 Chernobyl virus and the 2004 Witty worm were the first major uses of malware to carry destructive payloads;[10] however, they were both apparently released as an act of random vandalism rather than for any particular purpose.

That said, indiscriminate targeting is not an *inherent* characteristic of all cyberattacks. A number of cyberattacks we have seen to date—on Estonia, Georgia, Iran, and Sony Pictures (discussed in more detail later in the chapter)—used weapons that were carefully targeted and, for various reasons, did not cause significant damage beyond the original target. In three of these cases (Estonia, Georgia, and Iran), the cyberattacks appear to have helped accomplish the goals of the attackers—and did so without loss of life. None of the four attacks used weapons that were "inherently indiscriminate."

These attacks mark the beginning of the use of cyber in nation-state clashes. Cyberattacks are likely to be used by many parties, including nation-states, to accomplish their goals, both in circumstances of overt and acknowledged armed conflict and in circumstances short of overt and acknowledged armed conflict.

Constraints on Targetable Cyber Weapons

As noted, inherently indiscriminate weapons are incapable of being used in accordance with the principles of distinction and proportionality. The phrase "incapable of being used" is essential—nearly all weapons are *capable* of being used discriminately because their significantly harmful effects can be limited to areas in which only known enemy entities are present.

What is technically necessary for a cyber weapon to be capable of being used discriminately? Two conditions must be met: (1) The cyber weapon must be capable of being directed against explicitly designated targets; that is, the cyber weapon must be targetable; and (2) when targeted on an explicitly designated entity, the weapon must minimize the creation of significant negative effects on other entities that the attacker has not explicitly targeted.

Successful Targeted Cyberattacks

The first publicly visible cyberattack on a country as a country, as opposed to on specific targets within a country, was a massive denial-of-service attack on Estonia in 2007.[11] The attack—most observers either hold the Russian government responsible or believe that the Russian government either supported or tolerated it—did no permanent damage; however, internet links and servers in Estonia were flooded by malicious traffic, leaving them unusable. The cyberattack the following year against Georgia was similar, both in attribution and effect, although in the Georgian case the cyberattack was only one part of a larger conflict that involved conventional Russian and Georgian military forces.

The attacks on Estonia and Georgia were denial-of-service attacks that disrupted those nations' connections to the internet. They did not, however, cause long-term damage to computers and data (though cutting off access to the internet during the attack was, of course, damaging).[12] The Stuxnet attack on Iran and North Korea's attack on Sony Pictures did cause damage, and it is to these that we now turn our attention.

Stuxnet is a computer worm that spread from machine to machine but did harm to only very specific targets. Though Stuxnet was found on computers in Iran, Indonesia, India, and the United States,[13] because of the way the weapon was constructed the only destruction it caused was in Natanz, where it caused centrifuges to spin too fast and break.

Stuxnet is a sophisticated cyber weapon that relied on several zero-day vulnerabilities to penetrate systems not connected to the internet, which meant that it had to function largely autonomously after injection. The authors had very precise knowledge of the target environment, and Stuxnet used that knowledge for very precise targeting. It also manipulated output displays to deceive the plant's operators into believing that the centrifuge complex was operating properly. Although Stuxnet appeared both inside and outside of Iran, its destructive payload was only activated within the Natanz centrifuge plant.[14]

Although Stuxnet could operate autonomously, its controllers did not treat it as "fire and forget." Rather, they developed several versions, with enhanced features (and probably also bug fixes) that added new functionality, exploited newly learned information about the target, and adapted to changes in the operating environment.

Stuxnet carried the malware payload—but first there were intelligence activities to determine what systems Stuxnet should attack and what their characteristics were. There is no clear public evidence on how this intelligence was gathered. It could have been through a human operator (an insider, for example); it could have been electronic (obtained by hacking into Siemens systems, the supplier of the specific programmable logic controllers [PLCs] used in Natanz and that signaled Stuxnet that it was at the target system); or some other methods or combination of methods.

Iran apparently retaliated for Stuxnet by attacking the Saudi Aramco oil company. The cyber weapon Iran used, named Shamoon, erased the disks of infected computers. It was triggered by a timer set to go off at 11:08 A.M. on August 15, 2012; the malware had apparently been installed by an insider in the corporate network and not in a separate, disconnected net that ran the oil production machinery.[15] Because Shamoon spread via shared network drives, its damage was limited to the targeted corporation.[16]

The North Korean attack on Sony Pictures in 2014 was quite different in nature. Standard techniques were used, both for the initial penetration and for the destructive activities that followed. The initial penetration of Sony was via "spear-phishing,"[17] a technique that often involves sending a plausible-sounding email to a target to induce him or her to click on a link; once activated, this link then installs the malware. The attackers then spent months exploring and investigating Sony's network, learning where the interesting files were and planning how to destroy its systems. The actual destruction of the disks within Sony was performed by a worm.[18] At least some parts of the destruction software used commercial tools to bypass operating system protections.

In other words, and in contrast to Stuxnet, the attack on Sony was largely manual. The attackers allegedly exfiltrated a very large amount of information (100 terabytes), without being noticed;[19] they have publicly released 200 gigabytes of it. Carelessness on the part of the defender seems to have played an important role.

Distinctions between the Profiled Cyberattacks

There are a number of different types of cyberattack. The goal might simply be to "clog" the internet to prevent work from getting done, or it might be to destroy computers, or even physical devices attached to computers. We consider each in turn.

Denial-of-service attacks. One common form of online harassment is to launch a distributed denial-of-service (DDoS) attack. Usually, it is just that—harassment—though in certain circumstances preventing communication can have more serious consequences. Generally speaking, a denial-of-service attack involves exhausting some resource required by the target; these resources can include central processing unit (CPU) capacity, network bandwidth, and the like. The attacks can be direct, against the site itself, or indirect, by attacking some other site required by the target. In a distributed denial-of-service attack, the resources of many computers are dedicated to attacking a single target. A single home computer, with perhaps 10 million bits per second (bps) of upstream bandwidth, cannot clog the link of a commercial site with perhaps a 500 million bps link, but a few hundred attackers can do so easily. Estonia and Georgia were seriously affected by large-scale DDoS attacks in 2007 and 2008 respectively.

Although DDoS attacks are by their nature highly targeted, the potential for collateral impact is high, especially in indirect attacks. Assume, for example, that 10,000 such home machines focused their bandwidth on a single target. The aggregate bandwidth, 100 billion bps, could flood some of the internet service provider (ISP) links into the router complex serving that customer and thereby affect other customers.[20] Even if the ISP links are not flooded, there can still be collateral impact; most smaller websites are hosted on a shared infrastructure.[21]

The risk of collateral damage is especially high in indirect DDoS attacks. One common example is an attack against the domain name system (DNS) servers that handle the target's name.[22] Because DNS servers normally require far less bandwidth than, say, a website, the operators of such servers make use of lower-bandwidth (and lower-cost) links; they are thus much easier to clog. However, a DNS server may handle many other domains than just the one target; a DDoS perpetrated on such a server could take many other sites off the air as well.

File damage. Attacks that delete or damage files on the target's computers are arguably more significant than DDoS attacks. This sort of attack usually requires that the target computers be penetrated—that is, that the attacker be able to run destructive code on each one. It may be possible to launch one attack that effectively penetrates multiple computers—for example, by planting malware on a shared file server—but the attacker's ability to do so will be situation-dependent.

In practice, the amount of damage actually done to files is often the least important part of the attack. On well-run sites, all important disks are backed up, so little data will be lost. Furthermore, best practice after even "normal" incidents is to wipe the disk, reformat, and reinstall, regardless of what is perceived to have taken place; disinfecting a system is difficult, time-consuming, and not foolproof. Thus, whether files are damaged or not, the response to a penetration should be the same: start over and restore important data from backup media.

That said, data manipulation can be very disorienting, especially when it occurs in the midst of a kinetic attack. Indeed, during the 2016 U.S. presidential election, there was great concern over data manipulation on the day of the election.

Again, the risk of collateral damage depends on the quality of intelligence available. It is often straightforward to identify interesting target machines; however, identifying indirect dependencies can be difficult. Suppose, for example, that a mail server used by an opponent's foreign ministry is hacked, preventing it from sending and receiving mail. However, if the health ministry relies on the same server, then its ability to function will be damaged as well.

Physical damage. The most serious kind of attack is one that causes physical damage to computers or the equipment attached to them. (That, of course, was the effect of Stuxnet.) Computers are cheap and plentiful; although having to restore files is annoying, a cyberattack is unlikely to be fatal if the company has adequate backups. Consider Sony and the South Korean banks that were attacked, both apparently by North Korea: despite destruction of files, all are still in business, and none spent more than an inconsequential amount of time recovering.[23]

Physical damage, however, requires repair or replacement of physical items. This is likely to be far more expensive and far more time-consuming than restoring files. In 2007 a demonstration attack by the Department of Homeland Security on an electrical generator showed that elements of the power grid could be damaged by a cyberattack.[24] This point was underscored by the cyberattacks in 2015 and 2016 on three Ukrainian power distribution systems, which demonstrated that a well-planned attack on the grid could shut the systems down.[25] These three systems were restored to full functionality in a few hours, but a similar attack on U.S. power systems might cause damage that would take significantly longer to repair. It is likely that other forms of cyber-dependent critical infrastructure—dams, pipelines, chemical plants, and more—are equally vulnerable.

The risk of collateral damage from cyberattacks on physical assets may be high. The attacker may find it difficult to make good and reliable estimates of collateral damage. For example, if a pipeline is destroyed, might there be an explosion that kills many people? Will an attack on a hydroelectric power plant damage the dam and cause massive downstream flooding?

Why Some Attacks Stay Targeted

Despite their differences, the attacks on Estonia, Georgia, Iran, and Sony Pictures share a crucial similarity: none of them caused significant damage past the designated targets. There was of course an overriding policy reason to avoid attacks that would spread. But how was it achieved in practice?

The DDoS attacks on Estonia and Georgia were aimed directly at entities of those two nations. DDoS attacks executed in such a manner do not spread beyond their intended targets.[26]

There was no need for the attack against Sony to be self-spreading. To a fair extent, automation simply was not part of the attack strategy. During the initial stages of setting up the attack, people actively determined which systems to penetrate and decided what information to exfiltrate.

The attack on Iran provides another example of an interesting dimension in targeting. To achieve the strategic goal of delaying the Iranian effort to build a nuclear weapon, the Stuxnet weapon had to be used repeatedly; doing so only once could destroy some centrifuges, but not enough to seriously set back the Iranian effort. Thus, so that it could continue to destroy additional centrifuges, it was crucial that the weapon remain undetected.

Because the centrifuges at Natanz were not connected to the internet, Stuxnet had to be introduced into the Natanz complex without the benefit

of a network connection. In the absence of a cooperative insider at the Natanz complex, a method had to be found that would bridge the air gap. Stuxnet was designed to spread in virus-like fashion. Once inside the Natanz
complex, Stuxnet could use worm-like characteristics to spread on the internal network. At the same time, to maintain its covert nature, the program
had to avoid doing damage elsewhere that might be noticed and investigated.
Thus Stuxnet also had to avoid spreading too virulently from the original
injection point.[27]

These requirements point to two important aspects of Stuxnet: very careful targeting to prevent spread (and thus discovery) and extremely precise
intelligence on the configuration of the target machines. For the weapon to
be successful, its designers needed to know exactly what to do and when.
They may have developed several iterations, with spyware or perhaps human
intelligence gathering the necessary data (including blueprints and other
design documents). The weapon had an extreme need for intelligence, precise characterization of how the attack should work, and high-quality
damage-limiting software.

Technical Issues in Targeting

A precisely targeted attack will not affect other computers. Precise intelligence is necessary. As we shall describe, some of this intelligence gathering
must be built into the weapon.

In general, determining what will happen if a particular computer or network link is attacked is not easy. In some cases, knowing this may not
matter much; if a link serves only a military base that contains the target
computer, the other machines that are likely to be affected are also military
and hence legitimate targets. Other situations are more difficult. A server
that distributes propaganda or serves as a communication node for terrorists
may be located in a virtual machine in a commercial hosting facility. In such
a case, civilian machines will easily be affected by a weapon used against the
legitimate target. Understanding the interactions with the other computers
will require an initial analytic penetration. That is, the attacking force would
need to conduct cyber exploitation *on the target computer* to detect an underlying virtual machine hypervisor or to determine which other computers are
communicating to or through it.

In some cases, cyber weapons must operate autonomously, without real-
time control by a human operator. As noted, Stuxnet was designed this way

because the target network was physically separated from the internet.[28] Autonomous operation poses particular challenges for precise targeting. So that operators can account for the limits of what it can do, the weapon itself may need to do automated intelligence gathering and analysis. An analogy would be to a camera in a smart bomb that is used not only to guide the weapon but also to detect, say, the presence of children. In other situations, the cyber weapon's controller may need to monitor for impending collateral damage. Consider a DDoS attack that could flood other links. Simple network diagnostics could reveal if computers "near" the target are being affected to any undue extent. Note, though, that the success of such monitoring presumes that the dependencies are understood; one cannot monitor the behavior of a connection not known to exist.

Technical considerations also affect the extent and nature of collateral damage that might be expected when a cyber weapon is used in a specific operation against a particular target; these considerations pertain both to weapons design and intelligence support for using that weapon. Issues related to collateral damage have legal, ethical, tactical, and technical dimensions.

From an ethical perspective, an attacker has an obligation to minimize the harm to noncombatants that may result from a legitimate attack against a military objective. Legally, this ethical obligation is codified in the laws of armed conflict as the proportionality requirement of *jus in bello*.

In the Defense Department formulation, the likely collateral damage from the use of a weapon is one factor that is weighed in deciding whether to employ the weapon at all. The other factor is the military advantage that would accrue should the attack be successful. If the likely collateral damage from the attack is too high given its military value, the attack is either altered in some way to reduce the likely collateral damage or scrubbed entirely.

The tactical reason for minimizing collateral damage is that an attack that spreads far and wide is more likely to be discovered,[29] which may lead the defenders to take countermeasures. Martin Libicki has considered a related issue, that of limiting the size and scope of an attack for the same purpose: to reduce the likelihood that the defender will notice the attack. Some of the techniques he describes, such as opting for smaller effects (to enable a longer-term attack) or exploiting a vulnerability particular to a target, apply to minimizing collateral damage.[30]

Launching cyberattacks that minimize collateral damage requires a commensurate degree of precise intelligence about the target environment.

Kinetic attacks have a similar requirement—most friendly-fire incidents and inadvertent attacks on protected facilities are due to incorrect or incomplete information.[31] However, the volume of intelligence information needed for targeted cyberattacks is usually significantly larger.

We now discuss certain technical requirements our conditions impose on the design and use of targetable cyber weapons.

Condition 1: The Weapon Must Be Targetable

Targetable kinetic weapons must be designed to hit a designated target. Article 36 of Additional Protocol I of 1977 of the Geneva Conventions requires that parties to the convention conduct a legal review of weapons that are intended to be used to ensure that they meet this condition.[32] But how to meet condition 1 in practice depends on specific details of the weapon in question; for cyber, as our discussion of successful targeted attacks makes clear, the details are both complex and important.

As noted earlier, in order for a cyber weapon to be usable only on intended targets, the location and technical specifications of the intended target must be sufficiently precisely determined that they uniquely identify the intended target. For example, intelligence might provide an internet protocol (IP) address at which a putative target is located. Thus a cyber weapon might be provided with capabilities that enable it to be directed to a specified set of IP addresses.[33]

Even after the cyber weapon reaches an entity within which it can release its payload, the weapon must then be able to examine technical characteristics of the environment in which it finds itself. It must be able to determine if it has, in fact, arrived at the correct place. Detailed information concerning the desired target (for example, PLC type and configuration, as was used in Stuxnet) must be available in advance so that the weapon has a baseline against which to compare its environment.

The more detailed such information is, the better. In the limiting case, intelligence may reveal the serial numbers of various components in the environment—if serial numbers are known and are machine-readable, the probability that the weapon is in the targeted environment is surely high enough to allow its use.

One step that can be taken to increase the likelihood that damage will be confined to the intended target(s) is to direct the weapon only at systems that are intended to be damaged or that are important to the systems' proper functioning. In figure 11-1, I is the intended target. I is connected to a num-

FIGURE 11-1   An Attack on a Target "I," Passing through "J" and "K"

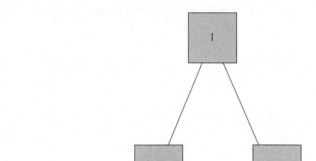

ber of other systems J and K, so a weapon should be directed at I but not at J and K. The weapon may pass through J or K on the way to I, but proper design of the weapon will mean it does not cause damage to J or K.

But in another possible configuration I may have other systems A and B attached to it, and perhaps A is the intended target and B consists of systems that the attacker does not wish to damage (see figure 11-2). But in this case we assume that both A and B rely on I for their proper functioning—and thus damage to I will also damage A and B.

Under the laws of war, the legitimacy of directing a weapon against I would depend on whether damage to B would be disproportionate to the military advantages gained by damage to A. This comparison is known as the proportionality test.

In certain cases, would-be targets may be protected from attack by international law or agreement. For example, hospitals are regarded as having special protection under the Geneva Conventions, though they must be clearly labeled (for example, with a Red Cross symbol). To the extent that nations can agree that certain entities should be protected against cyberattack, cooperative measures may serve to identify these entities (box 11-1).

Having reached its set of targets, the cyber weapon must be designed so that if the payload exits the target's machines it does not cause damage

FIGURE 11-2　An Attack on a Target "I," Passing through "J" and "K," but Where "A" and "B" Rely on "I" for Their Own Functions

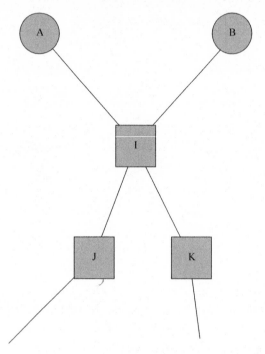

elsewhere—including through denial-of-service attacks. In addition, and especially for a cyber weapon that propagates autonomously, the method of propagation must not itself become a major disruptor of nontargets.[34] The Morris worm would fail this test, but Stuxnet passes easily.

Condition 2: The Targeted Weapon Must Avoid Inflicting Collateral Damage

It is easy to avoid inflicting collateral damage if the target is not connected to other systems. Consider the possibility that causing a harmful effect on the target (call it A) might have harmful effects on other systems (B, C, etc.) connected to it. Of course, A can be destroyed by kinetic means, and B may or may not be damaged as a result. (In some scenarios, B will see the kinetic destruction of A as simply losing its connection to A, and it will handle the destruction of A as it would the loss of that connection.) Such scenarios are common in kinetic warfare, and a well-developed legal and policy regime has emerged to deal with such questions.

But computer systems are often interconnected in complex ways that make clarity more difficult than for kinetic systems. Damaging but not destroying one computer system can have unforeseen effects on other, seemingly unrelated ones.[35] Furthermore, the negative impact on connected computers B and C may be greater when A is merely damaged in some way rather than completely destroyed; B and C may well be programmed to know what to do when the connection to A is broken, but they may not be able to recognize when data coming from A are corrupted in some way or even seriously delayed (for example, as the result of an attack on A). Thus, in the latter case, B and C may continue operating but slowly or with bad data—which may be more consequential than if the flow of data from A is simply stopped.[36]

Proliferation of Cyber Weapons

For a variety of reasons, proliferation of cyber weapons is potentially much easier than proliferation of kinetic weapons. Unlike kinetic weapons that explode and destroy themselves as well as the target, a cyber weapon does not necessarily destroy itself upon use. Such a weapon, used to attack one target, is relatively easily recovered, and some components may be repurposed. Thus, unless special precautions are taken to prevent the reuse of a cyber weapon, proliferation to other parties may enable those other parties to use the weapon for their own purposes—and thereby cause damage to other entities.

In addition, manufacturing cyber weapons is much cheaper and faster than manufacturing typical kinetic weapons. Once a cyber weapon has been reverse-engineered and its mechanism of deployment and use recovered, making more of the same is far easier than manufacturing other types of weapons.

With cyber weapons, however, simply the *use* of a weapon could supply the attacker with necessary information—technical or otherwise—to construct its own version if precautions are not taken to prevent such an outcome. In the cyber weapon context, the nonproliferation objective seeks to prevent others from being able to use code snippets, information on zero days, techniques for weapons design, or even new classes of weapon. The risk of

---

BOX 11-1   On Cooperative Measures to Differentiate Protected and Unprotected Entities in Cyberspace

Possible cooperative measures can relate to locations in cyberspace—for example, nations might publish the IP addresses associated with the information systems of protected entities, and cyber weapons would never be aimed at those IP addresses.* Alternatively, a system could have a machine-readable tag (such as a special file kept in common locations) that identifies it as a protected system. Cyber weapons could be designed to check for such tags as part of their assessment of the environment.

Such cooperative measures are problematic in many ways. For example, a scheme in which tags are applied to protected entities runs a strong risk of abuse—a military computer system could easily be equipped with a tag indicating that it is used by a hospital. (Of course, on the kinetic battlefield, a Red Cross symbol could also be improperly painted on a building that contains ammunition.)

The notion of tagged protected facilities raises a number of difficult research questions. For example, how can a cyber weapon query the tag when the act of querying is easily detected and would thus reveal an intrusion? How can protected facilities be listed publicly when the existence of one might give away the fact of an associated military computing complex?

Yet another tension would result in the event that the cyber weapon sensed that it was in the vicinity of its intended target (on the basis of

---

proliferation that may arise from these efforts varies substantially, with some posing little or no risk, and some posing a great deal.

These considerations also apply to prepositioned cyber weapons, which are sometimes called logic bombs. Such weapons are implanted into an adversary's computers in advance of hostilities, and they are intended to cause damage not upon implantation but at a later time when some condition has been met. The triggering condition can be that a specified amount of time has elapsed, the occurrence of a specific time and date, the receipt of a message from the owner or operator of the weapon, or the sensing of a particular condition in the environment in which the weapon has been prepositioned.

Assuming the process of prepositioning is executed properly, a prepositioned cyber weapon causes no damage before it is triggered. Once triggered, intelligence information gathered for this specific purpose) but also found a tag indicating that it was a protected facility. Should the weapon release its attack payload, despite the presence of a tag designating it as a protected entity? Or should it refrain from doing so despite intelligence information indicating that it is indeed in the environment of a valid target? Note that the same problem occurs in noncyber situations when, for example, an ambulance is being used to transport weapons.

A scheme to label unprotected entities also creates problems. For example, publicly listing the IP addresses of military computing facilities is an invitation to the outside world to target those facilities. The legal need to differentiate unprotected (military) and protected (civilian) facilities arises only in the context of the laws of war, which themselves come into force only during armed conflict. Thus, we confront the absurdity of a situation in which, before the outbreak of hostilities, lists of military entities are kept secret, but upon initiation of hostilities they are made public.

---

* Relying on third-party lists of IP addresses—for example, a country's national registry of protected computers—is a fragile defense. While servers' IP addresses are much more stable than those of desktops or laptops, they can and do change for many reasons: for example, they can be replaced (a new server is likely to be brought online before the old one is decommissioned), or network topology might change (for technical reasons, address assignment has to mirror the physical interconnections of different networks). System administrators tend to keep current only those entries necessary for day-to-day functioning of their computers and networks; a national registry important only in time of war does not qualify.

the damage it causes to intended or unintended targets is subject to the same considerations as any other weapon. But prepositioning a cyber weapon poses a risk that it will be discovered before it is triggered and then recovered intact. Once discovered, reverse-engineering attempts on the recovered weapon will surely be undertaken, and thus proliferation of that weapon becomes a distinct possibility. Furthermore, the owner or operator of the weapon is unlikely to know if the weapon has been discovered.

Mechanisms for Proliferation

As we have suggested, the actual use of a cyber weapon may lead to proliferation: the target will convert the weapon used against it into its own weapon and turn it back on the attacker. There are several ways in which this can happen.

The simplest is through knowledge that a particular technique works. It has been said that the only real secret of the atomic bomb was whether one could be built; after that, it "merely" required applied physics and engineering (and, of course, the expenditure of a large sum of money). The same is true in the cyber domain. For example, although C. A. R. Hoare had warned in 1981 of the dangers of not checking array indices,[37] it was not until the 1988 Morris Worm that most people realized that the security risk was quite real. Similarly, although using USB flash disks to jump an air gap was conceivable as an attack possibility, few thought it could be done in practice until Stuxnet showed that it worked.

A second route to proliferation involves code that reuses the specific, low-level techniques of an existing weapon. IRONGATE is an example: it has been called a "Stuxnet copycat," but was quite clearly not written by the same group.[38] CIA documents leaked in 2017 describe the existence of a program to reuse malware obtained from other sources, including other nations' cyber operations.[39] If the CIA is doing this, presumably other intelligence agencies are as well.

Finally, the actual code used can be reverse-engineered. Doing this requires significant effort by skilled individuals, but it can be done. The reverse-engineering of Stuxnet, the only sophisticated cyber weapon that we have described, was accomplished by a handful of researchers in private sector firms working essentially in their spare time. The expertise at intelligence agencies is at least as good—and probably significantly better—because they are handling sophisticated attacks from other nations. Agencies responsible for national security can be expected to be as equally professional in reverse engineering of cyber weapons as the Stuxnet teams were in constructing Stuxnet.

Taking Steps to Limit Proliferation

A state wanting to limit future damages caused by a given kind of cyberattack should take into account proliferation issues and take actions that effectively diminish the risks of proliferation. From a technical standpoint, meeting the nonproliferation objective is thus the problem of either (1) obfuscating the code of the weapon so that an adversary cannot make use of it, or (2) changing the environment of those who might be harmed by successful proliferation so that they will not be harmed. Problem (1) can be solved unilaterally by the actions of the weapons designer; problem (2) requires action on the part of both the attacker and others.

It is useful to divide the issue of proliferation into the immediate aftermath of an attack and those events that may occur due to proliferation in the longer term—perhaps days or weeks later. The simplest way to conceal the exploit is to use a "loader/dropper" architecture. In such a design, a small piece of code takes advantage of a security hole to penetrate a system, downloads the actual payload, and then deletes itself. An adversary who later determines that a system is infected will find only the payload and not the part of the code that actually effects the penetration of the target.

Attackers can also take steps to obfuscate their code. For example, they can encrypt the important parts of the code; the decryption key is derived from values specific to the target machines.[40] When encryption is used for obfuscation, it becomes very difficult to decrypt it without access to the target machines. The Gauss spyware employed such a scheme.[41] Obfuscation is the technique of choice for preventing an adversary from using it.

Preventing proliferation from occurring over the long term is the focus of changing the environment of potential victims, and is much harder because the solution is not entirely under the attacker's control. One approach—perhaps the only approach—to preventing proliferation is to provide to potential victims the information they need to prevent the repurposed weapon from being used against them. Specifically, the attacker would disclose the mechanisms used to effect penetration (that is, the vulnerabilities) after the weapon had served its original purpose.[42]

If disclosure of the penetration mechanisms were done entirely publicly, any potential victim could patch its systems to prevent the weapon from being used against it.[43] In this case, the weapon might well be unusable in the future. Also, widespread disclosure could make information available that would make it easier for attacks to occur much faster than they might have otherwise.[44] Alternatively, the disclosure could be limited to the extent possible only to friendly parties, thus increasing the likelihood that the same penetration mechanisms would be useful against other targets in the future. These issues are at the heart of the Vulnerabilities Equities Process, a process established by the executive branch in the United States to determine whether a given vulnerability should be disclosed (to enable its repair) or not disclosed (to enable it to be used by the U.S. government in the future).[45]

Whether the long-term nonproliferation objective should dominate over other policy concerns is something to be determined on a case-by-case basis.

Conclusion

Contrary to a belief held in many quarters, cyber weapons as a class are not inherently indiscriminate. But designing a cyber weapon so that it can be used in a targeted manner is technically demanding and requires a great deal of intelligence about the targets against which it will be directed. When the technical demands can be met and the requisite intelligence is in hand, it is possible to conduct cyberattacks that are precisely targeted to achieve a desired effect and with minimal damage to entities that should remain unharmed.

A second consideration in limiting damage from using a cyber weapon is that of proliferation. Proliferation does not arise as the direct result of using a cyber weapon in an attack. Rather, it is the result of the fact that a cyber weapon, once used, may become available for others to examine, copy, and reuse for their own purposes.

Whether Stuxnet was a factor in bringing Iran to the bargaining table over the development of nuclear weapons is hard to determine. What is clear is that the United States was able to attack a well-defended site at Natanz; that undoubtedly demonstrated to the Iranians the depth of U.S. capabilities. What is notable about the U.S. attack on the nuclear facility is that it was accomplished without loss of life.

The scope and nature of the ability to narrowly target a cyber weapon are crucial aspects of how, if at all, it can or should be used. The laws of armed conflict require the use of weapons that are not inherently indiscriminate, and furthermore that all weapons be used in a discriminating manner. This chapter has described how some cyber weapons can be used in a discriminating manner—that is, such weapons can be directed against specifically designated entities. But designing and using a cyber weapon in the requisite manner requires effort—perhaps significantly more effort, both on development and on intelligence gathering, than might be necessary to design and use a weapon in a less discriminating manner.

In this chapter we have sought to begin the conversation on how targetable cyber weapons can be developed from a technical standpoint and what policy issues need to be part of the considerations in both design and deployment. As far as we are aware, this is the first discussion in the open literature of targeting cyber weapons and ways to avoid proliferation. We hope this work engenders further discussion of these issues.

Notes

1. BBC History, "Britain Bombs Berlin" (www.bbc.co.uk/history/events/britain_bombs _berlin).

2. Cyber weapons can be instantiated in hardware as well. Tampering with hardware can result in widespread or narrow effects, depending on the mechanism and how it is activated. Backdoors can be embedded in hardware and installed at any point in the supply chain, from initial fabrication as commodity hardware to the process of shipping a finished system to an end user. See, for example, Samuel T. King and others, "Designing and Implementing Malicious Hardware," in *LEET '08: Proceedings of the First Usenix Workshop on Large-Scale Exploits and Emergent Threats* (Berkeley, Calif., 2008), pp. 1–8.

3. An analogy could be drawn to an airplane carrying a payload: the airplane is the penetration mechanism by which the attacker gains access to an adversary's territory. Once there, the airplane can drop high-explosive bombs, incendiaries, and nuclear weapons— or leaflets. Similarly, the same plane could simply take pictures.

4. Some analysts include a third class of nation-state intrusion known as "preparing the battlefield." Roughly speaking, it involves planting software that will be useful in the event of a conflict but leaving it dormant until then. The nearest analogy is prepositioning munitions in enemy territory before a war.

5. Department of Defense, Office of General Counsel, "Weapons," in *Law of War Manual* (2015), p. 340.

6. Ibid.

7. This chapter also distinguishes between two methods through which a cyber weapon can propagate. A worm is a cyber weapon that propagates through a network. By contrast, a virus propagates through non-network mechanisms such as infected files and human assistance, witting or unwitting, to carry the infection from an infected machine to an uninfected one. Because human assistance is needed, viruses propagate most readily and virulently within affinity groups. A given piece of malware can be designed as a worm or a virus, or it can make use of both mechanisms to propagate.

8. The Morris worm ultimately spread to a large number of systems on the internet (at the time, about 10 percent, or about 6,000). For an account of the Morris worm, see Katie Hafner and John Markoff, *CYBERPUNK: Outlaws and Hackers on the Computer Frontier*, revised updated ed. (New York: Simon & Schuster, 1995.

9. Robert A. Guth and Daniel Machalaba, "Computer Viruses Disrupt Railway and Air Traffic," *Wall Street Journal*, August 21, 2003.

10. For the Chernobyl virus, see Graham Cluley, "Memories of the Chernobyl Virus," *Naked Security*, April 26, 2011 (https://nakedsecurity.sophos.com/2011/04/26/memories -of-the-chernobyl-virus/). For the Witty worm, see Colleen Shannon and David Moore, "The Spread of the Witty Worm," *IEEE Security and Privacy* 2, no. 4 (2004), pp. 46–50.

11. During NATO's bombing campaign against Serbia, NATO systems were the target of low-grade attacks. Some of these are believed to have been launched by the Serbian military; see Jason Healey, "Cyber Attacks against NATO: Then and Now," Atlantic Council, September 6, 2011 (www.atlanticcouncil.org/blogs/new-atlanticist/cyber-attacks -against-nato-then-and-now). There are also reports that Israel's air strike on a purported North Korean–built nuclear reactor in Syria was aided by a cyber intrusion that disabled Syrian air defense radars. See David A. Fulghum, Robert Wall, and Amy Butler, "Cyber-Combat's First Shot," *Aviation Week & Space Technology*, November 26, 2007, pp. 28–31. No details have emerged; nor has there been independent confirmation.

12. There were some minor website defacements.

13. Kim Zetter, *Countdown to Zero Day: Stuxnet and the Launch of the World's First Digital Weapon* (New York: Crown, 2014).

14. Stuxnet was designed to unlock its malware payload only after it had checked the target system for a specific configuration of this plant: the model of PLC (programmable logic controller), the type of frequency converters, the layout of the units, and so on. If this check did not indicate that Stuxnet was inside a plant that matched this configuration, Stuxnet would remain on the compromised system in the plant, but Stuxnet's payload would not be decrypted. See ibid., pp. 28–29.

15. Nicole Perlroth, "Cyberattack on Saudi Firm, U.S. Sees Iran Firing Back," *New York Times*, October 23, 2012.

16. Dan Goodin, "Mystery Malware *Wreaks* Havoc on Energy Sector Computers," *Ars Technica*, August 16, 2012 (http://arstechnica.com/security/2012/08/shamoon-malware -attack/).

17. David E. Sanger and Martin Fackler, "N.S.A. Breached North Korean Networks before Sony Attack, Officials Say," *New York Times*, January 18, 2015.

18. Sean Gallagher, "Inside the Wiper Malware That Brought Sony Pictures to Its Knees," *Ars Technica*, December 3, 2014 (http://arstechnica.com/security/2014/12/inside -the-wiper-malware-that-brought-sony-pictures-to-its-knees/).

19. James Cook, "Sony Hackers Have Over 100 Terabytes of Documents," *Business Insider*, December 16, 2014 (www.businessinsider.com/the-sony-hackers-still-have-a-massive -amount-of-data-that-hasnt-been-leaked-yet-2014-12).

20. For complex reasons involving shared resources and network dynamics, the full 100G bps is unlikely to be realized; still, the effect would be considerable.

21. One example is a virtual machine hosted by a cloud provider such as Amazon; another could be a separate website hosted on a large dedicated web server.

22. The DNS (domain name system) is a distributed database that converts user-friendly names like www.stanford.edu into the IP addresses used by the network protocols.

23. Choe Sang-Hun, "Computer Networks in South Korea Are Paralyzed in Cyberattacks," *New York Times*, March 20, 2013.

24. "Sources: Staged Cyber Attack Reveals Vulnerability in Power Grid," CNN, September 26, 2007 (www.cnn.com/2007/US/09/26/power.at.risk/index.html).

25. Electricity Information Sharing and Analysis Center, *Analysis of the Cyber Attack on the Ukrainian Power Grid: Defense Use Case*, March 18, 2016 (https://ics.sans.org/media /E-ISAC_SANS_Ukraine_DUC_5.pdf).

26. Note, however, that other kinds of DDoS attacks can affect entities beyond those directly targeted. For example, on October 21, 2016, a large DDoS attack targeted Dyn, an internet infrastructure company that served many large consumer-facing firms, such as the *New York Times*, Spotify, Twitter, and Amazon, among others. This attack prevented many consumers from being able to access their desired web pages, even though the consumer-facing firms were not directly targeted. For accounts of this attack, see Lily Hay Newman, "What We Know about Friday's Massive East Coast Internet Outage," *Wired*, October 21, 2016 (www.wired.com/2016/10/internet-outage-ddos-dns-dyn/), and Kyle York, "Read Dyn's Statement on the 10/21/2016 DNS DDoS Attack," *Dyn Blog*, October 22, 2016 (http://dyn.com/blog/dyn-statement-on-10212016-ddos-attack/).

27. "Once the removable drive has infected three computers, the files on the removable drive will be deleted." See Nicolas Falliere, Liam O Murchu, and Eric Chien, *W32.Stuxnet Dossier*, Version 1.4, Symantec Corporation, February 2011, p. 29 (www.symantec.com /content/en/us/enterprise/media/security_response/whitepapers/w32_stuxnet_dossier.pdf).

28. Under certain conditions, attacks on networks that are air-gapped from the internet can simplify targeting—that is, if they only activate once certain conditions are met, all other computers within reach are part of the same isolated—and likely targeted—networks.

29. For example, according to David E. Sanger, Stuxnet was detected and then nullified precisely because it had spread too far ("Obama Order Sped Up Wave of Cyberattacks against Iran," *New York Times*, June 1, 2012) This analysis is somewhat controversial and contradicted by other accounts.

30. Martin C. Libicki, "Second Acts in Cyberspace," *Journal of Cybersecurity* 3, no. 1 (2017), pp. 29–35.

31. Camila Domonoske, "Attack on MSF Hospital a '*Tragic but* Avoidable Accident,' Pentagon Finds," NPR, November 25, 2015 (www.npr.org/sections/thetwo-way/2015/11/25/457370761/attack-on-msf-hospital-a-tragic-but-avoidable-accident-pentagon-finds).

32. Article 36 of Additional Protocol I of 1977 of the Geneva Conventions states, "In the study, development, acquisition or adoption of a new weapon, means or method of warfare, a High Contracting Party is under an obligation to determine whether its employment would, in some or all circumstances, be prohibited by this Protocol or by any other rule of international law applicable to the High Contracting Party." This article is widely regarded as imposing legal requirements to conduct reviews of weapons before they are adopted for use. See, for example, H. Parks, "Conventional Weapons and Weapons Reviews," in *Yearbook of International Humanitarian Law* 8 (2005), pp. 55–142.

33. This is not always sufficient to prevent collateral damage, especially if shared resources—network links, computers, and others—exist.

34. It is necessarily a minor disruptor in the sense that the attacked system is using resources to spread the attack and that it is not normal behavior for the system under attack.

35. AT&T's internet service once suffered an outage due to an erroneous change by another ISP. See Denise Pappalardo, "Internet Access Outage Burns AT&T; WorldNet Customers," CNN, December 6, 1999 (https://web.archive.org/web/20040810055011/http://www.cnn.com:80/1999/TECH/computing/12/06/att.outage.idg/index.html).

36. There are many ways in which this can occur. For example, TCP is designed to slow down drastically in the presence of packet loss (see V. Jacobson, "Congestion Avoidance and Control," *ACM SIGCOMM Computer Communication Review* 18, no. 4 [1988], pp. 314–29), since under normal conditions packet loss indicates network congestion. A carefully modulated denial-of-service attack could induce such behavior.

37. Charles Anthony Richard Hoare, "The Emperor's Old Clothes," 1980 ACM Turing Award Lecture, *Communications of the ACM* 24 (1981), pp. 75–83.

38. IRONGATE is a piece of control system malware that appeared post-Stuxnet and appears to reuse a number of Stuxnet's techniques; see Joseph Cox, "There's a Stuxnet Copycat, and We Have No Idea Where It Came From," *Motherboard*, June 2, 2016 (http://motherboard.vice.com/read/theres-a-stuxnet-copycat-and-we-have-no-idea-where-it-came-from).

39. Kim Zetter, "Wikileaks Files Show the CIA Repurposing Hacking Code to Save Time, Not to Frame Russia," *The Intercept*, March 8, 2017 (https://theintercept.com/2017/03/08/wikileaks-files-show-the-cia-repurposing-foreign-hacking-code-to-save-time-not-to-frame-russia/).

40. A cryptographic key is a long, usually random number. Most files encrypted with modern cryptosystems are unreadable unless the key is known. Computers have a variety of unique, unguessable numbers present, such as manufactured-in serial numbers and network hardware addresses.

41. Dan Goodin, "Puzzle Box: The Quest to Crack the World's Most Mysterious Malware Warhead," *Ars Technica*, March 14, 2013 (http://arstechnica.com/security /2013/03/the-worlds-most-mysteriouspotentially-destructive-malware-is-not-stuxnet).

42. This approach to preventing proliferation is not effective in all cases. The reason is that an independently developed cyber weapon based on an attack technique revealed from a proof-of-concept demonstration may not use the same vulnerabilities that the demonstration used.

43. Experience shows that not all potential victims install patches to known vulnerabilities. Indeed, the successful North Korean attack against Sony used well-known techniques and exploited unpatched systems. Furthermore, older systems are often not patchable: the hardware is incapable of running the newer versions of the code.

44. In the days immediately after a patch is announced, hostile parties reverse-engineer the patch to discover the vulnerability being fixed and launch attacks that take advantage of that vulnerability against a wide range of targets, many of whom will not have installed the patch by the time their attack occurs.

45. Michael Daniel, "Heartbleed: Understanding When We Disclose Cyber Vulnerabilities," *White House Blog*, April 28, 2014 (www.whitehouse.gov/blog/2014/04/28/heart bleed-understanding-when-we-disclose-cyber-vulnerabilities).

12

Rules of Engagement for Cyberspace Operations

A View from the United States

C. ROBERT KEHLER, HERBERT LIN,
and MICHAEL SULMEYER

As cyber weapons are incorporated into U.S. military planning, policymakers and field commanders will increasingly confront a core issue: how to formulate the rules of engagement (ROEs) for U.S. forces with regard to military operations that may use such weapons.[1] This chapter addresses ROEs from the perspective of U.S. military operators.[2] It is informed by practitioner experience rather than empirical research.

The U.S. Department of Defense (DoD) defines ROEs as "directives issued by competent military authority that delineate the circumstances and

C. Robert "Bob" Kehler thanks Theodore Richard for reviewing an early draft of this chapter. Herbert Lin thanks Taylor Grossman for critical assistance. Michael Sulmeyer thanks Peter Pascucci for reviewing an early draft of this chapter and Olivia Zetter for excellent research assistance. This work was supported by the Cyber Policy Program of Stanford University's Center for International Security and Cooperation and the Hoover Institution. All views expressed in this chapter are only those of the authors.

limitations under which U.S. forces will initiate and/or continue combat engagement with other forces encountered."[3] ROEs also provide authorization for and place limits on the use of weapons, the positioning and posturing of military forces, and the use or nonuse of certain specified capabilities (for example, specific weapons systems). However, they are not usually used to assign missions or to give tactical instructions.

Understanding Rules of Engagement

U.S. military commanders act within a complex network of authorities derived from law, policy, and regulation.[4] Authorities provide commanders with the permission needed to conduct military operations. Such authorities include the authority to use force, of which ROEs are one critical component.

ROEs reflect constraints on the use of force imposed by the law of armed conflict (LOAC). These constraints include *military necessity*, which permits only acts of force necessary to accomplish legitimate military objectives; *distinction*, which distinguishes between combatants and civilians; and *proportionality*, which counsels that the anticipated loss of life or injury to civilians or damage to civilian objects not be in excess of military advantages anticipated from a specific act.

In addition, senior leaders may wish for policy reasons to impose constraints that go beyond LOAC requirements. For example, they may wish to influence world opinion, to not antagonize an adversary unnecessarily, to conform to host-country law, or to not escalate a conflict. Commanders may use ROEs to place upper bounds on the scope and intensity of operations to reduce the chances of undesired conflict escalation.

U.S. forces operate under three types of ROEs. Standing rules of engagement (SROEs) provide a set of always-operative rules related to self-defense for forces in peacetime as well as a template for operation-specific ROEs. Supplemental ROEs (also known as mission-specific ROEs) are tailored for a region, a mission, or a specific operation and may elaborate on or interpret the SROEs for a given mission without contradicting them. Standing rules for the use of force (SRUFs) govern military actions inside the United States.

Standing Rules of Engagement

The SROEs empower commanders at all levels to protect their forces from hostile acts and demonstrations of hostile intent. Unit commanders always retain the inherent right and obligation to exercise unit self-defense in response to a hostile act or demonstrated hostile intent, whether or not a state of armed conflict is acknowledged to exist.

The SROEs allow a U.S. commander to use all necessary means available and to take all appropriate actions in self-defense, provided these actions do not violate the LOAC requirements of necessity and proportionality. However, they allow only those immediate actions minimally required (with respect to nature, duration, and scope of force) to end the immediate threat. Some weapons and tactics require specific approval from the president or the secretary of defense before they can be used (for example, only the president can authorize the use of nuclear weapons).

Self-defense includes passive and active defense measures. Passive defense refers to actions taken to "reduce the probability of and to minimize the effects of damage caused by hostile action without the intention of taking the initiative," whereas active defense refers to the "employment of limited offensive action and counterattacks to deny a contested area or position to the enemy."[5]

In practice, the on-scene commander must make judgments about what constitutes hostile intent, a difficult task in a fluid and fast-moving tactical situation. Commanders are asked to use their best judgment when considering available intelligence, political and military factors, indications and warnings, and other relevant information concerning possible threats in their area. But there is no checklist of indicators that will conclusively determine hostile intent. Proactive measures (such as issuing warnings and firing warning shots) are encouraged if practical because entities that do not alter their behavior as a result are regarded as more likely to be showing hostile intent.

Supplemental Rules of Engagement
Supplemental ROEs are mission-specific and do not restrict the appropriate use of force in self-defense. Supplemental ROEs may be used to elaborate on how the SROEs should be interpreted in situations likely to occur during a specific mission. For example, a given mission might call for deployed forces to interact with civilians. If such interactions are unfriendly (for example, an encounter with an unarmed mob), the risk of escalating a conflict may be high, and so a supplemental ROE might direct that the unit should withdraw or use smoke to camouflage itself, but should not use its weapons to fire on the mob.

Some supplemental ROEs permit a specific tactic, weapon, or operation. Others clarify action allowed under the SROEs. For example, they may limit specific types of artillery, who may use certain weapons, or the targets that may be attacked.

Because they are mission-specific, supplemental ROEs are an important focus of mission planning, a process that defines specific objectives, establishes lists of targets to be attacked to achieve those objectives, and develops courses of action and options for attacking each target. Mission planning is usually done well in advance of actual military action, but the existence of a mission plan does not have operational significance until commanders are given the authority to execute that mission. By contrast, the SROEs are always in effect and thus always have operational significance.

Standing Rules for the Use of Force

Standing rules for the use of force (SRUFs) govern military actions *inside* U.S. territory. Such actions can include those associated with Defense Support of Civil Authorities (DSCA), land homeland defense missions, and law enforcement and security measures at DoD installations. SRUFs are inherently restrictive: unless specific weapons and tactics are explicitly approved, they cannot be used without the authorization of the secretary of defense.

Defense Support of Civil Authorities during Hurricane Katrina offers one SRUF example. In that mission, SRUFs were used to help guide the actions of conventional forces from the Navy, Air Force, and Army that were assigned to support civilian authorities with search and rescue, aid delivery, and peacekeeping.

Rules of Engagement for Cyberspace Operations

ROEs for cyberspace operations have received growing attention as opportunities for achieving military objectives in and through cyberspace have become more plausible. To the extent feasible, the DoD has sought to apply the same principles that govern the use of kinetic weapons to the use of cyber weapons, while recognizing the special characteristics of the cyber domain and cyber weapons. This has proven to be a difficult challenge.

Many of the military's actual capabilities in the cyberspace domain and the ROEs corresponding to their use remain classified. That said, through inference, informed speculation, and an increasing public understanding of the underlying science and technology, a growing body of unclassified information is available regarding the principles and concepts that guide how DoD planners formulate ROEs for operations in cyberspace.

The Meaning of Self-Defense

The SROEs are based on an immediate threat (that is, the commander must determine that a hostile act has occurred or that hostile intent exists) and a need to respond to that threat. But an action that comes in or through cyberspace may not present an obvious threat to human life or critical capability. Rarely will a cyberspace operator confront a personal life-or-death decision similar to that of a soldier engaged in kinetic combat on a physical battlefield.[6] Thus cyberspace adds a new layer of complexity to the traditional concepts of self-defense.

The response to this new complexity has been a compromise. Military units are normally authorized to take passive defense measures within the systems or networks for which they are responsible. Examples include using intrusion detection systems (IDS—software that monitors the network or system for malicious activities), using firewalls that prevent traffic from passing through various ports or signature-based antivirus systems that screen incoming traffic for embedded malware, dropping connections that could be used for hostile purposes, or deleting malware found on the systems being defended. Such measures are analogous to evasive maneuvers by a ship facing an airplane that is apparently attacking.

On the other hand, a military unit experiencing a cyberattack would not be allowed on its own authority to conduct a cyberattack (or kinetic attack, for that matter) against the Ministry of Defense headquarters of the nation believed to be responsible. Such a response would be an overtly offensive action analogous to striking the airfield from which an attacking airplane was launched and would require separate authority.

Active defense occupies a large and uncharted gray area between passive defense and overtly offensive action. For all practical purposes, active defense can be defined as anything that is neither passive defense nor offensive action. As with all U.S. military operations, active defense measures must comply with the laws of war regarding distinction, proportionality, and the like. In addition, active defense must not go beyond measures that negate or mitigate the immediate threat to the defender. In the cyber context, active defense is complicated by several unique factors.

Active defense measures in cyberspace can fall into two categories: those that have effects on systems or networks inside the organizational span of control of the defender, and those that have effects on systems or networks outside that span of control.[7] Active defense measures in the first category (category 1) can include hunting within one's own network for malware, operating honeypots that attract adversary traffic, dynamically restricting privileges for suspicious users identified by an intrusion detection system, and so on. Such actions have few, if any, international legal implications. Category 1 active defense measures are analogous to launching intercept aircraft in response to an intruding enemy aircraft with orders to engage within the defender's airspace.

Active defense measures in the second category (category 2) are much more problematic from an international legal standpoint because they do have effects on or require access to systems or networks not under the defender's legitimate control. Category 2 active defense measures could include disabling the computer controlling the hostile action or beaconing (the practice of "bugging" files so that they report when the adversary opens them). Category 2 active defense measures would be analogous to an airplane flying in its own airspace that is illuminated by fire-control radar located in an adjacent country and firing an antiradiation missile at the radar. In all cases, differentiating between category 2 active defense and offensive action in cyberspace can be problematic.

Cyber-related self-defense takes another turn when considering responses with noncyber means. Indeed, the *Department of Defense Cyber Strategy* explicitly notes that the United States will "respond to cyberattacks against U.S. interests at a time, in a manner, and in a place of our choosing, using appropriate instruments of U.S. power."[8]

Thus, if the cyberattack originates from a nearby location, a unit might fire a missile to physically destroy the source of the attack. Although a kinetic response is not symmetrical to the incoming cyberattack, there is no prima facie reason why it could not be proportional. However, such a kinetic response could be escalatory, and escalation might be of significant concern to higher headquarters. Anticipating such a situation, higher authority might formulate restrictive ROEs on the unit so that explicit authorization is needed before responding in such a manner.

In addition, the effects of an active defense action are supposed to be limited to eliminating the immediate threat. Thus any category 2 active defense measure must employ weapons and techniques (cyber or otherwise) that confine damage to the threat entity and minimize damage to other systems. But such a task places great demands on intelligence, as discussed by Steven Bellovin, Susan Landau, and Herbert Lin in chapter 11 in this volume. A great deal of detailed intelligence information about the target of a category

2 active defense action is needed to limit effects to the threat entity. Such information may not be available in a timely way.

To a certain extent, development of ROEs will inform intelligence-gathering efforts about the possible targets, and therefore shape what entities may be targeted for category 2 active defense.

Another problematic scenario involves a tactical unit using a cyberattack as a response to incoming kinetic fire—the responsive cyberattack launched in self-defense would be targeted on the computers powering the opponent's equipment. With just these facts, such a cyber response might or might not be escalatory. And it is not clear that such a response would be any more (or less) narrowly tailored than a kinetic response. If the cyber response knocks out the firing weapon but also regional internet traffic that connects civilian infrastructure, the cyber option might be no better or worse than the non-cyber options. These scenarios present important wrinkles to be considered when commanders prepare ROEs pertaining to self-defense in cyberspace.

Commanders typically prefer permissive (and clear) ROEs for military operations. Allowing units to respond with a range of capabilities (regardless of whether they are cyber or noncyber) with permissive ROEs that are sensitive to the unique aspects of cyberspace is arguably the most efficient method to shape how units react. But from a policymaker's perspective, the risks of inadvertent escalation and collateral damage may well argue for restrictive rules, especially when considering responses with noncyber means.

A final point on self-defense: the more individualized notion of unit self-defense must be distinguished from the broader concept of defending the country, its interests, or its property.[9] Self-defense in the latter case is functionally distinct from the type of self-defense envisioned in the SROEs. Separate authorities (that is, supplemental ROEs) would have to be crafted to cover cyber actions taken in conjunction with DoD actions to defend the nation, or SRUFs would have to be developed to cover DSCA activities.

In general, active defense measures and deadly force through cyberspace could be authorized to protect people or capabilities that, if damaged or destroyed, would reasonably threaten death or serious bodily injury. Deadly force could not be used to defend most kinds of property, although passive defense measures can usually be taken (move the property, house it, lock it up, build a fence around it, and so on). However, according to the SRUFs, certain special categories of property can be protected with deadly force. These include:

- Assets vital to national security, such as nuclear weapons, nuclear command and control, designated restricted areas containing strategic operational assets, sensitive codes, or special-access programs.

- Inherently dangerous property, such as portable missiles, rockets, arms, ammunition, explosives, chemical agents, and special nuclear materials.

- National critical infrastructure, which include presidentially designated public utilities or similar critical infrastructure vital to public health or safety, the damage to which would create an imminent threat of death or serious bodily harm.[10]

Given that deadly force is authorized to protect these kinds of property, it is likely that the use of cyber weapons for the same purpose would be allowable under the standing rules for the use of force. But the considerations described in the following section may weigh against such use in many circumstances.

Ambiguous Intent

"Hostile intent"—the imminent use of or threat of force—is a foundational concept on which the SROEs are built.[11] However, in the cyber domain, determining the intent behind network activity can be confounding. For example, differentiating between enemy reconnaissance in cyberspace and enemy preparation for an imminent attack is very difficult, as both operations entail essentially the same activities from a technical perspective. Distinguishing between reconnaissance and routine intelligence collection is even more problematic. The majority of adversary objectives in cyberspace have heretofore been to create access to systems and data, to maintain persistent presence on those systems, and to steal information and intellectual property. Thus, distinguishing hostile intent from these other activities is a challenge for operators trying to apply ROEs in a timely way.

As an example, an attempted intrusion against an important military facility may be motivated by the desire to collect information without tactical military value. Such intent, though certainly not friendly, most likely does not rise to the level of either a hostile act or the demonstration of hostile intent. But the intrusion may also be the precursor to a cyberattack that will cause actual damage, which *would* be a hostile act. When the intrusion is detected, it may not be entirely clear which of these possibilities is the case, and a delayed response may be too late.

The lack of clarity arises from an inherent characteristic of cyber instruments. Such instruments require a mechanism to penetrate the system of interest and a separate mechanism (usually called the payload) to create the desired effects. When the intrusion is first detected, the payload may not have yet executed, making determination of the intrusion's purpose difficult.

A second example is port scanning, an action that determines which ports are open at a given IP address. An IP address specifies the location of a specific computer system in cyberspace at a specific time, and ports are channels through which that computer can transmit and receive information. Specific ports are often but not always associated with certain functions—Port A is used for passing information to and from the World Wide Web, Port B is used for email, and so on. The system administrator can open or shut down ports depending on the needs of the system's user, but often ports that are left open unnecessarily are used by intruders to gain access to the system.

Should port scanning of a military facility's computer system be regarded as a hostile act in the meaning of the SROEs, even if nothing happens as the result of that scan? According to Rear Admiral Betsy Hight of the Joint Task Force on Global Network Operations, as reported in a 2009 report of the National Research Council, an action that resulted only in inconvenience to the probed unit or that appeared directed at intelligence gathering did not rise to the threshold of warranting an active defense measure.[12]

Ambiguity of intent need not preclude active defense responses, especially those in category 1. Even if it were possible to definitively prove a penetration had purely defensive (and therefore nonhostile) purposes, network defenders would still carry out all possible responses to remove it, given the risk of future exploitation or hostile action. Furthermore, passive and category 1 active responses are aimed at eliminating the threat without undertaking any activity outside of the defender's network. If, for example, malware is found on a computer and has not spread, disconnecting that computer from the network eliminates the threat without regard to an intruder's intent.

ROEs may therefore need to make greater accommodation for the ignorance of intent when defining when and under what conditions cyberspace operators may act, especially in comparison with the rules for kinetic operations.[13] Alternatively, the standard of evidence required to determine intent may need to be lower than kinetic operations.

Finally, resolving ambiguity is compounded by a definitional problem. When every bad thing happening is characterized as a cyber "attack," it is far more difficult to characterize anything as a real attack. Clarity in this definition is an important precursor to understanding intent.

The (Putative) Need for Speed in the Meaning of Self-Defense

In the kinetic world, reacting quickly is often necessary to eliminate an immediate threat. For example, illuminating an aircraft with fire-control radar often indicates that a missile is about to be launched against it, and delaying the destruction of that radar is likely to increase the probability that the aircraft will be attacked and destroyed.

Similar considerations have been applied to threats in cyberspace. Given the speed with which a cyber threat may cause harm, a response action may be needed very quickly to eliminate or disrupt it. In fact, the time scale in which action is needed may be so short as to preclude human intervention. However, automated response may lead to unintended and collateral effects for which the consequences are not fully understood.

Consequently, cyber ROEs must account for some likely combination of enhanced machine-based indications and warning, careful automated responses, and human decision making. In 2007 the U.S. Air Force sought proposals for a cyber control system to support automated active defense operations.[14] Today, policymakers are wary of demands for speedy (and thus automated) responses, concerned about machine-driven escalation.

Command and Control

In a traditional kinetic attack, conventional U.S. military forces normally possess some resources that they can use in self-defense. For example, ground combat units likely carry weapons that they can use to target and silence the source of incoming fire. In cyberspace operations, however, a unit subject to cyberattack may not have all the resources needed to respond effectively. For example, consider network administrators at U.S. Pacific Command (PACOM) who see their unclassified networks subjected to a denial-of-service attack. These individuals may have to rely on both internal and external sources of support, all of whom may be operating under separate authorities and ROEs.

Headquarters staff will be required to draft cyber ROEs with full awareness of evolving cyberspace command and control arrangements. According to a 2011 document, command and control structures may differ depending on combatant commander authority, operational control, tactical control, administrative control, supporting, and direct support relationships.[15]

Borderless Geography and Range of Effects

Internet routing protocols route data by and through routers according to a series of rules that seldom include distinctions based on geopolitical boundaries. This reality has two consequences. First, it is almost impossible to route traffic on the internet in a way that is confined to physical-world geographies. This factor makes it difficult (though not necessarily impossible) to contemplate cyber operations, whose planning necessarily includes routing considerations, that are wholly confined to a specific geographic area. Second, the same reality also enables adversaries to exploit compromised infrastructure both inside and outside the United States to attack U.S. networks.

Because hostile acts in cyberspace may cross national boundaries, the physical distance between where the attack originates and where it has its effects may be large. The same is true for any defensive response action, whose range may be similarly large, and a cyber response action may create effects thousands of miles away. This situation would be analogous to one in which a surface-to-air missile fired against an attacking airplane could have destructive effects on a city on the border of a neutral third country into which the airplane crashes, although in reality both an attacking airplane and a surface-to-air missile fired against it in defense of a ship have comparatively limited ranges.

Cyberspace ROEs must account for these geographic realities of cyberspace. Doing so may call for blending the SROEs and their homeland counterpart, the SRUFs. Arrangements between DoD and the Federal Bureau of Investigation and other relevant domestic agencies will be needed for situations when cyber activity implicates their jurisdiction. A coalition or alliance approach to creating ROEs may also be needed that acknowledges the potential of cyber operations to occur and create effects in multiple international political jurisdictions.

Pre-kinetic Military Operations in Anticipatory Self-Defense

The *Department of Defense Cyber Strategy*, released in April 2015, states explicitly that "during heightened tensions or outright hostilities, DoD must be able to provide the President with a wide range of options for managing conflict escalation."[16] By definition, periods of heightened tension occur before the outbreak of outright hostilities, and thus this statement suggests that offensive cyber operations may well *precede* kinetic operations.[17]

The United States takes the position that nations have "the right to take measures in response to imminent attacks."[18] An imminent attack is one that has not happened yet (that is, the first damage from such an attack has not yet been suffered) but is about to happen, and the United States—like many other nations—reserves the customary international law right of anticipatory self-defense. (This right is contested in the academic literature as well as by nations that believe they have unjustly been the targets of such a response.)[19]

An important question for anticipatory self-defense is the degree and nature of the evidence needed to make the determination that an attack is imminent, but there is no consensus on an answer to this question.[20] A determination of imminence could be based in part on information provided by human intelligence (such as an informant embedded with an adversary), technical intelligence (such as photos showing the massing of military forces in critical areas), or signals intelligence (such as interceptions of adversary communications suggesting an imminent attack). In cyberspace, signals intelligence could include information derived from sensors that have been prepositioned inside adversary networks.

However, once a determination of imminence is made, SROEs relating to cyber operations may state that commanders are authorized to conduct such operations as part of an anticipatory self-defense effort. Other guidance or advice may or may not constrain how that determination of imminent attack is made—for example, by reiterating to the commander the need for high confidence in the determination or giving him or her access to sources of intelligence that might not otherwise be made available.

Under this doctrine, exercising the right of anticipatory self-defense requires necessity and proportionality.[21] While meeting the necessity requirement is the threshold for acting in anticipatory self-defense, meeting the proportionality requirement is almost certainly easier using cyber operations that shut down adversary military capabilities than destroying them kinetically (for example, by inhibiting adversary missile launches through cyberattacks against their launch facilities or their command and control systems).

Finally, operational preparation of the cyber battlefield (OPB) is likely to be an ongoing activity as routine as peacetime reconnaissance or surveillance of potential adversary activity. OPB involves an active search for vulnerabilities in and access paths to adversary systems and networks and when possible, implantation of "hooks" that will facilitate later overtly destructive cyber action should such action be necessary. The key characteristic of OPB is that it is not a destructive act in any way; even so, the scope and nature of OPB is likely to receive attention from higher authority because of its sensitivity and escalatory potential.

Forms of Offensive Operations in Cyberspace

The U.S. Cyber Mission Force may conduct two forms of operations that could be characterized as offensive. The first is the mission of "generating integrated cyberspace effects in support of operational plans and contingency operations."[22] For example, in February 2016, Secretary of Defense Ash Carter described how cyber operations are supporting the broader campaign against the Islamic State of Iraq and Syria (ISIS).[23] This form of offensive cyberspace operation may be seen as supporting or enabling other, probably kinetic, activities.

U.S. Cyber Command is also charged with defending the nation from a cyberattack of significant consequence. Just how it is to accomplish this mission is not publicly discussed at great length, but the DoD strategy document and other statements imply action beyond blocking and after-action mitigation.[24] Furthermore, the document's implementation objectives for the defend-the-nation mission refer multiple times to the need to deter cyberattacks of significant consequence. Though the deterrence by denial has a relationship to more defensive-type actions, deterrence by cost imposition can imply more offensive steps. The implication for commanders is that both types of offensive missions may need to be accounted for in ROEs.

Escalation of Force

In physical space, escalation-of-force (EOF) measures are a set of actions, taken in sequence, that begin with nonlethal force measures such as visual signals (for example, flags, spotlights, lasers, and pyrotechnics) and may graduate to lethal measures (direct action) such as warning, disabling, or deadly shots to defeat a threat and protect the force.[25] EOF measures support ROE objectives by helping soldiers to evaluate whether an approaching threat presents hostile intent and to decide the appropriate level of response.

Even in traditional operations, the decision to escalate force is highly subjective to the commander under threat. Subjectivity is compounded in cyberspace, where intent is harder to establish and certain individual acts may not be inherently more escalatory than others. To be sure, if a cyberattack wipes 30,000 hard drives[26] or causes physical destruction,[27] it would be higher on the ladder of escalation than a low-level denial-of-service attack. But which is most escalatory: opening a seemingly innocuous port, asking a foreign server to retrieve data, injecting code to access a hidden database, or installing a rootkit that enables administrator-level access on a compromised computer? Context will always shape the answer to this question, but ambiguities in escalation will complicate interpretations of ROEs.

As such, EOF measures will need to be adopted to account for the uncertain nature of escalation within cyberspace. One method of doing so is to use the confidentiality, integrity, and availability framework.[28] For example, it may be more important for a logistics support operation to maintain data availability than to pursue other objectives, whereas an intelligence operation may prioritize confidentiality instead. Compromises to lower priority objectives would be treated as lower levels on an escalation ladder.

Attribution

In the context of responding to a hostile act or a demonstration of hostile intent, determining the party responsible for an intrusion may be difficult. This is the well-known attribution problem in cyberspace. Certain passive defense actions, such as raising one's own defensive posture, are almost always appropriate because they do not cause harmful effects on systems without the permission of the owners of those systems. But causing harmful effects outside one's own systems or without permission on the systems of others has many implications, political and otherwise.

Attribution of a hostile act in cyberspace is often possible when analysts have time to draw on multiple sources of information, both historical and collected in the wake of the hostile act in question. But time may not be available in a tactical situation involving a hostile act, which may play out in seconds or minutes. The information available in these circumstances is unlikely to support a high-quality attribution judgment, and time lines will be short. How these considerations are ultimately addressed in cyber ROEs is a key matter for consideration and resolution.

Reconciliation of Rules of Engagement and Standing Rules for the Use of Force

As noted in the previous sections, the standing rules for the use of force govern behavior of U.S. military forces within the United States, while ROEs govern behavior outside U.S. boundaries. But cyberspace—and operations within it—increasingly blurs the line between national and international boundaries. In such instances, the SRUFs and the SROEs have to be reconciled or integrated.

As an example of a potentially problematic scenario, imagine a foreign nation that takes control of a computer within the United States and uses it to launch a cyberattack of significant consequence against the Pentagon. If the identity of the foreign nation is known with a high degree of confidence (a big if!), SROEs may allow a category 2 active response against the computer originating the attack even if it is located in that country. But if not, the only active response possible might be against the computer in the United States, an action that would implicate SRUFs.

Discussion

ROEs provide military forces with guidance from higher authority about when and under what circumstances they may take action without further orders. As such, ROEs must be sufficiently clear to provide guidance in situations or circumstances that military forces are likely to encounter, since tragedy may befall units that encounter situations that are not anticipated or that cannot be handled under their ROEs.

Accordingly, key terms such as "hostile act" and "demonstration of hostile intent" must have clear definitions. In the world of kinetic weapons, the understanding of how ROEs should be interpreted has evolved with the accumulation of practical experience over a period of many years. Experience has demonstrated that exceptional or unusual circumstances not anticipated in the interpretation of ROEs occur frequently. Commanders and military lawyers have accordingly learned more about such "edge" cases and have developed operationally useful interpretations based on these experiences, even as kinetic weapons evolved much more slowly.

By contrast, cyber weapons are relatively new, and most unit commanders have not accumulated a comparable experience base for understanding how any given ROE might apply in cyberspace. Furthermore, many possible adversaries are acquiring offensive cyber capabilities, and their number is growing, increasing the urgency of developing such understanding. One approach to meeting this urgent need is to provide intensive experiential training for unit commanders in responding to scenarios that mimic as closely as possible the range of scenarios that they may encounter.

A second important point is that many of the problematic issues for interpreting the SROEs in cyberspace arise from category 2 active defense actions. Active defense against kinetic weapons focuses on negating the immediate threat, a fact with two implications. First, the immediate threat is most often near the entity being defended, and thus action taken against it need not affect anything else that may be farther away. Second, speedy negation is essential—because the threat is physically near the defended entity, there is only a short time available to eliminate it. In some situations involving kinetic weapons, an automated response may be necessary. For example, the Phalanx Close-In Weapon System (a radar-guided Gatling gun intended for defense against incoming supersonic cruise missiles) has a fully autonomous mode in which it will shoot automatically at any target that meets certain specified parameters (for example, if a missile has a speed, range, and bearing that would put it on an intercept course toward the defended entity).

But cyber weapons are of a different character. The threatening cyber weapon is a software or hardware artifact that is physically located somewhere—either on the defender's own computer systems, on the attacker's computer systems, or perhaps on the computing infrastructure of a third party. Taking action against one's own systems (such as shutting down computers) is not problematic from a policy point of view, but taking action against an attacker's computer systems may be, as discussed earlier.

In addition, one important reason—perhaps the most important reason— for having ROEs in the first place is to inhibit the unintended escalation of conflict. ROEs help to ensure that U.S. actions do not lead the military forces of a potential opponent to escalate their response.[29] Actions that are considered and deliberate are less likely to result in unintended escalation than actions that are reflexive. Given the potential escalatory consequences of an automated response that has damaging or destructive effects on the attack-originating entity, rapid responses may not be desirable from a policy perspective.

Put differently, policy considerations may well dictate—or at least suggest—that category 2 active defense actions—that is, those that have damaging effects on systems outside the unit's organizational purview— should not be allowed in certain circumstances. Although emerging U.S. military doctrine seeks to integrate cyber weapons into an effects-based framework that applies to all weapons, applying the requirement for speedy action in a category 2 active defense response to a cyber threat—a requirement that may necessarily entail automated responses—may not serve U.S. interests in reducing the likelihood of escalation.

A third issue is the actual utility of category 2 active defense actions in negating cyber threats. Negating a cyber threat can only mean one of two things: preventing an initial threat from seriously affecting the unit's computer systems, or preventing follow-on threats from doing so. If SROEs allow category 2 active defense actions only when the threat rises to the level of impairing mission performance capabilities (as was true in 2007), it is highly likely that the damage will already have been done by the time it is possible to launch a response.

That leaves the possibility that a category 2 active defense response might be able to disrupt the computer systems responsible for the original attack so that further attacks will not take place. But this scenario is for all practical purposes indistinguishable from taking overtly offensive action—and it has one added complication. After the initial attack, an informed adversary can simply take the originating computers offline to make them immune to any response, and others can be brought online from different locations in cyberspace should further attacks be needed.

Given that category 2 active defense measures involving destructive or damaging action against adversary computers will require both rapid response and significant intelligence to be available, such measures are likely to be undesirable in many operational scenarios.

Conclusion

This discussion has suggested that when the principles guiding the formulation of ROEs for kinetic weapons are applied to cyber weapons, some ROE considerations are quite similar and others are considerably different. As commanders gain greater experience with cyber operations, how to interpret ROEs and indeed to formulate them will become clearer.

At the same time, ROEs in other domains have evolved over many years of operational experience. Because the potential significance of cyber operations, both defensive and offensive, is rapidly growing, the U.S. military does not have the luxury of time to develop such experience for such operations. So an important policy issue today is how to help commanders (and planning staffs, including their Judge Advocate Generals) gain the experience that will help them use cyber weapons effectively—a key part of which is developing good ROEs for their use. In the past, the use of cyber weapons has been impeded more by legal and policy considerations than by the unavailability of the requisite technical or operational capabilities.

We believe that tabletop exercises and war games with senior leaders and practitioners (including industry and commercial operators) are one way to help military commanders (and others in both the government and private sectors) gain the necessary experience for formulating good ROEs for using cyber weapons. Such activities will force the participants to focus on definitions, boundaries, and the other issues raised in this chapter. They will also force greater sharing of information and help bridge the natural gaps between domains and sectors. In addition, they will help familiarize commanders with realistic cyber options: what it is possible to do with cyber, and most important, how to instruct their forces on the use of those options. As an example of such an exercise, it may be useful to develop ROEs and SRUFs appropriate for a distributed-denial-of-service activity using compromised infrastructure both inside and outside the United States.

To be useful, these exercises and games will require the personal involvement of the actual individuals that will be engaged in conflict. No serious military leader would expect soldiers to learn their combat craft primarily by reading reports of exercises involving others, and so the U.S. military stresses a philosophy of units training as they expect to fight. There is no reason that cyber training should be any different.

Tabletop exercises and war games have the further advantage that they are framed around specific scenarios. No one scenario captures the full range of possibilities that commanders may face in combat, but commanders that participate in a number of exercises and games will be exposed to many more eventualities.

The authors expect that the most difficult scenarios for formulating appropriate ROEs are likely to be those involving active defense measures that may have effects on or that require access to systems or networks not under the defender's control (category 2 active defense measures). The reason that active defense measures may be the most difficult is that they are likely to be at issue mostly during times that are not characterized by overt and acknowledged hostilities. During hostilities, of course, it is expected that military operations, both cyber and noncyber, will be conducted that affect entities under the other side's control. Other scenarios may be less problematic, but that does not mean it will be easy to formulate ROEs for them. ROEs for cyber capabilities do present issues that are different in practice from those encountered in noncyber operations, and until U.S. commanders and their planning staffs are more familiar with operations in cyberspace, they will be unduly constrained in their combat roles.

APPENDIX A A Primer on Rules of Engagement

Military Commanders and Authority to Act

United States military commanders act within a complex network of authorities derived from law, policy, and regulation. Authorities provide commanders with the permissions needed to conduct military operations as well as forming the basis of domestic and international legitimacy for those operations.

The authority to use force is common to virtually every military operation; other authorities might include authority to organize forces to accomplish a mission, or authority to delegate operational or tactical control of those forces.[30] Typically, "the use of force is governed by international law (chiefly the principles of the Law of Armed Conflict), national law, national and coalition ROE (and Rules for the Use of Force in Domestic Operations), national caveats, and guidance and intent from superior commanders."[31] ROEs make up one critical component of a commander's authority to use force. Commanders must understand and apply other sources of authority to establish context for those ROEs.

The Scope and Nature of Rules of Engagement

ROEs reflect three forms of influence:

- *International over national*: Principles of the law of armed conflict are often incorporated in ROEs in ways that govern how national forces employ force, thus restraining a commander's actions so that they are conducted in a manner consistent with such law. As a matter of policy, sometimes the ROEs impose greater restraints on behavior than those required by international law, as indicated in the next item.

- *Civilian over military*: Motivated by considerations of policy and politics, civilian authorities such as the president of the United States and the secretary of defense issue ROEs to combatant commanders to govern the conduct of military operations, including the use of force.[32] That is, ROEs are part of ensuring that the actions of commanders in the field are consistent with national policies and objectives. For example, for various policy reasons such as a desire to influence world opinion, not antagonize an adversary unnecessarily, conform to host-country law, or not escalate a conflict, national policymakers may issue ROEs that restrict the engagement of certain targets or forbid the use of particular weapons systems.

- *Military over military*: Combatant commanders may issue ROEs to their component and subordinate commands from a perspective of tactics. These ROEs provide the parameters within which the commander must operate to accomplish the assigned mission. They place an upper bound on operations so that the commander's actions do not result in undesired escalation of a conflict. They also grant or withhold the commander's authority to employ certain weapons or tactics.

The three types of influence described above are listed in order of specificity, with "international over national" being most general, and "military over military" being most specific.

ROEs for U.S. forces are informed by principles of international law, such as: *military necessity*, which permits only acts of force necessary to accomplish legitimate military objectives; *distinction*, which distinguishes between combatants and civilians; and *proportionality*, which counsels that the anticipated loss of life or injury to civilians or damage to civilian objects not be in excess of military advantages anticipated from a specific act. Among most modern states, these principles are uncontroversial. But how these principles of international law are interpreted in practice is the subject of much debate.

U.S. forces operate under standing rules of engagement (SROEs), which provide a set of always-operative rules related to self-defense for forces in peacetime as well as a template for operation-specific ROEs.[33] SROEs are always operative and impose limits on the actions of units in the field. Standing rules can be augmented by supplemental ROEs (also known as mission-specific ROEs), which can be tailored to a region, a mission, or a specific operation.[34] Supplemental ROEs may elaborate on or interpret the SROEs for a given mission, but supplemental rules should not contradict standing rules. Supplemental ROEs can apply to specific operations (like cyberspace operations) and to the employment of specific types of weapons (like cyberspace capabilities).[35] Finally, the standing rules for the use of force (SRUFs) govern U.S. military actions inside the homeland.

Standing Rules of Engagement

The SROEs are issued by the uniformed chairman of the Joint Chiefs of Staff and approved by the civilian secretary of defense. The current version of the SROEs came into force on June 13, 2005.[36] While much of that document is classified, the following discussion is derived from unclassified portions of the 2005 document, as well as its antecedent from 2000.

The SROEs provide "implementation guidance on the inherent right of self-defense and the application of force for mission accomplishment."[37] The former give commanders authorities such that they always retain the inherent right and obligation to exercise unit self-defense in response to a hostile act or demonstrated hostile intent,[38] whether or not a state of armed conflict is acknowledged to exist. The authorized means and methods of self-defense can also be limited based on concerns relating to the political environment, resources, and the like. For example, "Don't fire until you see the whites of their eyes" would be an SROE limitation based on resource conservation. National leadership may limit the use of certain weapons in certain situations as well.

Under the SROEs, U.S. forces may use all necessary means available and all appropriate actions in self-defense, as long as they are consistent with the LOAC requirements of necessity and proportionality. This interpretation is usually understood to mean taking action that is minimally required (with respect to nature, duration, and scope of force) to end the immediate threat. Note, however, that some weapons and tactics require approval from the president or secretary of defense before they can be used (for example, only the president can authorize the use of nuclear weapons).

In practice, on-scene commanders must exercise good judgment in interpreting how ROEs apply in specific situations: while ROEs provide guidance and some limitations, they must avoid excessive constraints on forces operating in the field. This point is especially important when commanders are unable to communicate with higher authority in a timely fashion. Clarity and specificity are often sought by subordinate units, but breadth and generality are often provided at first to account for the broadest array of circumstances.

Ascertaining hostile intent is often difficult in a fluid and fast-moving tactical situation. Commanders are asked to use their best judgment when considering available intelligence, political and military factors, indications and warnings, and other relevant information concerning possible threats in the area of operations. However, there is no checklist of indicators that will conclusively determine hostile intent.[39]

Commanders are encouraged to use proactive measures, if practical, to determine the intent of an entity that poses a threat, such as issuing verbal warnings, sending visual or auditory signals, making use of physical barriers, changing course and speed to determine if the entity is continuing on an attack profile, illuminating the threat with fire-control radar, or firing warning shots. Entities that do not alter their behavior are regarded as more likely to be showing hostile intent.

A canonical example of applying the SROEs would be a Navy ship in peacetime circumstances that observes an inbound airplane that it has reason to suspect poses a threat.

- Under the SROEs, the ship would always be allowed to take evasive action by maneuvering, to warn the airplane not to approach further, or to activate electronic countermeasures to jam the airplane's radar. (Such action would be regarded as "passive defense.")[40] These measures may eliminate the apparent threat. They are also nondestructive and as such do not escalate unnecessarily.

- Under the SROEs and depending on circumstances, the ship may be allowed to launch a surface-to-air missile to destroy the airplane. (Such action would be regarded as "active defense.")[41] For example, active defense may be appropriate only when passive defensive measures have failed.

- Under the SROEs, the ship would not be authorized to launch a land-attack missile against the airbase from which the airplane was launched. (Such action would exceed that which is needed to eliminate the immediate threat and would constitute offensive action.) However, such a measure could be allowed under certain mission accomplishment ROEs or after obtaining higher-level approval for doing so.

ROEs—especially the SROEs—tend to be more restrictive before the outbreak of hostilities. They are more open-ended during hostilities, and they return to being more restrictive after hostilities cease. Such transitions from less to more restrictive, or vice versa, do not necessarily reflect specific principles of international law, but rather the policy prerogatives of senior U.S. leadership.

To illustrate, consider a developing crisis in which U.S. military forces are initially dispatched as advisers with a specific mission to train and assist indigenous forces. These U.S. forces would maintain their inherent right to self-defense, but the ROEs may limit their geographic movement, the conditions under which they may open fire, or when different categories of personnel (civilian, combatant) may be detained.[42] If the mission for these U.S. forces changes to reflect combat-related objectives, such as killing and capturing enemy combatants, the ROEs may relax limitations on geographic movement, on detention, or on the types of weaponry employed. When a specified area is cleared of combatants, U.S. forces may be called upon to provide stability in the absence of functioning local governance. A less militarized presence may be desirable under these circumstances, and so the ROEs may again limit movement, detention, and munitions use.

Thus, ROEs may change as a conflict evolves. Such changes also entail an even greater level of complexity for subordinate units, as these units must interpret evolving ROEs from higher headquarters as the nature of a particular mission evolves. In this dynamic environment, supplemental ROEs are particularly important.

Supplemental Rules of Engagement

Supplemental ROEs are mission-specific. They seek to further limit or enable distinct actions for mission accomplishment and require additional approval from higher authority. Supplemental ROEs pass these authorities to the relevant commanders.

There are two types of supplemental ROEs: permissive and restrictive. Supplemental ROEs set by the president, secretary of defense, or combatant commander are generally permissive in that they permit a specific tactic, weapon, or operation.[43] As a template for specific missions, Enclosure I of the standing rules details supplemental measures (and is primarily classified) and includes a list of weapons requiring approval by a combatant commander or someone of higher rank.[44]

All other supplemental ROEs seek to restrict action allowed under the SROEs or preexisting supplemental ROEs.[45] For example, they may limit specific types of artillery, who may use certain weapons, or the targets that are acceptable to strike. However, supplemental ROEs apply only to mission accomplishment and do not restrict the use of force in self-defense. In 2010, when General David Petraeus issued new ROEs for Afghanistan

restricting aerial bombardments and artillery strikes, he took care to remind commanders of their right to use force in self-defense.[46]

In general, supplemental ROEs reflect policy judgments about how deployed forces should behave to best support national interests. Supplemental ROEs can be used to elaborate on how the SROEs should be interpreted
in situations likely to occur during a specific mission. For example, a given
mission might call for deployed forces to interact with civilians. If such interactions are unfriendly (for example, an encounter with an unarmed mob),
the risk of escalating a conflict may be high, and so a supplemental ROE
might direct that the unit should withdraw or use smoke to camouflage itself, but should not use its weapons to fire on the mob.

Because they are mission-specific, supplemental ROEs are an important
focus of mission planning, which is a process that involves specific objectives, lists of targets to be attacked to support those objectives, and various
courses of action and options for attacking each target. Pros and cons of attacking each target with each option are analyzed and commanders make
decisions about which option is better in any given set of circumstances, or
whether none are acceptable (at which point his or her staff must develop
another option for consideration). Offensive cyber options have, in principle, the same status as offensive options in the physical domains such as
land and air—the pros and cons of each option factor into the commander's
decision.

Mission planning results in an operation plan, defined by the DoD as "a
complete and detailed joint plan containing a full description of the concept
of operations, all annexes applicable to the plan, and a time-phased force and
deployment data."[47] Mission planning may also take place long in advance
of actual military action; in fact, it usually does. However, the mere fact that
a mission has been planned in advance (and that possible options and courses
of action have been identified) does not automatically mean that commanders have the authority to execute it. Commanders can take action only when
they receive an explicit order from higher authority to do so. Such an order is
called an execute order (or EXORD), which the DoD defines as "an order
issued by the Chairman of the Joint Chiefs of Staff, at the direction of the
Secretary of Defense, to implement a decision by the President to initiate
military operations."[48]

As an example, consider a situation in which potentially hostile forces
from Country X face U.S. military forces on land. One important scenario
of interest to the United States is how it would respond to a surprise large-

scale attack by Country X across the zone separating the two forces. An effective U.S. response would entail a great deal of pre-planning—the plan for the response is designated in a formal operational plan, most likely containing supplemental ROEs. Execution of the actions contemplated in the plan would require an explicit order from the president or secretary of defense, and such an order would be transmitted as an EXORD. Nevertheless, under the SROEs, the commander of these forces may act in self-defense to a hostile act from Country X without additional authorization; and if that hostile act is large rather than small, the U.S. response may well be large as well if that is needed to neutralize the immediate threat. But the commander would not be authorized to act independently—that is, without an EXORD or other authority—to go beyond the needs of immediate self-defense and capture the capital of Country X. Of course, this hypothetical situation would become even more complex with the inclusion of allied and coalition partners.

Thus it is important not to conflate the existence of operation plans with SROEs. Nevertheless, an execute order remains valid until either the mission is accomplished or the operation is explicitly terminated,[49] and under some circumstances, an execute order is for all practical purposes a "standing" order that grants authorities to act in certain ways in accordance with a given operation plan. Furthermore, because an operation plan describes actions that are to be taken before actual conflict, the issuance of an execute order does not mean that conflict is about to break out.

Standing Rules for the Use of Force

Standing rules for the use of force (SRUFs) are similar to the SROEs in that they provide a general set of rules governing U.S. military action. The primary differences lie in their intent and geographic applicability.

Unlike the SROEs, which are essentially permissive in nature, SRUFs are inherently restrictive. Unless specific weapons and tactics are explicitly approved under the SRUFs, they cannot be used without the authorization of the secretary of defense.[50]

The SROEs apply to actions taken *outside* U.S. territory, as well as to air and maritime homeland defense missions.[51] SRUFs govern military functions *inside* U.S. territory. They include Defense Support of Civil Authorities (DSCA), land homeland defense missions, and law enforcement and security measures at DoD installations. However, the SRUFs do not apply to the

National Guard when it is operating in a state rather than under federal authority. The National Guard acts primarily as a "federally-recognized state government entity" and is usually called to service in support of state civil authorities.[52] Thus each state has its own set of rules that guide the National Guard based on the laws of that state.[53]

DSCA offers one example of how SRUFs are applied. In that mission, conventional forces from the Navy, Air Force, and Army were assigned to support civilian authorities with search and rescue, aid delivery, and peace-keeping.[54] SRUFs have not received much attention over the years because situations where DoD supports civil authorities infrequently involve the use of force.

Notes

1. In this chapter, cyber "weapons" and "capabilities" are used interchangeably for readability, even though not all cyber capabilities constitute cyber weapons.

2. Coalition activities whereby the United States conducts operations with allies and partners would be informed by this analysis, at least in part. Under some circumstances, U.S. military forces also develop rules of engagement with local law enforcement as well. For example, the *U.S. Army/Marine Corps Counterinsurgency Field Manual* notes that "to work effectively together, the police and military coordinate rules of engagement." U.S. Army and U.S. Marine Corps, "Police in Counterinsurgency," in *The U.S. Army/Marine Corps Counterinsurgency Field Manual*, 2nd ed. (University of Chicago Press, 2007), p. 233.

3. Department of Defense. "Terms and Definitions: Rules of Engagement," in Joint Publication 1-02, *Department of Defense Dictionary of Military and Associated Terms* (2018), p. 202 (www.jcs.mil/Portals/36/Documents/Doctrine/pubs/dictionary.pdf).

4. This section summarizes appendix A at the end of this chapter, which is a primer on rules of engagement and related concepts and provides the foundation for understanding the development of cyber-specific ROEs.

5. Department of Defense, Joint Publication 1-02, *Department of Defense Dictionary of Military and Associated Terms*.

6. This chapter uses "kinetic" as an approximate synonym for "noncyber" or "conventional."

7. Note that these categories are not terms recognized in U.S. military doctrine or literature; they are introduced here only for ease of exposition in this chapter.

8. "II. Strategic Context," in *Department of Defense Cyber Strategy* (2015), p. 11 (www.defense.gov/Portals/1/features/2015/0415_cyber-strategy/Final_2015_DoD_CYBER_STRATEGY_for_web.pdf).

9. "Standing Rules of Engagement," in *Operational Law Handbook* (Charlottesville, Va.: International and Operational Law Department of the Judge Advocate General's Legal Center and School, 2015), chap. 5, appendix A, p. 91 (www.loc.gov/rr/frd/Military_Law/pdf/operational-law-handbook_2015.pdf).

10. Department of Defense Joint Chiefs of Staff, "Enclosure L: Standing Rules for the Use of Force for U.S. Forces," CJCSI 3121.01B (2005) (https://navytribe.files.wordpress.com/2015/11/cjcsi-3121-01b-enclosure-l.pdf).

11. "Self Defense," in *Operational Law Handbook*, chap. 5, appendix A, p. 91.

12. W. Owens, K. Dam, and H. Lin, eds., *Technology, Policy, Law, and Ethics Regarding U.S. Acquisition and Use of Cyberattack Capabilities* (Washington: National Academies Press, 2009), p. 170.

13. An approximate analogue from kinetic operations might be a scenario in which soldiers are involved in urban combat where armed civilians and insurgents are intermingled. Rules of engagement in this scenario might specify that soldiers are authorized to fire their weapons when—and only when—fire is being directed at them, rather than when fire is occurring without singling them out as specific targets. This example is inspired by the film *Black Hawk Down*.

14. Air Force Materiel Command, Department of the Air Force, "70—Cyber Control System," FedBizOpps.gov, December 20, 2007 (www.fbo.gov/index?s=opportunity&mode =form&id=e80b7d909c5fa5107528a05bdf51d1bd&tab=core&_cview=1).

15. "Transitional Cyber C2 Construct," in *Operations Order 11-002, Operation Gladiator Shield* (United States Cyber Command, 2011), p. 44 (http://nsarchive.gwu.edu/dc.html ?doc=2692120-Document-12).

16. "III. Strategic Goals," in *Department of Defense Cyber Strategy*, p. 14.

17. A good discussion of offensive operations in cyberspace as they relate to kinetic conflict, especially in times of crisis, can be found in Martin C. Libicki, *Crisis and Escalation in Cyberspace* (Santa Monica, Calif.: RAND Corporation, 2012).

18. See Department of Defense, Office of General Counsel, "1.11.5.1 Responding to an Imminent Threat of an Attack," in *Department of Defense Law of War Manual* (2016), pp. 46–47 (www.defense.gov/Portals/1/Documents/DoD_Law_of_War_Manual-June _2015_Updated_May_2016.pdf). Also, in a 2015 article, Geoffrey DeWeese argues that anticipatory and preemptive self-defense "can be applied against imminent [cyber] threats in a similar manner to kinetic threats," but also that "putting a measure on how to determine imminence against threats in cyberspace presents challenges which States have not previously confronted from conventional threats." Geoffrey S. DeWeese, "Anticipatory and Preemptive Self-Defense in Cyberspace: The Challenge of Imminence," paper presented at the 7th International Conference Cyber Conflict: Architectures in Cyberspace, Tallinn, Estonia, 2015 (Tallinn, Estonia: NATO Cooperative Cyber Defense Centre of Excellence), pp. 81–92.

19. K. Tibori Szabó, "Introduction," in *Anticipatory Action in Self-Defence: Essence and Limits under International Law* (New York: Springer, 2011), pp. 6–8.

20. As noted by Terry Gill and Paul Ducheine, "The ICJ employed a stringent standard that rejected 'suggestive' and 'highly suggestive' evidence of Iranian involvement in attacks on international shipping in the Persian Gulf. *Oil Platforms (Iran v. U.S.)*, 2003 I.C.J. 161, ¶¶ 59, 71 (Nov. 6). This and other aspects of the judgment were vigorously criticized by a number of judges in their individual opinions. See id., ¶¶ 30–39 (separate opinion of Judge Higgins); id., ¶¶ 21–30 (separate opinion of Judge Kooijmans); id., ¶¶ 33–46 (separate opinion of Judge Buergenthal); id., ¶¶ 33–40 (separate opinion of Judge Owada)." See Terry D. Gill and Paul A. L. Ducheine, "Anticipatory Self-Defense in the Cyber Context," *International Law Studies* 89 (2013), p. 452 (www.usnwc.edu/getattach ment/f041ec70-19af-4df4-bf59-be73ec0fe493/Anticipatory-Self-Defense-in-the-Cyber -Context.aspx).

21. In this context, proportionality is the requirement that the degree and kind of forceful response must not exceed that which is minimally needed to forestall the imminent attack. This *jus ad bellum* proportionality is different from *jus in bello* proportionality

in conducting attacks discussed earlier. See, for example, Gill and Ducheine, "Anticipatory Self-Defense in the Cyber Context"; and Department of Defense, Office of General Counsel, "2.4.2 Examples Where Proportionality Is Reflected in Law of War Rules," in *Department of Defense Law of War Manual* (2016), pp. 61–62.

22. "I. Introduction," in *Department of Defense Cyber Strategy*, p. 5.

23. Ash Carter, Department of Defense Press Briefing by Secretary Carter and Joint Chiefs of Staff General Joseph F. Dunford, Pentagon Briefing Room, February 29, 2016 (www.defense.gov/News/Transcripts/Transcript-View/Article/682341/department-of -defense-press-briefing-by-secretary-carter-and-gen-dunford-in-the).

24. "III. Strategic Goals" and "IV. Implementation Objectives," in *Department of Defense Cyber Strategy*, pp. 14 and 24–26.

25. Center for Army Lessons Learned (CALL), *Escalation of Force Handbook* (Fort Leavenworth, Kans.: United States Army Combined Arms Center, 2007) (www.global security.org/military/library/report/call/call_07-21.pdf).

26. In 2012 the Shamoon virus infected the computer network of Saudi Arabia's national gas company, Aramco. The attack rendered over 30,000 machines unusable by overwriting their master boot records. Shamoon is speculated to have been carried out by Iran, but this remains unproven. C. Bronk and E. Tikk-Ringas, "The Cyber Attack on Saudi Aramco," *Survival* 55 (2013), p. 85.

27. For example, in 2007 the Idaho National Laboratory conducted the "Aurora" experiment to highlight vulnerabilities in the electrical sector. The experiment used a cyberattack to change the operating cycle of a generator, causing the generator to break down. J. Meserve, "Sources: Staged Cyber Attack Reveals Vulnerability in Power Grid," CNN, September 26, 2007 (www.cnn.com/2007/US/09/26/power.at.risk/index.html?iref=topnews# cnnSTCVideo).

28. A description of the confidentiality, integrity, and availability framework (also known as the CIA triad) can be found in many places. See, for example, Seymour E. Goodman and Herbert S. Lin, eds., *Toward a Safer and More Secure Cyberspace* (Washington: National Academies Press, 2007).

29. *Operational Law Handbook*, p. 81.

30. Deployable Training Division of the Joint Staff J7, "Authority to Use Force," in *Insights and Best Practices Focus Paper: Authorities* (Joint Staff J7, 2016), p. 9 (www.jcs.mil /Portals/36/Documents/Doctrine/fp/authorities_fp.pdf).

31. Ibid.

32. A "combatant commander" is the commander of one of the unified or specified combatant commands, At present, the unified commands of the Department of Defense include U.S. Africa Command, U.S. Central Command, U.S. European Command, U.S. Northern Command, U.S. Pacific Command, U.S. Southern Command, U.S. Special Operations Command, U.S. Strategic Command, U.S. Transportation Command, and U.S. Cyber Command. There are no specified commands today.

33. "Standing Rules of Engagement,"chap. 5, p. 82. This source notes that the SROEs, last revised in 2005, are under revision, so an update may be forthcoming.

34. Ibid., pp. 81–83.

35. Ibid., p. 84.

36. Ibid., p. 82.

37. Ibid.

38. Ibid., p. 91.

39. In some circumstances, one or more of the following actions may demonstrate hostile intent: aiming or directing weapons; adopting an attack profile; closing within weapon release range; illuminating the commander's unit with radar or laser designators; passing targeting information; or laying or preparing to lay naval mines.

40. The formal definition of "passive defense" is "measures taken to reduce the probability of and to minimize the effects of damage caused by hostile action without the intention of taking the initiative." Department of Defense. "Terms and Definitions: Passive Defense," in Joint Publication 1-02, *Department of Defense Dictionary of Military and Associated Terms*, p. 179.

41. The formal definition of "active defense" is the "employment of limited offensive action and counterattacks to deny a contested area or position to the enemy." Ibid., p. 1.

42. U.S. Army and U.S. Marine Corps, "Appendix D—Legal Considerations," in *The U.S. Army/Marine Corps Counterinsurgency Field Manual*, p. D-8.

43. "Standing Rules of Engagement," chap. 5, p. 84.

44. G. Solis, "Rules of Engagement-Formulating Mission-Specific ROE," in *The Law of Armed Conflict-International Humanitarian Law in War* (Cambridge University Press, 2010), p. 500.

45. "Standing Rules of Engagement," chap. 5, pp. 81 and 84.

46. J. Michaels, "Petraeus Reloads Rules of Engagement," *USA Today*, August 5, 2010.

47. Department of Defense, "Terms and Definitions: Operation Plan," in Joint Publication 1-02, *Department of Defense Dictionary of Military and Associated Terms*, p. 174.

48. Department of Defense, "Terms and Definitions: Execute Order," in Joint Publication 1-02, *Department of Defense Dictionary of Military and Associated Terms*, p. 83.

49. Department of Defense, *Joint Operation Planning*, Joint Publication 5-0 (2011). (http://www.jcs.mil/Portals/36/Documents/Doctrine/pubs/jp5_0_20171606.pdf).

50. "Standing Rules of Engagement," chap. 5, p. 86.

51. Ibid.

52. "II. Rules for the Use of Force for the National Guard," in *Operational Law Handbook*, p. 191.

53. There is no standard term used by states for rules of force. Some refer to them as rules for the use of force, as used here; however, others use rules of engagement and rules of interaction. Ibid.

54. For press accounts, see L. Arana-Barradas, "Air Force Rescues Top 4,000 Mark," *U.S. Air Force*, September 8, 2005 (www.af.mil/News/ArticleDisplay/tabid/223/Article /133434/air-force-rescues-top-4000-mark.aspx); and Commander, U.S. 2nd Fleet Public Affairs, "Norfolk Ships Deploy to Support Hurricane Katrina Relief Efforts," *U.S. Navy*, August 31, 2005 (www.navy.mil/submit/display.asp?story_id=19826). See also Gary Solis, *The Law of Armed Conflict: International Humanitarian Law in War* (Cambridge University Press, 2010), p. 494.

13

U.S. Offensive Cyber Operations in a China-U.S. Military Confrontation

ADAM SEGAL

Defense planners on both sides of the Pacific assume that offensive cyber operations will be part of any military confrontation between the United States and the People's Republic of China (PRC). The Defense Department's annual report on the People's Liberation Army (PLA) states that China is "focusing on counter-space, offensive cyber operations, and electronic warfare capabilities meant to deny adversaries the advantages of modern, informationized warfare." It continues that Chinese "offensive cyberspace operations could support A2/AD (anti access/area denial) by targeting critical nodes to disrupt adversary networks throughout the region." In addition, the PLA "would likely use EW [electronic warfare], cyberspace operations, and deception to augment counterspace and other kinetic operations during a wartime scenario to deny an adversary's attainment and use of information."[1]

Chinese defense analysts hold similar assumptions about U.S. operations. In open-source articles, PLA authors write extensively about how a technologically advanced competitor will use cyber operations to degrade computer and communication networks and refer to purported uses of cyberattacks by the U.S. military in Iraq, Kosovo, and Afghanistan. *The Science of Military*

Strategy, an authoritative study of the PLA's strategic thought published by the Academy of Military Science, argues, "The side holding network warfare superiority can adopt network warfare to cause dysfunction in the adversary's command system, loss of control over his operational forces and activities, and incapacitation or failure of weapons and equipment—and thus seize the initiative within military confrontation, and create conditions for . . . gaining ultimate victory in war."[2]

Not surprisingly, how the United State might deploy offensive attacks designed to deceive, deny, disrupt, degrade, and destroy information and information systems within the PRC and what impact these attacks might have on military and political goals is rarely discussed in public by U.S. officials or war planners. It seems a safe assumption, however, that during a conflict the United States is likely to consider striking two types of targets: tactical or operational targets that affect conventional military capabilities; and strategic targets directed at critical infrastructure or at the leadership and the political will to continue fighting. Put another way, cyberattacks in a U.S.-China military conflict can be designed for denial or punishment.

At first glance, attacks meant to block the PLA from using information systems are likely to be more effective and less escalatory than those designed to impose political costs on the regime. This chapter argues, however, that the dynamic of Sino-U.S. military competition as well as Chinese conceptions of deterrence and crisis management mean that any use of tactical cyberattacks is likely to heighten instability and lead to escalation. U.S. and Chinese policymakers and warfighters would also have to be concerned that third parties would launch cyberattacks, further complicating signaling and escalation control. Moreover, strategic attacks on the leadership's ability to control the flow of information are likely either to be missed or to be interpreted as existential threats. In the case of the latter, Beijing would quickly assume that the United States was trying to overthrow the Chinese Communist Party (CCP), thus significantly diminishing the chance that Washington could achieve more limited political goals.

Despite these significant risks, there can be little realistic expectation that either the PLA or the U.S. military will abstain from offensive cyber operations in a military conflict. Instead, this chapter concludes that these risks create shared incentives for preventing escalation from tactical to strategic attacks through dialogue and confidence-building measures. In particular, the two sides should work to expand discussions on operational planning, conceptions of deterrence and crisis management, and red lines.

Offensive Cyber Operations: Tactical Targets

The potential opportunities and challenges of offensive cyber operations have been well mapped by others. In comparison with conventional weapons platforms, offensive cyber tools may have lower research and development, maintenance, and operation costs. They can operate at high speed ("net speed") and are versatile, employable across the range of military operations.[3] Herbert Lin, for example, describes cyberattacks that threaten the integrity, authenticity, and availability of data. Data can be destroyed by manipulating electric networks and power generation or denying an opponent use of weapons platforms or systems. The injection of fake data into the system can create confusion in command and control, logistics, and intelligence networks. A denial-of-service attack could knock a communication system offline.[4] In addition, the National Academy of Sciences describes cyberattacks in support of psychological, information, traditional military, and other operations. Soldiers could be warned through email that their buildings were about to be bombed, networked air-defense systems suppressed, and smart munitions randomly altered.[5]

If these types of attacks are possible, then China is becoming an increasingly rich target environment for U.S. offensive cyber operations. The more successful the PLA is in adopting and deploying information and communication technologies, the more vulnerable it is to tactical attacks. Similarly, strategic vulnerability increases as the Chinese economy becomes more technologically developed and the polity more connected. Previously, the PLA, dependent on landline and sea-based fiber optics and mainland-based servers, routers, and transmission switches, appeared relatively insulated from cyberattacks. China's current military strategy, is, however, "winning informationized local wars," and it points to the growing prominence of the application of information technology in all aspects of military operations.

Informationized local wars, in the framing of the 2015 Chinese Military Strategy White Paper, is evolving toward the development and use of long-range, precision, smart and unmanned weapons and equipment.[6] The DoD notes that China continues to "prioritize C4I [command, control, communications, computers, and intelligence] modernization as a response to trends in modern warfare that emphasize the importance of rapid information sharing, processing, and decision-making." It is also trying to develop secure and reliable communication to fixed and mobile command posts as well as advanced automated command systems.[7] As the PLA depends more on networks, the more susceptible it becomes to cyberattacks. A 2015 RAND study argues that China's integrated air-defense systems (IADS); maritime intelligence, surveillance, and reconnaissance (ISR) systems; and dual-use networks (that is, networks shared by the military and civilian operators) would be "obvious targets" for U.S. cyber operations in the event of a conflict.[8] David Gompert and Phillip Saunders argue that "as PLA forces become more information-based—their stated goal—and extend into the Pacific to engage U.S. strike forces, they become more dependent on less secure computer networks."[9]

While many writings from the 1990s stress the asymmetric advantages to the PLA of cyber operations, more recent open-source Chinese writings display an increased concern about network vulnerability. Dr. Li Daguang, senior colonel and professor at the National Defense University, for example, echoes Gompert and Saunders's conclusion: "Sensor networks, command and control networks, and weapons platform networks are becoming the heart and an important support of informationized wars. If computer networks suffer attacks and are destroyed, the whole army's combat strength will be substantially decreased or even completely lost."[10] The 2015 edition of *The Science of Military Strategy* emphasizes that the PLA must plan for instances in which its military networks will be taken down by hostile adversaries and China's modernized command, control, communications, computers, intelligence, surveillance, and reconnaissance (C4ISR) networks cannot be relied upon.[11]

This greater vulnerability has motivated institutional change. The Chinese leadership announced in 2015 an increasing focus on network defenses in the PLA and the establishment of the Strategic Support Forces. These forces will combine space, cyber, and electronic warfare units and will be critical to China's ability to maintain information dominance in wartime. While Western analysts have focused on the offensive potential of the reorganization, Chinese writings have stressed the need for greater defense against cyberattacks on government, military, and civilian facilities.[12]

Offensive Cyber Operations: Strategic Targets

Changes in the economy will also make China more vulnerable to disruptive attacks by U.S. operations.[13] In President Xi Jinping's framing, "Without cybersecurity, there is no national security; without informatization (or advancing information technology), there is no modernization." The country's first internet White Paper described the internet's "irreplaceable role in accelerating the development of the national economy."[14] According to China's Academy of Information and Communications Technology and Ministry of Industry and Information Technology, China's digital economy in 2016 as a share of GDP was 30.3 percent, significantly higher than the average among developed economies. The total value of e-commerce in China alone, according to McKinsey, was $630 billion in 2015, nearly 80 percent higher than that of the United States.[15] New uses in the domestic market, such as wearables and the Internet of Things (IoT), could be responsible for 7 to 22 percent of China's incremental GDP growth through 2025, depending on adoption rates.[16]

Future economic growth will be dependent on greater interconnectivity. China's current growth model is coming to an end. Domestic consumption and innovation must replace labor-intensive exports and fixed asset investment. In his March 2015 "Work Report to the National People's Conference," Premier Li Keqiang explained that China "will develop the 'Internet Plus' action plan to integrate the mobile Internet, cloud computing, big data, and the Internet of Things with modern manufacturing, to encourage the healthy development of e-commerce, industrial networks, and Internet banking, and to guide Internet-based companies to increase their presence in the international market."[17] Another development plan, "Made in China 2025," sets out expansive targets for upgrading China's aging manufacturing base through smart manufacturing. This includes integrating automation, smart sensors, and IoT devices into Chinese industry. The market for the IoT in China may reach $168 billion by 2020.

China's leaders also have ambitious plans for cloud computing, big data, and artificial intelligence. The Next-Generation Artificial Intelligence Development Plan, for example, aims to turn China's artificial intelligence industry into a "world leader" worth RMB 400 billion ($60 billion) by 2025 and a "premier innovation center" worth RMB 1 trillion by 2030 ($150 billion).[18] China will upgrade and expand its existing digital infrastructure, from fiber-optic networks to satellite communications, to improve and boost data streaming ability, especially for rural areas. All of these development trends create a much larger potential target list for nations with offensive cyber capabilities.

Because China's internet infrastructure is relatively self-contained, Chinese policymakers may have felt themselves comparatively less vulnerable to attacks on their economy. That confidence must have been seriously dented in the light of Edward Snowden's revelations about the skills of the National Security Agency (NSA) in broaching air-gapped and other isolated networks. According to an interview Snowden gave a Hong Kong newspaper, the NSA hacked Chinese targets, including mobile phone operators and Tsinghua University (Xi Jinping's alma mater and home to one of the PRC's six major backbone networks, the China Education and Research Network).[19]

Moreover, articles in the Chinese press about the exposure of industrial control systems to damaging attacks are now common. In December 2014, China established its first laboratory to work on information security for industrial control systems.[20] According to the announcement that accompanied the creation of the lab, over 80 percent of China's economy and critical infrastructure involves some type of industrial control system (ICS). These systems are vulnerable to attack for at least three reasons: operators have low security awareness and ICSs are connected to the internet; Chinese industry is heavily reliant on foreign suppliers for its ICSs, and these suppliers have access in order to service or update software; and the country lacks a testing range or simulation environment to prepare for and defend against attacks.[21]

The increasing vulnerability of the economy overlaps with a political system that is both dynamic and fragile. On one hand, President Xi has consolidated power faster than his predecessors and is the head of four top-level leadership groups for economics, political reform, national security, and cybersecurity. In January 2016, China announced the reform of the PLA's four headquarters, the creation of a new joint command, and the reorganization of the military regions. Xi has launched an aggressive anticorruption campaign targeted at high-level "tigers" such as former security chief Zhou Yongkang, and tens of thousands of "flies," local bureaucrats. In January 2018, "Xi Jinping Thought on Socialism with Chinese Characteristics for a New Era" was added to the constitution as a guiding principle, and in March 2018, the Chinese Communist Party ended the ten-year presidential term limit, opening the way for Xi to remain in office indefinitely.

On the other hand, the Chinese Communist Party is exhibiting a high degree of anxiety about threats to its rule. China has tightened censorship of the internet and the media, mounted ideological campaigns in universities, and arrested rights lawyers, feminists, foreign nongovernmental organization workers, bloggers, and environmental activists. The state has rolled out a massive surveillance system based on big data, facial and voice recognition software, and artificial intelligence in the restive province of Xinjiang and is working to scale it up nationwide. For the first time, in 2013, China spent more on domestic security (769.1 billion RMB) than it did on national defense (740.6 billion RMB), and by 2017 spending on domestic security (1.24 trillion RMB) exceeded the national defense budget (1.02 trillion RMB).[22]

China's closed, authoritarian, but highly connected political system may provide more strategic targets than other less economically developed one-party states.[23] Moreover, given that the CCP's legitimacy depends on nationalism and continued economic growth, the leadership may be unable to withstand serious economic disruption caused by a major cyberattack. While Chinese data is opaque, often fake, and manipulated for political purposes, economic and social trends suggest the potential for rising domestic tensions.[24] In 2015, China's economic growth rate, 6.9 percent, was the slowest in twenty-five years. Widespread economic dislocation could produce greater unemployment and spark riots and social protests. The *China Labor Bulletin* recorded 2,700 strikes and protests in 2015, twice as many as in 2014.[25] China's elite youth, professionals, and middle class have high social and economic aspirations, and their disillusionment would be a threat to regime legitimacy.

In the wake of the hacking of the U.S. Office of Personnel Management, the *New York Times* reported that the White House was considering retaliating against China. One of the options discussed was breaching China's so-called Great Firewall so as to demonstrate to the Chinese leadership that the thing they value most—"keeping absolute control over the country's dialogue"—could be at risk.[26] Three types of attacks could be considered: hacks that expose personal or financial information embarrassing to the leadership; hacks that allow Chinese users access to blocked websites outside of China; and hacks that lessen or dismantle controls on information within China by attacking the technical, organizational, or personnel infrastructure of censorship.

The leak in 2016 of over 11 million documents from Panamanian law firm Mossack Fonseca, known as the Panama Papers, is the type of operation some have suggested could serve as a warning to Chinese leaders. Although similar information was discovered by previous reporting by Bloomberg and the *New York Times*, the Panama Papers revealed that the family members of eight current or former members of the Politburo Standing Committee of the Chinese Communist Party, including a brother-in-law of President Xi Jinping, had created secret offshore companies.[27] In response, Chinese censors moved quickly to remove any mention of the papers from social media.[28] A provincial government order instructed media outlets to "find and delete reprinted reports on the Panama Papers. Do not follow up on related content, no exceptions. If material from foreign media attacking China is found on any website, it will be dealt with severely."[29]

A strategic cyber operation may have occurred in the past. The drop of the Shanghai stock market by 64.89 points on the twenty-third anniversary of the Tiananmen Square massacre in Beijing (which occurred on June 4, 1989, or 6/4/89) may have been a weird coincidence, or an effort to show the Chinese leadership that their control over information and the domestic population was vulnerable.[30]

High Demands of Offense

Despite the wealth of potential targets for offensive cyber operations, there has been notable skepticism about the efficacy of tactical and strategic attacks. Determining the effects of an attack will require analysis and interpretation of an event at multiple targets.[31] While there is a widespread assumption that offense has the advantage over the attacker, Martin Libicki stresses the ability of the defender to respond: "Any assessment of computer network attacks must conclude that there are many available defenses, even if they are expensive and complex."[32] Defenders will respond quickly to successful attacks and cyber weapons are likely to be "one and done." Similarly, Thomas Rid and Peter McBurney conclude that the "offense has higher costs, a shorter-shelf life than defense, and a very limited target set" and Rebecca Slayton argues that "the advantages that complex information technology offers the offense do not extend to the physical world, making cyber offenses much more expensive for achieving physical effects than for conducting espionage and deception."[33]

Given the interconnectedness of networks, the attacker must also contend with the possibility of unexpected blowback or contagion. Media reports claim that an attack on the Iraqi financial system was considered in 2003 but eventually abandoned due to fear it would spread across the Middle East to Europe. "We are deeply concerned about the second- and third-order effects of certain types of computer network operations," said one senior officer.[34]

Defense analysts also worry about the impact of cyberattacks on crisis stability. The net effect of a successful attack on C4ISR may be the reduction of information available to the enemy. This is a positive in the effort to limit conventional capabilities, but also makes defense and civilian officials suspicious of their own information. This is likely to result in the degraded control over operators, and thus weaken the ability of policymakers to limit conflict if they so choose. Tactical strikes may quickly become strategic or kinetic, especially if the authority to escalate conflict devolves in the absence of connectivity.

The bar for a successful strategic strike seems even higher, moving beyond the "exquisite" intelligence, precise targeting, and tight political control needed for tactical attacks. As Thomas Mahnken argues, the proponents of cyberwar have "failed to offer a theory of victory for cyberwar, a chain of causal logic linking the use of cyber means to the achievement of political ends."[35] There is no guarantee that the attackers' intentions will be clear, or that the opponent will receive the desired signal amid all the noise.

Moreover, it is unlikely that the attacker understands the adversary's decision-making process well enough to design attacks that produce the desired outcome. On the technical side, a successful attack requires knowledge of networks. But to create strategic outcomes, the attacker must understand who the players are throughout the chain of command, what their interests are, and what information (or lack of access to information) might create specific outcomes. Libicki frames the challenge as the need to design an attack that creates more fear than anger. Fear persuades an opponent not to do something, anger convinces the opponent to do something that the attacker does not want it to do.[36] This type of knowledge is a major demand on attackers outside a system. As Peter Feaver notes, "any parent knows, having dominant battlespace awareness and an unquestioned advantage in perception management tactics does not necessarily lead to success in coercing a child into behaving as desired."[37]

Operations, Deterrence, and Crisis Management

The challenges for offensive cyber operation in a U.S.-China confrontation are both generic and specific to the Chinese context. The possible interaction of U.S. and Chinese military operations, Chinese views of deterrence and compellence in cyberspace, and Beijing's approach to crisis management would all combine to make limiting any cyber conflict difficult and raise the chances of escalation.

As several analysts have noted, the interaction of current U.S. and Chinese operational concepts meet the definition of crisis instability. The PLA has developed land-attack ballistic and cruise missiles to target U.S. forces in Japan and Korea; air-, land-, and sea-launched antiship ballistic and cruise missiles; surface-to-air missiles; surface ships, submarines, and aircraft; as well as space and cyber weapons designed to disrupt U.S. power projection in the Western Pacific. Countering these capabilities is very expensive and may not be possible. Instead, U.S. operations would involve long-range precision strikes on sensors, networks, launchers, weapons, and other parts of the "kill chain." The end result is both sides believe that defending against attacks is difficult, and that the initiator of conflict gains important warfighting advantages, creating incentives to strike first. The use of cyber weapons would heighten these dynamics since cyberattacks are likely to precede conventional strikes by hours or days.[38] Moreover, if each side believes that the other will try and gain information dominance at the beginning of a conflict, computer network operations in a crisis might be interpreted by the target as a more aggressive act than intended. *The Science of Military Strategy*, for example, stresses the importance of time in modern conflicts, and the need to reduce the space in the "awareness–decision making–operation" cycle.[39]

Instability would be further worsened if the PLA's nuclear and conventional forces share command and control infrastructure. Many Western observers believe they are co-located, and as a result an attack on conventional forces could be misinterpreted as an effort to take out China's strategic forces. M. Taylor Fravel and Fiona Cunningham, however, note that most Chinese experts believe that China's nuclear command and control infrastructure is separate from its conventional missile command and control facilities.[40] No matter the actual location of the networks, any disruption of surveillance and command networks may result in strategic forces being placed on higher alert.

Chinese conceptions of deterrence may also make it difficult for U.S. warfighters to control or limit escalation. The ability of the United States to deter actors in cyberspace remains a source of contention in policymaking and academic circles. In most definitions, deterrence refers to efforts to dissuade a potential adversary from taking a hostile action, often through the threat of retaliation or responsive action that imposes unacceptable costs. As many note, one of the central problems with deterring computer attacks is the difficulty of identifying the attacker in a timely manner. Former deputy secretary of defense William Lynn III writes, "Traditional Cold War deterrence models of assured retaliation do not apply to cyberspace, where it is difficult and time consuming to identify an attack's perpetrator."[41] Attacks can be masked and routed through multiple computers and networks. Digital forensics can take weeks or months and still may be inconclusive. The technical issues are compounded by the use of proxies by state actors and the frequent overlap between criminal and political actors. This blurring of lines makes it difficult to identify motives and for the defender to identify and hold at risk the resources the attacker values.

There is, however, a counterargument that a more nuanced, sociological approach to deterrence can be developed and applied to cyberspace. As with the deterrence literature dealing with nonstate actors and rogue states, the proponents of cyber deterrence argue for tailoring, denial, and layering.[42] The point of cyber deterrence is not to stop all attacks, but to reduce their intensity and to prevent certain types of computer operations. The Defense Science Board, for example, concludes that "The U.S. cyber deterrence posture must be 'tailored' to cope with the range of potential attacks that could be conducted by each potential adversary."[43]

The Science of Military Strategy defines deterrence as "the strategic operation, with the threat to use or the actual use of military capability in order to influence the adversary's strategic judgments by making the adversary feel it is difficult to achieve anticipated targets or the cost may exceed the benefit, conducted by countries or political groups for certain political goals."[44] Yet some Chinese analysts echo some of the questions about applying deterrence to cyberspace, arguing that "network deterrence" is different than conventional deterrence. *China Defense Daily*, for example, notes that attribution is hard, detection and monitoring underdeveloped, and that the efficacy of a cyberattack against a cyberattack is uncertain.[45] *The Science of Military Strategy* concludes that there is "very great diversity in different people's understandings of network deterrence, and the theory and practice of network deterrence both await further development and perfection."[46]

As Dean Cheng notes, Chinese defense analysts traditionally view deterrence, or *weishe*, both as deterrence in the Western sense—threats intended to raise the costs high enough so a potential adversary does not act in the first place; and as compellence—displays of military power or threats to use military power in order to compel an opponent to take an action or submit.[47]

Yuan Yi, a researcher at the Academy of Military Sciences, for example, describes "deterrence by combat operations." When one side believes the other is on the verge of initiating war, it may launch cyberattacks on critical defensive networks, thus conducting "preventive, restraining deterrence."

According to Yuan, a successful deterrence strategy requires preparation. Cyber forces must conduct comprehensive network reconnaissance and install backdoors and logic bombs to launch future attacks. Cheng argues that Chinese writers on offensive cyber operations stress the need "to remind an adversary of one's ability to plant viruses or otherwise undertake information attacks (*xinxi jingong*) in order to warn them to cease their policies or otherwise coerce them."[48] While Chinese authors might view a certain types of cyberattacks as a deterrent signal of last resort, U.S. analysts might see the event as a failure of deterrence and the beginning of a conflagration. Martin Libicki and Scott Harold also note that divergent conceptions of deterrence could lead to escalation or unwanted conflict.[49] They frame the United States (and its allies) as holding a more legalistic view of deterrence; deterrence either exists or it does not, and it involves clear no-go lines. Clearly communicating what those lines are and what one is willing to defend, in the U.S. perspective, minimizes the possibility of conflict as a consequence of error. By contrast, China (and others) prefers strategic ambiguity to no-go lines and places deterrence in a larger context of relative power relations. Chinese policymakers may choose to enforce a red line only if they think the outcome will be positive. This ambiguity, while making it more difficult for Washington to know where it must exercise restraint, increases Beijing's room for maneuver by allowing it to choose when it will and will not act.

Like much U.S. research, Chinese analysis closely links space and information systems. Writing in *Liberation Army Daily*, Senior Colonel Li Daguang observes that "information dominance cannot be separated from space dominance."[50] Conversely, others argue that it is only through achieving space dominance that the PLA can fully exploit C4ISR capabilities.[51] As in cyber, the two sides lack a shared understanding of deterrence and escalation control. As Dean Cheng argues, it is unlikely that China would engage in only space operations, or only cyber operations.[52] Conflict could quickly spill from one domain to the other.

The complications inherent in different views of deterrence are amplified by bureaucratic and organizational decisions. Signal sending and escalation control require tight political control of cyber forces. Although the structure of China's cyber forces is opaque to outside analysts, they appear scattered across services and headquarters. The Third Department of the PLA (3/PLA) is involved in cyber espionage and appears to have primary responsibility for computer network defense; the Fourth Department (4/PLA) is responsible for offensive computer operations, though there appears to be some overlap in roles.

In addition, Joe McReynolds argues that there are two other types of forces: PLA-authorized forces, which are teams of network warfare specialists in the Ministry of State Security and the Ministry of Public Security authorized to carry out network warfare operations; and nongovernmental forces, which are external entities that spontaneously engage in network attack and defense but can be organized and mobilized for network warfare operations.[53] Nigel Inkster argues that the cyber militia, situated within companies and universities, has a collective membership of close to 10 million people. Inkster believes it is unlikely that the militia would engage in offensive operations since doing so might undermine more advanced attacks conducted by the PLA, but the forces would provide defensive and logistic support.[54]

The recent reforms of the PLA should lead to a more unified leadership and command structure, as well as greater political control of the military, but they remain a work in process and face important obstacles. In 2015, in addition to supplanting the seven geographic military regions with five theater commands and replacing the General Staff, Political, Logistics, and Armaments Departments with new departments and commissions within the Central Military Commission, President Xi also announced the establishment of a new Strategic Support Force, whose responsibilities will include the "five domains" of intelligence, technical reconnaissance, electronic warfare, cyber offense and defense, and psychological warfare.[55] Phillip Saunders and Joel Wuthnow describe the reforms as "Goldwater-Nichols with Chinese characteristics"—that is, designed to rationalize the distinctions between operational and administrative chains of command, but where the CCP still plays a role in key decision making.[56]

John Costello notes that the Strategic Support Forces operate administratively like the former Second Artillery Forces and are under the direct command of the Central Military Commission. Such a structure allows "the CMC the benefit of technological progress without attendant loss of control."[57]

While these reforms may eventually improve the PLA's ability to conduct joint operations and its political control over the military, thus enhancing the capacity to send signals, Chinese approaches to crisis management would further complicate U.S. efforts to limit escalation. China, according to Michael Swaine, views itself as a uniquely nonaggressive great power, and sees its past efforts during territorial disputes as totally justifiable responses to the efforts of others to alter the status quo.[58] The United States is seen as offensively oriented, willing to violate the territorial integrity and sovereignty of other states. In past crises, China has used force to shape, deter, or reverse a situation, test intentions, and prevent escalation. These uses of force have required local superiority, tight control over troops, efforts to seize the initiative, use of pauses in communications, and the provision of "a way out" for both sides. At the same time, Beijing has preferred coercive actions over prolonged diplomatic, incremental action. But as Swaine notes, it is not clear how useful historical precedent is for predicting future behavior. Chinese decision making is much more complicated than it was under Mao and Deng, and China's leaders now have to respond to public sentiment.

Avery Goldstein lists additional conditions that make U.S.-China crisis management more difficult than the control of U.S.-Soviet competition.[59] First, Beijing and Washington lack the long, difficult history of crisis communication that Moscow and Washington experienced in the early years of the Cold War. In addition, Chinese analysts overestimate the ease and efficacy of using military actions to send signals. Second, unlike the Soviets, the Chinese appear to accept the instability-stability paradox—the belief that the possession of nuclear weapons by the two sides will limit conventional military conflict and thus act as a barrier to unwanted escalation. Third, as noted above, military technology has created a distinct offensive advantage. With emerging space and cyberwarfare capabilities, neither side can be confident in the durability and resilience of its C4ISR systems, inducing pressure to initiate the use of force.

Goldstein also argues that the continued advantages in U.S. conventional forces and in military intelligence provide strong incentives for Washington to strike first before Beijing has the opportunity to disperse its naval forces to deeper seas. Moreover, in a maritime conflict in the South China Sea or Taiwan Strait, Beijing would believe it was defending core sovereignty and territorial interests, while the United States would be upholding the principles of freedom of navigation and its reputation as a resolute ally. China is likely to believe that it values its interests more than the United States values the principles of free navigation and thus be tempted to strike first.

The region's political-military relationships heighten the incongruity of interests. The United States is involved in extended deterrence in the Asia Pacific as China directly confronts Taiwan, Japan, the Philippines, and others. Once again, Beijing is likely to believe that it values its sovereignty and territorial interests more dearly than Washington values reputational costs or the interests of its allies.

Third Parties

In addition to the effects of differing views of deterrence and crisis management, U.S. and Chinese policymakers and warfighters would have to worry about third parties engaging in cyberattacks, further complicating signaling and escalation control. Regional conflicts are now almost always accompanied by some forms of "patriotic hacking," individuals or groups engaged mainly in website defacement, the compromise of personal data, and distributed denial-of-service attacks. Libicki argues that "exchange of cyberattacks between states may also excite the general interest of superpatriot hackers or those who like a dog pile—particularly if the victim of the attack or the victim of retaliation, or both, are unpopular in certain circles."[60] During the war in Gaza in 2012, for example, the hacktivist collective group Anonymous launched its #OpIsrael Campaign, attacking websites belonging to the Israeli Defense Forces, the prime minister's office, Israeli banks, and airlines.

There is a long history of patriotic hacking in the U.S.-China relationship. In May 1999, after U.S. forces bombed the Chinese embassy in Belgrade during a NATO peacekeeping operation, Chinese hackers DoS attacked and defaced the websites of federal government agencies, temporarily knocking the White House website offline.[61] When a U.S. EP-3E reconnaissance aircraft collided in midair with a Chinese fighter jet seventy miles off the southern coast of China on April 1, 2001, Chinese hackers launched a campaign to deface U.S. websites, and U.S. hackers responded in kind.[62] There is also the possibility of a false flag operation, an attack designed to implicate a third party. Hackers claiming to represent the Islamic State, for example, interfered with the operations of the French news channel TV5Monde. French intelligence eventually attributed the attacks to Russia-based groups. Other regional actors with tensions with China might be tempted to hack U.S. targets in order to provoke retaliation against Beijing. They may also just serve to delay decision making as the defense wastes time trying to make the correct attribution. Vietnam in particular has allegedly been involved in attacks on other Southeast Asian countries as well as China. Its hackers have targeted information concerning territorial tensions in the South China Sea.[63]

Once cyber operations began, other nation-states could also be drawn into the conflict. PLA hackers are likely to target integrated air-defense systems; maritime intelligence, surveillance, and reconnaissance systems; and networks shared by the military and civilian operators in Japan and South Korea. Even if such attacks did not invoke the U.S.-Japan and U.S.-ROK defense treaties, they could spill over, creating damage to civilian targets and provoking Tokyo and Seoul to respond with their own strikes. In 2011 the U.S.-Australia alliance was extended to cover cyberattacks, and depending on the type, target, and severity of the attack, Australian forces could also be involved in a conflict. What started as a dispute between the United States and China could quickly expand to include other militaries and nonstate actors.

Ideological Struggle and the Difficulty of Strategic Targets

In a conflict that threatens vital national interests, the United States might also consider attacks on critical infrastructure. In response to written questions from the Senate Armed Services Committee about whether "U.S. Cyber Command and the military services [are] actively developing capabilities to threaten the critical infrastructure of peer adversaries," Lieutenant General Paul Nakasone, the nominee for head of U.S. Cyber Command, responded simply, "Yes."[64] These attacks, designed to cause widespread disruption or destruction, would be inherently escalatory and could be expected to provoke a similar set of attacks from Beijing on the United States. Even if the Chinese leadership wanted to slow down its response or de-escalate a conflict, it might face pressure from societal actors who want a more assertive response to a U.S. cyberattack after an event that causes widespread effects. While leaders often have incentives to overstate "the hurt feelings of the Chinese people," public opinion, and the internet in particular, creates new constraints on government leaders. As the administrator of the Chinese Ministry of Foreign Affairs website put it, "Policy-makers can't make decisions based on public opinion, but they can't ignore it either."[65]

U.S. policymakers might see an attack on the regime's legitimacy or reputation as a less escalatory strategic attack. The problem, however, is whether Beijing would interpret these attacks as less threatening. The Chinese leadership appears to believe that the two sides are already engaged in an ideological struggle in the information space, and that Washington is using the internet to undermine regime legitimacy. When Secretary of State Hillary

Clinton delivered three speeches on internet freedom between 2010 and 2011, asserting that users must be assured freedom of expression and religion online, as well as the right to access the internet and thereby connect to websites and other people, Beijing responded to the call for these four freedoms negatively and defensively. "Behind what America calls free speech is naked political scheming," read the headline of one article in *People's Daily*. "The United States," the article continued, "applies double standards in implementing freedom of information: for those who have different political views or values, it waves a 'freedom fighter's' club and leads a crusade against them."[66] The *PLA Daily* made a similar point: "If we do not occupy the online battlefield ourselves, others will occupy it; if we do not defend online territory ourselves, sovereignty will be lost, and it may even become a 'bridgehead' for hostile forces to erode and disintegrate us."[67]

An editorial in the *Global Times*, a highly nationalistic newspaper, frames the Panama Papers as part of this larger struggle without directly addressing claims that Chinese leaders had established shell companies. After questioning the independence of the investigators behind the reporting, and suggesting that some are U.S. intelligence agents, the editorial states, "Global information has inherent Western political elements. In the Internet era, the U.S. is very capable of fighting the war of public opinion."[68]

Moreover, with an attack directed at political control, such as visibly and publicly trying to dismantle the Great Firewall, it is unlikely that the United States could signal that it was designed to achieve political gains narrower than the overthrow of the CCP. In response to articles in the U.S. press that the Obama administration was considering developing a more creative response to Chinese cyber espionage, such as attacking the Great Firewall, *Xinhua* responded, "Just like protecting its territorial sovereignty and integrity, China is strongly determined to protect the safety of its cyber space and reserves all rights to counter any outside threats and intrusions."[69] Even if the United States hoped that an attack on the Great Firewall would lead to the cessation of hostilities or a return to the status quo, China is likely to view this type of attack as an existential threat.

Conclusion

Both the United States and China have an incentive to use cyberattacks early in a military confrontation. In addition, there are strong incentives to use the attacks broadly for denial and punishment. Every network that can support military operations is likely to be targeted. As Gompert and Saunders argue, "Tactical military calculations have to be combined with a strong possibility that cyber war could spread from the military to other realms, with imponderable economic and political effects for both sides."[70] Tactical cyberwar could easily become strategic cyberwar.

Since it cannot be expected that either the United States or China will eschew the use of offensive cyber operations, the two sides will want to consider how to prevent unwanted and unnecessary escalation from tactical to strategic. As many have noted, there is need for greater communication between the two militaries on crisis management and escalation control. Iain Johnston, for example, has suggested crisis-management dialogues and mechanisms be given a more central place in official U.S.-China military-to-military and political dialogue. Washington and Beijing also need discussions that help the other more clearly understand the other's red lines, which may include attacks on specific types of weapons platforms or military command and control systems.

The two sides will also want to discuss their command and control structures for cyber forces since tight political control over cyberattacks may keep attacks more precisely targeted and the risks of collateral effects lower. China's establishment of the Strategic Support Forces should result in tighter control of Chinese operators, and the United States could demonstrate its continued commitment to control over cyber operations in public statements and in training and exercises with allies. In addition, Beijing and Washington will want to build on the example of the cyber hotline that is being used by the U.S. Department of Homeland Security and China's Ministry of Public Security to investigate crime to establish communication lines between the relevant military commands and between political leaders.[71]

The two sides could also consider a ban on targeting and exploiting nuclear command and control systems, especially during periods of political tension.[72] These would be public statements by leaders in both countries, and, while masking and other deceptive techniques might make the declarations unverifiable, they could be used as part of a larger framework of confidence building. Such an agreement is not without precedent. In June 1998 Beijing and Washington announced a Nuclear Weapons De-Targeting Agreement, in which both sides agreed not to target each other's nuclear forces. Since U.S. weapons can be retargeted in minutes, this was mainly a symbolic gesture, though not without political value. As one U.S. official put it, "This will not have a lot of military significance, but we would like to do it as a political, confidence-building symbol."[73]

This type of agreement will also require creative technical thinking from Beijing and Washington on how to explicitly differentiate between conventional military and nuclear command and control systems, as well as differentiate between Chinese and U.S. exploits and those of third parties. Eventually these types of discussions should also be expanded to include France, the Russian Federation, India, and the United Kingdom.

The tempo of discussions between Beijing and Washington needs to be increased. China suspended a bilateral cyber working group after the United State indicted five PLA hackers for economic cyber espionage in May 2014. The two sides agreed to a new expert working group during the September 2015 summit between Presidents Xi and Obama, but that group only met once, in May 2016, led by the U.S. State Department and the Chinese Ministry of Foreign Affairs. President Xi and President Trump agreed to four dialogues, including the Law Enforcement and Cyber Strategic Dialogue and the Diplomatic and Security Dialogue. While the latter reportedly discussed in June 2017 issues of stability and international standards, the former, led by the Department of Justice and the Department of Homeland Security, focused on intellectual property theft and crime.[74] It is uncertain whether, without a more intensive engagement, China and the United States can avoid being locked into warfighting plans that are blind to many of the assumptions of the other side, and thus significantly raise the risk of escalation and spillover.

Notes

1. Office of the Secretary of Defense, *Annual Report to Congress: Military and Security Developments Involving the People's Republic of China 2016* (April 26, 2016) (www.defense .gov/Portals/1/Documents/pubs/2016%20China%20Military%20Power%20Report.pdf).

2. Research Department of Military Strategy, *The Science of Military Strategy*, 3rd ed. (Beijing: Military Science Press, 2013), p. 189.

3. Maren Leed, "Offensive Cyber Capabilities at the Operational Level" (Washington: Center for Strategic and International Studies, September 2013) (www.ciaonet.org /attachments/23730/uploads.

4. Herbert S. Lin, "Offensive Cyber Operations and the Use of Force," *Journal of National Security* 4, no. 1 (2010), p. 63.

5. William A. Owens, Kenneth W. Dam, and Herbert S. Lin, *Technology, Policy, Law, and Ethics Regarding U.S. Acquisition and Use of Cyberattack Capabilities* (Washington: National Academies Press, 2009).

6. M. Taylor Fravel, "China's New Military Strategy: 'Winning Informationized Local Wars,'" *China Brief* 15, no. 13 (2015) (www.jamestown.org/programs/chinabrief /single/?tx_ttnews%5Btt_news%5D=44072&cHash=c403ff4a87712ec43d2a11cf576f3e c1#.V1BLDPkrK70).

7. Office of the Secretary of Defense, *Annual Report to Congress*.

8. Eric Heginbotham, *U.S.-China Military Scorecard: Forces, Geography, and the Evolving Balance of Power 1996–2017* (Santa Monica, Calif.: RAND, 2015), pp. 259–83.

9. David C. Gompert and Phillip C. Saunders, *The Paradox of Power: Sino-American Strategic Restraint in an Age of Vulnerability* (Washington: National Defense University Press, 2011).

10. Daguang Li, "Constructs of Information System-Based Network Warfare" (in Chinese), *Space Power Magazine* (Winter/Spring 2010) (www.au.af.mil/au/afri/aspj /apjinternational/apj-c/2010/2010-4/2010_4_13_li.pdf).

11. Joe McReynolds, "China's Evolving Perspectives on Network Warfare: Lessons from the Science of Military Strategy," *China Brief* 15, no. 8 (2015) (www.jamestown .org/programs/chinabrief/single/?tx_ttnews%5Btt_news%5D=43798#.V1BM2_krK70).

12. Adam Segal, "Is China a Paper Tiger in Cyberspace?," *Net Politics* (blog), February 8, 2012 (http://blogs.cfr.org/asia/2012/02/08/is-china-a-paper-tiger-in-cyberspace/).

13. Gompert, and Saunders, *The Paradox of Power*.

14. "The Internet in China," White Paper (Information Office of the State Council of the People's Republic of China, June 8, 2010) (www.china.org.cn/government/whitepaper /node_7093508.htm).

15. "China's Digital Economy Surges 18.9%, Drives Growth," *China Daily*, July 20, 2017 (www.chinadaily.com.cn/business/2017-07/20/content_30179729.htm); Kevin Wei Wang, Alan Lau, and Fang Gong, "How Savvy, Social Shoppers Are Transforming Chinese e-Commerce," McKinsey Survey (April 2016) (www.mckinsey.com/industries/retail /our-insights/how-savvy-social-shoppers-are-transforming-chinese-e-commerce.

16. Jonathan Woetzel and others, "China's Digital Transformation" (McKinsey Global Institute, July 2014) (www.mckinsey.com/insights/high_tech_telecoms_internet /chinas_digital_transformation).

17. "Report on the Work of the Government" (draft copy), *China Daily*, March 5, 2015 (www.chinadaily.com.cn/china/2015twosession/2015-03/05/content_19729663_20 .htm).

18. Paul Mozur, "Beijing Wants A.I. to Be Made in China by 2030," *New York Times*, July 20, 2017.

19. Lana Lam, "NSA Targeted China's Tsinghua University in Extensive Hacking Attacks, Says Snowden," *South China Morning Post*, June 22, 2013 (www.scmp.com/news /china/article/1266892/exclusive-nsa-targeted-chinas-tsinghua-university-extensive -hacking).

20. Lili Fu, "China's Industrial Control System Information Security Situation is Grim" (in Chinese), *People's Daily*, December 2, 2014 (http://scitech.people.com.cn/BIG5 /n/2014/1202/c1057-26128680.html).

21. Adam Segal, "China and the Power Grid: Hacking and Getting Hacked," *Net Politics* (blog), December 3, 2014 (http://blogs.cfr.org/cyber/2014/12/03/china-and-the -power-grid/).

22. Josh Chin and Clément Bürge, "Twelve Days in Xinjiang: How China's Surveillance State Overwhelms Daily Life," *Wall Street Journal*, December 19, 2017; Ben Blanchard, and John Ruwitch, "China Hikes Defense Budget, to Spend More on Internal

Security," Reuters, March 5, 2013 (www.reuters.com/article/us-china-parliament-defence
-idUSBRE92403620130305); Josh Chin, "China Spends More on Domestic Security as
Xi's Powers Grow," *Wall Street Journal*, March 6, 2018.

23. Martin C. Libicki, "Pulling Punches in Cyberspace," in *Proceedings of a Workshop
on Deterring Cyberattacks* (Washington: National Academies Press, 2010), pp. 123–47.

24. "Chinese Data (sigh)," *Balding's World*, January 29, 2018 (www.baldingsworld
.com/2018/01/29/revisiting-chinese-data-sigh/).

25. Javier C. Hernandez, "Labor Protests Multiply in China as Economy Slows, Wor-
rying Leaders," *New York Times*, March 14, 2016.

26. David E. Sanger, "U.S. Decides to Retaliate against China's Hacking," *New York
Times*, July 31, 2015.

27. "Revolution to Riches," Bloomberg, December 2012 (https://www.sopawards
.com/wp-content/uploads/2013/05/45-Bloomberg-News1-Revolution-to-Riches.pdf);
David Barboza, "Billions in Hidden Riches for Family of Chinese Leader," *New York
Times*, October 25, 2012.

28. David Wertime, "Chinese Censors Rush to Make 'Panama Papers' Disappear,"
Foreign Policy, April 4, 2016.

29. Samuel Wade, "Minitrue: Panama Papers and Foreign Media Attacks," *China
Digital Times*, April 4, 2016 (http://chinadigitaltimes.net/2016/04/minitrue-panama-papers
-foreign-media-attacks/).

30. Adam Segal, *The Hacked World Order: How Nations Fight, Trade, Maneuver, and
Manipulate in the Digital Age* (New York: PublicAffairs, 2016), p. 94.

31. Lin, "Offensive Cyber Operations and the Use of Force."

32. Martin C. Libicki, *Conquest in Cyberspace: National Security and Information Warfare* (Cambridge University Press, 2007), p. 37.

33. Thomas Rid and Peter McBurney, "Cyber-Weapons," *RUSI Journal* 157, no. 1
(2012), pp. 6–13; Rebecca Slayton, "What Is the Cyber Offense-Defense Balance? Conceptions, Causes, and Assessment," *International Security* 41, no. 3 (2016/17), pp. 72–109.

34. John Markoff and Thom Shanker, "Halted '03 Iraq Plan Illustrates U.S. Fear of
Cyberwar Risk," *New York Times*, August 1, 2009.

35. Thomas Mahnken, "Cyber War and Cyber Warfare," in *America's Cyber Future:
Security and Prosperity in the Information Age*, vol. 2, edited by K. Lord and T. Sharp
(Washington: Center for a New American Security, 2011), pp. 53–62.

36. Libicki, "Pulling Punches in Cyberspace."

37. Peter D. Feaver, "Blowback: Information Warfare and the Dynamics of Coercion,"
Security Studies 7, no. 4 (1998), pp. 88–120.

38. Libicki, *Conquest in Cyberspace*.

39. Research Department of Military Strategy, *The Science of Military Strategy*,
p. 189.

40. M. Taylor Fravel and Fiona S. Cunningham, "Assuring Assured Retaliation: China's Nuclear Posture and U.S.-China Strategic Stability," *International Security* 40, no. 2
(2015), pp. 7–50.

41. William J. Lynn III, "Defending a New Domain: The Pentagon's Cyberstrategy,"
Foreign Affairs 89, no. 5 (September/October 2010), pp. 97–108.

42. Jeffrey W. Knopf, "The Fourth Wave in Deterrence Research," *Contemporary Security Policy* 31, no. 1 (2010), pp. 1–33.

43. Final Report of the Defense Science Board (DSB) Task Force on Cyber Deterrence (Department of Defense, February 2017) (www.acq.osd.mil/dsb/reports/2010s/DSB

-CyberDeterrenceReport_02-28-17_Final.pdf); Research Department of Military Strategy, *The Science of Military Strategy*, p. 134.

44. Research Department of Military Strategy. *The Science of Military Strategy*, p. 134.

45. "Experts Analyze U.S. Network Deterrence Strategy: It Is Difficult to Achieve Real Results" (in Chinese), *China News*, January 9, 2012 (www.chinanews.com/gj/2012 /01-09/3590771.shtml).

46. Research Department of Military Strategy, *The Science of Military Strategy*.

47. Dean Cheng, "Chinese Views on Deterrence," *Joint Force Quarterly* 60, no. 1 (2011), pp. 92–94.

48. Dean Cheng, "Prospects for Extended Deterrence in Space and Cyber: The Case of the PRC" (Washington: Heritage Foundation, January 21, 2016) (www.heritage.org /research/reports/2016/01/prospects-for-extended-deterrence-in-space-and-cyber-the -case-of-the-prc).

49. Martin C. Libicki and Scott Warren Harold, *Getting to Yes with China in Cyberspace* (Washington: RAND, 2016).

50. Quoted in Dean Cheng, "Prospects for China's Military Space Efforts," in *Beyond the Strait: PLA Missions Other Than Taiwan*, edited by Roy Kamphausen, David Lai, and Andrew Scobell (Carlisle, Pa.: Strategic Studies Institute, 2009), p. 215.

51. Ibid.

52. Cheng, "Prospects for Extended Deterrence in Space and Cyber."

53. McReynolds, "China's Evolving Perspectives on Network Warfare."

54. Nigel Inkster, *China's Cyber Power* (New York: Routledge, 2016), p. 108.

55. Chenxi Tu, "China's Strategic Support Force a Global First, May Oversee Shenlong Spacecraft" (in Chinese), *Global Times*, January 16, 2016 (http://mil.huanqiu.com /observation/2016-01/8392698.html).

56. Phillip Saunders and Joel Wuthnow, "China's Goldwater-Nichols? Assessing PLA Organizational Reforms," *Strategic Forum* (April 2016), p. 294 (http://ndupress.ndu.edu /Portals/68/Documents/stratforum/SF-294.pdf).

57. John Costello, "China's Strategic Support Force: A Force for a New Era," Testimony to the U.S.-China Economic and Security Review Commission (February 15, 2018) (www.uscc.gov/sites/default/files/Costello_Written%20Testimony.pdf).

58. Michael Swaine, "Chinese Crisis Management: Framework for Analysis, Tentative Observations, and Questions for the Future," in *Chinese National Security Decisionmaking under Stress*, edited by Andrew Scobell and Larry Wortzel (Carlisle, Pa.: Strategic Studies Institute, 2005), pp. 5–54.

59. Avery Goldstein, "First Things First: The Pressing Danger of Crisis Instability in U.S.-China Relations," *International Security* 37, no. 4 (2013), pp. 49–89.

60. Martin C. Libicki, *Cyberdeterrence and Cyberwar* (Washington: RAND, 2009) (www.rand.org/content/dam/rand/pubs/monographs/2009/RAND_MG877.pdf).

61. Ellen Messmer, "Kosovo Cyber-War Intensifies: Chinese Hackers Targeting U.S. Sites, Government Says," CNN, May 12, 1999 (www.cnn.com/TECH/computing/9905 /12/cyberwar.idg/).

62. Rose Tang, "China-U.S. Cyber War Escalates," CNN, May 1, 2001 (http://edition .cnn.com/2001/WORLD/asiapcf/east/04/27/china.hackers/).

63. Gordon Corera, "How France's TV5 Was Almost Destroyed by 'Russian Hackers,'" BBC, October 10, 2016 (www.bbc.com/news/technology-37590375); "Vietnam's Neighbors, ASEAN, Targeted by Hackers: Report," Reuters, November 7, 2017 (www

.reuters.com/article/us-cyber-attack-vietnam/vietnams-neighbors-asean-targeted-by
-hackers-report-idUSKBN1D70VU).

64. Advance Policy Questions for Lieutenant General Paul Nakasone, USA Nominee for Commander, U.S. Cyber Command and Director, National Security Agency/
Chief, Central Security Service, Senate Armed Services Committee (March 1, 2018)
(www.armed-services.senate.gov/imo/media/doc/Nakasone_APQs_03-01-18.pdf).

65. Quoted in Adam Segal, "Globalization Is a Double-Edged Sword: Globalization
and Chinese National Security," in *Globalization and National Security*, edited by Jonathan Kirshner (New York: Routledge, 2006), pp. 293–320.

66. Tania Branigan, "China Accuses U.S. of Online Warfare in Iran," *The Guardian*,
January 24, 2010 (www.theguardian.com/world/2010/jan/24/china-us-iran-online-war
fare); "Major Points Buried in the U.S. Cyberwar Strategy" (in Chinese), *Xinhua*, April 7,
2015 (http://news.xinhuanet.com/zgjx/2015-04/07/c_134128303.htm).

67. Rogier Creemers, "Cybersovereignty Symbolizes National Sovereignty," China
Copyright and Media, May 20, 2015 (https://chinacopyrightandmedia.wordpress.com
/2015/05/20/cybersovereignty-symbolizes-national-sovereignty/).

68. "Iceland PM Woes an Ad for Panama Papers" (editorial), *Global Times*, April 7, 2016
(www.globaltimes.cn/content/977535.shtml).

69. Linfei Zhi, "U.S. Should Think Twice before Retaliating against China over Un-
founded Hacking Charges," *Xinhua*, August 3, 2015 (http://news.xinhuanet.com/english
/2015-08/03/c_134475531.htm).

70. Gompert and Saunders, *The Paradox of Power*.

71. Alastair Iain Johnston, "The Evolution of Interstate Security Crisis-Management
Theory and Practice in China," *Naval War College Review* 61, no. 1 (2016), pp. 28–71.

72. Richard Danzig, *Surviving on a Diet of Poisoned Fruit: Reducing the National Security
Risks of America's Cyber Dependencies* (Washington: Center for a New American Security,
July 2014) (www.cnas.org/sites/default/files/publications-pdf/CNAS_PoisonedFruit_Danzig
_0.pdf).

73. Walter Pincus, "U.S., China May Retarget Nuclear Weapons," *Washington Post*,
June 16, 1998.

74. Secretary of State Rex Tillerson and Secretary of Defense Jim Mattis at a Joint
Press Availability (U.S. State Department, June 21, 2017) (www.state.gov/secretary
/remarks/2017/06/272103.htm); "First U.S.-China Law Enforcement and Cybersecurity
Dialogue: Summary of Outcomes, Department of Justice," October 6, 2018 (www.justice
.gov/opa/pr/first-us-china-law-enforcement-and-cybersecurity-dialogue).

14

Disintermediation, Counterinsurgency, and Cyber Defense

DAVID AUCSMITH

One of the major challenges in cyberspace is the disintermediation of government. Historically, governments have provided their value as intermediaries both within states and between them. They serve as intermediaries in disputes between people—civil, criminal, and international. Governments are also intermediaries in the physical world, protecting borders, investigating and prosecuting crimes, and creating much of the infrastructure upon which real-world interactions take place. This intermediary function of government is at the very core of the definition of government.

Following the Treaty of Westphalia in 1648, nation-states took on the sole legitimate authority to wage organized violence and the responsibility for the warlike acts of any of its citizens or agents.[1] The authorities and responsibilities of nation-states were linked to the geopolitical definitions of sovereignty. Governments defend their national territory. They prosecute criminals within their national territory. Likewise, they regulate commerce within their national territory and between their territory and the territories of other nation-states. The Treaty of Westphalia established the sovereign nation-state as the *sole* legitimate intermediary between individuals and between individuals and the state for matters of national security, military, and criminal justice, based on sovereignty over the geographic area in question. Of course in practice, state sovereignty has never been universally absolute.[2] However, the centrality of sovereign states in the conduct of international relations has been a defining characteristic of interstate relations for more than three centuries.

Cyberspace, however, is different than the physical world of the past. Cyberspace is a global commons; it is defined not by national boundaries, but by the telecommunications infrastructure. Though its components are present in the physical world, its instantiation is not governed by geography. All the richness of governments, companies, and individuals is equidistant from any point within cyberspace. The reach of the internet has made an organization's value accessible from anywhere, and disintermediation has directly connected that value to any consumer—without the traditional intermediary functions of government. There are no border checks, no customs, no neighborhood watch, and no wanted posters. In cyberspace, government has been further removed of its traditional functions of safety and security.

This fundamental shift accompanies a new reality: in cyberspace, weapons are also simply information. As several contributors to this volume note, cyberspace is the virtual environment created by the interconnected network of computing devices, communications channels, and the humans who use them. The value of information in cyberspace depends on the correct input, manipulation, and output of that information. Without information correctness (that is, data integrity), there is no value in information. Anything that disrupts this process or introduces ambiguity into it is a potential weapon. Cyber weapons cause the underlying system to perform in ways that are either unknown or unanticipated.

Cyberattacks exist because of *richness* and *reach*. The richness of information becomes the value and creates the target of the attack. Before the invention of the telegraph (arguably the beginning of telecommunications), seagoing ships carried information and trade goods. This commerce was so valuable that it led theorists such as Alfred Thayer Mahan and Julian S. Corbett to postulate that freedom of navigation was essential for national survival and the ability to interdict maritime commerce a key to projecting national interest. Now the command, control, communications, intelligence, surveillance, and reconnaissance of armies and the essential trade and commerce of nations all travel through cyberspace. Cyberspace has become, as Steven McPherson and Glenn Zimmerman argue, the global "center of gravity" for all aspects of national power, spanning the economic, technological, diplomatic, and military capabilities a country might possess.[3] Every part of a nation's existence ultimately depends on cyberspace. In this sense, cyberspace has become, as Carl von Clausewitz said regarding a center of gravity, "the hub of all power and movement on which everything depends."[4] Without access to cyberspace, a nation would have difficulty governing, conducting trade, communicating internally or externally, or understanding the intentions of other nations.

While the richness of information creates the target, reach creates the means of the attack. Cyberspace exists solely as lines of communications. It has no other expression. Alfred Thayer Mahan described the sea as a "great highway" passing in all directions, a domain of trade and international communication with tremendous social and political importance.[5] He observed that certain lanes of travel, seaports, and communication routes will inevitably be preferred over others, and become recognized as "trade routes," which over time can have a significant influence on national and international commerce, and the course of history.[6] Cyberspace is the "great highway" of our age. It, too, has "ports" (for example, data stores, sensors, weapons, and commercial systems) and "trade routes" (for example, fiber-optic cable and satellite links). It is a global common; defined not by national or geographic boundaries, but by the existence of the telecommunications infrastructure. The same reach that allows a publisher to download a book to a computer on the other side of the planet, free from the constraint of geography or intermediaries, also allows that computer to attempt to upload malicious code to the publisher in hopes of committing theft. The attacker, like the victim, is freed of the constraints of either geography or intermediaries. All points in cyberspace are effectively equidistant.

As government's richness and reach diminish, new entities with greater richness or greater reach arise to fill the void. These entities may be political, cultural, or ideological, or combinations of each, but the global nature of cyberspace allows for an inclusiveness independent of geography and outside the purview of government.

The Richness and Reach of Government Disintermediation

Disintermediation has made the traditional government responsibilities of safety and security far less relevant in cyberspace because of government's inability to match the richness and reach required of cyberspace. Government cannot be everywhere that needs protecting, so its reach in cyberspace is inherently limited, whether it is protection against war, espionage, or crime by the use, or threatened use, of physical force. Similarly, because no government is sovereign over all of cyberspace, its value is limited. Cyberspace was not designed to be controlled.

Starting with simple goals and an elegant design, cyberspace has evolved into a domain whose total structure is far too complex to be completely understood or analyzed. The structure of cyberspace, the consequence of its architecture and components, gives cyberspace inherent properties that limit the safety and security roles of government. For example, it limits both the ability to disambiguate network traffic at any single point and the capability to attribute actions to individuals or organizations, both of which are essential to the functions of safety and security.

Even in most developed countries there is no single point or collection of points from which all internet traffic into and out of the country can be observed. And if such a point existed, the volume of traffic would be far too great for content to be monitored. Cisco Systems, the global networking company, estimates that the total internet volume will reach 278 exabytes per month by 2021.[7] If such points of national ingress and egress existed and could ever be monitored, they would not have access to intercountry communications. Internet connectivity is highly redundant and interconnected. Many, many points would need to be monitored. Even if one could monitor some sizable percentage of internet traffic within a country, much communication is opaque from encryption (for example, with https://, IPSec VPNs, and other means) and not understandable to monitoring systems.

In addition to the problem of internet architecture and volume, in many countries, such as the United States, there is no government entity with the legal authority to monitor citizen communications without probable cause. Even if a government entity were monitoring a connection, distinguishing malicious activity from nonmalicious activity is an acknowledged hard problem, as exemplified by the continuous evolution of commercial products to perform the function.

The process of disintermediation has had both great and unanticipated effects. While disintermediation has fundamentally altered business, so too has it altered crime, espionage, and warfare. By connecting producer to consumer, disintermediation has directly connected criminal enterprises to the bank accounts of individuals. It has directly connected intelligence services to the national secrets of their adversaries, and it has connected the warfighting capacity of one nation to the critical infrastructure and military apparatus of another. Producers of information are connected to consumers of information, without intermediaries, without the traditional roles of safety and security once occupied by the representatives of government.

Nations can perform the functions of safety and security (the richness provided by governments) in limited scenarios (within the limited reach of which they are capable). Governments may defend their own infrastructure (for example, with .mil and .gov) and, perhaps, a limited subset of the national infrastructure, but governments do not have the reach to defend the totality of cyberspace upon which they depend. They do not have the reach to protect all of .com. They may be able to protect themselves, though that is doubtful, but they certainly cannot protect all of the businesses and citizens over which they have authority.

Who then defends the rest? The logical conclusion is that, in the global common of cyberspace, one must defend oneself. Whether this is possible, and what role private companies and governments can play to assist in self-defense in cyberspace are important questions. Answering these questions, in turn, requires a better understanding of the nature of conflict in cyberspace, a subject to which I turn next.

The Importance of Prepositions: Projecting Power from Cyberspace versus Projecting Power within Cyberspace

The cyber domain is unique among domains of war in that projecting power *from* the cyber domain to another domain is distinctly different from conflict solely *within* the cyber domain. To understand the difference, consider the air domain. Projecting power from the air domain to any other domain, such as attacking a target in the land domain, involves aircraft, missiles, squadrons, radar, and a myriad of other components. While the specifics of the systems involved may vary, it is roughly the same, in a strategic and tactical sense, as fighting air-to-air (conflict solely *within* the air domain). The cyber domain is not like this. Projecting power *from* the cyber domain to any other domain is network-centric warfare. By contrast, fighting solely *within* the cyber domain more closely resembles irregular war or a guerrilla insurgency.

Projecting Power from the Cyber Domain
In 1998, Admiral Arthur Cebrowski, then president of the Naval War College, proposed transforming the U.S. military by leveraging computer and

communications capabilities for warfare, as business had leveraged them for commerce.[8] He proposed the concept of network-centric warfare—a way to project power from cyberspace into the land, sea, air, and space domains.[9] With the advent of network-centric warfare, the cyber domain was born. As Cebrowski said, "Network-centric warfare enables a shift from attrition-style warfare to a much faster and more effective warfighting style characterized by the new concepts of speed of command and self-synchronization."[10] It enables "the wholesale and near instantaneous sharing of information within and among all elements of U.S. and allied armed forces, irrespective of their locality or mode of operation."[11] Carl von Clausewitz wrote, "War is the realm of uncertainty; three quarters of the factors on which action is based are wrapped in a fog of greater or lesser uncertainty."[12] The promise of network-centric warfare is, as Admiral William Owens argues, that it lifts the fog of war.[13]

Network-centric warfare envisions a "system of systems" that allows us to "sense" the battlefield with near perfect clarity, understand it, and strike with virtual impunity.[14] It is a strike *from* cyberspace. The strike is "sensed," planned, and directed from cyberspace, but the attack occurs in the physical world using weapons resident in the other domains of war that are uniquely enabled by cyber capabilities.

The first requirement of network-centric warfare is to ensure for oneself complete freedom of operation within the cyber domain. This gives rise to the requirement for what is termed "information superiority" or "information dominance," the complete freedom of operations within the domain while denying your adversary the same.

In this sense, the requirement for cyber domain superiority is similar to the call for sea domain superiority of Mahan and the air domain superiority of Douhet. Mahan argued that the need for command of the sea through naval superiority was a prerequisite for a nation's security.[15] Similarly, the argument for information superiority sounds very much like Douhet's statement about command of the air.[16] Both Mahan and Douhet based their arguments on the realization that one's adversary would likely possess the same technology and could similarly use the domain to project power. The only real way to stop them was to have superiority in or control of the domain itself. The logical means of creating superiority in a domain of war is to fight *within* that domain for that control.

Network-centric warfare is the way modern militaries conduct warfare. It is the essence of the "American way of war" and can be characterized as:

- Focused on a few decisive battles

- Technology-dependent

- Focused on firepower

- Large-scale

- Aggressive and offensive

- Profoundly regular

- Impatient

- Logistically excellent

- Highly sensitive to casualties[17]

In short, fighting from the cyber domain in network-centric warfare is expected to be quick, expensive, and highly lethal.

Projecting Power within the Cyber Domain

While *creating superiority* within the domain is required for network-centric warfare, *fighting* within the domain is not itself network-centric warfare. It is something different—more akin to guerrilla warfare or insurgency. Insurgency, a term coined by David Galula, is about the unseen force that, as Mao said, are the fish that swim in the sea of people.[18] By this, he meant that the adversary hides and flourishes among the people and it is among the people that an insurgent is in its natural habitat. In cyberspace, insurgents swim in the components of networks and computers. The goals and objectives of cyber insurgents are not necessarily the same as those of traditional real-world insurgents. But many of the tactics, techniques, and procedures used in real-world insurgency have direct analogues in cyber insurgency. More specifically, real-world insurgency is characterized by:

- Asymmetry between the insurgent and the counterinsurgent

- Fluidity of the insurgent, rigidity of the counterinsurgent

- Low costs (while counterinsurgency is costly)

- The population as target

- Discord as goal (the insurgent only has to sow discord anywhere while the counterinsurgent must maintain order everywhere)

- Protracted war which remains unconventional to the end[19]

The cyberspace analogues are obvious. There is a great asymmetry between the attacker and the defender, with the attacker having the advantage. The attacker has almost complete freedom of movement, able to choose the time, place, and method of attack, while the defender must rigidly defend assets everywhere. Cyberattacks are relatively cheap while cyber defense is costly. Cyberattacks focus on the defender's infrastructure, in many cases on less important or less critical systems from which to launch attacks at the defender's critical assets. Irregular warfare favors not one large blow, but many small ones. As Galula notes, "It hits suddenly, gnaws at the enemy's strength, achieves surprise, disengages, withdraws, disperses and hits again."[20] Cyberattacks seek to sow discord rather than maintain order, by eroding trust in the integrity of information, disrupting the availability of information, or compromising the confidentiality of information. And conflict within cyberspace has a protracted quality to it, with attackers new and old constantly on the hunt for new victims and vectors.

The low cost of entry means that states are by no means the only actors in cyber conflict. Instead, individuals and groups can pursue conflict within cyberspace using unconventional warfare. More important, relatively minor actors can fight within the cyber domain and have global reach. Irregular war in cyberspace can negate the wealth and technological advantage of Western states.

As former deputy secretary of defense William J. Lynn III observed:

> Cyberwarfare is asymmetric. The low cost of computing devices means that U.S. adversaries do not have to build expensive weapons, such as stealth fighters or aircraft carriers, to pose a significant threat to U.S. military capabilities. A dozen determined computer programmers can, if they find a vulnerability to exploit, threaten the United States' global logistics network, steal its operational plans, blind its intelligence capabilities, or hinder its ability to deliver weapons on target.[21]

Cyber Defense as Counterinsurgency

If attacking within cyberspace resembles an insurgency, defending attacks within cyberspace is analogous to counterinsurgency. David Galula was the first to systematically study counterinsurgency,[22] but many more have written on the topic.[23] For the purposes of a model in which to view cyber defense, it is helpful to use the recent work of David Petraeus, John Nagl, H. R. Mc-Master, and others[24] that led to the creation of the U.S. Army doctrine (fundamental principles) for tactical counterinsurgency.[25] U.S. Army counterinsurgency doctrine required a shift from the force-on-force doctrine epitomized by network-centric warfare to the population-centric, small-team, direct engagement doctrine that brought forces out of their bases and inserted them among the population.[26] That doctrinal shift was neither easy nor swift as it necessitated a change in both the object of defense and the prosecution of defense.

The sequence of objectives *clear–hold–build* is often used as a shorthand to describe the resultant counterinsurgency doctrine.[27] With a focus on the local population, a summation of the objectives is:

- Clear

  - Create a secure physical and psychological environment.

  - Establish firm government control of the populace and geographic area.

  - Gain the populace's support.

- Hold

  - Effectively and continuously secure the populace.

  - Establish host-nation government presence at the local level.

  - The safety and welfare of the population are the main focus.

- Build

  - Host-nation security forces continuously conduct patrols.

  - Use measured force against insurgent targets of opportunity.

  - Perform tasks that provide overt and direct benefit to the community.[28]

Obviously, the tactics used to achieve the clear-hold-build objectives are far more complex than this description indicates, but it is with these high-level objectives that a model for cyber defense emerges.

Government cannot defend against an insurgency by remaining in government-held defensive fortifications. Government must bring its expertise to bear within the general population. This lesson of counterinsurgency applies to cyberspace. In cyberspace, disintermediation prevents the government from being able to be effective in the general population of the internet. As the need for cyber self-defense follows from disintermediation, the form that self-defense must take follows from the counterinsurgency model of cyber defense. There are cyber counterinsurgency analogues to the real-world clear-hold-build.

- Clear
  - Create a secure cyber environment.
  - Establish control of vital services and information.
  - Gain support by demonstrating value.
- Hold
  - Effectively and continuously secure the cyber environment.
  - Establish collaboration with enterprise and industry partners.
  - The safety and welfare of critical systems are the main focus.
- Build
  - Teach enterprises how to defend and inform.
  - Use legal mechanisms to pursue targets of opportunity.
  - Help enterprises build cyber resiliency.

In cyberspace this amounts to clearing the adversary out of the contested cyber system, deploying enough resources to hold the adversary out, then building the necessary processes and procedures to keep the adversary out. In this context, clear-hold-build are the phased objectives of cyber defense. The last phase—building processes and procedures—is a continuous activity, heavily reliant on trained personnel, sensors, and intelligence.

Yet developing sufficient personnel, sensors, and intelligence is a daunting endeavor because governments have capabilities but not the reach to assist the general population. Training is critically important to the success of cyber self-defense, which is an adversarial contest whereby adversaries are engaged in a time-competitive, adaptive-learning, high-stakes struggle. Those who practice defense must stay informed of, and adapt to, the latest offensive techniques. These skills are difficult to acquire outside of the offensive cyber organizations of government. Similarly, sensing and intelligence capabilities that are sufficiently current and sufficiently comprehensive are difficult to obtain outside of government. The tactics, techniques, and procedures of the adversary—their tradecraft—are constantly evolving. Remaining cognizant of the adversary requires dedicated resources with sophisticated means. Some commercial organizations and individuals can develop some of these capabilities sufficient for cyber self-defense, but most cannot.

If organizations and individuals must defend themselves in cyberspace, and the counterinsurgency model demonstrates that training and intelligence are essential to success, how then can organizations and individuals actualize a viable cyber-defense capability? The answer is they may not be able to do so on their own. The logical conclusion is that organizations and individuals will have to contract with specialists to provide clear-hold-build cyber defense: incident response companies to *clear*, managed security companies to *hold*, and consultants to *build*, or companies that offer various combinations of services. The disintermediation of government has created a marketplace for cyber safety and security companies. These companies leverage the necessary training across multiple customers and acquire their own intelligence. The quality of both determines the efficacy of their offering.

A final note about active defense. In real-world counterinsurgency, militaries conduct strike operations in parallel, as needed, with clear-hold-build operations.[29] Strike operations are inherently offensive in nature and frequently external to the area subject to clear-hold-build. Strike operations are operations to find, fix, and finish insurgent forces in areas under insurgent control.[30] In cyberspace, the analogous operations would involve accessing the attacker's infrastructure to retrieve or destroy stolen information and to gather evidence for attribution. This is usually referred to as "hacking back," and the understanding is that the Computer Fraud and Abuse Act (CFAA)[31] *may* prohibit the cyber defender from offensive operations such as retrieving stolen information or collecting information for attribution.[32] The legality of "hacking back" seems to hinge on the definition of "authorized." The CFAA makes it illegal to enter a computer for which one does not have authorization yet never defines "authorization."[33] Whether CFAA can or should be modified is a critical question.

One fruitful way forward could be to apply the traditional restraints on self-defense, necessity, proportionality, and immediacy to cyberspace. This would mean interpreting the CFAA to give authorization to enter an attacker's computer for the purpose of retrieving or destroying stolen information and to compile evidence for attribution. Recklessly attacking the aggressor's computer would likely not meet the self-defense test of proportionality. The defender can give the acquired evidence to government authorities so that they can perform their traditional role of ensuring safety and security. If practiced by trained and informed specialized cyber defenders, privately collected evidence of unlawful acts could reinstate the deterrence previously provided by the disintermediated government functions of safety and security.

Conclusion

Disintermediation has removed the government from defending the cyberspace of the general populace and left people to defend themselves. Cyber self-defense is cyber counterinsurgency and requires specialized training and comprehensive intelligence that is out of reach for most organizations and certainly out of reach for individuals. Specialized cyber-defense companies that provide one or more services of clear-hold-build are filling the void. However, even these specialized companies are unlikely to be able to truly provide the safety and security that was once provided by the government.

Notes

1. Peter H. Wilson, *The Thirty Years War: Europe's Tragedy* (Cambridge, Mass.: Belknap Press of Harvard University Press, 2009), p. 754.

2. See, for example, Stephen D. Krasner, *Sovereignty: Organized Hypocrisy* (Princeton University Press, 1999).

3. Steve McPherson and Glenn Zimmerman, "Cyberspace Control," in *Securing Freedom in the Global Commons*, edited by Scott Jasper (Stanford, Calif.: Stanford Security Studies, 2010), p. 86.

4. Carl von Clausewitz, *On War*, edited and translated by Michael Howard and Peter Paret (Princeton University Press, 1989), p. 84.

5. Alfred Thayer Mahan, *The Influence of Sea Power upon History, 1660–1783* [with maps and plans] (New York: Dover Publications, 1987), p. 25.

6. Ibid.

7. Cisco, "The Zettabyte Era: Trends and Analysis," June 7, 2017 (www.cisco.com/c/en /us/solutions/collateral/service-provider/visual-networking-index-vni/vni-hyperconnec tivity-wp.html).

8. Arthur K. Cebrowski and John H. Garstka, "Network-Centric Warfare—Its Origin and Future," *U.S. Naval Institute Proceedings* 124, no. 1 (1998), p. 139.

9. Department of Defense, Office of Force Transformation, *The Implementation of Network-Centric Warfare* (2005).

10. Cebrowski and Garstka, "Network-Centric Warfare," p. 148.

11. Brice F. Harris, *America, Technology and Strategic Culture: A Clausewitzian Assessment* (New York: Routledge, 2009), p. 7.

12. Clausewitz, *On War*, p. 101.

13. William A. Owens, *Lifting the Fog of War* (Johns Hopkins University Press, 2001).

14. Thomas X. Hammes, *The Sling and the Stone: On War in the 21st Century* (Minneapolis, Minn.: Zenith Press, 2006), p. 190.

15. Jon Tetsuro Sumida, *Inventing Grand Strategy and Teaching Command: The Classic Works of Alfred Thayer Mahan Reconsidered* (Washington: Woodrow Wilson Center Press, 1999), p. 44.

16. Giulio Douhet, *The Command of the Air*, edited by Joseph Patrick Harahan and Richard H. Kohn (University of Alabama Press, 2009), p. 24.

17. Colin S. Gray, *Irregular Enemies and the Essence of Strategy: Can the American Way of War Adapt?* (Carlisle, Pa.: Strategic Studies Institute, U.S. Army War College, 2006), pp. 29–49.

18. Mao Tse-tung, "On the Protracted War," in *Selected Works of Mao Tse-tung*, vol. 2 (London: Lawrence and Wishart, 1954), p. 183.

19. David Galula, *Counterinsurgency Warfare: Theory and Practice* (Westport, Conn.: Praeger, 2006), pp. 1–10.

20. Ibid., p. xii.

21. William J. Lynn III, "Defending a New Domain: The Pentagon's Cyberstrategy," *Foreign Affairs* 89, no. 5 (September/October 2010), pp. 89–90.

22. Galula, *Counterinsurgency Warfare*.

23. C. E. Callwell, Sir Robert Thompson, Robert Taber, Dave Dilegge, and John Nagl to name but a few.

24. Fred M. Kaplan, *The Insurgents: David Petraeus and the Plot to Change the American Way of War* (New York: Simon & Schuster, 2013).

25. U.S. Department of the Army, *Field Manual FM 3-24.2 (FM 90-8 FM 7-98) Tactics in Counterinsurgency April 2009* (U.S. Government Printing Office, 2012).

26. Kaplan, *The Insurgents*.

27. U.S. Department of the Army, *Field Manual FM 3-24.2*.

28. *The U.S. Army Marine Corps Counterinsurgency Field Manual: U.S. Army Field Manual No. 3-24* (University of Chicago Press, 2007), pp. 174–80.

29. U.S. Department of the Army, *Field Manual FM 3-24.2*, p. 3-23.

30. Ibid.

31. 18 U.S. Code § 1030—Fraud and related activity in connection with computers (www.gpo.gov/fdsys/granule/USCODE-2010-title18/USCODE-2010-title18-partI -chap47-sec1030/content-detail.html).

32. Computer Crime and Intellectual Property Section Criminal Division, *Prosecuting Computer Crimes* (Washington: Office of Legal Education Executive Office for United States Attorneys, 2010), pp. 1–58 (www.steptoecyberblog.com/files/2012/11/ccmanual1.pdf).

33. "The Hackback Debate," *Steptoe Cyberblog*, November 2, 2012 (www.steptoecyber blog.com/2012/11/02/the-hackback-debate/).

15

Private Sector Cyber Weapons

An Adequate Response to the Sovereignty Gap?

LUCAS KELLO

The goal of national security policy is to preserve the safety of the state and its subjects against threats arising from other states. The organizing principle of international anarchy is that states are the supreme agents in this program of activity: they possess sovereign resources to carry out their own security policies against each other in the absence of world government. These are two classical tenets of international security studies; the central trends of cybersecurity challenge them. Previously the main question of security policy was: What actions of other independent states threaten vital national interests? This is increasingly supplanted by the concern: How do forces operating outside state confines imperil the nation? States to be sure retain their primacy. Nevertheless, new entrants on the international scene—hacktivists, criminal syndicates, militant groups, firms, and so on—can inflict great harm in cyberspace. Security policy now has to be conducted against and by not only states but also a growing universe of other players of unclear origin and identity.

The gradual flight of power away from state structures has produced a sovereignty gap: the private sector can no longer take for granted the ability of the government to protect it against all relevant threats if sovereignty means not just an interstate condition—that is, the state is subject to no other state in the ordering of its internal affairs, as international law commonly defines the notion,[1] but one also involving freedom from the interference of unaffiliated actors. A U.S.-based oil firm may reasonably expect that the U.S. military will be able to prevent the seizure of its property by pirate vessels in the Persian Gulf, but it may not have much confidence that the government can fend off sophisticated criminals seeking to capture or damage prized assets in cyberspace.[2] Offense superiority in the new domain widens the sovereignty gap. Because of enormous defense complications, the government is even less able to defend private subjects against "advanced persistent threats," or adversaries that are able to penetrate home defenses continuously and surreptitiously (think of China or Russia), than against private culprits (such as political or ideological militants). A remark by the chief of Cyber Command, General Keith Alexander, referring to a hypothetical cyber threat against Wall Street, conveys the problem: "[The] NSA and Cyber Command would probably not see it. We have no capability there."[3] A comment by John Chambers, the former executive chairman and CEO of Cisco Systems, captures the private sector's defensive agony: "There are two kinds of companies: those who have been breached and those who don't know they've been breached."[4] A further complication of the new domain is the confluence of criminal and national security activity, a blurring of the lines between hostile actions such as disruption of corporate functions that once implicated only private interests but which increasingly impinge on national security. As Joel Brenner puts it: "The boundary between economic and national security is also eroding—has eroded, in fact, almost completely."[5] The ideal types of "public" and "private" goods and actors, in short, are merging in ways that the conventional science of international relations is unaccustomed, possibly unequipped, to decipher.[6]

The challenge of cybersecurity, therefore, is essentially one of civil defense: how to equip the private sector to protect its own computer terrain in the absence of decisive government involvement.[7] Ordinarily, civil defense in the new domain has involved passive measures, such as resilience and redundancy, which aim to harden defenses and deflect offensive hits. But foiling a sophisticated offensive operation that is already in train is very difficult to do, particularly if deep exploitation of the target networks preceded the attack.[8] Denial of the adversary's arms has a higher chance of success if it occurs before they reach the defending line. Passive measures, therefore, will not redress the defensive gap unless they are complemented by a proactive approach—especially the techniques of "active defense," or offense-as-defense, which attempt to neutralize external threats before they are carried out. As a senior official in the British Cabinet Office put it: "Successful defense requires making life harder for the enemy." It demands a posture of aggressiveness: "We're not going to just sit there and let you get us—we will go after you in cyberspace and make your life more difficult. This is why one sees offensive actions."[9] Yet presently in the United States and Britain, as in many other jurisdictions, the authority to implement active defenses belongs exclusively to the government. Top U.S. officials have called for changes in U.S. law and policy that would bolster the private sector's use of active defenses such as "strikeback" or "hackback" technology: in effect, arming of the civilian quarters of cyberspace.[10] The main body of government opinion has successfully resisted these calls—so far.

This chapter asks: What are the possible strategic and other consequences of enabling the private sector to arm itself with active defenses? Little or no systematic analysis of this question exists. The chapter argues that while the potential defensive and other benefits of private sector arms are significant, the risks to defenders, innocent parties, and international conflict stability are notably greater.

But first, a clarification of key terms is in order. The label "private sector" in this paper denotes the entirety of nonstate groups and individuals who constitute the economy and society and who are not under direct state control but are possibly under its informal direction. Conceptually, the difference between formal state "control" and informal "direction" is subtle but crucial: the former implies membership of the state; the latter, exclusion from the state. On this basis, the private sector encompasses some forms of proxy actors such as criminal syndicates or privately owned firms (for example, Kaspersky Lab)[11] that have established informal working relationships with the government, but it excludes state-affiliated civilian actors such as paramilitary militias (for example, the Estonian Cyber Defense League) or publicly controlled firms (for example, Huawei).[12] The term "cyber weapon" or "arm" signifies the software and hardware instruments necessary to carry out a cyber exploitation or attack. The term "active defense"—a contested and ambiguous notion—is broadly construed to denote the use of such instruments outside the defender's or other friendly terrain to prevent or preempt attack. This interpretation of active defense does not imply the use of any specific kind of cyber weapon, merely that the activity takes place in extradefensive terrains (more on this later).

The chapter has three sections: first, it defines the concept of active defense; second, it reviews the current state of private sector active defense; and finally, it analyzes potential strategic benefits and risks associated with the development of private sector arms.

The Meaning of Active Defense

The first step in analyzing private sector active defense is to define active defense. The notion features prominently in national strategy papers and public debates about cybersecurity, yet it has never been satisfactorily defined. Within official policy circles, there is no clear or precise definition; or if there is such a definition, it is veiled by government secrecy: the research community does not know its full content. Official U.S. strategy papers supply only ambiguous meanings.[13] The Department of Defense describes "active cyber defense" as "[the] synchronized, real-time capability to deter, detect, analyze, and mitigate threats and vulnerabilities," but reveals very little about the types of action involved. Other nations have publicly claimed possession of a capability but fail to define it even vaguely.[14] This section attempts to define active defense so that it may serve as a useful tool of analysis.

Three defining characteristics of active defense stand out: defensive purpose, out-of-perimeter location, and tactical flexibility. These characteristics may apply to the concept of active defense in any domain of conflict; the focus here is on the cyber context.

Defensive Purpose

As the label implies, the aim of active defense is to enhance the security of the defender's assets: to deny proactively but not to penalize the attacker. The attacker, by definition, is affected only if he engages or prepares to engage or is perceived to engage the target. Thus the essence of active defense lies in the eye of the defender. It entails the reasonable *perception*—not necessarily the fact—of an adversary's intention and capability to attack. For this reason, retaliation to deter future attack does not qualify as active defense unless it seeks to degrade the attack sequence itself and transpires while the threat is still active.

Offensive activity that extends beyond the minimum threshold of action necessary to neutralize an imminent threat or endures after the threat has subsided also does not constitute active defense. Here the criterion of imminence is debatable: Does it include only tactical or also broader strategic threats? History provides a clue. As early as 1936, Japan presented a strategic threat to the United States by virtue of its intrinsic military potential and imperial designs in the Pacific, but it had few means to affect American interests directly. The Japanese threat did not become imminent until the Combined Imperial Fleet devised, in 1941, a viable tactical plan to attack Pearl Harbor. Thus the criterion of imminence demands the presence or the perception of a deployable, or nearly deployable, tactical capability to attack the defender.

What does imminence mean in the cyber domain? Two possibilities occur almost at once. The first and clearest scenario concerns the discovery within the defender's systems of sleeper malware: code customized to impair the target's functions but which has not yet struck. Of course, it may be difficult to ascertain the precise nature of the payload: Is it exploitative or destructive? But forensic testing may provide credible clues. A second scenario involves the detection of exploitative code whose aim the defender believes is to open a vector of access to attack or to harvest systems data that are relevant to the preparation of an attack. Whether the defender can infer from the activity an actual capability to disrupt the compromised system may depend on the activity's duration. The longer the length of action, the higher the chances the intruder will have harvested enough information to customize an attack payload. Here it may be difficult to ascertain the true intent of intelligence collection: Is it a case of stand-alone exploitation or a step in preparation for attack? The defender cannot penetrate the mind of the intruder. He may not even know the intruder's identity or location. Thus the perception of imminence will rest, inevitably, on the reliability of the defender's forensic knowledge of the intrusion and on the soundness of the reasoning upon which he construes the intruder's intent, both of which will remain open to interpretation.

Out-of-Perimeter Location

The "active" quality of the concept refers not to offensive activity, as some thinkers suppose, but to the activity's out-of-perimeter location. Passive measures are those the defender conducts within its own terrain; active measures are those the defender conducts *outside* it—that is, within adversarial or neutral terrain, including the terrain of innocent parties whose computer identity or functions the attacker has usurped. This characteristic of active defense features more prominently in British than in U.S. strategy papers, which do not clearly recognize it. For example, a report by the Joint Intelligence and Security Committee of Britain's House of Commons defines active defense as "interfering with the systems of those trying to hack into U.K. networks."[15]

The definition, it is important to realize, differs from the view of some information security professionals. One technical report described active defense as "the process of analysts monitoring for, responding to, learning from, and applying their knowledge to threats *internal to the network*." This definition, therefore, expressly excludes hacking back: "It is important to add the ending piece of 'internal to the network' to further discourage misrepresentation of the definition into the idea of a hack-back strategy. Analysts that can fall into this category include incident responders, malware reverse engineers, threat analysts, network security monitoring analysts, and other security personnel who utilize their environment to hunt for the adversary and respond to them."[16]

Any proactive measures such as honeypots or sinkholes that exist entirely within servers that the defender legitimately controls do not qualify as active defense.[17] For if they did, why the controversy over expanding private sector arms? Law and custom broadly recognize the right of a computer operator to take whatever measures within its own terrain are necessary to defend it.

Tactical Flexibility

There is one sense in which common ambiguities in the meaning of active defense are warranted: the concept implies nothing about the scale, type, or intensity of the defender's action. Tactically, active defense may involve a variety of actions: intelligence collection, disruption (including destruction), or some combination of the two. On this basis, it is possible to conceive of three broad sorts of active defense: *nondisruptive*, *disruptive*, or *mixed* (in other words similar to a "multistage" cyberattack that involves both preliminary exploitation and subsequent disruption).[18] It is therefore imprecise to define active defense simply as offensive action to defeat an ongoing attack (although some observers suggest this interpretation) because the concept could, in fact, involve entirely nondisruptive measures, such as the insertion of exploitative beacons in enemy networks to capture threat data.[19]

In sum, the chief distinguishing features of active defense are not the scale, intensity, or form of activity but rather *defensive* measures of threat

TABLE 15-1 Passive versus Active Defense in the Cyber Domain

	Within Perimeter: Passive	*Out of Perimeter: Active*
Undisruptive defense	Resilience, redundancy, organizational reform, information sharing	Stand-alone defensive exploitation (for example, to gain knowledge of the adversary's capabilities)
Disruptive defense	Honeypots, sinkholes, beacon neutralization	Disruption of the adversary's command and control systems (may require preliminary exploitation)

neutralization—whether nondisruptive or disruptive or both—that a defender implements *outside* its own or other friendly terrain. Table 15-1 summarizes and illustrates the differences between passive and active defense.

The Current State of Affairs

The current state of private sector active defense may be assessed from four viewpoints: law, policy, practice, and capability. From a legal viewpoint, in the U.S. federal context, the most important law is the Computer Fraud and Abuse Act of 1986 (CFAA). Of the CFAA's seven sections, two are directly relevant to the regulation of active defense: section (a)(2)(C), which forbids unauthorized access to a computer to obtain data in it; and section (a)(5), which forbids the intentional use of computer code to impair the operations of a protected computer system.[20] Moreover, the Federal Wiretap Act's section 2511(2)(a)(i) forbids the unauthorized interception or recording of electronic communication transiting between machines. The fines for infringement of these rules can be severe.

The legal consequences of the Cybersecurity Information Sharing Act of 2015 (CISA) for private sector active defense in the United States are unclear. Possibly the bill will broaden the monitoring powers of private actors, but only if they work in conjunction with government authorities—in other words, as an informal arm of the state. Probably the changes will not be drastic. Although the bill allows the deployment of "countermeasures" that legitimately target threats and damage data or machines on other networks, legally such countermeasures must be deployed within the defender's own network. Any resulting damage to external parties must therefore be unintentional.[21]

Thus the CISA's provision for countermeasures does not satisfy the out-of-perimeter criterion of active defense; it is beyond the scope of the present analysis.

There is little case law that elucidates the legal ramifications associated with the use of private sector arms.[22] Yet the prevailing legal viewpoint is clear: the practice of active defense is unlawful, if only because of the activity's second defining characteristic—that is, the intentional intrusion into or disruption of computers to which the defender lacks authorized access. Some officials have vocally pressed for changes in U.S. federal law that would allow the greater use of private active defense.[23] For now, however, the legal environment remains unequivocally proscriptive.

A second viewpoint concerns policy: official opinion reflects and supports the prevailing legal condition. The U.S. Department of Justice actively discourages exploitative active defense. One of its guidebooks states:

> A victimized organization should not attempt to access, damage, or impair another system that may appear to be involved in the intrusion or attack. Regardless of motive, doing so is likely illegal under U.S. and some foreign laws, and could result in civil and/or criminal liability. Furthermore, many intrusions and attacks are launched from compromised systems. Consequently, "hacking back" can damage or impair another innocent victim's system rather than the intruder's.[24]

Similarly, in a speech in 2015, Assistant Attorney General Leslie R. Caldwell publicly denounced the use of strikeback techniques of any kind by firms and other private actors.

Other officials have taken a more ambiguous position on the borderline between passive dissuasion and tacit acceptance. A comment in 2015 by Admiral Mike Rogers, director of the National Security Agency (NSA), embodies such ambiguity: "I'm not a big fan of the corporate world taking on this idea," he stated, but added: "It's not without precedence. If you go back to a time where nation states lacked capacity on their own, oftentimes they have turned to the corporate sector."[25] More revealingly, John Lynch, the head of the Justice Department's Computer Crime and Intellectual Property Section, in 2016 drew a distinction between different types of active defense and their varying tolerability. He endorsed the nondisruptive use of beacon technology as lawful but condemned disruptive instruments—for example, artifacts that gain root access to modify other machines.[26] Moreover, the FBI has shown selective tolerance of some uses of strikeback when it appeared urgent and proportionate to the security needs of the victim. Insofar as U.S. authorities are lenient toward private actors who employ defensive arms, they allow it not by changing the law but by evading it.

The third viewpoint is concerned with practice: What is actually happening regardless of the legal and policy conditions? The question is not easy to answer. Companies are no more transparent than governments when it comes to disclosing information about maneuvers within networks that they do not own or operate. The legal and reputational ramifications of disclosure are potentially high; they are not conducive to a culture of transparency on hacking and striking back. The near total absence of relevant case law reflects the prevailing culture of secrecy.

But if officials with knowledge of undisclosed cases are correct, the practice of active defense by the private sector far exceeds the record of it. As Tom Kellermann, a former member of the Commission on Cyber Security for the 44th Presidency, attested: "[Private] active defense is happening. It's not mainstream. It's very selective."[27] Of respondents to a 2012 poll at the Black Hat USA security conference, 36 percent claimed to have engaged in "retaliatory" hacking at least once (the poll was based on a sample of 181 conference attendees). Some American firms have recruited companies abroad to attack hackers on their behalf. At least a few times the freelancers provided strikeback as a courtesy to the victim. In brief, active defense activity by the private sector is increasingly common, if restrained, because of the moderate leniency of policymakers toward it.

Fourth, there is the question of capability: What is currently possible in the realm of private sector active defense, and what future developments await? Again, a wall of secrecy conceals many facts. Like governments, firms and other private actors rarely disclose information about their capacity to operate antagonistically in external networks. Nonetheless, observable cases of strikeback reveal that private sector arsenals are significant and growing.

Some technology firms conduct advanced research on and guardedly deploy active defense capabilities. For example, some have deployed "spamback" software (albeit without much success).[28] Microsoft possesses sophisticated measures to take down botnet command and control servers throughout the globe. In 2010, the company collaborated with the FBI to design and direct a remote "kill signal" to incapacitate machines infected with the Coreflood Trojan.[29] In 2014, Dell SecureWorks and Crowdstrike provided essential technical assistance to the FBI in an operation to take down the

"GameOver Zeus" botnet.[30] Juniper Networks has begun to integrate elements of strikeback into its products.

Whatever the state of the private sector's active defense capability, actors, particularly large technology firms, are caught in an inconsistency between the legal and policy conditions, which are broadly but not entirely prohibitive, and the state of practice, which seems far more indulgent. A remark by Juniper Network's chief technology officer captures the discrepancy: "The dirty little secret is if there were no worries ethically and legally, everyone [would want] a 'nuke from orbit' button."[31]

Arming of the Private Sector: Strategic Benefits and Risks

Would private sector active defense affect national and international security positively or negatively? In examining these consequences, this discussion considers effects on the defending players, their parent governments, innocent third parties, and international conflict stability.

Possible Benefits

The development of private sector arms may yield at least four positive consequences: improvement of strategic depth; closer civil–military integration; new options for plausible deniability by states; and a reduced defensive burden.[32]

One advantage involves *strategic depth*. Ordinarily, strategic depth in the cyber domain in the absence of active defense is very poor. The defender must wait until the attacker has made its move, after which the time to mount an effective defense is extremely short because the threat travels between machines at the speed of electrons and can achieve tactical results within a matter of seconds or even milliseconds. By contrast, the defensive response, unless it is automated, may require cumbersome procedures such as information sharing and coordination with law enforcement agencies, which in turn must take time to evaluate the legal, ethical, and tactical appropriateness of different policy options. For instance, it took the U.S. government several weeks simply to identify North Korea as the source of the attack against Sony Pictures in December 2014.[33] Moreover, detection itself may be very difficult to achieve. According to a report by Verizon, private firms take an average of 240 days to spot network intrusions.[34] The civilian sector owns or operates approximately 80–90 percent of critical computer systems and networks. Of U.S. government communications, including classified information, 98 percent travel over these networks.[35] It is therefore reasonable to assume that at all times some form of attack code resides undiscovered within much of the civilian sector's essential computer infrastructures.

One possible solution to the problem of strategic depth is greater information sharing between the private and public sectors. The Cybersecurity Information Sharing Act aims to foster such sharing.[36] So far, however, firms have been reluctant to share, on a regular basis, their incident and threat data with the government. They are even less willing to allow governments to monitor their networks directly owing to concerns about the privacy of proprietary information, the disclosure of which may harm corporate and client interests.

Private sector active defense could improve civilian strategic depth in a way that circumvents these concerns. It enables firms to identify and neutralize threats outside their networks without placing proprietary data at risk of government scrutiny. The insertion of beacons or "web bugs"—a form of exploitative active defense that some companies already use to track down stolen data—into adversary networks could enable these firms to design *disruptive* techniques that they can then use to neutralize threats at the point of origin, or, if the threat is in transit, in neutral systems. Here neutralization could be tactical—in other words a specific attack sequence is defeated but the attacker retains the ability to redeploy. Or it could be strategic—in other words, the attacker is dissuaded from or deprived of the ability to attack the target again. Exploitative tools could also support the government's *own* threat-monitoring and -neutralization efforts without themselves engaging in disruptive action. For example, third-party threat-intelligence companies may sell their services to the government, thereby serving as intermediaries between the victim and the government, an arrangement that could help to preserve the victim's anonymity.

A second advantage is enhanced *civil–military integration*. Western societies face an acute shortage of workers trained in technical disciplines relevant to cybersecurity, such as computer science and software engineering. The relevant skills base resides primarily in the private sector. Large technology firms (for example, Google, Apple, Microsoft) are able to offer salaries many times higher than military and security agencies can offer. "We are competing in a tough marketplace against a private sector that is in a position to offer a lot more money," lamented U.S. Secretary of Homeland Security Jeh Johnson in 2016. "We need more cybertalent without a doubt in D.H.S., in the federal government, and we are not where we should be right now, that is without a doubt."[37] Similarly, in Britain, the government skills gap is so severe that former Government Communications Headquarters (GCHQ) director Iain Lobban said that his agency might have to employ non-nationals for a brief period—that is, before they, too, are inevitably absorbed by the private sector.[38] Another drain on skills occurs when defense contractors hire the manpower of government agencies, only later to sell their services back to the government.

Governments have reacted to asymmetry in the technological skills base in two ways: first, by attempting to assimilate civilian talent into loose state structures such as military reserves; and second, by cooperating with private technology providers to develop joint capabilities.

In the first approach, the government assumes a direct role in equipping the private sector. It drafts, trains, arms, and retrains elements of the civilian population in the methods of cyber operations. This may be achieved by establishing a voluntary paramilitary defense force, such as Estonia's Cyber Defense League (*Küberkaitseliit*), a civilian defense organization that supports the military and Ministry of Defense;[39] or by way of conscription, as in Israel's Unit 8200, whose ranks include drafted servicemen who after an initial term of service enter the army reserves.[40] This approach has achieved moderate success in small nations such as Estonia and Israel, which have vibrant technological innovation hubs and a popular tradition of mass conscription. But it has paid only limited returns in large countries such as the United States and Britain where the National Guard or Reserves and the Territorial Army often fail to attract high-skilled elements of the civilian workforce.[41]

The second approach entails an extension of the concept of "private military companies" (PMCs) into the new domains. PMCs provide military and security services—even armed force—to the state or to other private entities.[42] This approach may be better suited to large nations with sizable private technology industries but poorly developed traditions of military service. It would, however, require a greater commitment on behalf of participating companies to develop the sorts of strategic and tactical technologies that governments need to achieve national security goals. Some firms already provide the U.S. and other governments with sophisticated surveillance tools such as tracking and eavesdropping software.[43] Few companies, however, have invested in the other side of active defense—advanced disruptive tools—because of the legal and policy prohibitions or because the business case for doing so is not clear. Yet the private sector is well poised to develop them. Cisco's dominance of the router market, Google's near monopoly of online searches, and Microsoft's dominance in the sale of desktop operating systems afford these firms tremendous (and legal) access to a significant proportion of internet traffic and global hardware components. Some of this access is directly relevant to the harvesting of zero-day vulnerabilities and to the design of access vectors and payloads that governments require to mount sophisticated cyber operations.[44] The CISA's relaxation of prohibitions against private sector exploitation performed under government sanction may foster more cooperation of this sort, although at present the structural incentives for such cooperation are not clear.

In brief, some elements of the technology sector possess merely by their existence a latent capacity to acquire sophisticated cyber weapons. The development of private sector cyber arms under informal government direction could enable governments to harness the civilian sector's technological prowess while avoiding the cumbersome organizational costs of traditional military formations.

Many firms, especially those with global commercial enterprises, may find the reputational costs of collaboration with government unacceptable, especially in a post–Edward Snowden world. Indeed, Google, Facebook, and other U.S. technology companies have sought to distance themselves from the perception that they work with the government to develop joint surveillance capabilities. But the alleged cooperation of RSA and Microsoft with the government proves that at least some level of complicity is acceptable even to large multinational firms with significant commercial interests abroad.[45] Most likely to succeed is the Israeli model of integrating the private sector into the national cyber establishment, which relies on the cultivation of ties with small startups that operate mostly in domestic markets—for example, NSO Group and Kaymera, which develop exploitative tools that allow the remote manipulation of smartphones.[46]

A third advantage is *plausible deniability*. Credible attribution of the source of a cyberattack is important because it enables the defender to inflict penalties on the attacker; without it the attacker can avoid them. States that develop offensive capabilities, therefore, have an incentive to devise means to complicate attribution (unless they desire positive attribution because they want to achieve a deterrent or demonstration effect). The more sophisticated the offensive operation, the smaller the universe of possible assailants; hence the higher the chances, a priori, that a defender who detects an attack will be able to credibly identify the attacker. This is a problem for the small number of states that possess the most advanced offensive weapons. After the Stuxnet attack became known, few people in Tehran asked: Did Jordan or Turkey do it? Similarly, no one asked: Was it Siemens (which built the Natanz nuclear facility's industrial control system) or Microsoft (the engineering stations)? Rather, the suspicion fell immediately upon the United States and Israel. Allowing the private sector to arm itself with sophisticated exploitative and disruptive tools would widen the field of theoretical attackers, thus complicating, in principle, the defender's attribution of the real attacker (a positive outcome for the attacker).

But the effect on attribution will be limited unless the firms in question are known to have offensive motives that seem credible to the adversary. Moreover, the development of PMCs may weaken the perception in the minds of adversaries of a neat separation between the public and private sectors. There is also the problem of "state responsibility," the principle of international law which stipulates that governments are responsible for harmful actions emanating from inside their jurisdictions. Thus the victim may attribute blame to the attacker's parent government even in the absence of direct government complicity.

Fourth is the reduction of the *defender's burden*. When a multinational firm is attacked, its possession of active defense capabilities could release the countries that host its headquarters or subsidiary branches from the burden of conducting defensive or retaliatory action against the offender. The transnational quality of modern production chains and commercial activity means that in contemporary society no large firm can enjoy the protection of a single state in all sectors of the global market within which it operates.[47] Firms may face attacks against interests and servers located in any one or in a variety of foreign jurisdictions. For example, considering the cyberattacks against Sony Pictures, a U.S.-based entertainment subsidiary of Sony, the Japanese technology conglomerate, the question is: In the absence of private sector arms, who strikes back, Washington or Tokyo? By enabling the company to respond itself, private sector arms would release the governments involved in the defensive response, assuming they desire one, from the burden of taking direct action.

The prospect of armed multinational enterprises acting under informal single-state direction recalls the partial successes of pirate merchants during the sixteenth and seventeenth centuries. Formally, pirates were unaffiliated (and thus differed from privateers, who operated under official government sanction). Yet occasionally they performed tasks at the direction of states, often changing flags in the process.[48] The use of pirates provided states with a means of waging undeclared and plausibly deniable war against other states.[49] Yet now, as then, the main obstacle to the success of the "piracy" model of public–private collaboration is the difficulty of aligning the goals of the state, which are usually political, with those of private firms, which are mainly economic.

Possible Risks

The use of cyber arms by the private sector entails at least three risks: foreign government penalties; innocent third-party harm; and inadvertent or accelerating international conflict. The last directly involves state interests and is potentially the gravest.

First is the danger of *foreign government penalties*. Even if CISA or other U.S. legislation permitted the private sector to deploy active defense tools, foreign domestic law will most likely continue to prohibit them; as noted earlier, almost all domestic penal codes presently criminalize active defense measures. Thus, in such a world, the activity would be legal only when the attack sequence originated in servers located exclusively within the defender's own jurisdiction and did not cross any national boundaries—that is, in a negligibly small number of conceivable cyberattack scenarios.

It is possible that some other countries could amend their laws to allow the private sector the use of weapons in select cases. Or else governments may cast a blind eye when a player based in a friendly foreign country conducts active defense within its own jurisdiction under controlled conditions for demonstrably defensive aims. Two considerations would nevertheless diminish the appeal of private sector active defense. First, because they are on friendly diplomatic terms with the defender's parent country, the nations likeliest to permit or tolerate the use of private sector arms in their virtual terrain are also the likeliest to offer legal and police assistance during an attack that implicates their jurisdiction, thus diminishing the need for private action in the first place. Second, and conversely, nations that have adversarial diplomatic relations with the defender's parent country are the least likely to permit or tolerate the use of private sector active defense against machines located within their jurisdiction. Even if they permitted the activity in some limited cases (for example, if the attacker is a common enemy), foreign nations would almost certainly penalize it in cases where they or their proxy agents were complicit in the attack. The difficulties of attaining certain attribution of the attack's sponsorship would mean that even if the defender *believes* the foreign government is not complicit, he may never be certain.[50] The possibility of punishment would remain agonizingly real, especially if the inhibition to punish a firm by imposing financial penalties is lower than the inhibition to penalize another government with weightier measures such as economic sanctions.

A second risk is the potential for *innocent third-party harm*. Recall one of the main distinguishing aspects of active defense: it takes place outside the defender's terrain, including, possibly, in neutral terrain. Now note two important features of offensive cyber operations: they can be very difficult to attribute; and they often use multiple neutral machines and networks to gain access to the target. Almost inevitably, therefore, active defense measures will impair to some degree the operations or data of third-party computer users, either because the defender misattributes the source of the attack to a machine that is in fact not involved because the attacker employs spoofing software that alters the compromise indicators (for example, the IP address); or because the defender correctly attributes the source or transit point of the attack but the identified machine is in fact innocent because the attacker has hijacked it. And as the number of injured parties multiplies, the potential for the conflict to accelerate and broaden grows.

The third type of danger is the gravest of all: *inadvertent and escalating conflict*, or the possibility of unwanted international crises. Some international relations thinkers have questioned the ability of private actors to destabilize the dynamics of interstate security competitions.[51] A world not far from the one in which we live challenges this view. Extending the private sector's ability to carry out active defense may produce instability in the following ways, among others:

1. A private actor based in country A executes a disruptive active defense action on an attacking machine in country B. The government of country B interprets the action as an offensive strike by the government of country A. It retaliates against the defender and the government of country A.

2. A private actor based in country A executes a disruptive active defense action on an innocent machine in country C whose identity an attacker in country B has in fact spoofed. The government of country C retaliates against both the defender and the government of country A.

3. A private actor based in country A executes exploitative active defense activities against a machine in country B because he suspects that the machine may be preparing an attack. The machine in country B misinterprets the defender's move as a prelude to attack and launches its own preemptive strike against the defender in country A.

4. The governments of countries A and B are engaged in an international exchange of cyber blows that both sides seek to de-escalate and terminate. Armed private technology firms recruited into the conflict by the two countries misinterpret or choose to ignore their government's instructions. The firms continue to launch strikes against targets located in the other side's territory. The governments of countries A and B misinterpret the strikes as actions conducted or condoned by the opposing country. Rather than de-escalate, the conflict rapidly and uncontrollably intensifies.

5. An ideologically motivated and technically savvy employee of a private firm in country A illegitimately employs (in other words, for offensive purposes) disruptive active defense tools against multiple innocent machines in country B while spoofing his identity to resemble a government player in country C (a hated country of the rogue employee). The government of country B misattributes the location of the attacker as country C. It attacks targets in country C. The government of country C retaliates in kind against targets in country B. The rogue employee repeats the deceptive maneuver but instead of attacking machines in country B targets those in country C. The cycle repeats.

Convergence as the Cost of Collision

Equipment of the private sector with cyber weapons would intensify a broader trend in the contemporary era: the partial fusion of the world of states and the world of citizens and other groups. Many thinkers traditionally treat these two worlds as separate behavioral universes; they customarily ban private agents from theoretical models of the states system. Legal scholars point to the prevailing positivist doctrine by which the consent of states, whether formal or customary, is the only true source of international law.[52] Political scientists normally emphasize the state's supreme political authority in the ordering of both domestic and international affairs. Yet the growing influence of a variety of nonstate actors in the twenty-first century challenges these rigid models of political order. Multinational firms influence, sometimes decisively, the fiscal and developmental agendas of states. Religious militant groups export pernicious ideologies and fighters to distant societies. Private military corporations affect the outcomes of foreign military occupations. Pirates scour the high seas and penetrate foreign coastlines. And so on.

The expansion of active defense activities to the private sector would intensify this flight of power away from the state. It would further challenge prevailing patterns of security competition and order in the international system. This disruptive trend could positively affect national security: by improving strategic depth in a framework of interaction where private players are especially disadvantaged in defense; by fostering civil-military integration in a domain where technological prowess is indispensable but scarce; by offering governments new options to deny responsibility for offensive actions; and by lessening the sovereign burden of governments in a domain where the protection of the private sector—their traditional duty—is increasingly difficult to guarantee. That is, it may generate new opportunities for convergence, or cooperation between states and nonstate actors who share objectives and enemies.

The trend also invites new perils, however. A world in which private firms and citizen groups are free to carry out the prerogatives of national security policy against each other and against states is a world in which the risks of harm to innocent parties and accelerating conflict are potentially grave. The international system is the product of centuries of evolution in the design of mechanisms to regulate and restrain conflict among the main units: states. Continued erosion of that model through the empowerment of players that are alien to the system and that may not share the goal or even comprehend the intricate requirements of international order invites not only the benefits of deeper convergence but also the dangers of collision between the fragile states system and the chaotic global system. Cyber civil defense should remain a reactive enterprise.

Notes

1. Case of the S. S. "Wimbledon," Permanent Court of International Justice, A 1 (1923) (www.worldcourts.com/pcij/eng/decisions/1923.08.17_wimbledon.htm).

2. The threat of piracy, however, has grown recently. The shipping industry has reacted by increasing the presence of armed security personnel onboard. M. N. Murphy, "Con-

temporary Piracy and Maritime Terrorism: The Threat to International Security," Adelphi Papers no. 388 (University of Michigan, 2007); P. Chalk, *The Maritime Dimension of International Security: Terrorism, Piracy, and Challenges for the United States* (Santa Monica, Calif.: RAND, 2008).

3. David E. Sanger, "NSA Director Says Snowden Leaks Hamper Efforts against Cyberattacks," *New York Times*, March 4, 2014.

4. Joseph Muniz, "Responding to Real-World Cyber Threats," Ciscopress.com (February 16, 2016) (http://www.ciscopress.com/articles/article.asp?p=2481826).

5. Joel Brenner, *America the Vulnerable: Inside the New Threat Matrix of Digital Espionage, Crime, and Warfare* (London: Penguin, 2011), p. 13.

6. The question of the salience of nonstate actors in international relations is not new. International relations theorists recognize the existence of nonstate actors. In Kenneth Waltz's words: "States are not and never have been the only international actors. . . . The importance of nonstate actors and the extent of transnational activities are obvious." Kenneth N. Waltz, *Theory of International Relations* (New York: McGraw-Hill, 1979), pp. 93–94. But mainstream thinkers argue that states are so important as to be the central—some say only—units of analysis.

7. Lucas Kello, "The Meaning of the Cyber Revolution: Perils to Theory and Statecraft," *International Security* 38, no. 2 (2013), p. 29.

8. This is often the case: for example, the handlers of the Stuxnet worm that hit the Natanz nuclear facility in Iran in 2009 may have compromised the industrial controller several years earlier. See David E. Sanger, *Confront and Conceal: Obama's Secret Wars and Surprising Use of American Power* (New York: Crown, 2012), chap. 8.

9. Author's interview with a senior official in the British Cabinet Office, February 17, 2017.

10. "Chairman of the U.S. House Intelligence Committee Mike Rogers in Washington Post Live: Cybersecurity 2014," *Washington Post*, October 2, 2014.

11. See Riley C. Matlack, M. Riley, and J. Robertson, "The Company Securing Your Internet Has Close Ties to Russian Spies," Bloomberg, March 15, 2015.

12. Huawei describes itself as an employee-owned "collective," but some commentators have questioned its freedom from Chinese state control. See Richard McGregor, *The Party: The Secret World of China's Communist Rulers* (New York: HarperCollins, 2010); and M. Rogers and C. A. D. Ruppersberger, *Investigative Report on the U.S. National Security Issues Posed by Chinese Telecommunications Companies Huawei and ZTE*, U.S. House of Representatives 112th Congress, Permanent Select Committee on Intelligence (October 8, 2012).

13. See *Department of Defense Strategy for Operating in Cyberspace* (July 2011), p. 7.

14. See *Cyber Security Strategy, 2014–2017* (Tallinn, Estonia: Ministry of Economic Affairs and Communications, 2014).

15. C. Green, "U.K. Becomes First Country to Disclose Plans for Cyber Attack Capability," *Information Age*, September 30, 2013.

16. Robert M. Lee, *The Sliding Scale of Cyber Security—A SANS Analyst Whitepaper* (Boston: SANS Institute, 2015), pp. 9–11.

17. Honeypots consist of decoy data that the defender uses to lure an attacker to study and disrupt the defender's methods. See Loras R. Even, *Honey Pot Systems Explained* (Boston: SANS Institute, July 12, 2000). Sinkholes refer to a DNS computer server that produces false data to prevent the attacker from using the true domain name. See Guy Bruneau, *DNS Sinkhole* (Boston: SANS Institute, August 7, 2010).

18. See David D. Clark and Susan Landau, "Untangling Attribution," *Harvard National Security Journal* (March 2011).

19. See, for instance, Alexander Klimburg and Jason Healey, "Strategic Goals and Stakeholders," in *National Cyber Security Framework and Manual*, edited by Alexander Klimburg (Tallinn, Estonia: NATO Cooperative Cyber Defence Centre of Excellence, 2012), pp. 74–75, 80; Tim Maurer and Robert Morgus, *Compilation of Existing Cybersecurity and Information Security Related Definitions* (Washington: New America, October 2012), p. 71; and Jay P. Kesan and Carol M. Hayes, "Mitigative Counterstriking: Self-Defense and Deterrence in Cyberspace," *Harvard Journal of Law and Technology* 25, no. 2 (2012), p. 460.

20. There are debates about the requirements of "authorization." See Department of Justice, Office of Legal Counsel, *Searching and Seizing Computers and Obtaining Electronic Evidence in Criminal Investigations*, 3rd ed. (Washington: Office of Legal Education, Executive Office for United States Attorneys, 2009).

21. It is unclear, however, whether intentional damage resulting from actions taken entirely within one's networks is lawful. See "Cyber-Surveillance Bill to Move Forward, Secretly" (Washington: Center for Democracy and Technology, March 4, 2015).

22. One notable case is *Susan Clements Jeffrey* v. *Absolute Software*, involving a company that used beacon technology to capture explicit data from a computer the operator did not know was stolen. The court ruled against the company. See "Absolute Software Settles Lawsuit over Nude Photos," *Forbes*, September 6, 2011.

23. See remarks by the Homeland Security Secretary, Janet Napolitano, in Joseph Menn, "Hacked Companies Fight Back with Controversial Steps," Reuters, June 18, 2012; and remarks by Chairman of the U.S. House Intelligence Committee Mike Rogers in "Washington Post Live: Cybersecurity 2014," *Washington Post*, October 2, 2014.

24. *Best Practices for Victim Response and Reporting of Cyber Incidents* (Washington: Department of Justice, April 2015), p. 12.

25. Michael S. Rogers, "Cyber Threats and Next-Generation Cyber Operations" (Keynote Speech at the Annual Cybersecurity Technology Summit, AFCEA, Washington, April 2, 2015).

26. Interview with John Lynch, Steptoe Cyberlaw Podcast, January 21, 2016.

27. Hannah Kuchler, "Cyber Insecurity: Hacking Back," *Financial Times*, July 27, 2015.

28. See Tom Spring, "Spam Slayer: Bringing Spammers to Their Knees," *PCWorld*, July 18, 2008.

29. See Kim Zetter, "FBI vs. Coreflood Botnet: Round 1 Goes to the Feds," *Wired*, April 11, 2011.

30. See Brian Krebs, "'Operation Tovar' Targets 'Gameover' ZeuS Botnet, CryptoLocker Scourge," *KrebsonSecurity*, June 2, 2014.

31. Kuchler, "Cyber Insecurity."

32. These consequences are positive from the perspective of private defenders and their parent governments; other players may not share this view.

33. The attackers activated the "Wiper" malware on November 24; the FBI publicly attributed the attack to North Korea on December 19. See "Update on Sony Investigation," Federal Bureau of Investigation (December 19, 2014) (www.fbi.gov/news/pressrel/press-releases/update-on-sony-investigation).

34. See Verizon, *2016 Data Breach Investigations Report* (April 24, 2016), pp. 10–11. This figure is a simplification. The lag time between compromise and detection depends on the class and effects of the hostile action. A higher figure applies to cyber exploitation rather

than cyberattacks. Indeed, some attacks—such as ransomware, which incapacitates the target machine—may be discovered immediately. The policy process from the time that investigators identified North Korea as the culprit to publicly outing it took longer than the time between when investigators first learned of the breach and when they identified North Korea.

35. See Peter W. Singer and Allan Friedman, *Cybersecurity and Cyberwar* (Oxford University Press, 2014).

36. To share information derived from classified sources the U.S. government resorts to four selective commercial service providers: AT&T, CenturyLink, Lockheed Martin, and Verizon. See Andy Ozment, *DHS's Enhanced Cybersecurity Services Program Unveils New "Netflow" Service Offering* (Washington: U.S. Department of Homeland Security, January 26, 2016) (www.dhs.gov/blog/2016/01/26/dhs%E2%80%99s-enhancedcybersecurity -services-program-unveils-new%E2%80%9Cnetflow%E2%80%9D-service-offering).

37. Ron Nixon, "Homeland Security Dept. Struggles to Hire Staff to Combat Cyberattacks," *International New York Times*, April 6, 2016.

38. See Oliver Wright, "GCHQ's 'Spook First' Programme to Train Britain's Most Talented Tech Entrepreneurs," *The Independent*, January 1, 2015; and Jamie Collier, "Proxy Actors in the Cyber Domain" (unpublished paper).

39. See Christian Czosseck, Rain Ottis, and Anna-Maria Talihärm, "Estonia after the 2007 Cyber Attacks: Legal, Strategic and Organisational Changes in Cyber Security," in *Case Studies in Information Warfare and Security*, edited by M. Warren (Reading, U.K.: Academic Conferences and Publishing International Limited, 2013).

40. See Lior Tabansky and Itzhak Ben Israel, *Striking with Bits? The IDF and Cyber-Warfare* (Cham, Switzerland: Springer, 2015).

41. See "National Guard to Stand Up 13 New Cyber Units in 23 States," *Army Times*, December 15, 2015.

42. See James Pattison, *The Morality of Private War: The Challenge of Private Military Companies and Security Companies* (Oxford University Press, 2014); and A. Alexandra, D.-P. Baker, and M. Caparini, eds., *Private Military Companies: Ethics, Policies and Civil-Military Relations* (London: Routledge, 2008).

43. See Sari Horwitz, Shyamantha Asokan, and Julie Tate, "Trade in Surveillance Technology Raises Worries," *Washington Post*, December 1, 2011.

44. See Lillian Ablon, Martin C. Libicki, and Andrea A. Golay, *Markets for Cybercrime Tools and Stolen Data* (Santa Monica, Calif.: RAND, March 14, 2014).

45. See James Vincent, "Edward Snowden Claims Microsoft Collaborated with NSA and FBI to Allow Access to User Data," *The Independent*, July 12, 2013.

46. See Gabrielle Coppola, "Israeli Entrepreneurs Play Both Sides of the Cyber Wars," Bloomberg, September 29, 2014.

47. See Stephen Krasner, "State Power and the Structure of International Trade," *World Politics* 28, no. 3 (1976), pp. 317–47; and Richard N. Rosecrance, *The Resurgence of the West: How a Transatlantic Union Can Prevent War and Restore the United States and Europe* (Yale University Press, 2013).

48. See Florian Egloff, "Cybersecurity and the Age of Privateering: A Historical Analogy," Cyber Studies Working Paper 1 (University of Oxford, March 2015).

49. See Fernand Braudel, *The Mediterranean and the Mediterranean World in the Age of Philip II* (University of California Press, 1995).

50. Some thinkers question whether attribution is as hard as many observers believe it to be. See Jon R. Lindsay, "Tipping the Scales: The Attribution Problem and the Feasibility

of Deterrence against Cyberattack," *Journal of Cybersecurity* 1, no. 1 (2015), pp. 53–67; and Thomas Rid, "Attributing Cyber Attacks," *Journal of Strategic Studies* 38, nos. 1–2 (2015), p. 38.

51. See Brandon Valeriano and Ryan C. Maness, *Cyber War versus Cyber Realities: Cyber Conflict in the International System* (Oxford University Press, 2015).

52. Legal scholars who support the "natural law" tradition developed by Aquinas, Locke, and Vattel have challenged the positivist doctrine's position as the legitimate source of international law. See James L. Brierly, *The Basis of Obligations in International Law* (Oxford: Clarendon Press, 1958); and Hersch Lauterpacht, *International Law and Human Rights* (London: Stevens and Sons, 1950).

16

Cyberwar Inc.

Examining the Role of Companies in Offensive Cyber Operations

IRV LACHOW *and* TAYLOR GROSSMAN

The private sector is an important driving force behind the development of cybersecurity products and services. National governments are the hubs for the creation and use of offensive cyber capabilities, both because of legal constraints around the use of force and because warfighting is usually considered to be the province of nation-states. At the same time, the lines between industry and government are blurring. Private sector actors are becoming increasingly influential in the international arena and governments are relying on companies for assistance with offensive as well as defensive operations—a development with profound implications for both domestic politics and international relations. This chapter seeks to identify pressing issues associated with the growing role of private companies in supporting offensive cyber operations. Its goal is to inform policymakers of the challenges they face while

The authors would like to thank Matt Venhaus for his thorough review and helpful suggestions. Thanks also to Herbert Lin and Marion Michaud for their guidance and support.

laying out a research agenda that can guide the work of scholars and practitioners.

The chapter begins with a description of cyber operations to set the stage for the analysis that follows. It then explores three areas where companies are providing cyberattack capabilities to governments: intelligence, surveillance and reconnaissance; the development of cyber weapons; and planning and support. The chapter then examines the implications of this development both domestically and internationally. It closes by offering recommendations for future research.

Understanding Offensive Cyber Operations

There is much confusion around the use of terms such as "cyberattack" and "cyber operations." For example, the word "cyberattack" is often applied to cyber espionage and cyber crime. According to the U.S. Department of Defense (DoD), "Cyber Operations" missions are categorized as offensive cyber operations (OCO), defensive cyber operations, and DoD information network operations based on their intent.[1] Offensive cyber operations, the primary focus of this chapter, are defined as "cyberspace operations intended to project power by the application of force in and through cyberspace."[2] Offensive cyber operations have various direct effects that include denying, degrading, disrupting, destroying, or manipulating information, computer systems, or networks of an adversary.[3] This chapter uses the terms "offensive cyber operations" and "cyberattack" interchangeably with the understanding that they both refer to force projection in and through cyberspace for the purposes of degrading, disrupting, or destroying a particular target.

Cyber operations conducted by governments, like military operations in general, require extensive preparations. As Chris Inglis notes in chapter 2, intelligence, surveillance, and reconnaissance (ISR) and operational preparation of the environment play especially important roles in cyberspace. Trey Herr and Drew Herrick echo this point:

> Cyber-enabled ISR focuses on gathering information on a specific adversary's systems, including their hardware/software configurations, personnel, and operational security. This information is critical for effective targeting, operational planning, and "weaponeering" or preparing capabilities to achieve their desired effects. Cyber [opera-

tional preparation of the environment], for its part, focuses on access to a target system, and on the means of preparing it for the specific operation.[4]

The cyber kill-chain model is a useful construct for understanding the steps that an attacker must go through to launch a successful cyber operation. Developed by several experts from Lockheed Martin, the cyber kill-chain is defined as "a systematic process to target and engage an adversary to create desired effects."[5] Simply put, a cyber intrusion requires an aggressor to develop a payload, breach a trusted boundary, establish a presence within a trusted environment, and take actions within that environment. More specifically, the attacker must accomplish seven steps in the cyber kill-chain:

1. Reconnaissance. The attacker starts by researching, identifying, and selecting targets. Reconnaissance may also involve examining vulnerabilities and exploits for possible use in later steps of the kill-chain.

2. Weaponization. Malware is coupled with an exploit and payload to create a cyber weapon.

3. Delivery. This step consists of transmitting a weapon to its target. Delivery can be accomplished via several means, including phishing emails and the use of infected USB drives.

4. Exploitation. After the weapon has been delivered to the target system, code is activated that enables the weapon to take advantage of the particular exploit it was designed to use.

5. Installation. After the exploitation code has been run, the weapon installs the payload into the target system. The code is now embedded in the trusted environment, often without the defender knowing that this has occurred.

6. Command and Control. The installed code is inside the target system, and most often it will beacon back out to let the attacker know that it is in place. The attacker can then send instructions to the malware.

7. Actions on Objectives. The attacker is now in a position to take actions within the target environment. These actions could focus on denial, degradation, disruption, destruction, or manipulation of data.

The seven steps of the cyber kill-chain can be grouped into three broad phases: pre-launch, launch, and post-launch. The pre-launch phase includes intelligence gathering and reconnaissance, planning, weaponization, and testing. The second phase focuses on delivery of the weapon via a propagation method.[6] The third phase consists of post-intrusion activities: installation of the malware on the target system (which may involve lateral movement within the target network), command and control of the malware (which may involve the downloading of additional malware), and actions on objectives. The attacker may also attempt to assess the damage of the operation.[7]

Because of legal and practical considerations, contractor support for OCO will likely focus on the pre-launch phase. Even within this phase, there may be constraints on the specific activities that private sector actors can perform. In many countries, domestic laws preclude companies from being actively involved in gathering intelligence or launching cyberattacks. For example, in the United States, the Computer Fraud and Abuse Act prohibits companies and individuals from accessing computers (inside or outside the United States) without the authorization of the owner or operator of those systems. There may also be limits based on international law. For example, as Oona Hathaway and Rebecca Crootof write, "States may not employ civilian contractors to carry out activities where they will exercise discretion that implicates the law of armed conflict [LOAC]."[8] Thus, American companies cannot be directly involved in any "hands-on keyboards," activities that would either violate the Computer Fraud and Abuse Act or LOAC. In practice, these laws may keep private sector actors from participating in actions that deliver a cyber weapon to a target or actions that involve delivering a malware payload for intelligence-gathering purposes.

Intelligence, Surveillance, and Reconnaissance

Intelligence, surveillance, and reconnaissance (ISR) are vital because cyberattacks are designed to penetrate particular networks and systems to create specific effects. As Paul Roberts writes, "The quality of the intelligence gathered on a particular target makes the difference between an effective cyber weapon and a flop."[9] Private sector activities in this phase could include understanding and mapping target networks and systems, identifying vulnerabilities in those targets, and possibly even gaining information on users who might be targeted by spear phishing and other delivery mechanisms.

The type of detailed intelligence needed to support OCO used to be solely the province of government spy agencies, but that is no longer the case. Shane Harris notes, "This kind of intelligence used to be the near-exclusive domain of government intelligence agencies. They alone had the access and the know-how to sniff out vulnerable computers with such precision . . . not anymore."[10] A recent RAND study has determined that some signals intelligence capabilities which were previously limited to governments are now "available to anyone."[11] These capabilities go beyond the spyware that is often associated with cyber monitoring. The RAND report notes, for example, that one university researcher built a rudimentary cyber surveillance system for less than $900 in one week that had the following capabilities: bulk data collection, search, cookie tracking, anonymous user identification, and malware injection.[12] Although this system has nowhere near the capabilities of sophisticated state actors, its development does suggest that cyber capabilities are spreading rapidly, while the costs of acquiring them are decreasing.

It should not be surprising that there is a market of companies providing extremely sophisticated cyber intelligence services. For example, the following description is taken from FireEye's website:

> FireEye iSIGHT cyber threat intelligence is unique in the industry. Our team of more than 160 intel experts span the globe and apply decades of experience in intelligence collection and analysis to their work. With native speakers in over twenty languages, the FireEye iSIGHT Intelligence team has the cultural and colloquial knowledge required to understand important nuances discussed in the underground. We produce deep, rich, contextual intelligence that includes motivation, intent, targets, attribution and methods, plus threat and technical tags. The FireEye iSIGHT Intelligence team employs a formal intelligence process, similar to a state-based intelligence organization, but optimized over nearly a decade, to rapidly collect and analyze findings and disseminate new intelligence to customers.[13]

CrowdStrike, a FireEye competitor, offers similar capabilities, promising to provide "the latest insights and indicators of compromise from an all-source methodology of intelligence gathering, analysis, and dissemination." The company notes that its "global intelligence team gathers, analyzes, and reports on over ninety threat actors that operate around the world."[14] Notably, both FireEye and CrowdStrike focus on public sector as well as private sector customers. And while they market their capabilities for defensive purposes, the types of intelligence they and other cybersecurity firms provide could be useful for offensive cyber operations as well.

In the United States, cyber ISR capabilities may also be provided by cleared defense contractors—private entities "granted clearance by the Department of Defense to access, receive, or store classified information for the purpose of bidding for a contract or conducting activities in support of any program of the Department of Defense."[15] There is an array of cleared defense contractors that provide a mix of cyber, intelligence, and operational capabilities to U.S. government sponsors.[16]

Finally, there are boutique firms that provide specific types of cyber intelligence that could be useful for OCO. For example, startups such as FlashPoint and Surfwatch Labs provide intelligence about the dark web—the hidden part of the World Wide Web that can only be accessed via specific applications and communications links. The following description of FlashPoint's capabilities focuses on cybersecurity, and yet one could easily imagine "actionable" intelligence being used to support offensive operations:

> Flashpoint illuminates the Deep and Dark Web. A pioneer in providing intelligence from these regions of the Internet, Flashpoint's software and data services help companies, governments, and consumers enhance their cyber and physical security. The company's unique blend of subject matter expertise and software engineering has changed the way meaningful and actionable intelligence is gleaned from the previously unmapped regions of the Internet.[17]

Weaponization

There is no single definition of a cyber weapon. For our purposes, it is useful to think about weaponization as the combination of three factors: a vulnerability, an exploit, and a propagation method. A vulnerability is a weakness or flaw in hardware or software that can be taken advantage of by an attacker. An exploit is code written to take advantage of a vulnerability to cause a specific effect, such as gaining access to a system or shutting down a piece of hardware.[18] In other words, vulnerabilities are properties inherent in the systems (hardware or software) that one seeks to "hack," while exploits are the programs written to take advantage of these weaknesses. A propagation method, finally, is how an exploit is delivered to a target, such as a phishing email.[19]

Weaponization depends on intelligence that has been gathered previously to identify and develop the most promising vulnerabilities, exploits, and propagation methods. Governments can receive private sector support in the weaponization process via several channels, most notably through markets.[20] Generally speaking, markets come in three types: white, gray, and black.[21] White markets focus on identifying vulnerabilities to improve cybersecurity. Those who operate in such markets turn over discovered vulnerabilities to the affected vendor or publicly announce their findings so that organizations can take steps to protect themselves. In gray markets, vulnerabilities and exploits are often kept private and sold to governments, militaries, or defense contractors for both offensive and defensive purposes. Black markets focus on providing vulnerabilities and exploits to criminal groups and other buyers who have illicit purposes.

Although governments understandably try to keep a low profile when it comes to purchasing vulnerabilities and exploits from the private sector, there is a growing body of evidence that such interactions are commonplace. For example, in 2015 a company called Hacking Team, which provides "surveillance and intrusion software," was breached and its records were made public, revealing that almost forty governments around the world had purchased their products.[22] Similarly, a recent profile of a startup from Australia called Azimuth Security claims that the company provides exploits to the "Five Eyes" countries: the United States, the United Kingdom, Canada, Australia, and New Zealand.[23] Finally, RAND has determined that "approximately two dozen companies are in the business of selling [exploits] to U.S. or U.S.-allied entities."[24]

There is also evidence that large government contractors may play a role in the development of cyber weapons. For example, a recent Request for Proposal from U.S. Cyber Command sought support for "the development, evaluation, analysis, and integration of cyber weapons/tools/capabilities."[25] This was part of a broader request for support that could only be provided by a large cleared defense contractor. This is discussed further in the next section. The key takeaway is that private sector actors play a role in providing governments with vulnerabilities and exploits that can support the development of cyber weapons.

Planning and Support

The previous discussion examined how private sector actors can support OCO by participating in the steps of the cyber kill-chain. Companies also help governments conduct cyberattacks by providing general support that enables such cyber operations to take place. For example, in the Request for Proposal described earlier, U.S. Cyber Command sought assistance in the following areas: operations, planning, training and exercises, strategy and policy, information technology, communications, business support, and engagement. These activities are important to the overall function of the Command, but they are not focused on operations per se.

It is likely that planning and general support for OCO will come from cleared defense contractors (or similar organizations in other countries). These companies work closely with the government across a range of functions, including cyber operations. They have a history of supporting the military, understand its culture, and usually have many employees with security clearances. Finally, there is the matter of scope. The ceiling of the U.S. Cyber Command solicitation is $460 million and requires the support of hundreds of people. This observation is supported by testimony from the former U.S. Cyber Command commander, Admiral Michael Rogers, before the Senate Armed Services Committee in which he noted that the 2016 U.S. Cyber Command budget had billets for 963 government employees (military and civilian) and 409 contract employees.[26] Small companies simply cannot provide that number of qualified and cleared personnel.

Although small companies can provide specialized services in specific areas, one would expect a large prime contractor to oversee the overall work program and provide the bulk of support services. In fact, this is exactly what happened in the U.S. Cyber Command solicitation described earlier in this chapter: KEYW Corporation; Vencore, Inc.; Booz Allen Hamilton, Inc.; Science Applications International Corporation; CACI, Inc. Federal; and Secure Mission Solutions, LLC[27] were all selected to support U.S. Cyber Command. Foreign governments likely rely on similar types of companies to support their versions of U.S. Cyber Command, especially if such government organizations are relatively large.

Implications

Private sector actors are playing an important role in supporting OCO, and that role is likely to grow. The implications of this trend affect both domestic policy and international relations. We discuss four key issues below: how offensive cyber operations may affect domestic work force shortages, oversight, international power dynamics, and the use of proxies.

Domestic Workforce Issues

Many arms of the U.S. government are using companies to fill staffing gaps across the spectrum of cyber support and operations. Private sector actors provide a crucial benefit by supporting staffing needs that cannot be satisfied through normal recruiting and hiring processes. The U.S government has been quite open about its challenge in hiring qualified cyber professionals. In 2018 a DHS official summed up this difficulty, stating, "It's really hard for us to maintain key people in cybersecurity areas when they could make maybe three or four times their salary in the government . . . it is a struggle for the government to keep good IT security people."[28]

Cyber workforce challenges are most acute for the armed services. The military faces greater hurdles in both finding and retaining highly skilled professionals than the intelligence community and other federal agencies do.[29] Notably, U.S. Cyber Command initially intended to build a workforce of six thousand cyber professionals by 2016 but was unable to meet this timeline and had to request delays.[30] In part to remedy this problem, the U.S. Army launched its own program to fill lingering workforce gaps.[31]

The skills shortage is relevant for OCO because these operations require intense levels of training to create cyber warriors who can develop and launch cyberattacks. Individuals with existing talent and training in this field are few and far between, and are usually courted by private sector companies. The federal government faces extreme challenges when competing with industry for top cybersecurity talent. As a *Politico* article put it in 2015, "if there's an employer less like the cash-rich, flex-time, playful ethos of Silicon Valley than the federal bureaucracy, it's hard to imagine what it is."[32]

Unfortunately for DoD and other agencies, the workforce problem is likely to get worse before it gets better. Even when the government can hire people into its ranks, retention remains a major challenge. The military may hire a young cyber analyst and train him or her at great expense to become a highly proficient cyber warrior, only to have that individual lured away by a private company after a few years of government service. Industry can offer higher salaries, the prospect of more rapid advancement, open working conditions, and stock options—perks that government agencies cannot match. Former NSA employees, one article noted, "are becoming a hot commodity in Silicon Valley . . . investors looking to ride the boom in cybersecurity are dangling big paydays in front of former NSA staffers, seeking to secure access to the insider knowledge they gained while working for the world's most elite surveillance agency."[33] The *Washington Post* has reported that the NSA has lost hundreds of hackers, engineers, and data scientists in just the last few years. According to government officials, "the potential impact on national security is significant."[34]

If the military cannot hire enough cyber warriors on its own, it may find itself in a position where it has no choice but to rely on contracting private sector actors to conduct OCO. There is a vast difference between *choosing* to use the private sector and *needing* to use the private sector. The latter situation raises important concerns of oversight; for example, the federal government may be forced to rely on contractors for exceedingly sensitive support roles, or even employ contractors that it may feel are not up to the task.

Oversight Issues

If the U.S. government employs a growing number of private sector actors for OCO, oversight issues may become increasingly challenging. Government contracting officers need to have a mix of subject matter expertise, contracting know-how, and general experience to properly manage cyber-related contracts to ensure that they are being carried out effectively, ethically, and legally. A contracting officer plays an enormous role in overseeing agreements between private sector actors and contracting agencies, providing "technical direction, clarification, and guidance with respect to the contract specifications and statement of work. The contracting officer is the technical liaison between the government and industry and is responsible for ensuring satisfactory performance and timely delivery as set forth in the contract."[35] This kind of expertise is not easy to develop, and the military must ensure it has enough specialists of high caliber to oversee the large number of contracts it is granting.

Precedent for concern exists here. The U.S. government, including both the DoD and the State Department, had major problems overseeing private military contractors during the Iraq and Afghanistan conflicts. Several reforms were implemented by both the executive branch and Congress, and the number of contracting and acquisition personnel was also greatly expanded.[36] However, cyber operations contracts may pose a unique challenge owing to their scope, complexity, and level of classification. Given the shortage of cyber expertise in the federal government, and the growing reliance on private sector actors to fill these gaps, it is possible that there will not be enough qualified contracting officers to effectively oversee contracts involving OCO.

This potential shortage could lead to two acute risks, one financial and the other operational.[37] The financial risk is straightforward: a lack of contract oversight could result in contractor fraud, waste, and abuse. Fraud was perpetrated by contractors in Iraq and Afghanistan, and has also occurred on many major contracts involving weapons systems and information technology. By one estimate, contract waste and fraud amounted to between $31 billion and $60 billion in the Iraq and Afghanistan engagements.[38]

The operational concern is a bit trickier. Cyber contractors could conceivably take actions that have international or strategic implications. Such an issue arose during the Iraq War, when the United States became embroiled in a controversy later known as the Nisour Square Massacre. Four employees of Blackwater, a private military contractor, were eventually convicted in federal court of killing fourteen unarmed civilians, and U.S.–Iraq relations were severely strained as a result. The legal battle over these Blackwater employees has only become more complicated over time.[39] While the chances of a "cyber Blackwater" event may be low, the consequences of such an occurrence could be significant.

Even if the U.S. government can oversee its contractors effectively, the government still has limited control over the business decisions that such firms make. A few laws and regulations are in place to limit undesirable outcomes, such as export controls around the transfer of certain specified technologies.[40] U.S. military contractors also want to avoid making business decisions that upset their government customers. Yet ultimately, these companies have a great deal of leverage in deciding whom they support and how. As Peter Singer writes, "The simple fact is that there are no guarantees over where or for whom the firms will work."[41] A private sector actor could conceivably conduct an offensive cyber operation outside the purview of any government. In addition, a company that decided to develop and sell the ability to conduct sophisticated and comprehensive cyberattacks could prove to be a wildcard in the international arena. Finally, the use of contractors may increase the risk that an insider will inadvertently or deliberately leak sensitive information.[42]

International Balance-of-Power Issues

Companies already provide advanced cyberattack capabilities to customers around the globe. This reality may have international implications. Singer writes that the privatized military industry creates "alternative patterns of power and authority linked to the global market, rather than limited by the territorial state."[43] These patterns, in turn, unavoidably affect domestic politics and international dynamics. The proliferation of private sector actors in OCO raises a key question about global power dynamics: Will private sectors actors level the playing field for offensive cyber operations or exacerbate the gaps between the haves and the have-nots?

Whether and how private sector actors will affect power differentials in cyberspace is widely debated among academics and practitioners. On the one hand, the availability of cyber know-how could level the playing field between countries. An expanded market of offensive cyber capabilities could make it more economically feasible for countries with limited in-house cyber capabilities to acquire and launch OCO.[44] Alternatively, the use of private sector actors could accentuate the gap between haves and have-nots in cyberspace. As discussed earlier, conducting OCO requires a wide range of supporting actions as well as some level of direction and oversight. Although companies can provide many of the capabilities needed to launch a sophisticated cyberattack, these capabilities must be embedded into a broader strategy and military structure to achieve desired results beyond simply sowing chaos. It is easy to acquire sophisticated cyber crime tools and to utilize "malware as a service" to avoid the need to build and maintain a large internal infrastructure for malware creation.[45] However, OCO that is part of a sustained strategic campaign requires additional support. For example, because cyberspace is a complex domain with rapidly changing technical features, cyber weapons require detailed and timely intelligence about the intended target.

Given these considerations, it may be difficult for a country with limited cyber resources and infrastructure to simply buy an off-the-shelf offensive capability from a private sector actor and effectively operationalize it to align with full-scale military operations. Actors attempting to base their entire cyber arsenal on market-available tools and services would look more like sophisticated cyber criminals than powerful nation-states. These countries would not be able to keep up with advanced players already possessing sophisticated internal capabilities. A more powerful state can easily acquire the same readily available off-the-shelf tool or service as the cyber novice.

Yet, where the novice has to rely solely on the ready-made tool, the expert can integrate it into existing capabilities to build a much more effective campaign.

In addition, the involvement of government players in the exploitation marketplace may drive up the prices for zero-day vulnerabilities, essentially forcing out poorer or less powerful countries from these kinds of exchanges. Wealthier countries tend to have more advanced cyber infrastructures and can afford to invest beyond defensive capabilities and into the offense-oriented realm: "The market for back-door exploits has been boosted in large part by the burgeoning demand from militaries eager to develop their cyber war-fighting capabilities . . . [and] the U.S. military's dominant presence in the market means that other possible purchasers cannot match the military's price."[46] This is yet another example of how private sector actors may exacerbate power differentials in cyberspace.

Private Sector Actors as Combatants

As private sector actors play an increasingly active role in enabling and supporting OCO, their status in conflict becomes murkier. Can states legitimately treat contracted private sector actors as combatants in cyber conflict under international law? In general, civilians are not legitimate targets in a military conflict. However, civilians can lose that protection if they directly participate in hostilities or act "in a continuous combat function."[47]

> The civilian designer of a weapons system has traditionally not been treated as a direct participant in hostilities. However, the programmer who works with military intelligence may tweak the code to enable the attack, right up until the moment of the attack. The actions of such a civilian—particularly of a civilian who regularly engages in such activity—could be considered a "continuous function [that] involves the preparation, execution, or command of acts or operations amounting to direct participation in hostilities." As a result, *civilians involved in cyber-attacks might be regarded as performing tasks that alter their status under the law of war, rendering them lawful targets of a counterattack.*[48]

To parse out the legal status of private sector contractors, one must determine whether the type of support provided by the actor can be considered direct participation in hostilities or a continuous combat function. Based on our earlier examination of the roles inhabited by the private sector in supporting OCO, these actors appear to be primarily focused on providing support activities before the launch of a cyber weapon. Even if those activities include intelligence gathering and military planning, private sector actors probably should not be viewed as legitimate targets for attack under the law of armed conflict.

However, this question cannot be put to rest quite so easily; it involves several legal, ethical, and practical considerations. For example, the majority of OCO will likely occur over the internet, which means that they will transit networks that are owned and operated by internet service providers (ISPs). What responsibility do ISPs have to identify and prevent such attacks from occurring? Could a country that suffers a cyberattack hold an ISP responsible, or view it as a legitimate target for retaliatory action? Do the answers to these questions differ from peacetime to wartime? The legal considerations surrounding contractor actions in cyberspace deserve continuing attention, especially as the role of companies continues to grow in both offensive and defensive cyber operations.

Further muddying the waters is the possibility that private sector actors could support both the offensive and defensive sides of a given operation. This occurrence is hardly a new phenomenon in warfare: hired hands have been fighting each other for hundreds of years. However, we have yet to fully understand the implications of this wrinkle in a cyber conflict featuring two cyber contractors facing off against each other in support of their respective government customers. One could imagine three scenarios with differing dynamics.

In the first scenario, a U.S.-based private sector actor supporting OCO might confront a foreign company that was hired to defend the organization that the operation is targeting. This situation is likely to occur because non-U.S.-based companies are becoming increasingly sophisticated and popular providers of cybersecurity products and services, even in the United States. Many countries are investing in home-grown cybersecurity markets, and several of these companies are known to be quite capable (for example, F-Secure of Finland, Kaspersky Lab of Russia, and Check Point Software Technologies of Israel).

A second scenario involves a U.S.-based private sector contractor facing off with another U.S. company. This situation is also quite likely as the United States boasts the world's largest and strongest market for cybersecurity services and products. In this situation, one company might need to find and exploit vulnerabilities in the software of another U.S. company to success-fully penetrate the target's computer systems. If one company identifies vul-nerabilities in another company's software or hardware, does it disclose that information to improve the security of all users? Or, does it choose to keep the information quiet so that it can succeed in its offensive mission?

A third and final scenario involves a U.S.-based private sector company becoming embroiled in both ends of an operation. This case is theoretically possible because some global defense contractors provide support to both of-fensive and defensive operations. A single company might support an OCO launched by the United States, while simultaneously providing defensive sup-port to countries around the globe—including the target country of that same initial OCO. For example, the consulting firm Booz Allen Hamilton is known to support the NSA[49] and provide cybersecurity services to coun-tries in the Middle East.[50] This situation is more likely to arise in the case of a cyber exploitation than a cyberattack. However, this scenario does raise interesting questions about the preeminence of offense versus defense, and the choices that companies may be required to make as they consider involve-ment both with the U.S. government and with governments abroad.

The position of private sector actors in cyber conflict is already compli-cated in the best of circumstances. In countries like the United States, private sector actors usually serve in well-scoped roles, as contractors who provide discrete support services. In many other countries, however, pri-vate sector actors operate in much murkier roles of "proxies." A nation-state may choose to hide its activities in the guise of a nonstate actor to avoid re-taliation or to maintain its ability to engage in other realms (diplomatic, economic) without acknowledging its hand in OCO. China uses a wide range of actors to conduct cyber espionage: "The Chinese government cre-ated a proxy hacking system precisely so that it could deny state involve-ment."[51] The Russian government relies on criminals to gather information and launch attacks on its behalf.[52] Russia also encourages hacktivist groups to take actions on behalf of the state—a practice that dates back to the 2007 cyberattacks against Estonia.[53] Finally, it appears that Iran is growing in-creasingly reliant on proxies to augment its national cyber capabilities.[54]

By relying on proxies, a country may be able to create at least *some* con-fusion as to its involvement with an OCO by shifting most of the blame to a nonstate actor, while still (potentially) achieving its larger offensive goals. This kind of subterfuge raises a host of questions related to a broader cyber-security debate: the role (and certainty) of attribution. A state that sanctions or sponsors a cyberattack may be able to avoid retaliation for its actions if attribution of such an operation remains uncertain.

Avenues for Future Research

Based on our findings, four avenues for research appear to be most promising and useful for policymakers. First, more attention needs to be paid to understanding how countries can balance the benefits and risks of reliance on private sector cyber capabilities. This area of research touches on topics such as recruitment and retention of cyber warriors, oversight for cyber contractors, and the role of cyber contractors in cyber conflict. Much work has been done to address a potential shortfall in cyber warriors.[55] However, most of the attention so far has focused on cyber defense. For example, The National Institutes of Standards and Technology has developed a detailed guideline on cybersecurity education.[56] More research is needed on how to attract and retain people who work on offensive cyber operations. A good first step would be a broader discussion around the magnitude of the problem, which is often shrouded in secrecy.

Additionally, the U.S. government needs to determine if there is a shortage of skilled contracting officers to oversee complex cyber projects, especially those involving offensive cyber operations. If there is a shortage, then steps should be taken to address that shortfall as soon as possible while putting in place a long-term plan for increasing the ranks of cyber-savvy contracting officers.

Second, developing a better understanding of state interests in and capabilities for OCO will shed useful light on whether, how much, and in which ways key states are likely to use private sector actors for such operations. For example, one could posit that the internal political landscape of countries will affect their willingness to engage in OCO. It is also important to explore whether the proliferation of cyber weapons and capabilities, partially abetted by the private sector, will level the playing field or exacerbate the gap between top tier and second tier cyber powers.

A related topic for exploration is determining whether the proliferation of cyber capabilities via private sector actors will increase or decrease global stability. It may be that global stability can be maximized by having a more equitable distribution of cyber capabilities. On the other hand, global stability may be improved by having a few dominant powers that "rule the roost." When one considers the impact of the private sector on both the global balance of cyber power and the stability of resulting power dynamics, four scenarios can be imagined. In the first scenario, a greater number of states develop offensive cyber capabilities, which leads to a more level playing field and greater stability. In the second scenario, the wide distribution of OCO capabilities evens out the distribution of power but ultimately leads to greater instability due to a lack of deterrence. The third scenario involves a world in which cyber restraint and stability reign even as the gap increases between cyber haves and have-nots. The fourth and final scenario features an unstable world where a few cyber powers dominate the playing field. This area is ripe for further research.

Finally, although there is a growing line of research examining the role that proxies can play in cyber conflict, more work needs to be done on how to distinguish between legitimate and illegitimate use of nongovernment actors to support cyber operations.[57] For example, is it acceptable for the United States to rely on cleared defense contractors but not acceptable for other countries to use proxies for their operations? What distinguishes the two? Is it a matter of attribution or command and control? What does international humanitarian law have to say about these issues? Should norms be developed, and if so, how can they be acceptable to the key players in the global arena?

Conclusion

There is a subtle but important change occurring in the cyber landscape: private sector actors are increasingly influential in protecting computer systems, and they are also beginning to affect the full range of both defensive and offensive cyber operations. As Jason Healey testified before Congress, "America's cyber power is not focused at Fort Meade with NSA and U.S. Cyber Command. The center of U.S. cyber power is instead in Silicon Valley, in Route 128 in Boston, in Redmond, Washington, and in all of our districts where Americans are creating and maintaining cyberspace."[58]

If current workforce and investment trends are indicators of what is to come, private sector actors will continue to grow in sophistication and will likely take on larger roles in offensive cyber operations. Understanding the implications of this development will be critical for both government and industry.

Notes

1. U.S. Department of Defense, *Cyberspace Operations*, Joint Publication 3-12 (R) (Washington, February 5, 2013).

2. Ibid.

3. Ibid. This definition is similar to the concept of a "cyberattack" used in the National Academy of Sciences report on offensive cyber operations: "'cyberattack' refers to the use of deliberate actions and operations—perhaps over an extended period of time—to alter, disrupt, deceive, degrade or destroy adversary computer systems or networks of the information and (or) programs resident in or transiting these systems or networks. Herbert S. Lin, "Offensive Cyber Operations and the Use of Force," *Journal of National Security Law and Policy* 4, no. 1 (2010), pp. 63–86, at 63.

4. Trey Herr and Drew Herrick, "Understanding Military Cyber Operations," in *Cyber Insecurity: Navigating the Perils of the Next Information Age*, edited by Richard M. Harrison and Trey Herr (London: Rowman & Littlefield, 2016), p. 261.

5. E. M. Huchins, M. J. Cloppert, and R. M. Amin, *Intelligence-Driven Computer Network Defense Informed by Analysis of Adversary Campaigns and Intrusion Kill Chains* (Bethesda, MD: Lockheed Martin, 2011).

6. Trey Herr, *PrEP: A Framework for Malware & Cyber Weapons*, Report GW-CSPRI-2014-2 (Washington: George Washington University, 2014).

7. See Ben Buchanan, *The Cybersecurity Dilemma: Hacking, Trust and Fear between Nations* (Oxford University Press, 2017).

8. Oona A. Hathaway and Rebecca Crootof, "The Law of Cyberattack," Faculty Scholarship Series 3852 (Yale University, 2012) (digitalcommons.law.yale.edu/fss_papers/3852).

9. Paul F. Roberts, "If This Is Cyberwar, Where Are All the Cyberweapons?," *MIT Technology Review*, January 27, 2014 (www.technologyreview.com/s/523931/if-this-is-cyberwar-where-are-all-the-cyberweapons/).

10. Shane Harris, *@War: The Rise of the Military-Internet Complex* (Boston: Houghton Mifflin Harcourt, 2014).

11. Cortney Weinbaum, Steven Berner, and Bruce McClintock, *SIGINT for Anyone: The Growing Availability of Signals Intelligence in the Public Domain* (Santa Monica, Calif.: RAND, 2017).

12. Ibid., p. 7.

13. See FireEye, "iSIGHT Intelligence: The Details" (www.fireeye.com/products/isight-cyber-threat-intelligence-subscriptions/isight-intelligence-details.html).

14. See CrowdStrike, "Cyber Threat Intelligence Solutions," 2018 (www.crowdstrike.com/solutions/threat-intelligence-solutions/).

15. See IT Law Wiki, "Cleared Defense Contractor," 2016 (itlaw.wikia.com/wiki/Cleared_defense_contractor).

16. Dana Priest and William Arkin, *Top Secret America: The Rise of the New American Security State* (New York: Little, Brown, 2011).

17. See Threat Connect, "Flashpoint," 2018 (www.threatconnect.com/partners/flashpoint-intelligence/).

18. Herr, *PrEP*.

19. Ibid.

20. The RAND Corporation has conducted two studies about the nature of these markets, and their findings have provided some light. One key finding is that "any serious attacker can likely get an affordable zero-day for almost any target." Lillian Ablon and Timothy Bogart, *Zero Days, Thousands of Nights: The Life and Times of Zero-Day Vulnerabilities and Their Exploits* (Santa Monica, Calif.: RAND, 2017). See also Lillian Albon, Martin C. Libicki, and Andrea A. Golay, *Markets for Cybercrime Tools and Stolen Data: Hackers' Bazaar* (Santa Monica, Calif.: RAND, 2014).

21. Ablon and Bogart, *Zero Days, Thousands of Nights.*

22. Joseph Cox, "The FBI Spent $775K on Hacking Team's Spy Tools since 2011," *Wired*, July 6, 2015 (www.wired.com/2015/07/fbi-spent-775k-hacking-teams-spy-tools -since-2011/).

23. Joseph Cox and Lorenzo Franceschi-Bicchierai, "How a Tiny Startup Became the Most Important Hacking Shop You've Never Heard Of," *Motherboard*, February 7, 2018 (motherboard.vice.com/en_us/article/8xdayg/iphone-zero-days-inside-azimuth -security).

24. Ablon and Bogart, *Zero Days, Thousands of Nights*, p. 25.

25. U.S. Cyber Command, *Attachment E, Seed Task Order 1 (TO1) for Cyberspace Operations Support Services*, GSC-QF0B-15-32959 (2016).

26. Senate Armed Services Committee, *Statement of Admiral Michael S. Rogers, Commander of the United States Cyber Command, before the Senate Armed Services Committee*, April 5, 2016.

27. Aaron Boyd, "CYBERCOM Awards Spots on New $460M Cyber Operations Contract," *Federal Times*, May 23, 2016 (www.federaltimes.com/2016/05/23/cybercom -awards-spots-on-new-460m-cyber-operations-contract/).

28. "Unfilled Cyber Positions in Government Continuing to Increase, DHS Official Says," *Inside Cybersecurity*, January 26, 2018 (insidecybersecurity.com/daily-briefs/unfilled -cyber-positions-government-continuing-increase-dhs-official-says).

29. David Barno and Nora Bensahel, "Can the US Military Halt its Brain Drain?," *The Atlantic*, November 5, 2015 (www.theatlantic.com/politics/archive/2015/11/us-military -tries-halt-brain-drain/413965/).

30. Ian Duncan, "Lawmakers Push to Make U.S. Cyber Command a Top Military Command," *Baltimore Sun*, May 22, 2016 (www.baltimoresun.com/news/maryland /politics/bs-md-cyber-command-combatant-command-20160522-story.html).

31. Morgan Chalfant, "Army Leaders Launch Program to Recruit More Cyber Warriors," *The Hill*, December 5, 2017 (thehill.com/policy/cybersecurity/363349-army -leaders-launch-program-to-recruit-more-cyber-warriors).

32. Darren Samuelsohn,"Inside the NSA's Hunt for Hackers," *Politico*, December 9, 2015 (www.politico.com/agenda/story/2015/12/federal-government-cyber-security-technology -worker-recruiting-000330).

33. Cory Bennett, "NSA Staffers Rake in Silicon Valley Cash," *The Hill*, February 24, 2015 (thehill.com/policy/cybersecurity/233740-nsa-staffers-rake-in-silicon-valley-cash).

34. Ellen Nakashima and Aaron Gregg, "NSA's Top Talent Is Leaving Because of Low Pay, Slumping Morale and Unpopular Reorganization," *Washington Post*, January 2, 2018 (www.washingtonpost.com/world/national-security/the-nsas-top-talent-is-leaving-because -of-low-pay-and-battered-morale/2018/01/02/ff19f0c6-ec04-11e7-9f92-10a2203f6c8d _story.html?utm_term=.f1c915ccae61).

35. See U.S. Army Medical Research Acquisition Activity, "Contracting Officer's Representative (COR) Program," 2016 (www.usamraa.army.mil/Pages/Cor.aspx).

36. Moshe Schwartz and Jennifer Church, "Department of Defense's Use of Contractors to Support Military Operations: Background, Analysis, and Issues for Congress" (Congressional Research Service, May 17, 2013).

37. Ibid.

38. Ibid., p. 8.

39. Scott Neuman, "U.S. Appeals Court Tosses Ex-Blackwater Guard's Conviction in 2007 Baghdad Massacre," *NPR*, August 4, 2017 (www.npr.org/sections/thetwo-ay/2017

/08/04/541616598/u-s-appeals-court-tosses-conviction-of-ex-blackwater-guard-in-2007 -baghdad-mass).

40. See U.S. State Department Directorate of Defense Trade Controls, "The International Traffic in Arms Regulations (ITAR)" (www.pmddtc.state.gov/regulations_laws /itar.html).

41. Peter Singer, *Corporate Warriors: The Rise of the Private Military Industry* (Cornell University Press, 2003).

42. Although the Snowden case is the best-known example of this phenomenon, it occurs with alarming frequency. For example, see Evan Perez, Jim Sciutto, and Laura Jarrett, "Contractor Charged with Leaking Classified NSA Info on Russian Hacking," CNN, June 6, 2017 (www.cnn.com/2017/06/05/politics/federal-contractor-leak-prosecution/index .html).

43. Singer, *Corporate Warriors*, p. 170.

44. Nicola Whiting, "Cyberspace Triggers a New Kind of Arms Race," *Signal*, February 1, 2018 (www.afcea.org/content/cyberspace-triggers-new-kind-arms-race).

45. Danny Palmer, "Criminals in the Cloud: How Malware-as-a-Service Is Becoming the Tool of Choice for Crooks," *ZDNet*, April 21, 2016 (www.zdnet.com/article/criminals -in-the-cloud-how-malware-as-a-service-is-becoming-the-tool-of-choice-for-crooks/).

46. Tom Gjelten, "First Strike: U.S. Cyber Warriors Seize the Offensive," *World Affairs Journal*, January/February 2013 (www.worldaffairsjournal.org/article/first-strike-us-cyber -warriors-seize-offensive).

47. U.S. Cyber Command, *Attachment E, Seed Task Order 1 (TO1)*.

48. Hathaway and Crootof, "The Law of Cyberattack"; emphasis added.

49. Drake Bennett and Michael Riley, "Booz Allen, the World's Most Profitable Spy Organization," *Bloomberg Businessweek*, June 21, 2013 (www.bloomberg.com/news/articles /2013-06-20/booz-allen-the-worlds-most-profitable-spy-organization).

50. See Booz Allen Hamilton, "Booz Allen Hamilton to Support Business and Economic Growth in the Kingdom of Saudi Arabia," February 18, 2013 (investors.boozallen .com/releasedetail.cfm?releaseid=749160).

51. Ethan Gutmann, "Hacker Nation: China's Cyber Assault," *World Affairs* 173, no. 1 (2010), pp. 70–79.

52. Brian Whitmore, "Organized Crime Is Now a Major Element of Russian Statecraft," *Business Insider*, October 27, 2015 (www.businessinsider.com/organized-crime-is -now-a-major-element-of-russia-statecraft-2015-10).

53. Tim Maurer, "Cyber Proxies and Crisis in Ukraine," in *Cyber War in Perspective: Russian Aggression against Ukraine*, edited by K. Geers (Tallinn: NATO CCD COE Publications, 2015), pp. 79–86.

54. Jordan Brunner, "Iran Has Built an Army of Cyber Proxies," *The Tower*, August 2015 (www.thetower.org/article/iran-has-built-an-army-of-cyber-proxies/).

55. Two examples of this: Franklin S. Reeder and Katrina Timlin, *Recruiting and Retaining Cybersecurity Ninjas* (Washington: Center for Strategic and International Studies, October 2016); and Center for Strategic and International Studies, *Hacking the Skills Shortage: A Study of the International Shortage in Cybersecurity Skills* (Washington: McAfee, July 2016).

56. See William Newhouse, Stephanie Keith, Benjamin Scribner, and Greg Witte, "National Initiative for Cybersecurity Education (NICE) Cybersecurity Workforce Framework," NIST Special Publication 800-181 (Washington: National Institute of Standards and Technology, 2017).

57. For a comprehensive discussion of this topic, see Tim Maurer, *Cyber Mercenaries: The State, Hackers, and Power* (Cambridge University Press, 2018).

58. U.S. Congress, House of Representatives, Armed Services Committee, *Cyber Warfare in the 21st Century: Threats, Challenges, and Opportunities—Testimony by Jason Healey*, 115th Cong., March 1, 2017.

Index

Academics and analysts: on offense-defense balance in cyberspace, 118–19; role in policymaking, 1, 4–5

Accesses: concealment of, 145–46; controls over, 137; disclosure of, to prevent proliferation, 283, 393; to encrypted files, 4; intelligence collection vs. cyberattack, 187; to missiles in development, 154, 155, 157–58, 166; to NC3, 200; to North Korea, 166; for OCO, 111, 116–19, 120–22; Russian, to U.S. networks, 181–82; to software and cybersecurity, 141–43

Active defense, 4; cybersecurity and, 228; defined, 359–60; disintermediation of government and, 353–54; escalatory scenarios of, 372–73; government authority over, 359; ISR and, 117; lawfulness of, 364; out-of-perimeter location of, 361–62; private sector and, 363–66, 371–72; purpose of, 360–61; rules of engagement and, 291, 293–95, 297–98, 303–06, 310; tactical flexibility of, 362–63; types of, 362

Adaptive planning, 120–21

Adjustment responses to cyberattacks, 10, 134–36; access to software and cybersecurity, 141–43; heuristic process of, 136–38; methods for slowing, 143–47; in missile development programs, 165–66; organizational culture and, 138–40; system characteristics and, 140–41

Adversaries: adaptation and adjustment responses of, 91, 134–36, 147–48, 165–66,

183; attack structures against, 112–15; capabilities and systems, 24, 26–28, 88, 176; deception operations by, 124, 125; in escalation scenarios, 93–95; intent, 11, 14, 27, 30–33, 81–82; norms of cyber conflict and, 65; signaling, 38, 40, 67–68, 176–78; threat perception of, 90–95; types of, 95–96; U.S. Cyber Command on, 85–87, 89

Agility as requirement of ISR, 31, 34, 36, 42

Air Force (U.S.), 117, 122–23, 127, 200, 298

Alexander, Keith, 81, 200, 358

Ali, Muhammed, 85–87, 95, 97–98

Alliances: China-U.S. military confrontation and, 334; as essential components of ISR, 35, 38, 41; instability from, 219; rules of engagement and, 299

Ambiguous intent, 11, 14; active defense and, 361; cyber capabilities and, 212; in "detect and respond" scenarios, 27; ISR and, 30–33, 40; rules of engagement and, 296–98

Anonymity, 25, 26, 29, 238, 367

Anonymous (hacktivist group), 237, 242, 252, 256, 333

Antiballistic missile systems, 208, 226

Anticipation and anticipatory self-defense: data analytics and, 36; in ISR, 28, 33; requirements for, 21, 27–28, 29–31; rules of engagement and, 299–300

Armed conflict. *See* Kinetic attacks

Armed Services Committee, 81–82

Contributors

David Aucsmith is Chief Scientist at root9B, where he works on science to support manned active cyber defense and adversary pursuit, and a Senior Principal Research Scientist at the Applied Physics Laboratory of the University of Washington, where he studies cyber-physical systems security. Aucsmith was the Senior Director of Microsoft's Institute for Advanced Technology in Governments from 2002 until 2014, where he was responsible for technical relationships with agencies of the U.S. and other governments. Aucsmith was the Chief Security Architect for Intel Corporation from 1994 to 2002. He has been an industry representative on the technical advisory boards of the National Security Agency, the National Reconnaissance Office, the National Academies, and the National Security Directorate of Pacific Northwest National Labs. He currently lectures at the Naval Postgraduate School, the Naval War College, and the Air Command and Staff College.

Steven M. Bellovin is the Percy K. and Vidal L. W. Hudson Professor of Computer Science at Columbia University, a member of the Cybersecurity and Privacy Center of the university's Data Science Institute, and an affiliate faculty member at Columbia Law School. He conducts research on security and privacy and related public policy issues. As a graduate student he helped create Netnews; for this he and the other architects were given the 1995 Usenix Lifetime Achievement Award (The Flame). Bellovin has served as Chief Technologist of the Federal Trade Commission, Technology Scholar at the Privacy and Civil Liberties Oversight Board, and as a member of the Department of Homeland Security's Science and Technology Advisory Committee. He is a member of the National Academy of Engineering and currently serves on the Computer Science and Telecommunications Board of the National Academies of Sciences, Engineering, and Medicine. He received the 2007 NIST/NSA National Computer Systems Security Award and has been elected to the Cybersecurity Hall of Fame. Bellovin is the author of *Thinking Security: Stopping Next Year's Hackers* (Addison-Wesley, 2016) and holds a number of patents on cryptographic and network protocols.

Daphna Canetti is Professor of Political Science at the University of Haifa and Director of the Graduate Program in Democracy Studies. Canetti's research examines the psychological challenges and policy implications of terrorism and political violence. She is the author of "A Checkpoint Effect? Evidence from a Natural Experiment on Travel Restrictions in the West Bank" (*American Journal of Political Science*, 2014) and "Conflict Will Harden Your Heart: Exposure to Violence, Psychological Distress, and Peace Barriers in Israel and Palestine" (*British Journal of Political Science*, 2014). She has also published in the *Journal of Conflict Resolution*, *Political Behavior*, *Political Psychology*, *Political Studies*, *Political Research Quarterly*, *Foreign Affairs*, and other leading academic journals. Her commentary has been featured on National Public Radio and in the *Washington Post*, *Ha'aretz*, and the *Times of Israel*.

Henry Farrell is Associate Professor of Political Science and International Affairs at George Washington University. He works on a variety of topics, including trust, the politics of the internet, and international and comparative political economy. He is the author of *The Political Economy of Trust: Interests, Institutions and Inter-Firm Cooperation* (Cambridge University Press, 2009) as well as numerous academic articles, book chapters, and nonacademic publications. He is a member of the Council on Foreign Relations.

Erik Gartzke is Professor of Political Science and Director of the Center for Peace and Security Studies (cPASS) at the University of California, San Diego. Previously he was on the faculty at Columbia University and the Pennsylvania State University. Gartzke's research focuses on war, peace, and international institutions. His interests include deterrence, nuclear security, the liberal peace, alliances, information and war, cyberwar, and the evolving technological nature of interstate conflict. He has written on the effects of global commerce, development, system structure, and climate change on warfare. Recent studies include the role of military automation on patterns of conflict, cross-domain deterrence, and research contributing to the intellectual foundations of cyber conflict. Gartzke's research appears in the *American Political Science Review*, the *American Journal of Political Science*, the *British Journal of Political Science*, and elsewhere.

Charles L. Glaser is Professor of Political Science and International Affairs and Director of the Elliott School's Institute for Security and Conflict Studies at George Washington University. His research focuses on international relations theory, including the security dilemma, defensive realism, the offense–defense balance, and arms races, and on international security policy, including U.S. policy toward China, energy security, and U.S. nuclear weapons policy. Before joining George Washington University, Glaser was the Emmett Dedmon Professor of Public Policy and Deputy Dean at the Harris School of Public Policy at the University of Chicago. He has served on the Joint Staff at the Pentagon and was a peace fellow at the United States Institute of Peace.

Michael L. Gross is Professor and Head of the School of Political Science at the University of Haifa. His fields of interest include applied normative theory, military and medical ethics, asymmetric war, and nonkinetic warfare. He is the author of *Moral Dilemmas of Modern War* (Cambridge University Press, 2010), *The Ethics of Insurgency* (Cambridge University Press, 2015), and, with Tamar Meisels, *Soft War: The Ethics of Unarmed Conflict* (Cambridge University Press, 2017).

Taylor Grossman was the Senior National Security Analyst at Clark Street Associates, a consulting firm in Silicon Valley that works with emerging technology companies. Previously she was Cyber Research Associate at the Hoover Institution, Stanford University, where she conducted research in cyber policy and cybersecurity. She has also served in the Office of the Assistant Secretary of Defense for Public Affairs.

Jason Healey is Senior Research Scholar at Columbia University's School for International and Public Affairs, specializing in cyber conflict and risk.

He started his career as a U.S. Air Force intelligence officer before moving to cyber response and policy jobs at the White House and Goldman Sachs. He was Founding Director for Cyber Issues at the Atlantic Council, where he remains a Senior Fellow and is the editor of the first history of conflict in cyberspace, *A Fierce Domain: Cyber Conflict, 1986 to 2012*. He served as Vice Chair of the Financial Services Informational Sharing and Analysis Center (FS-ISAC) and helped create the world's first cyber command in 1998. He is on the DEF CON review board and the Defense Science Board task force on cyber deterrence.

Chris Inglis currently serves as the U.S. Naval Academy's Robert and Mary M. Looker Distinguished Visiting Professor for Cyber Studies. He retired from the Department of Defense in 2014 after more than forty-one years of federal service, including twenty-eight years at the National Security Agency, where he was its senior civilian and Deputy Director. Inglis's career began at NSA as a computer scientist within the National Computer Security Center and was followed by tours in information assurance, policy, time-sensitive operations, and signals intelligence organizations. Promoted to NSA's Senior Executive Service in 1997, he held a variety of senior leadership assignments and twice served away from NSA Headquarters, first as a visiting professor of computer science at the U.S. Military Academy (1991–92) and later as the U.S. Special Liaison to the United Kingdom (2003–06).

Inglis's military career includes over thirty years in the U.S. Air Force, from which he retired as a Brigadier General in 2006. His significant awards include the Director of National Intelligence Distinguished Service Medal (2014) and the President's National Security Medal (2014).

C. Robert Kehler retired from the United States Air Force in December 2013 after almost thirty-nine years of distinguished service. From January 2011 until November 2013 he served as the Commander, United States Strategic Command (USSTRATCOM), where he was directly responsible to the secretary of defense and the president for the plans and operations of all U.S. forces conducting strategic deterrence, nuclear alert, global strike, space, cyberspace, and associated operations. Before commanding USSTRATCOM the general commanded United States Air Force Space Command and two operational space wings responsible for space launch, missile warning, and space control. He also commanded an intercontinental ballistic missile (ICBM) squadron and operations group. Kehler was the S. T. Lee Distinguished Lecturer at Stanford University's Freeman Spogli Institute for International Studies for the academic year 2014–15 and remains an Affiliate of Stanford's Center for International Security and Cooperation.

Lucas Kello is Senior Lecturer in International Relations at Oxford University. He serves as Director of the Centre for Technology and Global Affairs, a research initiative exploring the impact of modern technology on international relations, government, and society. He is also Co-director of the interdisciplinary Centre for Doctoral Training in Cyber Security in the Department of Computer Science. His publications include *The Virtual Weapon and International Order* (Yale University Press, 2017), "Security," in *The Oxford Companion to International Relations* (Oxford University Press, 2014), and "The Meaning of the Cyber Revolution: Perils to Theory and Statecraft," in *International Security* (2013).

Irv Lachow is Deputy Director of Cyber Strategy and Execution at The MITRE Corporation. He has spent over twenty years working at the intersection of technology and policy issues, focusing for the past fifteen years primarily on cybersecurity. He was a Professor of Systems Management at the National Defense University, a Senior Associate at Booz Allen Hamilton, a Policy Analyst at Rand Corporation, and a Defense Policy Fellow in the Department of Defense. He is also a Nonresident Fellow at the Center for Strategic and International Studies, a Visiting Fellow at the Hoover Institution, and an Affiliate at Stanford University's Center for International Security and Cooperation. Lachow is the author or coauthor of numerous books, articles, and reports and has appeared on *PBS NewsHour*, CNN, and CSPAN.

Susan Landau is Bridge Professor of Cyber Security and Policy at the Fletcher School of Law and Diplomacy and the School of Engineering, Department of Computer Science, Tufts University. She is the author of *Listening In: Cybersecurity in an Insecure Age* (Yale University Press, 2017) and *Surveillance or Security? The Risks Posed by New Wiretapping Technologies* (MIT Press, 2013). Landau has testified before Congress; written for the *Washington Post*, *Science*, and *Scientific American*; and appears frequently on National Public Radio and the BBC. She has been a Senior Staff Privacy Analyst at

Google; a Distinguished Engineer at Sun Microsystems; and a faculty member at Worcester Polytechnic Institute, the University of Massachusetts Amherst, and Wesleyan University. She was inducted into the Cybersecurity Hall of Fame in 2015.

Martin C. Libicki holds the Keyser Chair of Cybersecurity Studies at the U.S. Naval Academy. In addition to teaching, he conducts research in cyberwar and the effects of information technology on domestic and national security. He is the author most recently of *Cyberspace in Peace and War* (Naval Institute Press, 2016), as well as numerous Rand monographs, notably *Defender's Dilemma, Brandishing Cyberattack Capabilities, Crisis and Escalation in Cyberspace, Global Demographic Change and Its Implications for Military Power,* and *Cyberdeterrence and Cyberwar.* Prior employment includes twelve years at the National Defense University, three years on the Navy Staff as program sponsor for industrial preparedness, and three years for the Government Accountability Office.

Herbert Lin is Senior Research Scholar for cyber policy and security at the Center for International Security and Cooperation and Hank J. Holland Fellow in Cyber Policy and Security at the Hoover Institution, both at Stanford University. His research interests relate broadly to the policy dimensions of cybersecurity and cyberspace, with particular focus on the use of offensive operations in cyberspace as instruments of national policy. He is also Chief Scientist, Emeritus, for the Computer Science and Telecommunications Board, National Research Council of the National Academies, where he served from 1990 through 2014 as study director of major projects on public policy and information technology, and Adjunct Senior Research Scholar and Senior Fellow in Cybersecurity (nonresident) at the Saltzman Institute for War and Peace Studies of the School for International and Public Affairs at Columbia University.

Jon R. Lindsay is Assistant Professor at the Munk School of Global Affairs and Public Policy and the Department of Political Science at the University of Toronto. He studies the impact of technology on international security, focusing on military innovation, cybersecurity, and grand strategy. His publications include *China and Cybersecurity: Espionage, Strategy, and Politics in the Digital Domain* (Oxford University Press, 2015), and his work has appeared in *International Security, Security Studies,* the *Journal of Strategic*

Studies, and *Technology and Culture*. He has served as a U.S. naval reserve intelligence officer in Europe, Latin America, and the Middle East.

Austin Long is a Senior Political Scientist at the Rand Corporation. His research interests include low-intensity conflict, intelligence, military operations, nuclear forces, military innovation, and the political economy of national security. Long previously was an Associate Professor at Columbia University's School of International and Public Affairs. He also was an analyst and adviser to the U.S. military in Iraq (2007–08) and Afghanistan (2011 and 2013). He was a Council on Foreign Relations International Affairs Fellow in Nuclear Security, serving in the Joint Staff J5. His research has appeared in *International Security*, *Security Studies*, the *Journal of Strategic Studies*, the *Journal of Cold War Studies*, *Orbis*, and *Survival*. He is also the author of *The Soul of Armies: Counterinsurgency Doctrine and Military Culture in the United States and United Kingdom* (Cornell University Press, 2016).

Adam Segal is the Ira A. Lipman Chair in Emerging Technologies and National Security and Director of the Digital and Cyberspace Policy Program at the Council on Foreign Relations (CFR). An expert on security issues, technology development, and Chinese domestic and foreign policy, Segal was the project director for the CFR-sponsored Independent Task Force report *Defending an Open, Global, Secure, and Resilient Internet*. His most recent book, *The Hacked World Order: How Nations Fight, Trade, Maneuver, and Manipulate in the Digital Age* (PublicAffairs, 2016), describes the increasingly contentious geopolitics of cyberspace. His work has appeared in the *Financial Times*, *The Economist*, *Foreign Policy*, the *Wall Street Journal*, *Foreign Affairs*, and elsewhere. He currently writes for the blog *Net Politics*.

Max W. E. Smeets is a cybersecurity postdoctoral fellow at Stanford University's Center for International Security and Cooperation. He is also a nonresident Cybersecurity Policy Fellow at New America and Research Associate at the Centre for Technology and Global Affairs, Oxford University. He was awarded the annual 2018 Amos Perlmutter Prize of the *Journal of Strategic Studies* for the most outstanding manuscript submitted for publication by a junior faculty member. In 2015 he also received the Young Writers Award of the German Marshall Fund for an article written with George

Bogden. Smeets has held research positions at the Oxford Cyber Studies Programme, Columbia University's School of International and Public Affairs, Sciences Po CERI, and NATO Cooperative Cyber Defence Centre of Excellence.

Michael Sulmeyer is the Cyber Security Project Director at the Belfer Center, Harvard Kennedy School. He served several years in the Office of the Secretary of Defense, most recently as the Director for Plans and Operations for Cyber Policy. He was also Senior Policy Adviser to the Deputy Assistant Secretary of Defense for Cyber Policy. In these jobs he worked closely with the Joint Staff and Cyber Command on a variety of efforts to counter malicious cyber activity against U.S. and Department of Defense interests. For this work he received the Secretary Medal for Exceptional Public Service. Previously he worked on arms control and the maintenance of strategic stability between the United States, Russia, and China.

Dana R. Vashdi is Senior Lecturer in the Division of Public Administration and Policy at the University of Haifa. Vashdi's research focuses on the well-being of citizens, especially employees in public organizations, as well as on teamwork, organizational learning, and healthcare policy. She has published articles in a wide variety of academic journals, including the *Academy of Management Journal*, *British Medical Journal*, *Human Resource Management*, and *Public Administration Review*.

Amy Zegart is the Davies Family Senior Fellow at the Hoover Institution, a Senior Fellow at the Center for International Security and Cooperation, and Professor of Political Science, by courtesy, at Stanford University. She is also a contributing editor to *The Atlantic*. Her research examines U.S. intelligence challenges, cybersecurity, drone warfare, and American foreign policy. Her publications include *Spying Blind: The CIA, the FBI, and the Origins of 9/11* (Princeton University Press, 2007) and, with Condoleezza Rice, *Political Risk: How Businesses and Organizations Can Anticipate Global Insecurity* (Twelve, 2018). Before coming to Stanford in 2011 she was Professor of Public Policy at UCLA's Luskin School of Public Affairs and spent several years as a McKinsey & Company management consultant.